Production Volume Rendering

Production Volume Rendering

Design and Implementation

Magnus Wrenninge

CRC Press
Taylor & Francis Group
Boca Raton London New York

CRC Press is an imprint of the
Taylor & Francis Group, an **informa** business
AN A K PETERS BOOK

Cover design by Vincent Serritella.

CRC Press
Taylor & Francis Group
6000 Broken Sound Parkway NW, Suite 300
Boca Raton, FL 33487-2742

First issued in paperback 2020

© 2013 by Magnus Wrenninge
CRC Press is an imprint of Taylor & Francis Group, an Informa business

No claim to original U.S. Government works

ISBN-13: 978-1-56881-724-8 (hbk)
ISBN-13: 978-0-367-65919-6 (pbk)

Library of Congress Cataloging-in-Publication Data

Wrenninge, Magnus.
    Production volume rendering : design and implementation / Magnus Wrenninge.
      p. cm.
    Includes bibliographical references and index.
    ISBN 978-1-56881-724-8 (hardcover : alk. paper)
      1. Computer animation. 2. Rendering (Computer graphics) I. Title.

    TR897.7.W746 2012
    006.6'96--dc23

                                                                                                    2012019339

Visit the Taylor & Francis Web site at
http://www.taylorandfrancis.com

and the CRC Press Web site at
http://www.crcpress.com

To Chia-Chi.

Contents

Preface

Production volume rendering, described in less than 15 words, refers to rendering of nonsurfaces for the purpose of creating images for film or animation production. A slightly longer explanation might include some examples, such as the creation and rendering of virtual smoke, fire, dust, and clouds. The "and" in "creation and rendering" is also an important point: production volume rendering refers just as much to the *modeling* of the effects as it refers to the actual *rendering*, and in fact, the modeling side is often the lesser known part of the two.

No matter which way you look at it, production volume rendering is an esoteric subject. Volume rendering in the general sense encompasses everything from medical visualization to real-time game graphics, but production volume rendering has very little overlap with these subjects. There are only a few publicly available pieces of software, and to make matters more complicated, there is also very little research or other documentation available, due to the fact that most development is done in-house at visual effects and animation production houses around the world.

The consequence of this lack of information is that each person who is tasked with working on a production volume renderer, or who just happens to be interested in the topic, has to start out from scratch, inventing most of the puzzle pieces that he or she needs to make their systems work.

A certain frustration with this lack of documentation and systemization led to a 2010 SIGGRAPH course called *Volumetric Methods in Visual Effects*, and the course, in turn, led to the book you now hold in your hand.

The course tried to give an overview of all the different techniques and ideas that are used in the volume-rendering solutions at some of the largest production facilities, and it also covered a wide range of concrete examples of those techniques, as they are implemented at those facilities.

This book takes over where the first part of the course left off and goes into all the same fundamental topics. But where the course stayed in a generic context, with simple examples, this book provides and describes a systematic implementation of the techniques.

The book's approach is highly pragmatic. Its scope is limited to the techniques and algorithms that are actively used in production work. It leaves out much of the available research into photorealistic volume rendering, but the reason for doing so is simply that those techniques rarely get used in production work.

In order to ensure that enough detail is provided on how each technique works, the book is written around an open source renderer called PVR, which can be downloaded, compiled, and modified by the reader. This approach hopefully means that whatever questions are left by the book can be answered by looking at how the code is implemented.

Goals

The goal of the book is to provide two paths towards understanding production volume rendering. On one side, it describes the techniques used for modern production volume rendering in a generic context. It shows how the techniques fit together, and how the modules that make it up are used to achieve real-world goals. But it wouldn't be a complete book if it did not also describe an implementation of those techniques. Showing how to translate the abstract set of concepts into concrete, working code is an important part of the equation. It shows that the ideas work. And it shows that they work together to create a complete system.

Throughout this book, the illustrations and rendered images are all created using the code that the book describes. In fact, the scripts and the data used for all the examples are freely available (along with the source code) at http://www.github.com/pvrbook.

The aim with this approach is to let the readers explore the book in two ways: Someone who is curious about how production volume rendering works in the big picture can start with reading the chapters that describe the fundamental ideas at play. At the same time, if the reader comes across an interesting image, he or she can go straight to the lowest level, starting with the script that created it. The reader can then trace his or her way back through the rendering code and the modeling primitives, which then hopefully illustrates the bigger picture that ties all the steps together.

The primary goal of the book is to be illustrative, and an important step towards that goal is making sure that the translation of the techniques and concepts into the working code is clear and that the code's modular structure properly reflects the ideas presented in the book. Secondly, the concepts outlined in the book and implemented in the code must be completely integrated, in the sense that each part of the system should work with all the others, using the same fundamental concepts. There should not be any isolated ideas that only work on their own and cannot be integrated into the system.

Efficiency is not the primary concern of the system. In the choice between simpler code or faster performance, PVR strives to be easy to understand. That is not to say that the system's performance is ignored. On the contrary, scalability is a very important aspect of any system that is to be used in production. The goal of the system is instead to show how various design considerations have an impact on both scalability, extensibility, generality, and performance, but to do so in a straightforward and understandable way.

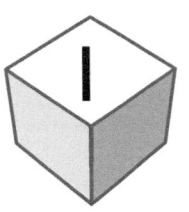

The PVR System

The system described in this book is called PVR, standing simply for production volume rendering. Because production volume rendering is a fairly esoteric topic, it was clear early on that a working example of the algorithms and techniques in action had to be included. To not include one would be to rob the reader of the understanding that can sometimes only be had by seeing how a set of techniques covering different areas work in conjunction with one another.

1.1   C++ and Python

PVR is implemented entirely in C++. The choice of C++ was simple; although the PVR renderer isn't built primarily for speed, the amounts of data it needs to process makes C or C++ the only real choice. And because the system needed to be modularized so that concepts from the book could map cleanly to code, the object-oriented nature of C++ made it the best candidate.

While C++ has many strengths, runtime configurability isn't necessarily one of them. In order to make it easy for the reader to create scene descriptions, PVR also includes a Python module that wraps the entire code base (or at least the relevant 99% of it) so that scenes can be created and rendered with a few lines of Python code.

To exclude the Python interface (or some other scripting language bindings) would mean that the reader would have to compile a full C++ application in order to create a scene. We assume that the reader takes no pleasure in decoding GCC's template error messages and, therefore, provide the bindings as a convenient, but powerful, scene-modeling and rendering language.

The intent of this book is to describe a simple but complete volume-modeling and rendering system. The focus is on illustrating the most important concepts as clearly as possible, and on describing a modular system where parts can easily be replaced to show the impact of different techniques and system design decisions. Performance, although very important in a production renderer, is not the primary goal of PVR. The system doesn't use any hard-to-understand or obfuscating optimization techniques, but where algorithmic optimizations are possible, those are discussed and implemented.

The system does use some programming concepts that are advanced in nature, but an effort has been made to keep this in the supporting code. The key parts of the system have all been designed to be as simple and instructive as possible.

1.1.1 Use of Namespaces

Namespaces are an important part of writing production code. If we consider some common classes one might write for a render, **Ray**, **Vector**, **Curve**, **Polygon**, etc., it is not unlikely that one of the other libraries that our system uses might have similarly named classes. If this occurs, the compiler will throw up its hands in confusion and tell you that you already created a **Vector** class, and it is not impressed that you are trying to do so again.

C++ provides a concept called *namespaces* that addresses this problem by changing the internal (C++ calls this *mangled*) name of a symbol to include the name of the namespace. This way, the compiler will know the difference between **Imath::Vec3<T>** and your **MyLibrary::Vec3<T>**. For this reason, all of the C++ source code is wrapped in a **pvr** namespace.

PVR also uses namespaces to divide its classes into broad modules, although more for organizational purposes than to prevent symbol name clashes. Representations of geometry, such as polygons, particles, and attributes, are all in the **pvr::Geo** namespace. Modeling-related classes are in **pvr::Model** and so on.

pvr::Accel	Acceleration data structures
pvr::Geo	Geometry-related classes and functions
pvr::Math	Math-related functions
pvr::Model	Volume-modeling classes

pvr::Noise	Noise and fractals
pvr::Render	Rendering-related classes
pvr::Sys	System-related classes
pvr::Util	Various utility functions and classes

1.1.2 Use of External Libraries

Where possible, existing libraries have been used to accomplish tasks not central to the functionality of the system and for components not directly related to volume modeling and rendering.

OpenEXR/Imath	Used as the main math library. Contains basic classes such as vectors and matrices.
OpenImageIO	A library for image input and output. Gives PVR the ability to read and write a variety of image formats.
Field3D	Provides voxel data structures and routines for storing voxel data on disk.
GPD	A library that enables reading and writing of Houdini's **geo** and **bgeo** formats.
boost	After the Standard Template Library, probably the most commonly used library in the world. PVR uses a variety of classes from **boost**, from smart pointer classes through timing utilities to Boost.Python.

1.2 Python Bindings

The use of Python in production pipelines has exploded over the last five to ten years. It is most commonly used for general scripting, but due to the ease of creating bindings for existing C/C++ libraries, it has also replaced the internal scripting languages of several major applications, for example, hscript in Houdini, MEL in Maya, and Tcl in Nuke.

PVR uses Boost.Python for its bindings, which exposes PVR's internal classes and function directly. Boost.Python makes it very simple to build the bindings and supports advanced memory management and object lifetime techniques, such as smart pointers, deep and shallow copying, etc.

As an example, the following code snippet builds a Python class that exposes the **Renderer** class, automatically manages its lifetime using **Renderer::Ptr**, and also replaces Python's default constructor with a custom one.

Code 1.1. Creating Python bindings for the **Renderer** class using Boost.Python

```
class_<Renderer, Renderer::Ptr>("Renderer", no_init)
    .def("__init__",       make_constructor(Renderer::create))
    .def("clone",          &Renderer::clone)
    .def("setCamera",      &Renderer::setCamera)
    .def("setRaymarcher",  &Renderer::setRaymarcher)
    .def("addVolume",      &Renderer::addVolume)
    .def("addLight",       &Renderer::addLight)
    .def("execute",        &Renderer::execute)
    .def("saveImage",      &Renderer::saveImage)
    ...
    ;
```

Boost.Python also makes it easy to expand the flexibility of the C++ code when creating bindings. For example, Python has no concept of **const** objects. To make the C++ code play nice with the Python bindings, Boost.Python provides a function that instructs the binding layer that some extra type conversions are legal, for example converting a non-**const** object to a **const** one.

Code 1.2. Instructing Boost.Python that a non-**const** pointer is convertible to a **const** pointer

```
implicitly_convertible<Renderer::Ptr, Renderer::CPtr>();
```

Boost.Python also makes it simple to adapt C++'s rigid type structure to work within Python's loosely typed classes. For example, we can tell it to allow conversions from Python's **list** and **dict** types to C++'s **std::vector** and **std::map**.

Code 1.3. Converting a Python type to a C++ type

```
template <typename T>
std::vector<T> pyListValues(boost::python::list l)
{
  using namespace boost::python;
  using namespace std;

  vector<T> hits;

  for (boost::python::ssize_t i = 0, end = len(l); i < end; ++i) {
    object o = l.pop();
    extract<T> s(o);
```

```
    if (s.check()) {
      hits.push_back(s());
    }
  }

  return hits;
}

// Convert a python list, grabbing only float values
boost::python::list l = some_list();
std::vector<float> floatVec = pyListValues<float>(l);
```

The bindings for PVR reside in the libpvr/python folder.

1.3   Rendering with PVR

To give an example of how rendering is accomplished with PVR, we first look at an example of a Python script that uses the **Modeler** class to build a voxel buffer and then renders it using the **Renderer** class. In the example, references have been made to each of the relevant chapters and sections. The final image is shown in Figure 1.1.

PVR's Modeling Pipeline, 91
Voxel Buffers, 33
PVR's Rendering Pipeline, 203

Figure 1.1. The result of our PVR example.

First, the **pvr** module is imported into the script. The `from pvr import *` syntax is used instead of `import pvr` so that the symbols in the library become visible without always having to prefix them with the library name.

Code 1.4. A simple modeling and rendering example

```
#! /usr/bin/env python

from pvr import *
```

The next step is to create instances of the classes that are used in the volume-modeling process. The **Modeler** is responsible for taking inputs in the form of **ModelerInput** instances and turning them into voxel buffers. Each modeler input contains the definition of a *volume primitive* (also known as *volumetric primitive*), in this case, a **PyroclasticPoint**, and a **Geometry** instance, which is the underlying geometric representation of the volume primitive. Pyroclastic points are a type of rasterization primitive, and their geometric representation is a **Particles** instance.

Code 1.5. A simple modeling and rendering example

```
# Modeling classes
modeler = Modeler()
parts   = Particles()
geo     = Geometry()
prim    = Prim.Rast.PyroclasticPoint()
input   = ModelerInput()
```

The particles object is configured with a single point, which by default sits at the origin. The particles instance is then hooked up to the geometry container, and the two are added to the modeler input along with the volume primitive. In a normal render, the volumetric primitive would be configured with a set of *attributes* to drive its appearance. In this simple example the default parameters will be used.

Code 1.6. A simple modeling and rendering example

```
# Create a modeling primitive with a single input point
parts.add(1)
geo.setParticles(parts)
input.setGeometry(geo)
input.setVolumePrimitive(prim)
```

The final step in the volume-modeling process is to add the **Modeler Input** to the **Modeler** and then update the *bounds*, which configure the voxel buffer so that it encloses all of the primitives in the modeler's list of inputs. Once the final resolution of the voxel buffer has been set, the modeler is executed, which runs each of its inputs and lets them write their data to the voxel buffer.

Code 1.7. A simple modeling and rendering example

```
# Add input to modeler and rasterize
modeler.addInput(input)
modeler.updateBounds()
modeler.setResolution(200)
modeler.execute()
```

Next, we create the rendering-related objects. The **Renderer** is the most important one, responsible for firing the rays that are turned into the pixel values of the final image. Any render requires that a camera be present; in this example, a **PerspectiveCamera** is used.

PVR uses raymarching to integrate the volumetric properties in the scene, but the task is broken into two separate parts. The **Raymarcher** takes steps along each ray fired from the final image's pixels, but the radiance and transmittance change at each step is determined by a **RaymarchSampler**.

Various types of light sources may be used in PVR to produce illumination of the scene. The task is divided between two classes. Each **Light** determines the illumination intensity and direction present at various points in the scene, but answering queries about how much light actually arrives at any given point is done by the **Occluder** rather than the light itself.

Although the modeler produces a voxel buffer after the **execute()** method has been called, it is not in a form that the renderer can handle. Instead, we first wrap it in a **VoxelVolume** instance, which makes the buffer renderable.

Code 1.8. A simple modeling and rendering example

```
# Rendering classes
renderer       = Renderer()
camera         = PerspectiveCamera()
raymarchSampler = PhysicalSampler()
raymarcher     = UniformRaymarcher()
occluderCamera = SphericalCamera()
occluder       = OtfTransmittanceMapOccluder(renderer, occluderCamera, 8)
light          = PointLight()
volume         = VoxelVolume()

# Configure rendering objects
camera.setPosition(V3f(0.0, 0.25, 6.0))
camera.setResolution(V2i(320, 240))
```

```
raymarcher.setRaymarchSampler(raymarchSampler)
light.setPosition(V3f(10.0, 10.0, 10.0))
light.setIntensity(Color(1.5))
occluderCamera.setPosition(light.position())
light.setOccluder(occluder)
volume.addAttribute("scattering", V3f(4.0, 6.0, 8.0))
volume.setBuffer(modeler.buffer())
```

Before the final image can be rendered, the camera, raymarcher, volume, and light all need to be added to the **Renderer**. Taken together, the **Volume** and **Light** instances make up the **Scene** of the render.

The last step before executing the render is to print the scene information. The **execute()** call will then start firing rays through the scene, which ultimately results in an image that can be saved to disk.

Code 1.9. A simple modeling and rendering example

```
# Connect the renderer with the raymarcher, camera, volume and light
renderer.setRaymarcher(raymarcher)
renderer.setCamera(camera)
renderer.addVolume(volume)
renderer.addLight(light)

# Print scene structure and start render
renderer.printSceneInfo()
renderer.execute()

# Save image to disk
renderer.saveImage("out/image.png")
```

PVR reports progress and status information at each step in the pipeline. The example code above generates the following log output, which gives feedback on each of the steps in the process.

Code 1.10. The log file generated by the above rendering example

```
23:01:33 [pvr] Updated bounds to: ((-3 -3 -3), (3 3 3))
23:01:33 [pvr] Creating dense buffer
23:01:33 [pvr] Using uniform/matrix mapping
23:01:33 [pvr] Setting voxel buffer resolution to: (200 200 200)
23:01:33 [pvr] Pyroclastic point primitive processing 1 input points
23:01:35 [pvr]    Rasterization: 22.68%
23:01:38 [pvr]    Rasterization: 45.09%
23:01:40 [pvr]    Rasterization: 67.70%
23:01:43 [pvr]    Rasterization: 90.19%
23:01:44 [pvr]    Time elapsed: 11.2419996
23:01:44 [pvr] Voxel buffer memory use: 91MB
23:01:44 [pvr] Scene info:
23:01:44 [pvr]    (VoxelVolume)
23:01:44 [pvr]      a scattering
```

```
23:01:44 [pvr]     i scattering : (4 6 8)
23:01:44 [pvr]     i Empty space optimization disabled
23:01:44 [pvr]     p Isotropic
23:01:44 [pvr]    (PointLight)
23:01:44 [pvr]     i (1.5 1.5 1.5)
23:01:44 [pvr]     o OtfTransmittanceMapOccluder
23:01:44 [pvr] Rendering image (320 240) (1 x 1)
23:01:46 [pvr]    44.23%
23:01:49 [pvr]    88.77%
23:01:49 [pvr]    Time elapsed: 5.51499987
23:01:49 [pvr] Writing image: out/image.jpg
23:01:49 [pvr]    Done.
```

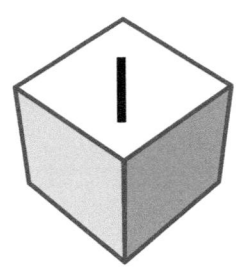

Fundamentals

The Basics

2.1 Time and Motion Blur

One of the key requirements of a production renderer is that it must handle the effects of time-varying properties robustly. Because a camera shutter (see Figure 2.1) stays open over a finite amount of time, we must account for changes in the scene during that time period. Attributes that often change with time are object position (transformation motion blur), object shape (deformation motion blur), and camera position and orientation (camera motion blur). For a rendering solution to be useful in a production context, each of these must be handled.

Time itself can have multiple different reference frames, each of which can be useful in a renderer. Film and television rely on showing a sequence of images that change quickly enough to give the illusion of motion. Each of these images is referred to as a *frame*, and an integer number can be assigned to each frame, making for a convenient reference frame for time.

Time can, of course, also be measured in seconds. If we consider an animation containing 48 frames, running at 24 frames per second, we have two seconds of material, given that the *frame rate* is the standard 24 frames per second (often abbreviated fps). If we start numbering frames at 1, we can convert between time (t) and frame number (F) using a simple formula:

$$t = \frac{F - 1}{\text{frames per second}}.$$

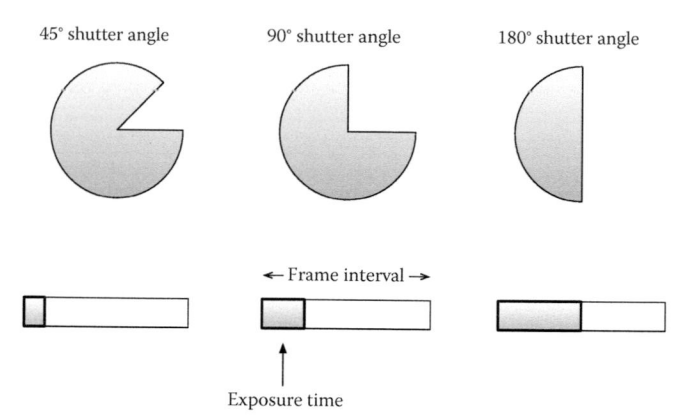

Figure 2.1. A motion picture camera shutter uses a rotating disk as its shutter. By varying the size of the open section, a certain shutter angle and exposure time is achieved.

A third way of looking at time is to define it in the time interval bounded by the camera shutter opening and closing. Here we can consider a parametric measure of time that is unitless and is defined only within a $[0,1]$ interval.

The shutter is usually not open for the entire duration of a frame. Most motion pictures are filmed using a *shutter angle* of 180° [Burum 07], a notion that warrants some explaining. A motion picture camera's shutter is most often a rotating disk with an adjustable slot, which in turn controls how long the exposure of each film frame is. The degree measure refers to the angle the slot occupies on the disk, meaning that at 180° the shutter is open 50% of the time and is closed 50% of the time. In computer graphics, this is more often expressed as a fraction called *shutter length* or *motion blur length*, and the corresponding value to 180° is 0.5.

We often refer to the actual time that the camera shutter is open as dt, and we can find it using the frame rate and shutter angle or motion blur length:

$$dt = \frac{\text{motion blur length}}{\text{frames per second}} = \frac{\text{shutter angle}/360°}{\text{frames per second}}.$$

A strict and consistent definition and handling of the various time frames is important in a renderer, and in PVR, they are actual class types, which prevents accidental misinterpretation. Time in seconds is defined by the `Time` class, whereas shutter open/close time is defined by `PTime`. PVR does not deal with frame time directly.

Code 2.1. The **Time** class

```
class Time
{
public:
  explicit Time(const float t)
    : m_value(t)
  { }
  operator float() const
  { return m_value; }
  float value() const
  { return m_value; }
private:
  float m_value;
};
```

Code 2.2. The **PTime** class

```
class PTime
{
public:
  explicit PTime(const float t)
    : m_value(t)
  { }
  operator float() const
  { return m_value; }
  float value() const
  { return m_value; }
private:
  float m_value;
};
```

Geometry Attributes, 24

In PVR, the motion of particles and geometry is represented using the v (for *velocity*) point attribute (see Section 2.4). Velocity vectors are always defined in m/s, meters per second. *Motion vectors* are different from velocity vectors; they refer to motion in the current shutter open/close interval and thus only have the length unit m. Any velocity vector can be converted to a motion vector through the formula

$$\vec{m} = \vec{v} \cdot dt.$$

2.1.1 Render Globals

When designing a renderer, there is always a certain amount of information that pertains to all parts of the renderer. Rather than passing a set of variables to every single rendering function, it is quite common to use an object that is globally accessible to store such information. In PVR, this class is called `RenderGlobals`.

The `RenderGlobals` class stores pointers to the current scene as well as to the render camera. Information relating to time is also available in the class. When a new render frame is initiated, the rendering class configures `RenderGlobals` by calling the static `setupMotionBlur()` method. After that, any of PVR's components can access *dt* through the `RenderGlobals::dt()` method.

Code 2.3. `RenderGlobals`

```
class RenderGlobals
{
public:
  // Typedefs
  typedef boost::shared_ptr<const pvr::Render::Scene> SceneCPtr;
  typedef boost::shared_ptr<const pvr::Render::Camera> CameraCPtr;
  // Exceptions
  DECLARE_PVR_RT_EXC(BadFpsException, "Bad frames per second value:");
  DECLARE_PVR_RT_EXC(BadShutterException, "Bad shutter value:");
  // Main methods
  static void      setupMotionBlur(const float fps, const float shutter);
  static void      setScene(SceneCPtr scene);
  static void      setCamera(CameraCPtr camera);
  // Accessors
  static float     fps();
  static float     shutter();
  static float     dt();
  static SceneCPtr scene();
  static CameraCPtr camera();
private:
  // Data members
  static float     ms_fps;
  static float     ms_shutter;
  static float     ms_dt;
  static SceneCPtr ms_scene;
  static CameraCPtr ms_camera;
};
```

2.1.2   Function Curves

So far, we have mentioned motion blur, but we have not yet showed how time-varying properties can be represented. PVR treats properties that change with time as one-dimensional functions that are linearly *interpolated* to find sub-sample values. (See, for example, Figure 2.2.)

In most cases, time-varying properties change gradually and smoothly over time and can be described well using only two time samples: one at the shutter open time and one at shutter close. In other cases, such as

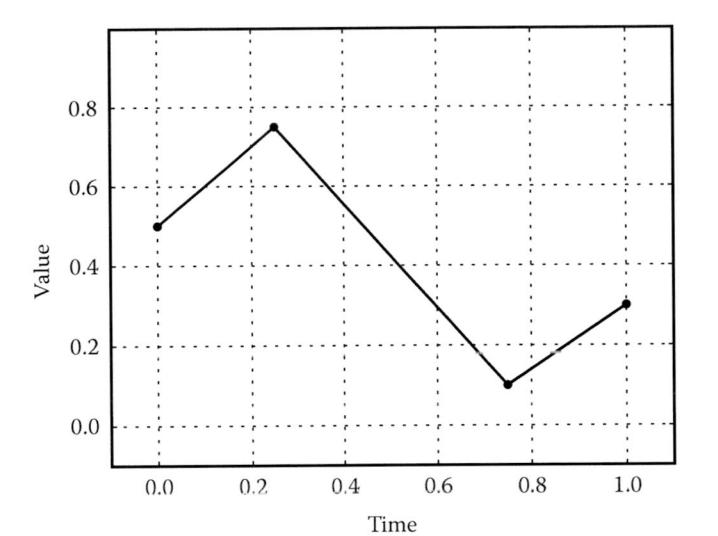

Figure 2.2. A function curve using four samples and linear interpolation.

a camera with "shake" applied, the changes can be drastic and sudden, requiring more than two samples to accurately describe the change in position, orientation, etc. In order to support arbitrary intra-frame motion, PVR handles these time-varying properties using the **Util::Curve** class. Each **Curve** can contain as many samples as is necessary, and in-between values are then linearly interpolated.

Code 2.4. Curve

```
class Curve
{
public:
...
  // Main methods
  void              addSample(const float t, const T &value);
  T                 interpolate(const float t) const;
  size_t            numSamples() const;
  const SampleVec&  samples() const;
  std::vector<float> samplePoints() const;
  std::vector<T>    sampleValues() const;
  void              removeDuplicates();
  static CPtr       average(const std::vector<CPtr> &curves);
private:
...};
```

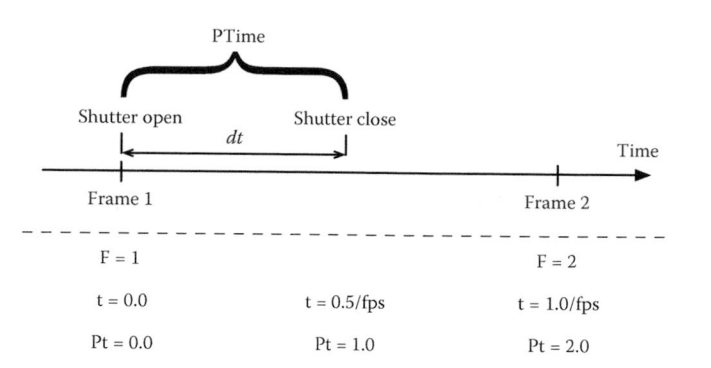

Figure 2.3. PVR's temporal coordinate frames.

The **Curve** class is templated and can theoretically be used to store any type of data that can be interpolated. The most commonly used types, however, are

```
typedef Curve<float>  FloatCurve;
typedef Curve<Color>  ColorCurve;
typedef Curve<Vector> VectorCurve;
typedef Curve<Quat>   QuatCurve;
```

When a **Curve** is used in PVR, the time dimension is assumed to line up with **PTime**, such that $t = 0.0$ refers to the start of the frame and the shutter open time. The end of the shutter interval falls at $t = 1.0$, which matches the **PTime** definition. When constructing a curve, it is most common to have information about how a given attribute changes from frame to frame. If we let $t_P^i = 0.0$ be the **PTime** of the current frame start, then the equivalent **PTime** for the next frame start can be found through the expression

PTime, 15

$$t_P^{i+1} = \frac{1}{\text{motion blur length}}.$$

Figure 2.3 illustrates PVR's definition of time reference frames for a motion blur length of 0.5.

2.2   Cameras

The camera classes in PVR are very simple, and their implementations should provide no surprises to the reader. Most parameters are assumed to be temporally varying, meaning that properties such as position, orientation, and field of view may change over the course of the current frame. In support of this, all of the calls to the camera that depend on time use the **PTime** concept, where 0.0 is assumed to be the start of the current frame, i.e., when the shutter opens, and 1.0 is the time that the shutter closes.

This book assumes the reader is familiar with common computer graphics conventions for camera projection calculations. For a thorough introduction to cameras in computer graphics, [Watt 00] and [Pharr and Humphreys 10] are good sources.

2.2.1 Camera Coordinate Spaces

PVR's world space is right-handed, but its camera space is left-handed. By default, a camera with no rotation looks down the negative z-axis in world space, and down positive z in camera space. The camera's x- and y-axes line up with the world space, with x to the right and y facing up. (See Figure 2.4.)

Screen space defines the projected view of the camera, with $x = 1$ indicating the left edge of the camera's view, $x = 1$ the right edge, $y = 1$ the bottom edge, and $y = 1$ the top edge. The depth dimension has no negative range, instead putting $z = 0$ at the near plane of the projection and $z = 1$ at the far plane. (See Figure 2.5.)

PVR also uses a second projection space, which is called NDC space. NDC stands for normalized device coordinates and changes the x and y ranges of the projection to the $[0, 1]$ range. (See Figure 2.6.)

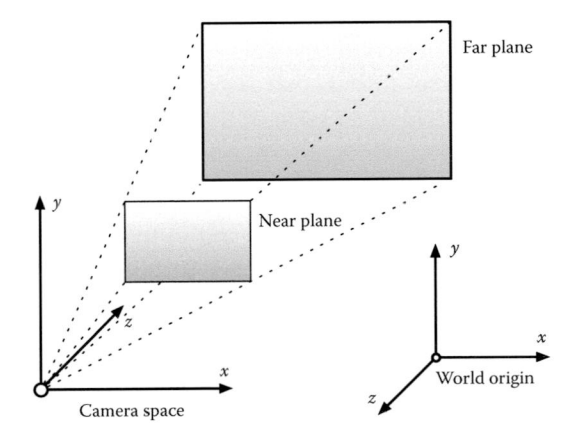

Figure 2.4. PVR's camera space conventions.

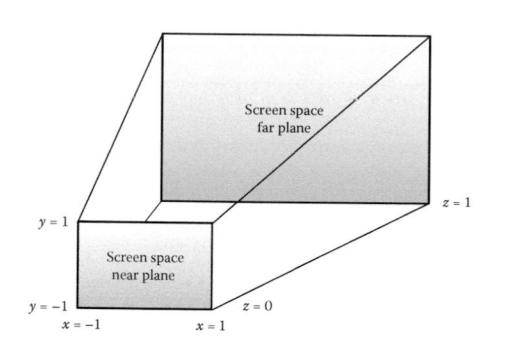

Figure 2.5. PVR's screen space conventions. **Figure 2.6.** PVR's NDC space conventions.

2.3 Geometry

Most of PVR's modeling operations take geometry as their inputs. The geometry may be a point cloud (particles), splines (or polygonal lines), and/or *meshes* (connected grids of $M \times N$ dimensions). Each type has an associated class in PVR, and the classes all reside in the **pvr::Geo** namespace.

Common for all the geometry types is that they store multiple instances of the data types they represent. For example, **Meshes** stores N number of mesh instances, and **Particles** stores N number of particle instances.

The topology[1] of each instance is configured when it is added to the collection. Once the topology is in place, all of the properties of the geometry are handled by attributes (see Section 2.4). Per-point attributes are always accessed through the **pointAttrs()** call, which contains all per-point varying properties, including point positions. It is, in general, safe to add extra attributes directly to the **AttrTable** that **pointAttrs()** returns but not to change its size; rather, that should be accomplished with the dedicated functions provided by each of the geometry container classes.

2.3.1 The **Geometry** Class

The **Geometry** class wraps up all of the individual geometry types that PVR is able to process. It contains one instance each of **Particles**, **Polygons**, and **Meshes** (see below) and also carries *global attributes* (in the form of another **AttrTable**) that apply to the geometry as a whole. The class also provides the **Geometry::read()** call, which loads geometric data from a variety of formats.

---

[1]For example, the number of points for a polygon or the number of rows and columns for a mesh.

Code 2.5. The **Geometry** class

```
class Geometry
{
public:
  ...
  // Main methods
  static Geometry::Ptr read(const std::string &filename);
  void              setParticles(Particles::Ptr particles);
  void              setPolygons(Polygons::Ptr polygons);
  void              setMeshes(Meshes::Ptr meshes);
  Particles::Ptr    particles();
  Particles::CPtr   particles() const;
  Polygons::Ptr     polygons();
  Polygons::CPtr    polygons() const;
  Meshes::Ptr       meshes();
  Meshes::CPtr      meshes() const;
  AttrTable&        globalAttrs();
  const AttrTable&  globalAttrs() const;
protected:
  ...};
```

2.3.2 The **Particles** Class

AttrTable, 25

The **Particles** class is used to represent point clouds and particle systems. It is represented as a single **AttrTable**, which contains all the information properties of the point cloud, including position. It provides calls for changing the number of particles (**Particles::resize()**) and appending extra points to the existing particle system (**Particles::add()**). All of PVR's modeling algorithms that are point based use the **Particles** class as their data representations and utilize any number of per point and global attributes. Figure 2.7 shows an example.

Code 2.6. The **Particles** class

```
class Particles
{
public:
  ...
  // Main methods
  void              resize(const size_t size);
  void              add(const size_t numItems);
  size_t            size() const;
  void              setPosition(const size_t idx, const Imath::V3f &pos);
  AttrTable&        pointAttrs();
  const AttrTable&  pointAttrs() const;
private:
  ...};
```

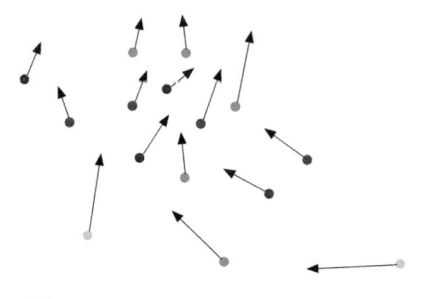

Figure 2.7. A particle system with per-point color and velocity vectors.

2.3.3   The **Polygons** Class

The **Polygons** class is used to represent all sorts of basic polygon primitives, both open (such as lines) and closed (triangles and higher point-
count polygons). (See Figures 2.8 and 2.9.)

The most common way to construct a **Polygons** object is **Polygons::**
addPolygon(), which returns the index of the new polygon. Once the
polygon exists, the properties of the individual points (the polygon's
vertices) can be configured by querying **Polygons::pointForVertex()** and
using the point index to manipulate items in the **AttrTable** returned by   **AttrTable**, 25
Polygons::pointAttrs().

Code 2.7. The **Polygons** class

```
class Polygons
{
public:
...
  // Main methods
  size_t           size() const;
  size_t           addPoint();
  size_t           addPolygon(const size_t numVertices);
  size_t           numVertices(const size_t polyIdx) const;
  void             setVertex(const size_t polyIdx, const size_t vertIdx,
                            const size_t pointIdx);
  void             setVertices(const size_t polyIdx,
                            const std::vector<size_t> pointIndices);
  size_t           pointForVertex(const size_t polyIdx,
                            const size_t vertIdx) const;
  bool             isClosed(const size_t polyIdx) const;
  void             setIsClosed(const size_t polyIdx, bool closed);
  AttrTable&       pointAttrs();
  const AttrTable& pointAttrs() const;
  AttrTable&       polyAttrs();
  const AttrTable& polyAttrs() const;
...
protected:
...};
```

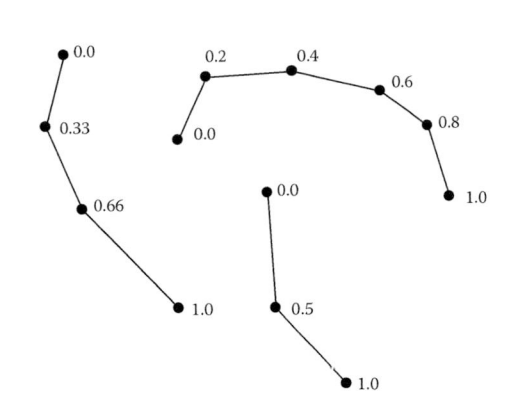

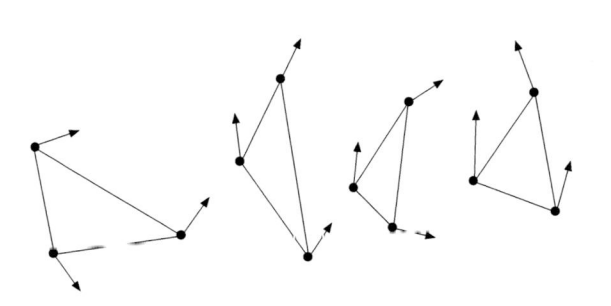

Figure 2.8. A set of poly lines with UV coordinates.

Figure 2.9. Triangles with velocity vectors.

2.3.4   The **Meshes** Class

The **Meshes** class represents a collection of meshes, which are connected quadrilaterals attached in grids of $M \times N$ rows and columns. Each mesh in a **Meshes** instance can have different dimensions. (See Figure 2.10.)

Polygons, 22

Similar to the **Polygons** class, a **Meshes** instance is normally built by first calling **Meshes::addMesh()**, which returns the index of the new mesh, and then setting up the per-point and per-mesh properties using **Meshes:: pointForVertex()** and the **AttrTable** instances provided by **Meshes::point Attrs()** and **Meshes::meshAttrs()**.

Code 2.8. The **Meshes** class

```
class Meshes
{
public:
...
  // Main methods
  size_t          size() const;
  size_t          addMesh(const size_t numRows, const size_t numCols);
  size_t          numRows(const size_t meshIdx) const;
  size_t          numCols(const size_t meshIdx) const;
  size_t          startPoint(const size_t meshIdx) const;
  size_t          pointForVertex(const size_t meshIdx,
                                 const size_t row, const size_t col) const;
  AttrTable&      pointAttrs();
  const AttrTable& pointAttrs() const;
  AttrTable&      meshAttrs();
  const AttrTable& meshAttrs() const;
  void            computeDerivatives();
...
protected:
...};
```

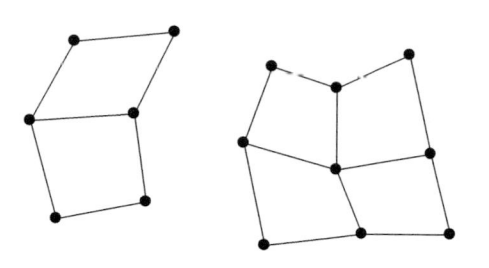

Figure 2.10. Two meshes of dimensions 3×2 and 3×3.

2.4 Geometry Attributes

A fundamental part of production rendering, both surface rendering and volume rendering, is the use of *attribute data* for driving various aspects of shaders and other rendering parameters. Attributes can, for example, be used to alter the color of a surface or pass texture and noise coordinates to a shader.

A typical subdivision surface might include the following attributes:

- P – position,
- N – normal,
- uv – texture coordinates,
- crease – crease amount,
- color – point color.

However, a typical particle simulation would have a different set of attributes:

- P – position,
- v – velocity,
- a – acceleration,
- age – age of particle (since birth),
- color – particle color.

It would be impractical to predict all attributes the user might possibly need; instead, production rendering systems almost always allow the user to input any number of arbitrarily named attributes along with their geometries. This is especially true for volume rendering, since almost all of the modeling primitives use some form of procedural techniques and/or shaders for adding detail, and the shaders require parameters to be controlled by attributes on the geometry.

Attributes in PVR are divided into different categories. For example, a point cloud or a particle system may have not only attributes that change from point to point but also attributes that affect the primitive as a whole, i.e., ones that are common for all of the points. Throughout the book, we will come back to a few specific types:

Point attributes. These are properties that assume different values for different parts of the geometric primitive. Point attributes often need to be interpolated across the geometry.

Primitive attributes. When a property is constant for an entire primitive (for example, noise scale), it is more efficient to store that attribute once, rather than duplicated for each point in the primitive.

Global attributes. Properties that are shared between all of the primitives in the *input geometry* are referred to as global attributes.[2]

Because adding, manipulating, and reading attribute values are such a common process in PVR, a set of classes is available for storing attributes (**AttrTable**), for referring to attributes (**AttrRef**), for accessing the values of attributes (**Attr**), and for conveniently traversing all the attribute values in a collection (**AttrVisitor**). The following sections will describe each of the classes.

2.5   Attribute Tables

The **AttrTable** class represents a collection of attributes and an arbitrary number of instances that carry those attributes. It is easiest thought of as a two-dimensional array, where each column is an attribute, and each row is an instance. For example, the properties of a particle system with 100 points and 4 attributes would be represented as a 4×100 table.

An **AttrTable**'s *size* refers to the number of items in the table, i.e., the number of rows.

Code 2.9. **AttrTable**'s main methods

```
class AttrTable
{
public:
...
  // Main methods
  void    addElems(const size_t numItems);
  void    resize  (const size_t size);
  size_t  size    () const;
...
private:
...};
```

---

[2]Global attributes are sometimes also called *object attributes*.

The **AttrTable** class supports several types of attributes:

- int – integer attributes (can be of any length),
- float – float attributes (can be of any length),
- vector – vector attributes (always stores three float values),
- string – string attributes (always stores a single variable-length string).

Each attribute in the **AttrTable** has a unique name. Before accessing an attribute value, the name must be known. The **AttrTable** class also provides routines for getting the names of all attributes of a given type:

Code 2.10. Access to attribute names

```
class AttrTable
{
public:
...
  // Attribute names
  StringVec intAttrNames   () const;
  StringVec floatAttrNames () const;
  StringVec vectorAttrNames() const;
  StringVec stringAttrNames() const;
...
private:
...};
```

When creating a new attribute, the name of the attribute must be provided, as well as its default value. Defaults are important: existing table rows need to have a value filled in, and conversely, when new table rows are added, a value must be assigned for each existing attribute.

Code 2.11. Adding attributes

```
class AttrTable
{
public:
...
  // Adding attributes
  AttrRef addIntAttr   (const std::string &attrName, const size_t size,
                        const std::vector<int> &defaults);
  AttrRef addFloatAttr (const std::string &attrName, const size_t size,
                        const std::vector<float> &defaults);
  AttrRef addVectorAttr(const std::string &attrName,
                        const Imath::V3f &defaults);
  AttrRef addStringAttr(const std::string &attrName);
...
private:
...};
```

Before reading or writing an attribute value, we need to get a *reference* to it. References can be had either by adding the attribute as described in the previous section, in which case the reference is returned, or, if an attribute already exists, by retrieving a reference through an **AttrTable** call. In this case, only the attribute name is required, as attribute names are unique identifiers.

Code 2.12. Attribute references

```
class AttrTable
{
public:
...
  // Attribute references
  AttrRef intAttrRef   (const std::string &attrName) const;
  AttrRef floatAttrRef (const std::string &attrName) const;
  AttrRef vectorAttrRef(const std::string &attrName) const;
  AttrRef stringAttrRef(const std::string &attrName) const;
...
private:
...};
```

Once we have the reference to an attribute, we can access its value using the following functions:

Code 2.13. Attribute read access

```
class AttrTable
{
public:
...
  // Attribute read access
  int         intAttr   (const AttrRef &ref, const size_t elem,
                         const size_t arrayIdx) const;
  float       floatAttr (const AttrRef &ref, const size_t elem,
                         const size_t arrayIdx) const;
  Imath::V3f vectorAttr(const AttrRef &ref, const size_t elem) const;
...
private:
...};
```

Writing attribute values is very similar to reading them.

Code 2.14. Attribute write access

```
class AttrTable
{
public:
  ...
```

```
  // Attribute write access
  void setIntAttr    (const AttrRef &ref, const size_t elem,
                      const size_t arrayIdx, const int value);
  void setFloatAttr (const AttrRef &ref, const size_t elem,
                      const size_t arrayIdx, const float value);
  void setVectorAttr(const AttrRef &ref, const size_t elem,
                      const Imath::V3f &value);
  ...
private:
...};
```

2.5.1   String Attributes

String attributes are handled differently than other attribute types. Because strings are variable length, they can not efficiently be stored directly in the table. Rather, a separate *string table* is used to store the strings, and a reference index to the string is stored as the string attribute value. Storing strings indirectly also has the benefit of allowing identical strings to be shared, reducing the cost of storage to just a single **size_t**.

Code 2.15. String attribute access

```
class AttrTable
{
public:
...
  // String attribute access
  size_t             stringIdxAttr    (const AttrRef &ref,
                                       const size_t elem) const;
  void               setStringIdxAttr(const AttrRef &ref,
                                       const size_t elem,
                                       const size_t value);
  const std::string& stringAttr       (const AttrRef &ref,
                                       const size_t elem) const;
  void               setStringAttr    (const AttrRef &ref,
                                       const size_t elem,
                                       const std::string &value);
  const std::string& stringFromTable  (const AttrRef &ref,
                                       const size_t strIdx) const;
  size_t             addStringToTable(const AttrRef &ref,
                                       const std::string &s);
...
private:
...};
```

The easy, but slow, way to read and write string attributes is to use **AttrTable::stringAttr()** and **AttrTable::setStringAttr()**. These do the work of adding strings to the string table, setting index values, and reading strings back from the string table. A more efficient way, at least when adding many identical strings, or when comparing string values between different table rows, is to read and write the string index directly using **AttrTable::stringIdxAttr()** and **AttrTable::setStringIdxAttr()**.

2.6   Attribute References

Although a reference to an attribute is nothing more than an array index, the **AttrRef** class wraps up this index along with another important piece of information: whether the reference is indeed a *valid* reference. The various **AttrTable::<type>AttrRef** calls may not necessarily find an attribute of the given name, in which case it needs to report this failure. Rather than return a boolean or throw an exception, it marks the **AttrRef** as being invalid. In practical code, it is used as follows:

```
AttrTable at;
AttrRef positionRef = at.vectorAttrRef("P");
if (positionRef.isValid()) {
  Imath::V3f position = at.vectorAttr(positionRef, pointNum);
}
```

The **AttrRef** also contains information about the size of array attributes (integer and floating-point attributes may contain N values in a single attribute).

```
AttrTable at;
AttrRef idxRef = at.intAttrRef("indices");
if (idxRef.isValid()) {
  for (int i = 0; i < idxRef.arraySize(); ++i) {
    int value = at.intAttr(idxRef, pointNum, i);
    ...
  }
}
```

2.7   Attribute Iteration

AttrTable, 25

One of the most common tasks in PVR is to iterate over the attribute values in an **AttrTable**. While it would be possible to write the loop as seen below, this is both terse and inefficient.

```
AttrTable at;
AttrRef pRef = at.vectorAttrRef("P");
if (pRef.isValid()) {
```

```
  for (size_t i = 0, end = at.size(); i < end; ++i) {
    V3f p = at.vectorAttr(pRef, i);
    ...
  }
}
```

Things are further complicated when we introduce the concept of global attributes. In many cases, an attribute is the same for all primitives that are being iterated over; the noise function may be the same even if its amplitude changes across the primitive. It is unnecessary and costly to store these attributes once for each point in the geometry, so instead, a global set of attributes can be used, which reduces memory overhead. A second case occurs when the user knows that a given per-point varying attribute is constant for all primitives. In this case, the person writing the code can't be sure if a given attribute will come in as a global or per-point attribute (ideally we want to support both), so the code becomes more complex as a result:

```
AttrTable  at;
ParamMap   globalAttrs = getGlobalAttrs();
AttrRef    pRef = at.vectorAttrRef("P");
AttrRef    attr1Ref = at.floatAttrRef("attr1");
AttrRef    attr2Ref = at.floatAttrRef("attr2");
float      attr1Def = globalAttrs["attr1"];
float      attr2Def = globalAttrs["attr2"];
for (size_t i = 0, end = at.size(); i < end; ++i) {
  V3f p = at.vectorAttr(pRef, i);
  if (attr1Ref.isValid()) {
    float attr1 = at.floatAttr(attr1Ref, i);
    ...
  } else {
    float attr1 = globalsAttrs["attr1"];
    ...
  }
  ...
}
```

A better way to accomplish the same goal is to use the **AttrVisitor** and **Attr** classes. The class **AttrVisitor** is a utility class that makes it simple to traverse all of the items in an **AttrTable**. It is used in conjunction with the **Attr** class, which represents the current value for one of the attributes in the **AttrTable**.

AttrTable, 25

An equivalent version of the above code example would be

```
AttrTable   at;
ParamMap    globalAttrs = getGlobalAttrs();
AttrVisitor visitor(at, globalParams);
```

```
Attr<V3f>   p("P");
Attr<float> attr1("attr1");
Attr<float> attr2("attr2");
for (AttrVisitor::const_iterator i = visitor.begin(), end = visitor.end();
     i != end; ++i) {
   i.update(p);
   i.update(attr1);
   i.update(attr2);
   ...
}
```

We note that the **AttrVisitor** class itself handles global attributes, and it hides whether the current attribute value comes from the **AttrTable** itself or from the global **ParamMap**. Most importantly, no iteration actually takes place when reading the attribute value from the global attributes. Not only is the latter option easier and cleaner to code, performance is also better than the first two examples.

Voxel Buffers

3.1 Introduction to Voxel Buffers

Production volume rendering systems vary in how they are structured and what techniques they use for creating images, but they generally have one thing in common, which is the use of *voxel buffers*. Some volume renderers use procedural volumes (and PVR can do so as well), but in general, production volume rendering revolves around the *modeling* of voxel buffers and around how those buffers then get *rendered* into images.

A voxel is the three-dimensional extension of a pixel, and the word supposedly stems from *volume pixel* or *volumetric pixel*. Where images are two-dimensional arrays of pixels, voxel buffers are three-dimensional arrays of voxels. (See Figure 3.1.)

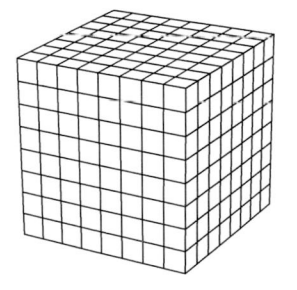

Figure 3.1. A voxel buffer with $8 \times 8 \times 8$ voxels.

3.1.1   Voxel Indexing

Just as with a two-dimensional image, we can access the contents of a voxel by its coordinate. The bottom-left corner of the buffer has coordinate $(0\ 0\ 0)$ in the *voxel coordinate space*, and its neighbor in the positive direction along the x-axis is $(1\ 0\ 0)$. When referring to the index along a given axis, it is common to label the variable i, j, and k for the x-, y-, and z-axes, respectively. In mathematic notation, this is often written using subscripts, such that a voxel buffer B has voxels located at $B_{i,j,k}$.

In code, this translates directly to the integer indices given to a voxel buffer class's accessor method, such as the following:

```
struct VoxelBuffer
{
  float value(int i, int j, int k);
  // ...
};

float a = buffer.value(0, 0, 0);
```

3.1.2   Extents and Data Window

Voxel indices do not need to start at $(0\ 0\ 0)$. In some cases, only a portion of the voxel buffer is of relevance to a particular scene or problem, and if the voxel buffer could be defined so that only those voxels existed in memory, there would be less overhead. As a parallel, images in the OpenEXR file format [ILM 12] have a *display window* and *data window* that specify the intended size and the allocated pixels of an image. The same concept translates well to voxel buffers, where we will refer to the intended size of the buffer as *extents* and the region of legal indices as data window. (See Figure 3.2.)

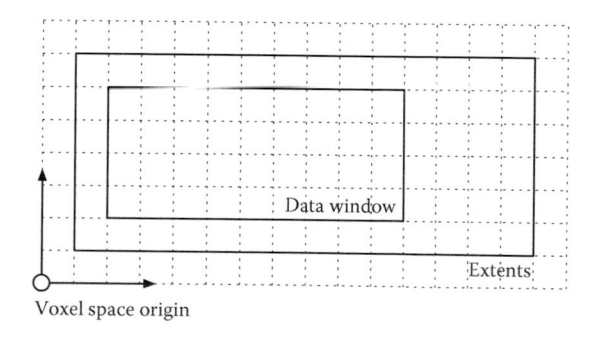

Figure 3.2. Two-dimensional example of extents and data window.

In the illustration above, the extents is greater than the data window. It would be the result of the following code:

Code 3.1. Setting the extents and data window of a voxel buffer

```
Box3i extents(V3i(1, 1, 0), V3i(15,7,10));
Box3i dataWindow(V3i(2, 2, 0), V3i(11, 6, 10));
buffer.setSize(extents, dataWindow);
```

Using separate extents and data window can be helpful for image processing (a blur filter can run on a padded version of the field so that no boundary conditions need to be handled), interpolation (guarantees that a voxel has neighbors to interpolate to, even at the edge of the extents), or optimizing memory use (only allocates memory for the voxels needed).

3.1.3   Coordinate Spaces and Mappings

The only coordinate space we've discussed so far is the voxel buffer's native coordinate system. (See Figure 3.3.) In the future, we will refer to this coordinate space as *voxel space*. In order to place a voxel buffer in space, we also need to define how to transform a position from voxel space into *world space* (which is the global reference frame of the renderer). Besides voxel and world space, a third space is useful, similar to RenderMan's NDC space but local to the buffer. This *local space* defines a $[0, 1]$ range over all voxels in the buffer's extents and is used as a resolution independent way of specifying locations within the voxel buffer. Although local space is defined so that it lines up with the extents, it is still perfectly valid to transform points that lie outside the extents into and out of the local space.

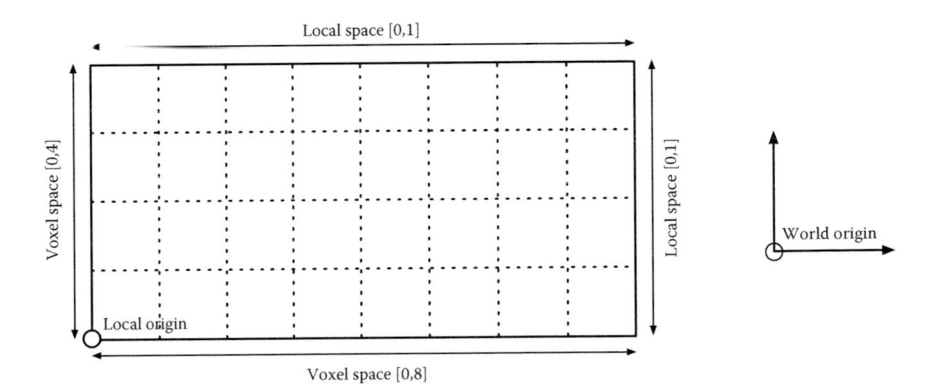

Figure 3.3. A voxel buffer's coordinate spaces.

When constructing a voxel buffer, we define a *local-to-world transform* in order to place the buffer in space. This transform is also called *mapping* and defines the transformation between the voxel buffer's local space and the renderer's world space. Section 3.4 will describe mappings in more detail, but for now we can assume that they simply answer how a given point in the buffer maps to a position in the global reference frame of the renderer. We also note that the transformation from local space to voxel space is the same regardless of the buffer's location in space.

Transformations and Mappings, 43

To sum things up, the following are the coordinate spaces we will be interacting with:

World space. The global coordinate system of the renderer. Exists independently of any voxel buffer.

Local space. A resolution-independent coordinate system that maps the full voxel extents of the buffer to a $[0, 1]$ space.

Voxel space. Used for indexing into the underlying voxels of a field. A field with 100 voxels along the x-axis maps (100.0 0.0 0.0) in voxel space to (1.0 0.0 0.0) in local space.

As a matter of convenience and clarity, we will prefix variables in code and pseudocode with an abbreviated form of the coordinate space. A point `P` in world space will be called `wsP`, in voxel space `vsP`, and in local space `lsP`. This convention helps remind us when a function parameter is presumed to be in a given coordinate space, and hopefully prevents us from introducing subtle bugs where coordinate systems get mixed up.

3.1.4   What Are the Coordinates of a Voxel?

Voxel space is different from local and world space in that it can be accessed in two ways: using integer or floating-point coordinates. Integer access is used for direct access to an individual voxel, and floating-point coordinates are used when interpolating values. It is important to take care when converting between the two. The center of voxel (0 0 0) has floating-point coordinates (0.5 0.5 0.5). Thus, the edges of a field with resolution 100 are at 0.0 and 100.0 when using floating-point coordinates, but when using integer indexing, only 0 through 99 are valid indices. An excellent overview of this can be found in an article by Paul S. Heckbert, "What Are the Coordinates of a Pixel?" [Heckbert 90]

In practice, it is convenient to define a set of conversion functions to go from floating-point to integer coordinates and vice versa, so that a `float` may be converted to an `int` appropriately, and `Vec3<float>` to `Vec3<int>`, etc. We will refer to these conversion functions as `discToCont()` and `contToDisc()`.

Code 3.2. Utility functions for correctly transforming floating-point voxel coordinates to integer coordinates

```
int contToDisc(float contCoord)
{
  return static_cast<int>(std::floor(contCoord));
}
float discToCont(int discCoord)
{
  return static_cast<float>(discCoord) + 0.5f;
}
```

3.2   Implementing a Simple Voxel Buffer

If we consider the simplest possible voxel buffer, it only needs to carry two properties: its resolution along each dimension and its data. It also only needs to perform two tasks: reading values from the data set and writing values to the data set. This can all be implemented in 14 lines of C++ code.

Code 3.3. A trivial voxel buffer class

```
struct VoxelBuffer {
  VoxelBuffer(int sizeX, int sizeY, int sizeZ)
    : m_sizeX(sizeX), m_sizeY(sizeY), m_sizeZ(sizeZ)
  { m_data.resize(sizeX * sizeY * sizeZ); }
  float read(int i, int j, int k) const
  { return m_data[index(i, j, k)]; }
  void write(int i, int j, int k, float value)
  { m_data[index(i, j, k)] = value; }
private:
  int index(int i, int j, int k)
  { return i + j * m_sizeX + k * m_sizeX * m_sizeY; }
  int m_sizeX, m_sizeY, m sizeZ;
  std::vector<float> m_data;
};
```

Of course, to do interesting work, one needs to position the voxel buffer in space. This can be done by providing a 4×4 matrix during construction, which specifies how coordinates in the local coordinate system maps to coordinates in world space (see Section 3.1.3).

Coordinate Spaces and Mappings, 35

Code 3.4. Adding a local-to-world transform to the trivial voxel buffer class

```
struct VoxelBuffer {
  VoxelBuffer(int sizeX, int sizeY, int sizeZ, float *localToWorld)
    : m_sizeX(sizeX), m_sizeY(sizeY), m_sizeZ(sizeZ),
```

```
      m_localToWorld(localToWorld)
  { m_data.resize(sizeX * sizeY * sizeZ); }
  float* localToWorld() const
  { return m_localToWorld; }
  ...
private:
  ...
  float *m_localToWorld;
  ...
};
```

It would also be useful if the data sets could be written to and read from disk:

Code 3.5. Adding read and write capabilities to the trivial voxel buffer class

```
struct VoxelBuffer {
  ...
  void read(const char *filename)
  {
    std::ifstream in(filename);
    in >> m_sizeX >> m_sizeY >> m_sizeZ;
    std::copy(std::istream_iterator<float>(in),
              std::istream_iterator<float>(),
              std::back_inserter(m_data));
  }
  void write(const char *filename)
  {
    std::ofstream out(filename);
    out << m_sizeX << " " << m_sizeY << " " << m_sizeZ << std::endl;
    std::copy(m_data.begin(), m_data.end(),
              std::ostream_iterator<float>(out, "\n"));
  }
  ...
};
```

At 34 lines, the code is still not long, but we can see how the complexity grows with each feature that needs to be added.

3.3   Field3D

In the interest of keeping PVR's code base simple and short, it uses many existing libraries to perform functions that it would otherwise have to implement itself. Some examples are Boost.Python [Abrahams 12] and OpenImageIO [Gritz 12]. For voxel buffers, one open source alternative is Field3D [Wrenninge 12], which Sony Pictures Imageworks released in 2009. Field3D provides both voxel-buffer data structures and I/O routines for reading and writing the data to disk. Since Field3D and the book you are currently reading share an author, it seemed somewhat redundant to implement a new set of classes for accomplishing the same work. Instead, PVR uses Field3D for all of its voxel buffer needs. In the next few sections, we will look at how each of the major components works and what features set production-honed code apart from simple tests, such as the example above.

3.3.1 The DenseField Class

The simplest kind of voxel buffer (similar to the trivial example above) is implemented in the **Field3D::DenseField<T>** class. All of the voxels in the buffer are allocated in a single contiguous memory block, using a simple **std::vector<T>**. The class uses very little memory apart from the voxel data itself, so the amount of memory used at various sizes is very close to $R^3 \cdot$ sizeof(T), where R is the resolution of the field.

DenseField memory use	
64^3	1 MB
128^3	8 MB
256^3	64 MB
512^3	512 MB
1024^3	4096 MB

Traversing DenseField	
64^3	0.001 s
128^3	0.008 s
256^3	0.06 s
512^3	0.5 s

Field3D provides some helper classes for efficiently traversing the voxels in the buffer. Instead of writing explicit for loops over each dimension, **DenseField<T>::iterator** provides a more convenient way of traversing the voxels.

Code 3.6. Traversing the voxels in a field explicitly

```
for (int k = 0; k < size; k++) {
  for (int j = 0; j < size; j++) {
    for (int i = 0; i < size; i++) {
      float value = field.fastValue(i, j, k);
    }
  }
}
```

Code 3.7. Traversing the voxels in a field using iterators

```
DenseField<float>::const_iterator i = field.cbegin();
DenseField<float>::const_iterator end = field.cend();
for (; i != end; ++i) {
  sum += *i;
}
```

Using the **iterator** approach is approximately 20% faster than the explicit loop because the loop no longer needs to compute the array index at each voxel.

3.3.2 The SparseField Class

One of the main limitations with **DenseField<T>**'s approach is that it allocates memory indiscriminately; even voxels that never have a value written to them still use up memory. If it was possible to know exactly how many nonzero voxels the final buffer would contain, it would theoretically be possible to allocate only those. Of course, knowing this ahead of time is next to impossible,[1] so the question is rather how one can get close to the optimal memory footprint, without resorting to time travel.

SparseField memory use	
64^3	2.4 KB
128^3	16.4 KB
256^3	128.4 KB
512^3	1 MB
1024^3	8 MB

Traversing SparseField	
64^3	0.002 s
128^3	0.015 s
256^3	0.12 s
512^3	0.97 s

Field3D's **SparseField<T>** class gets around the problem by deferring the allocation of memory until it is clear that it is needed, i.e., when a voxel is first written to. This would be an expensive approach (not considering the memory fragmentation) if each voxel was allocated individually, so **SparseField<T>** instead allocates memory in *chunks*, or *blocks*, of M^3 voxels. Whenever the buffer is resized (e.g., to N^3), a *block grid* is constructed at a resolution of $(N/M)^3$, with each block containing an unallocated array. Figure 3.4 illustrates the relationship.

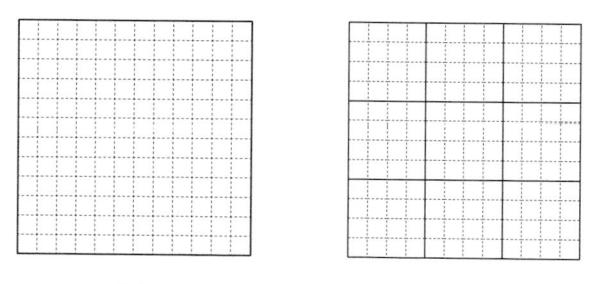

(a)   (b)

Figure 3.4. Slice of 12^3 voxel buffer. (a) Virtual voxels before any data are written to the buffer. (b) Blocks outlined. The block field resolution is 3^3.

---

[1]Except for cases where the exact domain of evaluation is known.

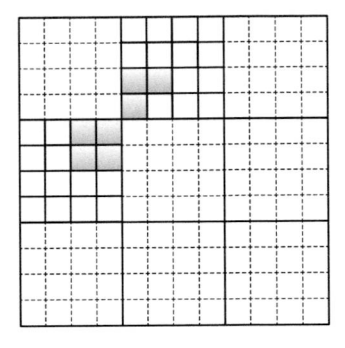

Figure 3.5. A sparse voxel buffer with two allocated blocks. As soon as one voxel in a block is written to, the entire block must be allocated in memory. Virtual voxels are indicated with dashed lines.

Using the coarse block grid means that voxel access is somewhat more complicated than for a regular **DenseField<T>**. First, we must find which block a given voxel is located in. With the block known, we must check if this is the first time it is being accessed, in which case the data array must be allocated. (See Figure 3.5.) With the array in place, we must then find the right voxel within the block before we can return a result to the caller. All of this work makes sparse buffers somewhat slower than their dense counterparts, which only need to compute an array index. At the same time, **SparseField<T>**'s use of memory is more conservative than **DenseField<T>**. For an unused field where all values are zero, it takes up only 0.2% as much space as the corresponding **DenseField<T>**.[2] The memory use then scales linearly with the number of allocated blocks, until all blocks are allocated, at which point the memory use is 100.2% of **DenseField<T>**.

Code 3.8. SparseField<T>'s voxel access method

```
template <class Data_T>
Data_T SparseField<Data_T>::fastValue(int i, int j, int k) const
{
  // Find block coordinate
  int bi, bj, bk;
  getBlockCoord(i, j, k, bi, bj, bk);
  // Find coordinate in block
  int vi, vj, vk;
  getVoxelInBlock(i, j, k, vi, vj, vk);
  // Get the actual block
  int id = blockId(bi, bj, bk);
  const Block &block = m_blocks[id];
```

---

[2] At the default block size of 16^3.

```
  // Check if block data is allocated
  if (block.isAllocated) {
    return block.value(vi, vj, vk, m_blockOrder);
  } else {
    return block.emptyValue;
  }
}
```

Similar to **DenseField<T>**, **SparseField<T>** offers iterators to optimize and simplify the traversal of its voxels. The **SparseField<T>::iterator** and **SparseField<T>::const_iterator** classes work exactly like **DenseField<T>**'s, guaranteeing the same traversal order. Compared to **DenseField<T>**, the iteration is slower because there is more bookkeeping required and we can only touch M voxels in a row before we reset the internal pointer to a row of voxels in a different **SparseBlock**. Fortunately, **SparseField<T>** offers a more efficient approach through the **block_iterator** type. The iterator takes advantage of the block structure during iteration and ensures that all voxels in a block (which are contiguous in memory) are visited linearly, before stepping to the next block.

By using the **block_iterator**, we can request iterators that traverse only the voxels belonging to a single **SparseBlock**, which are then traversed continuously in memory, rather than skipping from block to block, as is the case with the ordinary **iterator** type. (See Figure 3.6.)

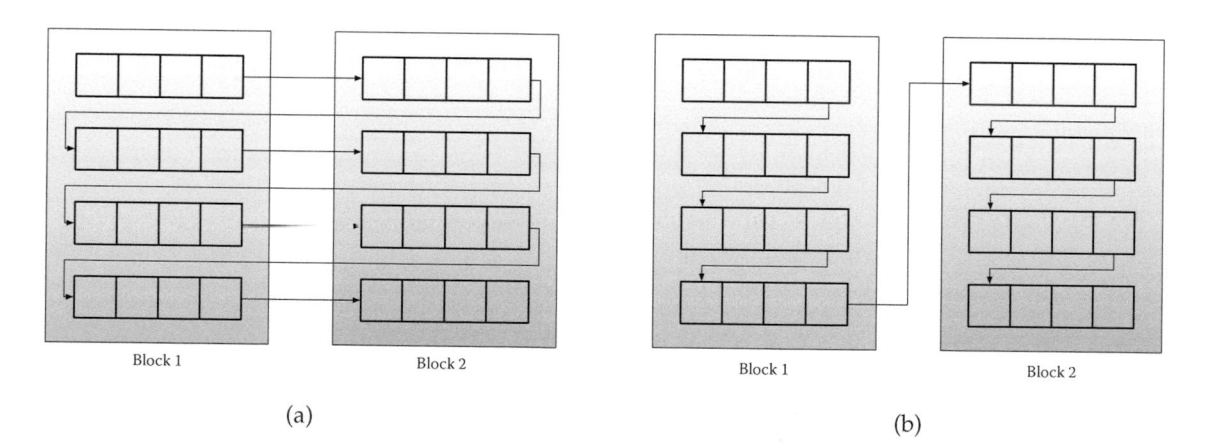

| Block 1 | Block 2 | | Block 1 | Block 2 |
| (a) | | | (b) | |

Figure 3.6. Iterating over voxels in a sparse buffer. (a) The access pattern of the **iterator** class. (b) The access pattern when using **block_iterator** in conjunction with **iterator**.

Code 3.9. Traversing the voxels in a **SparseField<T>** using block iterators

```
SparseField<float>::block_iterator b = field.blockBegin();
SparseField<float>::block_iterator bEnd = field.blockEnd(),
for (; b != bEnd; ++b) {
  Box3i block = b.blockBoundingBox();
  SparseField<float>::iterator i = field.begin(block);
  SparseField<float>::iterator end = field.end(block);
  for (; i != end; ++i) {
    *i = 0.0;
  }
}
```

3.4   Transformations and Mappings

In Section 3.1.3 we looked at the various coordinate systems that the renderer uses for voxel buffers, but we did not go into detail about which types of transforms exist and how one implements them.

3.4.1   Uniform Transforms

In practice, two types of transforms are the most common. The first is the classic *uniform transform*, which performs a simple translate/rotate/scale and preserves the orthogonal shape of the voxel buffer. (See Figure 3.7.) Field3D provides an implementation of this transform type in the **MatrixFieldMapping** class.

Uniform transformations are usually described by a single property, which is the local-to-world transformation matrix M_{lsToWs}. The matrix encodes all of the properties of the transformation, including translation, rotation, and scale. When a point needs to be transformed from local space to world space, the mapping simply multiplies the local space

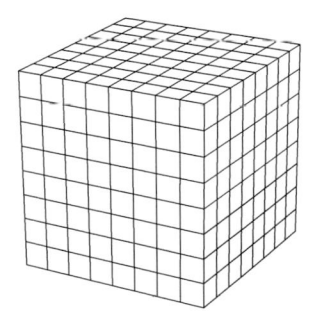

Figure 3.7. A uniform voxel buffer.

coordinate by the matrix

$$P_{\text{world}} - P_{\text{local}} \cdot \mathbf{M}_{\text{lsToWs}}.$$

Conversely, when a point needs to be transformed from world space to local space, it is multiplied by the inverse of the matrix

$$P_{\text{local}} = P_{\text{world}} \cdot \mathbf{M}_{\text{lsToWs}}^{-1}.$$

To keep things efficient, this inverse is usually precomputed and stored in the transformation class and then reused every time the inverse transformation is requested. We also note that transformations from local space to voxel space are unaffected by the type of mapping, since it is a transformation that simply scales the $[0,1]$ range into a $[0,R]$ range. In Field3D, this is performed by the **FieldMapping** base class through the **localToVoxel()** and **voxelToLocal()** member functions.

There is no single correct way to specify a local-to-world transform for use with uniform buffers. It is up to the person writing the renderer to decide what conventions should be used, in terms of rotation orders, pivot points, etc. This is also the reason why the interface to the mapping is a simple transformation matrix, rather than specific controls for translating, rotating, and scaling the buffer. In PVR, uniform transforms are constructed in the **Modeler::setupUniformMapping()** method.

In order to handle voxel buffers that move, the local-to-world transform can be made to vary with time. In this case, a series of transform matrices are used, each one at a different time sample. Later, when a point needs to be transformed, a transformation matrix is interpolated and then used to multiply the point, executing the transformation.

```
void MatrixFieldMapping::localToWorld(const V3d &lsP, V3d &wsP, float time)
  const
{
  if (!m_isTimeVarying) {
    m_lsToWs.multVecMatrix(lsP, wsP);
  } else {
    M44d lsToWs = m_lsToWsCurve.linear(time);
    lsToWs.multVecMatrix(lsP, wsP);
  }
}
```

3.4.2 Frustum Transforms

The second common type of transform is called a *frustum transform*, and it transforms the local voxel space into the view frustum of a camera.

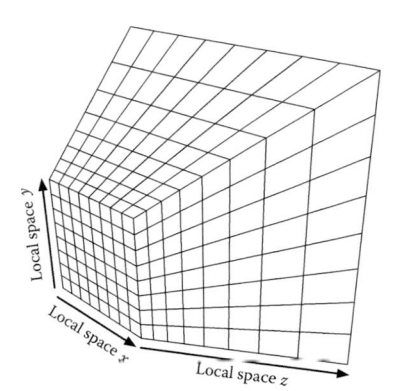

Figure 3.8. Voxel buffer using a frustum transformation. PVR and Field3D's convention for the local coordinate system is indicated.

(See Figure 3.8.) Just as with uniform mappings, Field3D provides an implementation in the **FrustumFieldMapping** class.

Frustum transforms are similar in function to shadow maps, and they are described by two required transformation matrices: a screen-to-world transform and a camera-to-world transform. Just as with the uniform mappings, there are many ways to construct the perspective matrix used to place the voxel buffer in world space. All that the **FrustumFieldMapping** requires is that the screen space be defined as $[-1, 1]$ in the x- and y-dimensions and as $[0, 1]$ in the z- or depth dimension. In PVR, frustum transforms are constructed by **Modeler::setupFrustumMapping()**.

When transforming between local space and world space, there are two ways to determine the z-coordinate. The first option is to use the screen-to-world transform directly, which gives the distribution of z-coordinates a nonuniform spacing that inherits the properties of the perspective transformation.[3] The second option is to use a uniform spacing of z-coordinates in world space, and this is achieved by taking the x- and y-coordinates from the screen-to-world transform and selecting a z-coordinate based on the point's projection through the camera-to-world transform.

3.5   Interpolating Voxel Data

With the data structures in place, the next thing to consider is how we read the voxel data from the buffer. The **Field<T>::value()** function lets

---

[3]This distribution is pictured in Figure 3.8.

us read the data in individual voxels, but it is only relevant if the point we wish to sample lies exactly at the voxel center. In all other cases, an estimate must be made regarding what the density value should be, based on the values of the neighboring voxels.

In the following sections, we will look at various interpolation schemes and the impact they have on visual quality as well as performance.

3.5.1 Nearest-Neighbor Interpolation

The simplest form of interpolation is called *nearest neighbor* and is arguably not even an interpolation scheme. Instead of blending together neighboring voxel values, it simply picks the value of the voxel center it is closest to. (See Figure 3.9.) This results in an image that clearly shows the extents of each individual voxel. (See Figure 3.10.)

Given a discretely sampled function $\mathbf{d}$ and a position x, nearest-neighbor interpolation in one dimension can be written as

$$I_n(x, \mathbf{d}) = \mathbf{d}_{\lfloor x+0.5 \rfloor}.$$

In code, we have a one-dimensional array A and a floating-point coordinate x. Assuming that x lies within the valid index range of A, the implementation is as follows:

Code 3.10. Implementing nearest-neighbor interpolation in one dimension

```
float nearest1D(float x, float *A)
{
  const int idx = static_cast<int>(floor(x + 0.5));
  return A[idx];
}
```

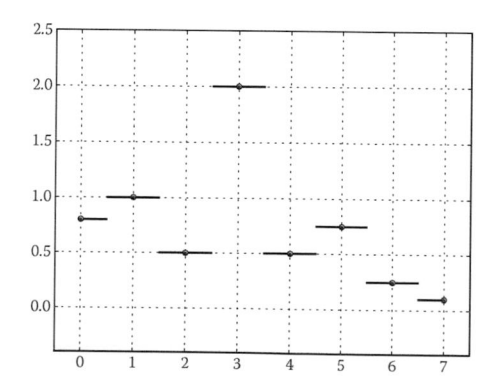

Figure 3.9. Nearest-neighbor interpolation.

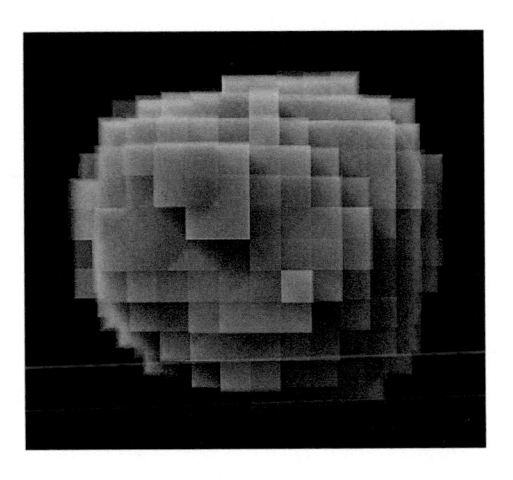 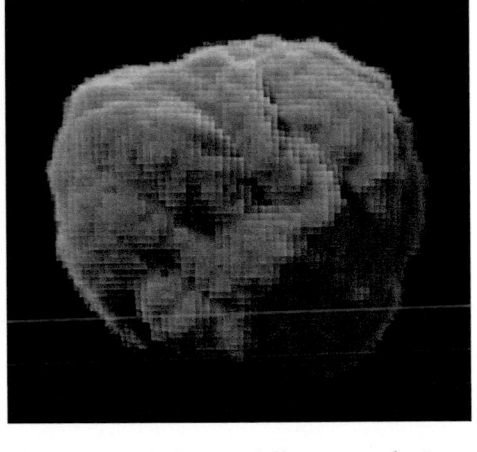

Figure 3.10. Images rendered using nearest-neighbor interpolation at different resolutions: low (left) and high (right).

What Are the Coordinates of a Voxel?, 36

Rounding the floating-point coordinate of a voxel in order to find the integer coordinate should seem familiar: the function **contToDisc()** from Section 3.1.4 performs exactly that routine. For the three-dimensional case, we simply call the existing function, rather than implementing it again.

Code 3.11. Implementing nearest-neighbor interpolation in three dimensions

```
float nearest3D(const Imath::V3f &vsP, const VoxelBuffer &buf)
{
  // Convert voxel-space coordinates to discreet voxel-space coordinates
  V3i dvsP = contToDisc(vsP);
  return buf.value(dvsP.x, dvsP.y, dvsP.z);
}
```

3.5.2 Linear Interpolation

For interpolation schemes that actually do compute in-between values, the most basic one is the linear interpolation method. It computes values by weighting the nearby samples linearly by distance, such that the contribution is 1.0 if the sample point is aligned with the voxel center and is 0.0 when the distance to the voxel center is 1.0.

Given the same $\mathbf{d}$ and x as above, linear interpolation can be written as

$$I_l(x, \mathbf{d}) = (1 - \alpha) \cdot \mathbf{d}_{\lfloor x \rfloor} + \alpha \cdot \mathbf{d}_{\lceil x \rceil},$$
$$\alpha = x - \lfloor x \rfloor.$$

Code 3.12. Implementing linear interpolation in one dimension

```
float linear1D(float x, float *A)
{
    const int floorX = static_cast<int>(floor(x));
    const int ceilX = static_cast<int>(floor(x));
    float alpha = x - floorX;
    return (1.0 - alpha) * A[floorX] + alpha * A[ceilX];
}
```

In three dimensions we need to do a little bit more work. The integer indices need to be found just as in the nearest-neighbor case, but while we previously only touched one voxel, linear interpolation requires the eight neighboring voxel values. In general, the larger the neighborhood that needs to be sampled, the slower the interpolation will be. We refer to the size of the neighborhood as the interpolation scheme's *support* (S), and for linear interpolation $S_{\text{linear}} = 2$. The number of voxel values a given interpolation scheme needs to sample is S^d, where d is the number of dimensions. Thus, linear interpolation in three dimensions requires $2^3 = 8$ samples.

Looking at Figure 3.11, although it may look like the discontinuities that are visible indicate the edges of the voxel, similar to nearest-neighbor interpolation, this is not the case. Instead, the discontinuity occurs when the sample point changes from interpolating in the interval $[d_{i-1}, d_i]$ to $[d_i, d_{i+1}]$. This happens at the voxel centers, rather than at the voxel edges. (See also Figure 3.12.)

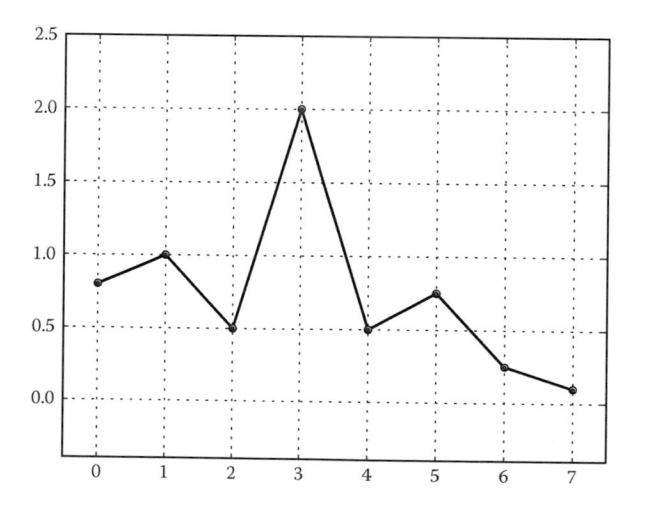

Figure 3.11. Linear interpolation.

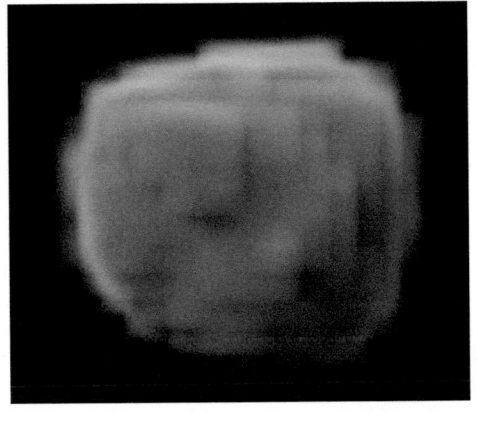 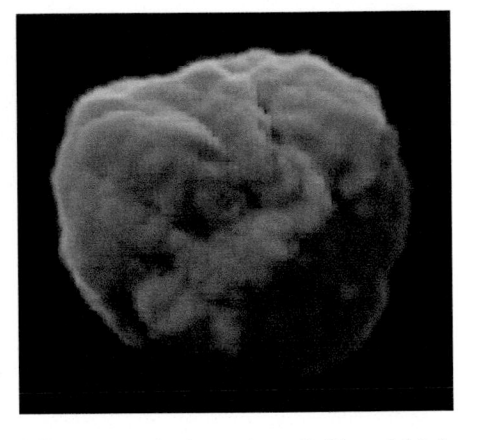

Figure 3.12. Comparing linear interpolation at different resolutions: low (left) and high (right).

Code 3.13. Implementing linear interpolation in three dimensions

```
float linear3D(const Imath::V3f &vsP, const VoxelBuffer &buf)
{
  const int fX = static_cast<int>(floor(vsP.x - 0.5));
  const int fY = static_cast<int>(floor(vsP.y - 0.5));
  const int fZ = static_cast<int>(floor(vsP.z - 0.5));
  const float aX = vsP.x - 0.5 - fX;
  const float aY = vsP.y - 0.5 - fY;
  const float aZ = vsP.z - 0.5 - fZ;
  const float bX = 1.0 - aX;
  const float bY = 1.0 - aY;
  const float bZ = 1.0 - aZ;
  return bX * (bY * (bZ * buf.value(fx,     fy,     fz) +
                     aZ * buf.value(fx,     fy,     fz + 1)) +
               aY * (bZ * buf.value(fx,     fy + 1, fz) +
                     aZ * buf.value(fx,     fy + 1, fz + 1))) +
         aX * (bY * (bZ * buf.value(fx + 1, fy,     fz) +
                     aZ * buf.value(fx + 1, fy,     fz + 1)) +
               aY * (bZ * buf.value(fx + 1, fy + 1, fz) +
                     aZ * buf.value(fx + 1, fy + 1, fz + 1)));

}
```

3.5.3 Cubic Interpolation

Linear interpolation uses a first-order (i.e., linear) polynomial to compute in-between values, but its result is not smooth. By using higher-order polynomials, we can achieve smoother interpolation, at the cost of speed. The next step up from linear interpolation is called *cubic interpolation*, and it looks at a neighborhood of four values when interpolating:

$$I_c(x, p_{i-1}, p_i, p_{i+1}, p_{i+2}).$$

To derive the formula for cubic interpolation we first consider the basic form of a third-order polynomial and its derivative:

$$f(x) = ax^3 + bx^2 + cx + d,$$
$$f'(x) = 3ax^2 + 2bx + c.$$

The points that we are interested in interpolating lie in the $[0, 1]$ range, and the four points that are the inputs to the interpolation function are assumed to lie at

$$p_{i-1} = -1,$$
$$p_i = 0,$$
$$p_{i+1} = 1,$$
$$p_{i+2} = 2.$$

Evaluating the function and its derivate at 0 and 1, we get

$$f(0) = d,$$
$$f(1) = a + b + c + d,$$
$$f'(0) = c,$$
$$f'(1) = 3a + 2b + c.$$

Rewriting each of the equations to solve for a, b, c, and d, we get

$$a = 2f(0) - 2f(1) + f'(0) + f'(1),$$
$$b = -3f(0) + 3f(1) - 2f'(0) - f'(1),$$
$$c = f'(0),$$
$$d = f(0).$$

We know the values of $f(0)$ and $f(1)$, but the derivate values were not directly passed to the function. Fortunately, we can easily compute them since we have $f(-1)$ and $f(2)$ available:

$$f(0) = p_i,$$
$$f(1) = p_{i+1},$$
$$f'(0) = \frac{p_{i+1} - p_{i-1}}{2},$$
$$f'(1) = \frac{p_{i+2} - p_i}{2}.$$

Combining the last two sets of equations, we can find simple closed-form values for a, b, c, and d:

$$a = -\frac{1}{2}p_{i-1} + \frac{3}{2}p_i + \frac{3}{2}p_{i+1} + \frac{1}{2}p_{i+2},$$

$$b = p_{i-1} + \frac{5}{2}p_i + 2p_{i+1} - \frac{1}{2}p_{i+2},$$

$$c = -\frac{1}{2}p_{i-1} + \frac{1}{2}p_{i+1},$$

$$d = p_i,$$

which brings us to the solution to our original function,

$$I_c(x, p_{i-1}, p_i, p_{i+1}, p_{i+2}) = \left(-\frac{1}{2}p_{i-1} + \frac{3}{2}p_i + \frac{3}{2}p_{i+1} + \frac{1}{2}p_{i+2}\right)x^3 +$$
$$\left(p_{i-1} + \frac{5}{2}p_i + 2p_{i+1} - \frac{1}{2}p_{i+2}\right)x^2 +$$
$$\left(-\frac{1}{2}p_{i-1} + \frac{1}{2}p_{i+1}\right)x +$$
$$p_i.$$

Cubic interpolation uses two values below and two values above the sample point, so the scheme has a support of $S_{\text{cubic}} = 4$, as seen in Figure 3.13. In three dimensions, this wider support requires $4^3 = 64$ lookups in order to compute a single interpolated value.

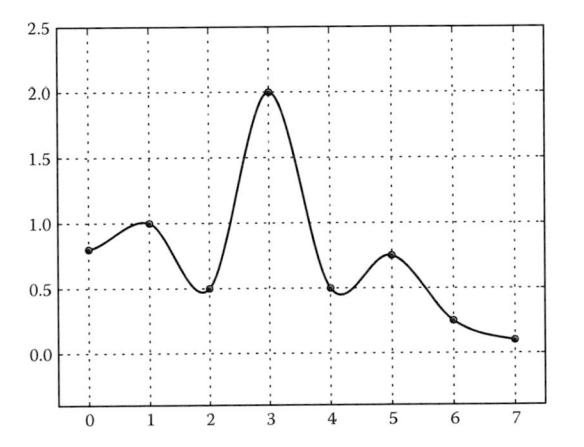

Figure 3.13. Cubic interpolation.

Code 3.14. Cubic interpolation in one dimension

```
template <class Data_T, class Coord_I>
Data_T cubicInterp(Coord_T x, Data_T p[4])
{
  return p[1] + 0.5 *
    x * (p[2] - p[0] +
      x * (2.0 * p[0] - 5.0 * p[1] + 4.0 * p[2] - p[3] +
        x * (3.0 * (p[1] - p[2]) + p[3] - p[0])));
}
```

To interpolate in two and three dimensions, we can reuse the one-dimensional case and interpolate each dimension independently.

Code 3.15. Cubic interpolation in two dimensions

```
template <class Data_T, class Coord_T>
Data_T bicubicInterp(Coord_T x, Coord_T y, Data_T p[4][4])
{
  Data_T yInterps[4];
  yInterps[0] = cubicInterp(y, p[0]);
  yInterps[1] = cubicInterp(y, p[1]);
  yInterps[2] = cubicInterp(y, p[2]);
  yInterps[3] = cubicInterp(y, p[3]);
  return cubicInterp(x, yInterps);
}
```

Code 3.16. Cubic interpolation in three dimensions

```
template <class Data_T, class Coord_T>
Data_T tricubicInterp(Coord_T x, Coord_T y, Coord_T z, Data_T p[4][4][4])
{
  Data_T yzInterps[4];
  yzInterps[0] = bicubicInterp(y, z, p[0]);
  yzInterps[1] = bicubicInterp(y, z, p[1]);
  yzInterps[2] = bicubicInterp(y, z, p[2]);
  yzInterps[3] = bicubicInterp(y, z, p[3]);
  return cubicInterp(x, yzInterps);
}
```

One of the downsides to the cubic interpolation scheme is that it suffers from *overshoots*. Where large gradients exist in the discrete data, the interpolation scheme can assume values that are larger or smaller than any of the samples in the actual data set. Looking carefully at Figure 3.14, we can see that some ghost density values are visible outside, and detached from, the main density cloud. For rendering of density functions, this is usually OK, but when using the cubic interpolator for velocity fields or levelset data, the overshoots are unacceptable. The next

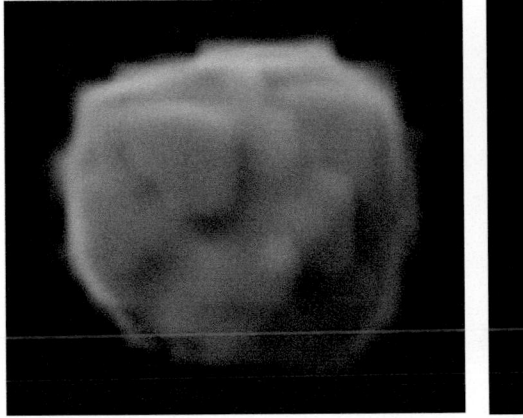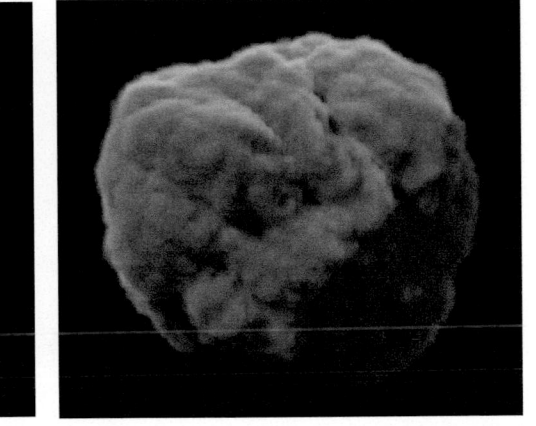

Figure 3.14. Comparing cubic interpolation at different resolutions: low (left) and high (right).

section, monotonic cubic interpolation, shows how we can address the problems.

3.5.4 Monotonic Cubic Interpolation

In a fluid simulation paper called "Visual Simulation of Smoke" [Fedkiw et al. 01], Fedkiw et al. showed how the overshoot problem could be solved for cubic interpolation. The paper called the solution *monotonic* cubic interpolation, and for their fluid-simulation problem, it helped solve a stability issue by ensuring that the magnitude of the interpolated values never exceeded the existing data points. (See Figures 3.15 and 3.16.)

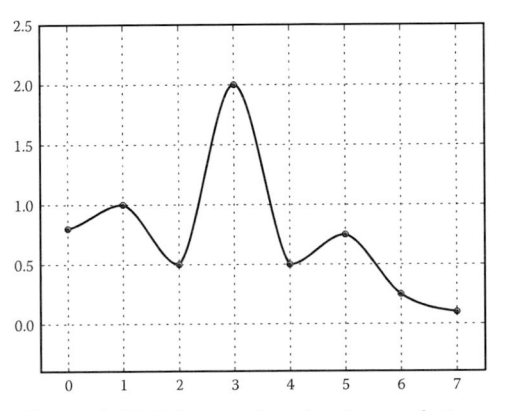

Figure 3.15. Monotonic cubic interpolation.

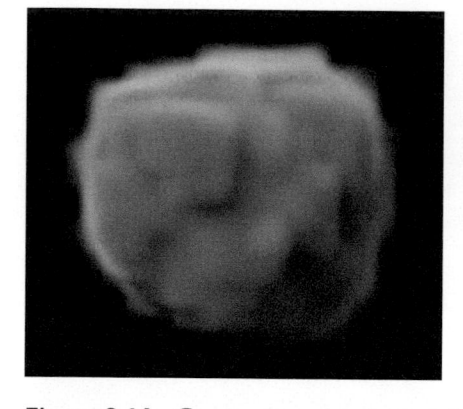 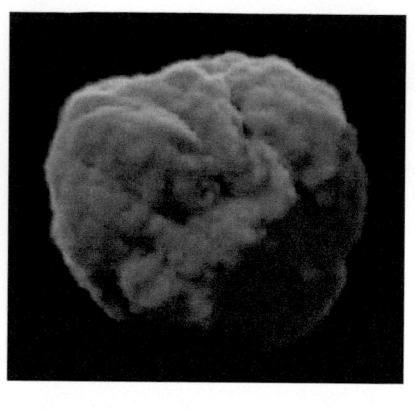

Figure 3.16. Comparing monotonic interpolation at different resolutions: low (left) and high (right).

For volume rendering, the problem with overshoots has more to do with visual quality than numerical stability, but the technique is still relevant, as it solves the problem of visual artifacts due to overshoots in the cubic interpolator.

Field3D's implementation of monotonic cubic interpolation follows the algorithm presented in the original paper.

Code 3.17. Monotonic cubic interpolation in one dimension

```
template<class T>
T monotonicCubic(const T &f1, const T &f2, const T &f3, const T &f4,
                 double t)
{
  T d_k = T(.5) * (f3 - f1);
  T d_k1 = T(.5) * (f4 - f2);
  T delta_k = f3 - f2;

  if (delta_k == static_cast<T>(0)) {
    d_k = static_cast<T>(0);
    d_k1 = static_cast<T>(0);
  }

  T a0 = f2;
  T a1 = d_k;
  T a2 = (T(3) * delta_k) - (T(2) * d_k) - d_k1;
  T a3 = d_k + d_k1 - (T(2) * delta_k);

  T t1 = t;
  T t2 = t1 * t1;
  T t3 = t2 * t1;

  return a3 * t3 + a2 * t2 + a1 * t1 + a0;
}
```

3.6   Filtered Lookups

An alternative to using interpolation is to instead treat the problem of in-between values as a reconstruction problem. In rendering, reconstruction filters are used to turn unstructured arrays of point samples (the image samples) into regularly sampled arrays (the final image). But taking linear interpolation as an example, the same result would be achieved by considering the voxel buffer as a set of regularly spaced sample points, with a continuous function reconstructed using a triangle filter.[4] Although interpolation is more common in production volume rendering, filtered lookups are also useful, and PVR supports both methods in the `VoxelVolume` class.

VoxelVolume, 243

To implement filtered lookups we can break the task in two parts: looping over the relevant voxels and computing the contribution using the filter function, which can be any normal image-reconstruction filter kernel.

Code 3.18. The filtering loop

```
for (z) {
  for (y) {
    for (x) {
      float weight = filter(x, y, z);
      total += weight * buffer.value(i, j, k);
      totalWeight += weight;
    }
  }
}
return total / totalWeight;
```

3.6.1   Gaussian Filter

One common reconstruction filter is the Gaussian filter. It uses the Gaussian function, also known as the *bell curve*, and has the form

$$g(x, \alpha) = e^{-\alpha x^2}.$$

The pure Gaussian function is nonzero for all values of x (i.e., $x \in [-\infty, \infty]$), so when used in image reconstruction, a width parameter w is added, which specifies a distance at which the kernel value is zero. Past this width, the value is clamped at zero, making for a windowed function

---

[4]Indeed, all the interpolation methods covered in Section 3.5 can be implemented as reconstruction filters, with the exception of the monotonic cubic interpolator.

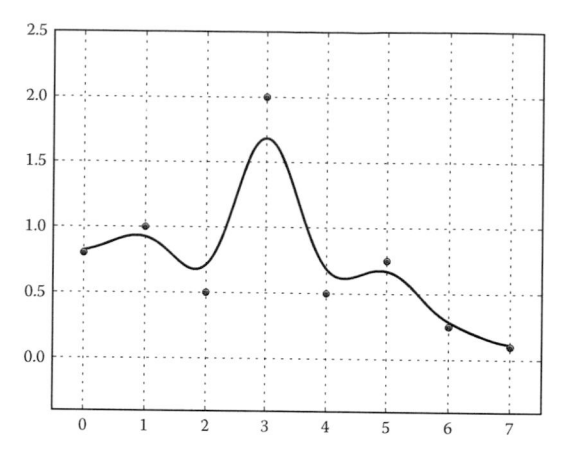

Figure 3.17. Gaussian filtered lookups.

with well-defined bounds:

$$g(x, \alpha, w) = e^{-\alpha x^2} - e^{-\alpha w^2}.$$

As we can see in Figure 3.17, the Gaussian kernel smooths the under-lying sample value significantly, and any peaks and valleys are averaged out towards their neighbor values. While this may sometimes be a desirable effect, it usually gives a too-smooth result with details wiped out. (See Figure 3.18.)

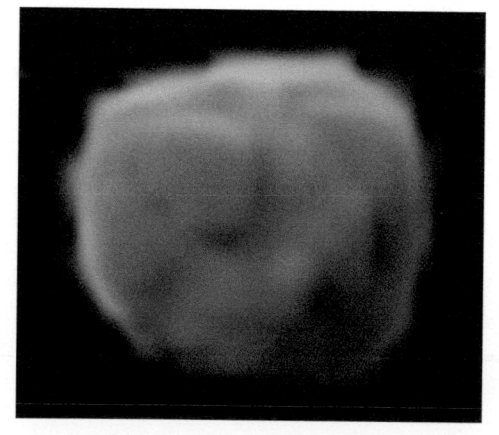 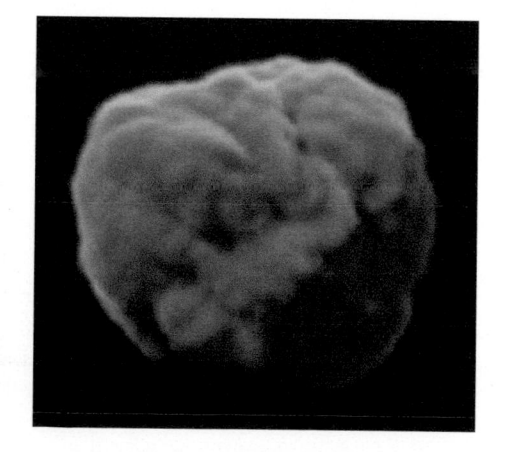

Figure 3.18. Comparing Gaussian filter at different resolutions: low (left) and high (right).

The Gaussian filter kernel has a support of $S_{\text{Gaussian}} = 4$, but the exponential function is more expensive to evaluate than the cubic function's polynomials, so the execution speed is slower.

Code 3.19. Gaussian filter in one dimension

```
float gaussian(float x, float alpha, float width)
{
    return std::max(0.0f, std::exp(-m_alpha * x * x) -
                          std::exp(-m_alpha * width * width);
}
```

An important property of the Gaussian kernel is that it is *separable,* so we can use it in higher-dimension contexts by simply multiplying the result of each individual dimension separately.

Code 3.20. Gaussian filter in three dimensions

```
float gaussian(float x, float y, float z, float alpha, float width)
{
    return gaussian(x, alpha, width) *
           gaussian(y, alpha, width) *
           gaussian(z, alpha, width);
}
```

3.6.2 Mitchell-Netravali Filter

As we have seen, there is a trade-off between sharpness and smoothness in the different interpolation and filtering methods. Different approaches give different visual results that suit different situations. In 1988, two engineers at Bell Labs, Mitchell and Netravali, decided to run a survey with their computer graphics peers. The survey asked, for a large set of images that had been filtered, which one looked best? At the same time, they had developed a parametric filter function that could be tuned to achieve various amounts of smoothing and sharpening. The winner, or rather the combination of filter parameters that most people found pleasing, became known as the Mitchell-Netravali filter [Mitchell and Netravali 88]. (See Figures 3.19 and 3.20.)

The filter is made up of two separate polynomials, one for $x \in [0,1]$ and another for $x \in [1,2]$. It has two parameters, B and C, that have been carefully selected to give control over the smoothing and sharpening aspects of the filter. The authors suggest that parameters be chosen such

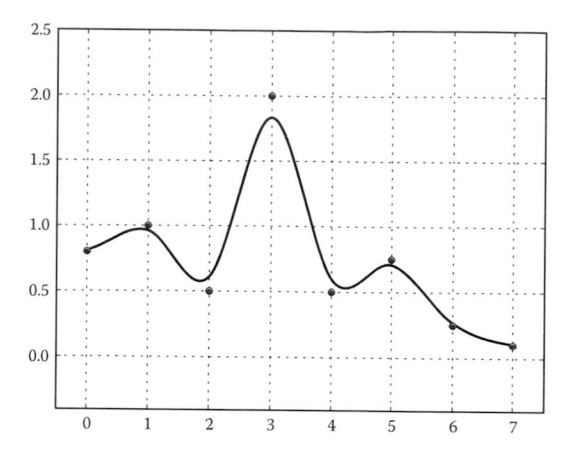

Figure 3.19. Mitchell-Netravali filtered lookups.

that $B + 2C = 1$, but this is not strictly enforced.

$$f(x, B, C) = \begin{cases} \dfrac{|x|^3(12-9B-6C)+|x|^2(-18+12B+6C)+(6-2B)}{6}, & |x| \in [0,1); \\[2ex] \dfrac{|x|^3(-B-6C)+|x|^2(6B+30C)+|x|(-12B-48C)+(8B+24C)}{6}, & |x| \in [1,2); \\[1ex] 0, & |x| \geq 2. \end{cases}$$

The Mitchell-Netravali filter kernel has a support of $S_{\text{Mitchell}} = 4$.

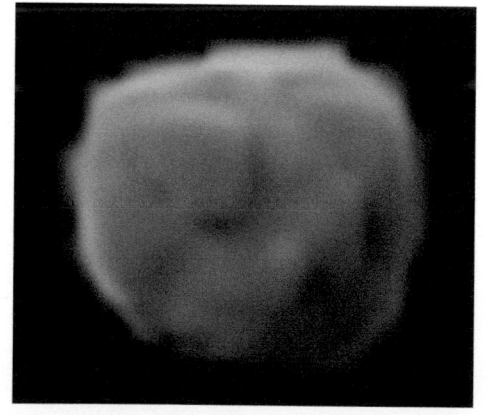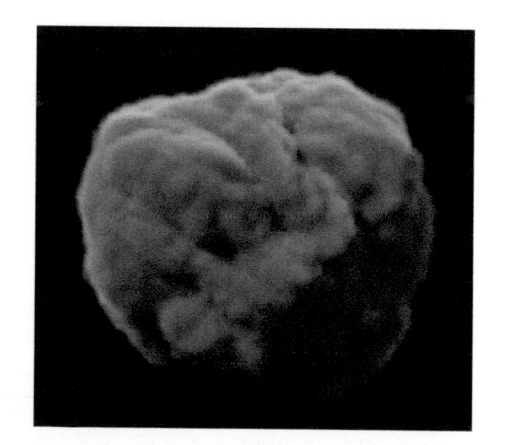

Figure 3.20. Comparing Mitchell-Netravali filter at different resolutions: low (left) and high (right).

Code 3.21. Mitchell-Netravali filter in one dimension

```
float mitchellNetravali(float x, float B, float C)
{
  float ax = std::abs(x);
  if (ax < 1) {
    return ((12 - 9 * B - 6 * C) * ax * ax * ax +
            (-18 + 12 * B + 6 * C) * ax * ax + (6 - 2 * B)) / 6;
  } else if ((ax >= 1) && (ax < 2)) {
    return ((-B - 6 * C) * ax * ax * ax +
            (6 * B + 30 * C) * ax * ax + (-12 * B - 48 * C) *
            ax + (8 * B + 24 * C)) / 6;
  } else {
    return 0;
  }
}
```

Similar to the Gaussian filter, Mitchell-Netravali can be evaluated for each dimension independently:

Code 3.22. Mitchell-Netravali filter in three dimensions

```
float mitchellNetravali(float x, float y, float z, float B, float C)
{
  return mitchellNetravali(x, B, C) *
         mitchellNetravali(y, B, C) *
         mitchellNetravali(z, B, C);
}
```

3.6.3 Performance Comparison

There are two costs involved with interpolation and filtered lookups: the cost of accessing memory locations that hold sample values and the cost of evaluating the filter or interpolation function. A filter or interpolation scheme with a wide support is slower because it needs to access more data points, but the computation speed of the filter kernel or interpolation means that schemes with identical support still run at different speeds.

To compare the relative speed of the filters, the following table lists the time taken to sample 1 million randomly chosen points in a 100^3 dense voxel buffer.

Filter performance in seconds	
Nearest neighbor	0.021039
Linear	0.093818
Cubic	0.467335
Mitchell	1.32077
Gauss	1.90725

Noise

4.1 Procedural Textures

In computer graphics, textured surfaces have been around since Ed Catmull's pioneering work in the 1970s [Catmull 74]. His breakthrough discovery was to place images onto geometric shapes, thereby drastically increasing the perceived complexity of the rendered surface. Although image mapping can be useful in production volume rendering, what we are interested in are *procedural* textures.

When we employ procedural textures, we go past the use of explicit data and instead concern ourselves with procedural functions that produce coherent patterns or images using nothing more than a set of parameters. That is, the image they produce is never stored within the function itself, but rather is an emergent pattern based on evaluating the procedural function over some given domain. A trivial example would be the function

$$\text{stripes}(x, y) = \max(\sin x, 0).$$

There are many excellent texts on procedural texturing techniques for computer graphics, and this chapter will only introduce PVR's specific implementation of noise and fractal functions. For a thorough background to noise, fractals, and procedural textures, the best source is *Texturing and Modeling: A Procedural Approach* [Ebert et al. 02].

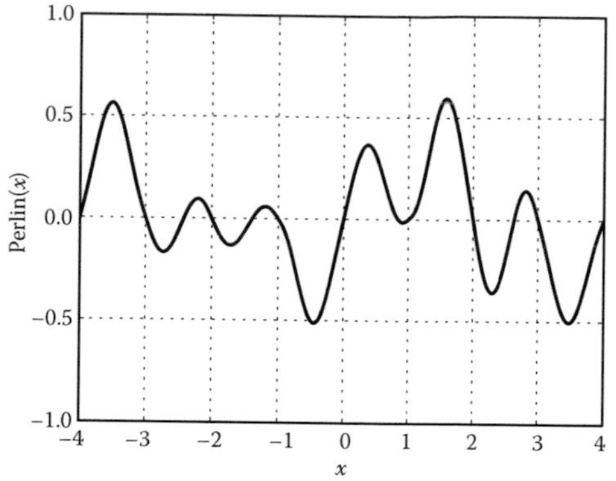

Figure 4.1. Perlin noise in one dimension.

4.2   Perlin Noise

Ever since Ken Perlin introduced his now-classic noise function in 1985 [Perlin 85], it has been a staple in visual effects production. Perlin noise is a band-limited random value function that can be sampled in any number of dimensions, although only the first four dimensions are commonly used. The basis of the function is gradients, which are randomly (but coherently) placed at integer coordinates of an infinitely repeating grid. In between the integer coordinates, the slope of the gradients is used to produce a varying function that has a known frequency content. (See Figure 4.1.)

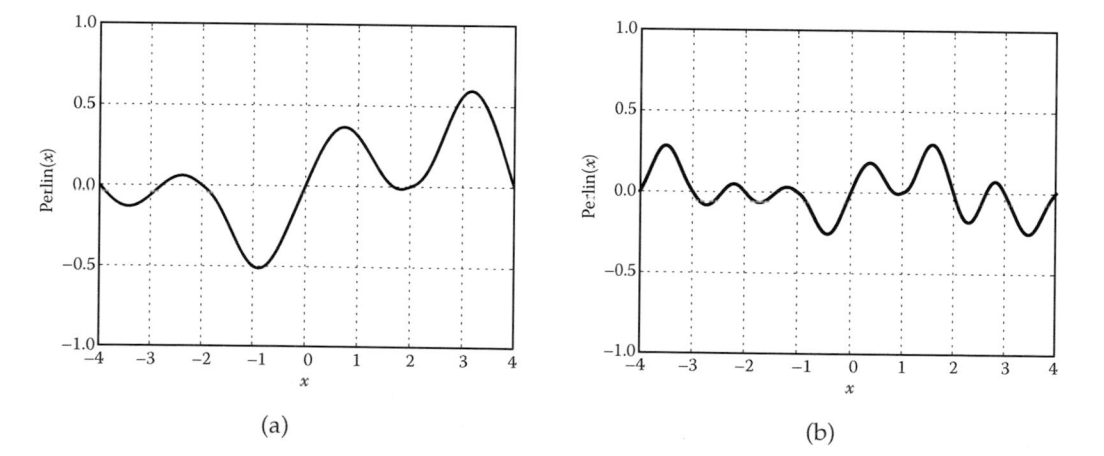

(a)   (b)

Figure 4.2. (a) Varying the frequency of Perlin noise. (b) Varying the amplitude of Perlin noise.

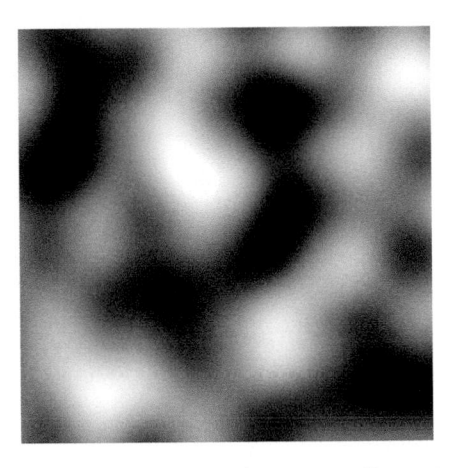

Figure 4.3. Perlin noise evaluated as a two-dimensional image.

The basic Perlin function has no parameters other than the coordinates at which it is sampled. In order to produce specific patterns, however, the frequency and amplitude are often modulated, which changes the behavior and appearance of the function. Figure 4.2 illustrates these changes. (See also Figure 4.3.)

4.3   Noise Functions

PVR supports multiple types of noise functions, and the base class for each of them is **NoiseFunction**.

A noise function must be able to return both scalar- and vector-valued samples in one, two, and three dimensions, which it does through **eval()** and **evalVec()**. It must also be able to tell the renderer what its value range is.

Code 4.1. The **NoiseFunction** base class

```
class NoiseFunction
{
public:
  // Typedefs
  PVR_TYPEDEF_SMART_PTRS(NoiseFunction);
  typedef std::pair<float, float> Range;
  // To be implemented by subclasses
  virtual float      eval(const float x) const = 0;
  virtual float      eval(const float x, const float y) const = 0;
  virtual float      eval(const float x, const float y,
                          const float z) const = 0;
```

```
virtual Imath::V3f evalVec(const float x) const = 0;
virtual Imath::V3f evalVec(const float x, const float y) const = 0;
virtual Imath::V3f evalVec(const float x, const float y,
                           const float z) const = 0;
virtual Range      range() const = 0;
// Utility member functions
float              eval(const Imath::V3f &p) const;
Imath::V3f         evalVec(const Imath::V3f &p) const;
};
```

PVR provides two variants of Perlin noise. The **PerlinNoise** class is a slightly modified version of the original Perlin implementation that produces signed values in the range $[-1, 1]$. The **AbsPerlinNoise** class is a variation of **PerlinNoise** that returns the absolute value of the Perlin function.

4.4   Fractal Functions

In the procedural texturing context, fractals[1] are constructed by combining multiple noise functions at different scales. A very simple fractal function is the *fractional Brownian motion, or fBm* function, which can be implemented as

```
float fBm(point P, int octaves, float octaveGain, float lacunarity)
{
  float value = 0;
  for (int i = 0; i < octaves; i++) {
    value += noise(P) * pow(octaveGain, i);
    P *= lacunarity;
  }
  return value;
}
```

The result of the fBm function is a sum of noise functions at successively higher frequencies. Each noise function in the fractal is referred to as an *octave*, and the relative amplitude of each successive octave is called *octave gain*. Usually, each octave has a frequency roughly twice as high as the previous octave, and this spacing between frequencies is called *lacunarity*. Although it may be tempting to set lacunarity to be exactly 2.0, to produce frequency content that really is an octave in musical terms, this has the unwanted side effect of lining up the zero-value integer coordinate points between octaves. It is better to use a value close to, but not quite, 2.0. PVR generally uses 1.92 as its default lacunarity value. Figure 4.4 shows a plot of fBm in one dimension.

---

[1]Here, we only discuss fractals in the context of noise functions and shaders. General fractals, such as the Mandelbrot set, are a different concept.

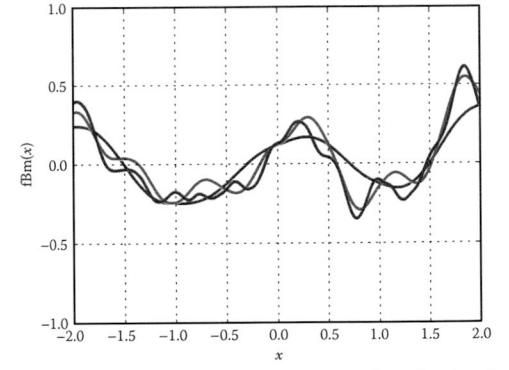

Figure 4.4. The fBm fractal using $R = 1$, $G = 2$, $B = 3$ octaves.

A common variation on the fBm fractal is *turbulence*. It uses the absolute value of a noise function and is implemented as

```
float turbulence(point P, int octaves, float octaveGain, float lacunarity)
{
  float value = 0;
  for (int i = 0; i < octaves; i++) {
    value += abs(noise(P)) * pow(octaveGain, i);
    P *= lacunarity;
  }
  return value;
}
```

Figure 4.5 shows the difference between fBm and turbulence.

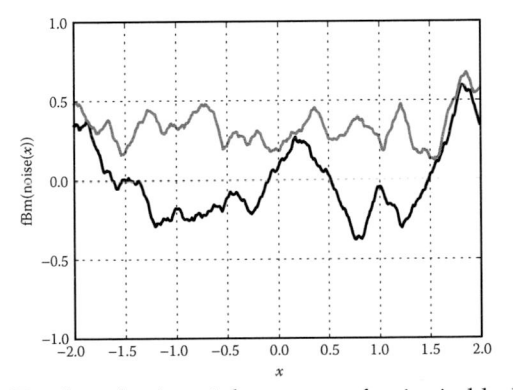

Figure 4.5. The fBm fractal using eight octaves of noise in black and the turbulence function using eight octaves of $|\text{perlin}(x)|$ in gray.

4.5   The `Fractal` Base Class

Just as with noise functions, PVR allows for fractals to be defined arbitrarily, as long as they can be point sampled and they can provide a bound on their value range.

Code 4.2. The `Fractal` base class

```
class Fractal
{
public:
  // Typedefs
  PVR_TYPEDEF_SMART_PTRS(Fractal);
  typedef std::pair<float, float> Range;
  // To be implemented by subclasses
  virtual float      eval(const Imath::V3f &p) const = 0;
  virtual Imath::V3f evalVec(const Imath::V3f &p) const = 0;
  virtual Range      range() const = 0;
  // Utility member functions
  float      eval(const float x) const;
  float      eval(const float x, const float y) const;
  float      eval(const float x, const float y, const float z) const;
  Imath::V3f evalVec(const float x) const;
  Imath::V3f evalVec(const float x, const float y) const;
  Imath::V3f evalVec(const float x, const float y, const float z) const;
};
```

Rather than implement a separate fractal type for turbulence, which is a fractal function made from the absolute value of noise, fractal functions in PVR take a generic `NoiseFunction` pointer as their source of noise. That way, fractals can be built out of any noise function, even completely new ones, if the user adds one. And in the case of the turbulence function, it becomes a plain `Fractal` that uses `AbsPerlinNoise` as its input.

4.6   Fractional Brownian Motion: fBm

PVR's `fBm` class implements the standard fractional[2] Brownian motion loop with a few improvements and additions. Instead of evaluating `pow(octaveGain, i)` at each loop iteration, which is expensive, a variable called `octaveContribution` is used in the loop. The octave contribution is scaled by `octaveGain` at each iteration and will produce a result identical to the power function, but only incurs the cost of a multiplication.

The PVR implementation also adds one important feature that the simpler example did not have: a continuous parameter for the number of

---

[2]Fractional Brownian motion is sometimes also called *fractal* Brownian motion.

octaves. If an integer parameter is used to control the number of octaves, it is impossible to animate the setting without causing visible jumps in the animation. PVR instead uses a common approach where the last, partial octave is added to the final result, but at only a fraction of its full contribution. Using this approach makes it possible to smoothly introduce or remove higher-frequency content over time, for example, if a camera moves closer or farther away from an object.

Code 4.3. The fBm fractal loop

```
float fBm::eval(const Imath::V3f &p) const
{
  // Scale the lookup point
  Imath::V3f noiseP(p / m_scale);
  // Initialize iteration variables
  float result = 0.0f;
  float octaveContribution = 1.0f;
  float octaves = m_octaves;
  // Loop over octaves
  for (; octaves > 1.0f; octaves -= 1.0f) {
    // Add in noise function
    result += m_noise->eval(noiseP) * octaveContribution;
    // Scale amplitude of next octave
    octaveContribution *= m_octaveGain;
    // Scale lookup points of next octave
    noiseP *= m_lacunarity;
  }
  // If there is a partial octave left, apply fraction of last octave
  if (octaves > 0.0f) {
    result += m_noise->eval(noiseP) * octaveContribution * octaves;
  }
  return result ;
}
```

4.6.1 Octaves

The user can control the amount of high-frequency content in a fractal by changing the number of octaves used. Increasing the number of octaves adds more detail but also makes the fractal more expensive to evaluate. The number of noise evaluations increases, as does the value range of the fractal, which can have an impact on displacement bounds in the renderer. Figure 4.6 illustrates the effect of changing the number of octaves.

4.6.2 Scale

Fractal functions have a primary *scale*, or *frequency*, that indicates the most prominent feature size. This scale refers to the size of the lowest octave in

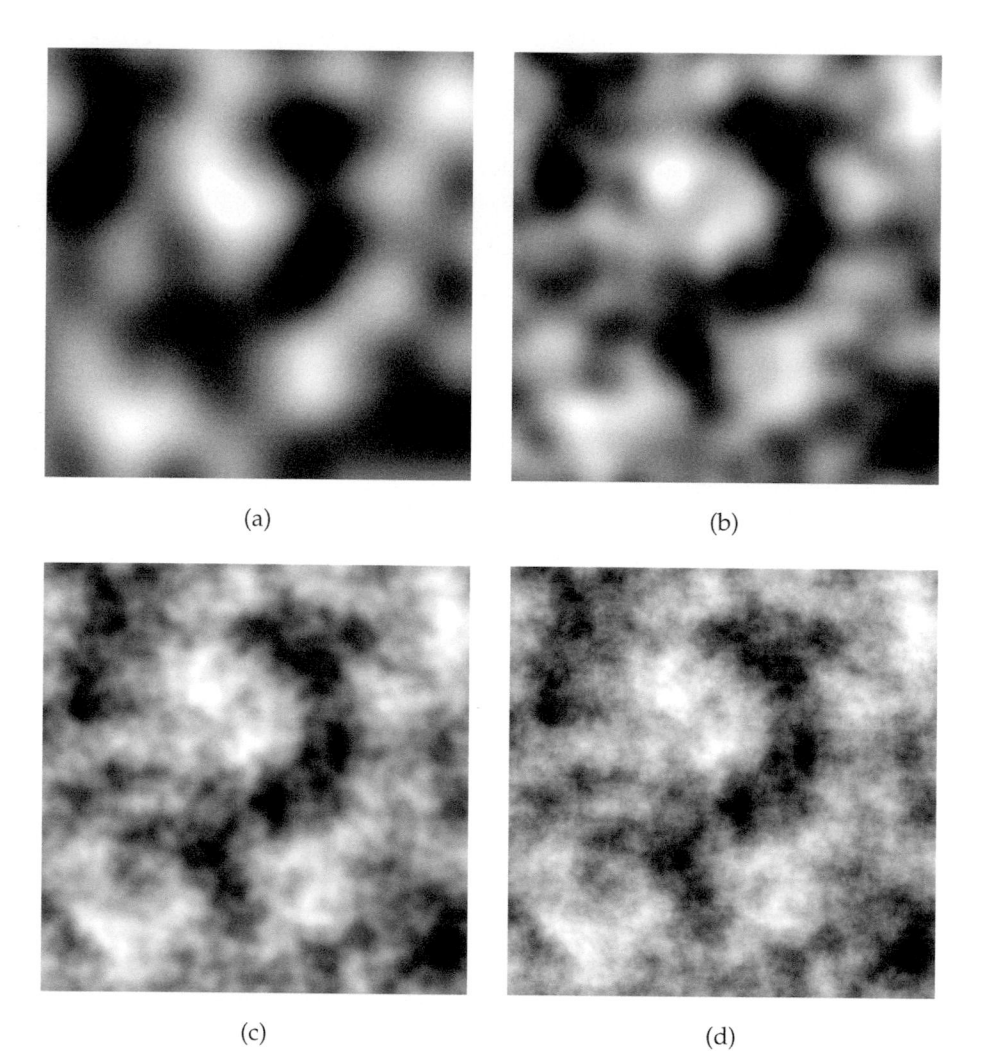

(a)   (b)

(c)   (d)

Figure 4.6. Changing the number of octaves of the fBm fractal: (a) one, (b) two, (c) four, and (d) six.

the fractal, which is where most of the function's energy lies. Figure 4.7 shows how changing this parameter affects the appearance of the fractal.

Whether the user parameter should be exposed as a scale or frequency is largely a matter of taste, which is probably why both approaches are seen in production code. Throughout PVR, scale is used rather than frequency, since feature sizes for typical production scenes tend to be on macroscopic rather than microscopic scales.

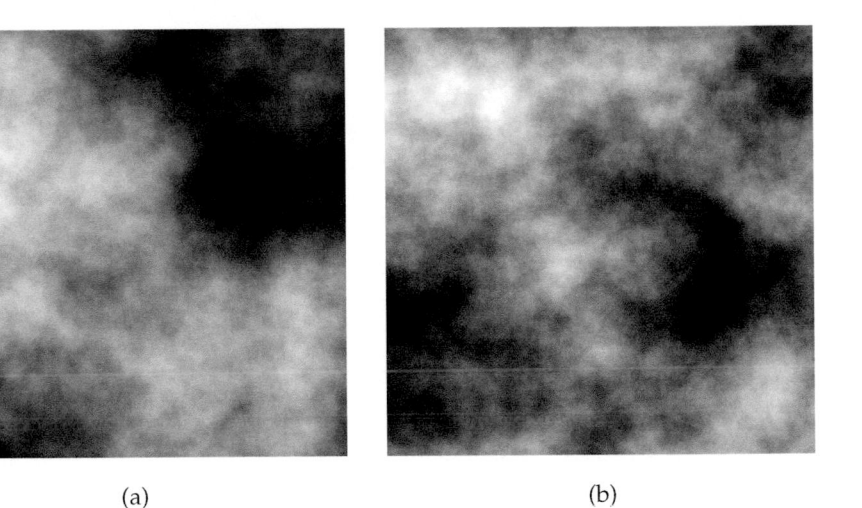

(a)   (b)

Figure 4.7. Changing the scale of the fBm fractal: (a) scale = 1.0 and (b) scale = 0.5. We note that features in the noise move as the scale changes.

Scale is incorporated into the fractal function by transforming the lookup point prior to entering the fractal loop.

Code 4.4. Controlling the scale of the fractal

```
// Scale the lookup point
Imath::V3f noiseP(p / m_scale);
```

4.6.3   Octave Gain

When combining octaves of noise into a fractal, the user is often given control over the amplitude of the higher octaves. The amplitude is usually expressed as a relative measure (in the range $[0, 1]$) of each octave's contribution compared to the one immediately preceding it. In PVR, this relative amplitude is called octave gain. Figure 4.8 shows how changing this parameter affects the appearance of the fractal.

Code 4.5. Controlling the relative amplitude of each octave

```
// Scale amplitude of next octave
octaveContribution *= m_octaveGain;
```

(a)   (b)

Figure 4.8. Changing the amplitude of each successive octave: (a) octave gain = 0.5 and (b) octave gain = 0.75. We note that that the overall features are the same, but high frequency detail is exaggerated.

4.6.4 Lacunarity

Lacunarity controls the relative scale between each octave in the fractal. It is the least commonly changed parameter for noise functions, and although it is certainly not wrong to change, we generally leave it at its default of 1.92 in the examples of fractals used throughout this book. Figure 4.9 shows the affect of a couple other values.

Code 4.6. Controlling the relative scale of each octave

```
// Scale lookup points of next octave
noiseP *= m_lacunarity;
```

4.6.5 Value Range of Fractal Functions

As we will see in the modeling chapters, it is important to know the *range* of noise and fractal functions. The range depends on which noise function drives the fractal: using absolute noise as the input means the lower bound is zero regardless of how many octaves of noise are used.

In practice, determining the range is just a matter of replicating the fractal loop itself, but instead of sampling the value of noise at each octave, the function sums up the upper and lower bounds of the noise func-

 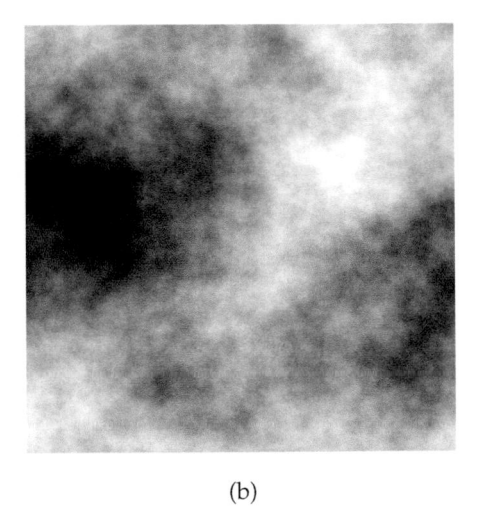

(a)   (b)

Figure 4.9. Changing the relative scale of each successive octave: (a) lacunarity = 1.75 and (b) lacunarity = 2.25. Here, features in the lowest frequencies remain, but high frequency content changes.

tion. While this requires a loop, there are no expensive noise-function computations to compute.

Code 4.7. Computing the range of the fBm fractal

```
Fractal::Range fBm::range() const
{
  Range noiseRange = m_noise->range(), range = std::make_pair(0.0f, 0.0f);
  float octaveContribution = 1.0f;
  float octaves = m_octaves;
  // Loop over octaves
  for (; octaves > 1.0f; octaves -= 1.0f) {
    range.first += noiseRange.first * octaveContribution;
    range.second += noiseRange.second * octaveContribution;
    octaveContribution *= m_octaveGain;
  }
  if (octaves > 0.0f) {
    range.first += noiseRange.first * octaveContribution * octaves;
    range.second += noiseRange.second * octaveContribution * octaves;
  }
  return range;
}
```

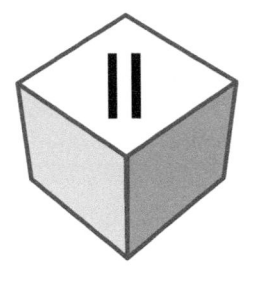

Volume Modeling

Fundamentals of Volume Modeling

This chapter looks at the basics of volume modeling, with the goal of outlining the different techniques used in the modeling stage. The next chapters will describe how PVR actually implements these techniques, but this one focuses on the fundamental techniques.

Volume modeling is in itself an almost limitless topic. In surface rendering, the difference between *geometry* and *shader* is well defined, but in volume rendering, the distinction is blurred. Volumetric primitives will often use geometry as a form of control, but complex shader operations are what give the primitive its final appearance, making the relationship much closer between the underlying geometry and the code that turns it into volumetric data. Because of this intertwined relationship, it is especially important to characterize the different modeling stages and the approaches that are used, in order to provide a language for volume modeling and a set of basic design patterns.

5.1 Volume Modeling and Voxel Buffers

When we discuss volume modeling, voxel buffers are almost always an integral part, since they are the most common data structure used to store the output of the process. But not all volume modeling needs to involve voxel buffers. In the end, most volume-modeling techniques boil down to sampling some form of density function, and the voxel buffers only exist as a form of cache that holds a discretized version of these density functions. In fact, many of the techniques described here could equally well happen at render time, without first creating a voxelized representation of the modeling primitives.

Nonetheless, voxel buffers are still the most common way to handle volume modeling, and the following chapters covering the basics of volume modeling, as well as PVR's implementation thereof, all use voxel buffers.

5.2   Defining the Voxel Buffer

Before we can begin to populate the voxel buffer using one of the many modeling techniques, we must first define the bounds of the modeling primitives. The bounding process lets the modeling application know the domain over which the volumetric primitives have nonzero density. This is done before any primitive is given access to the voxel buffer, in order to guarantee that the voxel buffer spans all the space covered by the volumetric primitives. (See Figure 5.1.)

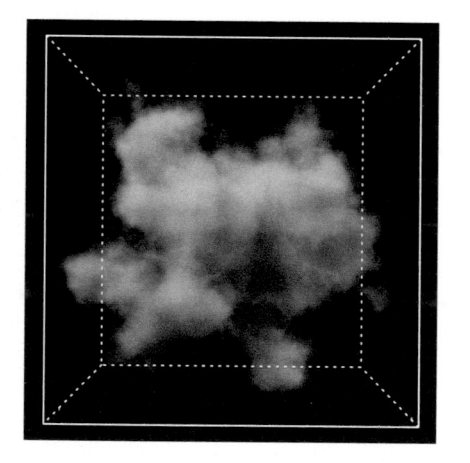

Figure 5.1. The bounds of a primitive.

5.2.1   Bounding Primitives

The modeling primitives we will study are driven by geometric inputs, such as point clouds or meshes, but because of their volumetric nature, the extents of the final result is greater than the bounds of the input geometry. For example, each point in a point cloud might produce a small "cloud puff" that has a finite, but nonzero, radius. It is very important to consider how far each primitive extends past its underlying geometry and to not simply look at the bounding box of the geometry itself.

This is a natural parallel to the concept of displacement bounds in surface rendering. Because the nature of the required padding is similar in both contexts, we will use the term *displacement bounds* in this book as well when referring to the added space required around a volumetric primitive.

To make matters more complicated, it is often the case that the padding required by a primitive is dependent on one or more user parameters. For example, the amplitude of a pyroclastic noise function influences how far into the space surrounding the geometry we will find nonzero densities. It would certainly be possible to let the user specify the displacement bounds explicitly, but this is usually a poor solution. Instead, the programmer or shader writer should take care to analytically decide what the bounds should be, given the input geometry and the specified user parameters. We will return to the topic in Chapters 7 and 8 to see how PVR handles this.

Rasterization Primitives in
PVR, 107

Instantiation Primitives in
PVR, 145

5.2.2 Boundless Voxel Buffers

Although it is outside the scope of this book, it is possible to design voxel buffer data structures that are *boundless*, i.e., that contain data over an infinitely large domain. In these cases, the bounding of primitives is no longer required in order to construct the voxel buffer, but it is still needed for some primitive types in order to know which part of the voxel buffer domain will be accessed. The rasterization family of primitives are one such case, where the density function of the primitive needs to be sampled across a finite domain.

5.3 Volume-Modeling Strategies

As mentioned earlier, the dual nature (primitive/shader) of volumetric primitives means that there are many different approaches to volumetric modeling. But while the number of possible techniques may be endless, most techniques can still be categorized and grouped into families of similar operations. Throughout the book, we will separate the various modeling primitives into one of the following categories. The categories are not disjoint; rather, they describe levels in a hierarchy, where the higher levels may employ the lower ones. The hierarchy is illustrated in Figure 5.2.

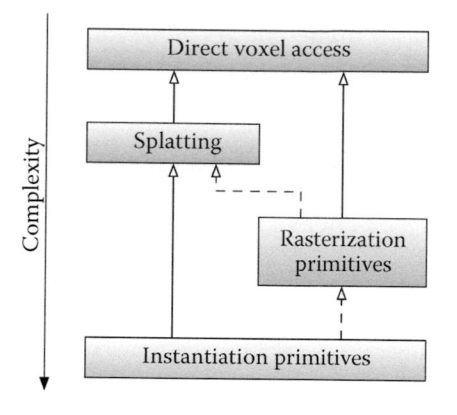

Figure 5.2. The hierarchy of modeling primitives.

5.3.1   Direct Voxel Access

The first category refers to direct voxel access using buffer's class interface, where the value of a single voxel is set explicitly. All higher-level
primitive types use this at some stage, so it can be considered (as may
be obvious) the base of all volume modeling. Section 3.1.1 describes this
part of the pipeline.

5.3.2   Splatting

The second category is *splatting*. It is used when primitives want to write
a specific value to the voxel buffer, but the position where the value is
known falls between the discrete positions of the voxels. Section 6.6 describes how PVR implements this in more detail.

5.3.3   Rasterization

Primitives that are converted voxel by voxel into volume data are called
rasterization primitives, a common example of which is pyroclastic point
primitives. Rasterization primitives normally use direct voxel access to
write values to the voxel buffer, since they have control over its sample positions and can align those with the voxel buffer. However, when
considering motion blur, splatting may also be used in order to draw
smeared lines. Section 5.4 outlines the basics of rasterization, and Chapter 7 shows how PVR implements several primitives of this type.

5.3.4 Instantiation

The last type of modeling approach uses instances of other primitive types in order to build a more complex primitive type and is referred to as *instantiation primitives*. The most common types instantiate large numbers of small points, using splatting or rasterization to write those points into the buffer. We refer to those types as *point-based instantiation*

primitives. Again, Section 5.5 looks at the basic premises of instantiation, and Chapter 8 illustrates how PVR implements it.

5.4 Rasterization Primitives

The common aspect of all rasterization primitives is that they visit a subset of the buffer, voxel by voxel, and compute some density function that represents the primitive. The density value is then written directly to the voxel buffer to produce the final result.

The rasterization algorithm is quite generic and can be used for any kind of primitive that can be built by considering what the density of each primitive is at a given point in space. The control method for placing the primitive in the buffer is independent of the rasterization process, and anything from no geometry through points to splines may be used as the underlying geometric primitive.

In pseudocode, the rasterization algorithm has the following structure:

Code 5.1. Simplified rasterization loop

```
for (int k = 0; k < kMax; k++) {
  for (int j = 0; j < jMax; j++) {
    for (int i = 0; i < iMax; i++) {
      Vector worldSpaceP = voxelToWorld(i, j, k);
      float density = primitive.density(worldSpaceP);
      buffer.writeValue(i, j, k, density);
    }
  }
}
```

If the input contains more than one primitive, the algorithm can be written to visit each primitive once:

Code 5.2. Visiting each primitive once

```
for (int prim = 0; prim < numPrims; prim++) {
  for (int k = 0; k < kMax; k++) {
    for (int j = 0; j < jMax; j++) {
```

```
      for (int i = 0; i < iMax; i++) {
        Vector worldSpaceP = voxelToWorld(i, j, k);
        float density = primitives[prim].density(worldSpaceP);
        buffer.writeValue(i, j, k, density);
      }
    }
  }
}
```

Alternatively, it can be written to visit each voxel once:

Code 5.3. Visiting each voxel once

```
for (int k = 0; k < kMax; k++) {
  for (int j = 0; j < jMax; j++) {
    for (int i = 0; i < iMax; i++) {
      Vector worldSpaceP = voxelToWorld(i, j, k);
      float density = 0.0;
      for (int prim = 0; prim < numPrims; prim++) {
        density += primitives[prim].density(worldSpaceP);
      }
      buffer.writeValue(i, j, k, density);
    }
  }
}
```

Each approach has its merits. If we consider a voxel data structure that is out of core, i.e., not all data are available in memory at once, it may be better to only visit each voxel once. On the other hand, the algorithm that deals with just a single primitive may be simpler to write, making for a more generic implementation. Throughout this book, the approach of visiting each primitive once will be used. Chapter 7 describes PVR's implementation of the rasterization algorithm in detail.

Rasterization Primitives in PVR, 107

When is rasterization used? The rasterization algorithm is well suited to primitives that are continuous in nature, such as clouds, fog and smoke. It becomes less efficient when large portions of a primitive's bounds are unoccupied, since even noncontributing voxels must be visited and computed.

5.5   Instantiation Primitives

Rasterization primitives work well for modeling phenomena that are inherently continuous in nature and where density fills the majority of the space the primitive occupies. Rasterization can, however, be inefficient in cases where primitives contain a lot of negative space, since it is difficult to decide if the computation of a voxel can be skipped, unless the world-to-local transform and potential fractal functions have already been computed. Trying to optimize for those sparse cases is also difficult and risks incurring as much overhead as the potential savings would be. Another drawback of rasterization primitives (as discussed in the next section) are the difficulties in transforming from world space into a primitive's local space because of potential ambiguities.

Instantiation primitives avoid many of these drawbacks by taking the opposite approach to modeling: decide first what densities should make up the volume, and only then calculate where in the voxel buffer those densities should be written. This approach *pushes* density into a voxel buffer, and it avoids the waste of performing computations that contribute no visual result, since instantiated primitives with zero density can be skipped early. It also means that the cost of a given primitive is proportional to the amount of density that is actually seen, instead of proportional to the size of the primitive's bounding domain.

A very simple instantiation primitive that fills a solid box in the coordinate range $(-1 \ -1 \ -1)$ to $(1 \ 1 \ 1)$ could be implemented as follows:

Code 5.4. A trivial instantiation loop

```
for (int i = 0; i < numInstances; i++) {
  Vector worldSpaceP;
  worldSpaceP.x = randomNumber(-1.0, 1.0);
  worldSpaceP.y = randomNumber(-1.0, 1.0);
  worldSpaceP.z = randomNumber(-1.0, 1.0);
  float density = 1.0f;
  buffer.splat(worldSpaceP, density);
}
```

The above example, which creates a number of splats (effectively small dots) in a voxel buffer, is a point-based instantiation primitive. In fact, all the instantiation primitives in PVR are of this type. Although less common, and not covered in this book, it is possible for an instantiation primitive to create higher-level volumetric primitives, including rasterization primitives and even other instantiation primitives. This means that complex (and potentially recursive) shapes can be constructed, making this fourth type of modeling primitive quite flexible and powerful.

When is instantiation used? The instantiation algorithm works best for effects that are somewhat granular in nature, i.e., things that can be considered as discrete pieces at roughly the scale of a voxel. It is nonetheless possible to achieve smooth-looking effects as well, simply by instantiating enough points, which makes instantiation primitives very versatile.

5.6   Using Geometry to Guide Volumetric Primitives

Although not required, it is common to use various types of geometry to control volumetric modeling primitives. We call these types of primitives *geometry-based primitives* and refer to the geometry used to drive them as *underlying geometry* or *underlying primitives*. Most rasterization and instantiation primitives are geometry based.

5.6.1   Coordinate Systems

In order to use geometry to drive volumetric primitives, we need to be able to parameterize them in two ways. First, we need to be able to express some form of coordinate system on the geometry itself, which is what is done in ordinary texturing operations common to all forms of surface rendering. We also need to parameterize the space surrounding the geometry, so that the volume can extend beyond the otherwise infinitely thin surface. This is the key to creating volumetric primitives: using lower-dimensional primitives to control three-dimensional primitives that are, in turn, embedded in a three-dimensional volume.

If we consider a simple local coordinate system defined by vectors $(\vec{u}, \vec{v}, \vec{w})$ at position p (Figure 5.3) defined in the world reference frame $(\hat{x}, \hat{y}, \hat{z})$, then the matrix $\mathbf{M}$ that transforms from local space coordinates to world space coordinates is

$$\mathbf{M} = \begin{pmatrix} u_x & u_y & u_z & 0 \\ v_x & v_y & v_z & 0 \\ w_x & w_y & w_z & 0 \\ p_x & p_y & p_z & 1 \end{pmatrix}.$$

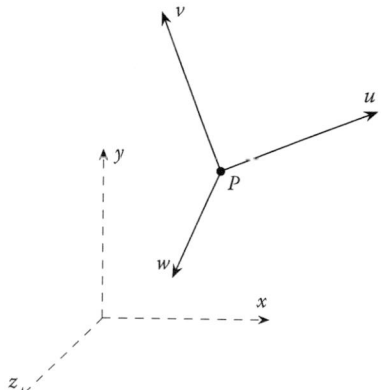

Figure 5.3. The set $(\vec{u}, \vec{v}, \vec{w}, p)$ forms a coordinate system in $(\hat{x}, \hat{y}, \hat{z})$.

In addition to this local-to-world transformation, we will need two projections $(C(p), L(p))$ and one transformation $(P(p))$:

$C(p)$ finds the closest point p'_{world} on a primitive given an arbitrary point p_{world}.

$L(p)$ finds the closest local-space point p'_{local} on the primitive given a point in local space p_{local} that may lie away from the primitive.

$P(p)$ transforms a point p_{local}, lying on the primitive, to p_{world}. This is used to find the world-space position for points on a geometric primitive.

The strategy for transforming from local-space coordinates to world space is similar for all of our underlying geometric primitives:

1. Let $p_{local} = (a\ b\ c)$ be the coordinates in the primitive's local coordinate system. These may lie in the space around the primitive (i.e., not directly on the primitive).
2. Use $L(p_{local})$ to find p'_{local}
3. Use $P(p'_{local})$ to find the world-space position p'_{world}.
4. Find the basis vectors $\vec{u}, \vec{v}, \vec{w}$ at p'_{local}.
5. Construct matrix $\mathbf{M}$ as described above, using $(p_{world}, \vec{u}, \vec{v}, \vec{w})$.
6. Transform p_{local} to p_{world} using $\mathbf{M}$.

The inverse transform, going from world-space to local-space coordinates, is similar:

1. Let $p_{world} = (x\ y\ z)$ be the coordinates in world space.
2. Use $C(p_{world})$ to find the closest point p'_{world} on the primitive. At the same time, determine the local-space coordinates p'_{local}.
3. Find the basis vectors $\vec{u}, \vec{v}, \vec{w}$ at p'_{local}.
4. Construct matrix $\mathbf{M}$ as described above, using $(p'_{world}, \vec{u}, \vec{v}, \vec{w})$.
5. Transform p_{world} to p_{local} using inverse of $\mathbf{M}$.

5.6.2   Local-to-World versus World-to-Local

It is important to consider which transforms will be executed during the modeling process. Normally, it is only necessary to transform either into or out of the geometric primitive's local coordinate space, but rarely both. If we consider the two main modeling strategies described in Section 5.3, we will see that each corresponds directly to one transformation direction.

Volume-Modeling
Strategies, 77

Rasterization primitives first consider the domain that the primitive overlaps and then traverses each voxel in that domain. To sample the

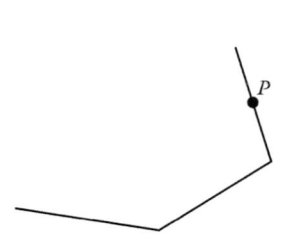

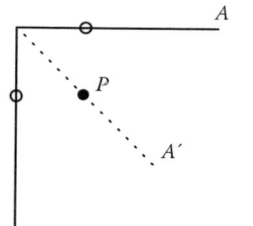
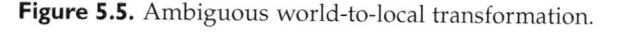

Figure 5.4. Point on a polygonal line.   **Figure 5.5.** Ambiguous world-to-local transformation.

density of the primitive, it is necessary to transform first from voxel space to world space, and then from the world-space position of each voxel into the local space of the primitive. Thus, rasterization primitives rely primarily on the world-to-local transform.

On the other hand, instantiation primitives first consider the parametric coordinate system of the underlying primitive used to drive them. A position in the local space is picked for each instantiated point (or other primitive), and it is then necessary to transform from the local space of the primitive to world space, and then from world space into the voxel space of the target voxel buffer. Instantiation primitives thus rely on the local-to-world transform.

There are some important implications to consider with each transformation direction. If we consider a polygonal line (Figure 5.4), we quickly see that one transformation is trivial: finding the world-space position given a parametric position on the line, i.e., the local-to-world transform, which is simply a linear interpolation between the polygon vertices. The inverse transformation, i.e., finding a position on the line given a position in world space, is much more involved. First, it is necessary to find which line segment is closest to the world-space point. Then, the closest point on the line segment can be computed.

There are two problems to consider. Finding the closest line segments naïvely involves visiting each segment once for testing, making the operation complexity $O(n)$. Using an acceleration structure can reduce the time complexity, but in contrast to the local-to-world transform, which is $O(k)$, it is an expensive operation.

The second problem comes from potential ambiguity in the distance query. If we consider a polygonal line A bent $90°$, there is a second line A' for which the nearest-point query has two equally correct answers (Figure 5.5). In this case, it is impossible to decide which point should be considered to be closest. For more intricate lines, there could be any number of potential closest points. Even if the ambiguity was addressed by looking at all possible solutions, what should be done when sampling the primitive? Should both density values be used? Just one? If so, which one? And for every point where the ambiguity exists, each neighboring sample will likely only have one closest point, creating a discontinuity where both values no longer get sampled.

In conclusion, using complex underlying geometry to drive rasterization primitives can be expensive, and also potentially difficult to control for the user due to unexpected behavior where the world to local transform is ambiguous. Instantiation primitives have neither of these limitations, since the local-to-world transform remains unambiguous for geometry that bends, or even self-intersects.

5.7   Common Coordinate Systems

In the previous section, we discussed finding basis vectors and doing closest-point queries for geometric primitives. This section will detail those for the basic types of geometry that the book uses.

5.7.1   Points/Spheres

The simplest geometric type is the *particle system*, or *point cloud*. It contains N points scattered in space, each with at least a position attribute. Although each point is a zero-dimensional entity, they can still possess an *orientation*, which can be described as a rotation using Euler angles, quaternions, or as orientation vectors. Each of these can be trivially converted to a rotation matrix $\mathbf{M}$. (See Figure 5.6.)

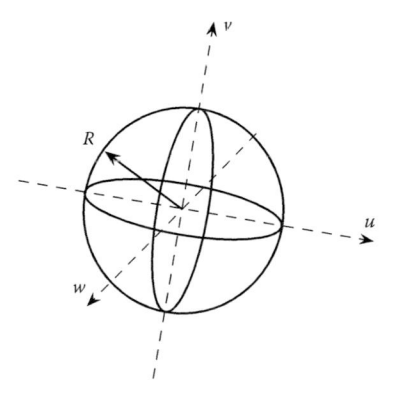

Figure 5.6. An oriented sphere of radius R.

Given the information of a point's position and orientation, the necessary properties to define a coordinate system are

$$
\begin{aligned}
p &= \text{position of point,} \\
\mathbf{M} &= \text{point's rotation matrix,}
\end{aligned}
$$

$$
\begin{aligned}
\vec{u} &= (1\,0\,0) \cdot \mathbf{M}, \\
\vec{v} &= (0\,1\,0) \cdot \mathbf{M}, \\
\vec{w} &= (0\,0\,1) \cdot \mathbf{M}, \\
C(p_{\text{world}}) &= p, \\
L(p_{\text{local}}) &= (0\,0\,0), \\
P(p_{\text{local}}) &= p.
\end{aligned}
$$

From these properties, we can see that the basis vectors $\vec{u}$, $\vec{v}$, and $\vec{w}$ can be found by rotating a vector aligned with each major axis by the rotation matrix $\mathbf{M}$. The closest point on a point to a point in space is the position of the point primitive itself. The closest local-space coordinate on the point primitive is always $(0\,0\,0)$, and the world-space position of a point p_{local} on the point primitive is also the position of the point primitive itself.

5.7.2 Lines

The second primitive type we will study is the line. Lines are one dimensional in their local coordinate space and can be either polygonal (linear interpolation between vertices) or higher order (spline interpolation). (See Figure 5.7.) PVR uses only polygonal lines for simplicity, but can still produce smooth results as long as the input geometry is subdivided appropriately.

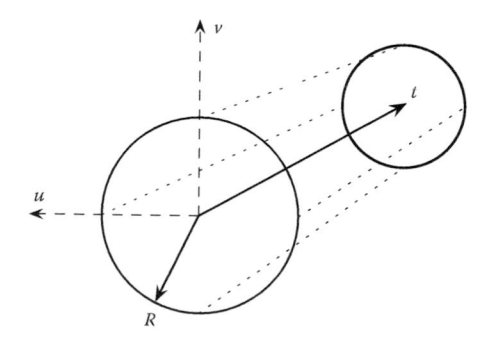

Figure 5.7. A line's local coordinate system.

A line's single dimension is parameterized by t, but to create a three-dimensional coordinate system that spans the space around the line, we also add the two normal directions $\vec{u}$ and $\vec{v}$. The following conventions are then used to construct the required local-to-world and world-to-local mappings:

$$
\begin{aligned}
t &\in [0,1] & &= & &\text{position along the length of the line,} \\
u &\in [-1,1] & &= & &\text{position right/left across line,} \\
v &\in [-1,1] & &= & &\text{position down/up across line,}
\end{aligned}
$$

$$
\begin{aligned}
p(t) &= &&\text{position in world space at parametric point } t \\
& &&\text{(linear- or spline-interpolated from control vertices),} \\
T(t) &= &&\text{world-space tangent at parametric point } t, \\
N(t) &= &&\text{world-space normal at parametric point } t,
\end{aligned}
$$

$$
\begin{aligned}
\vec{u} &= N(t) \times T(t), \\
\vec{v} &= N(t), \\
\vec{w} &= T(t), \\
C(\boldsymbol{p}_{\text{world}}) &= \text{nearestPointQuery}(\boldsymbol{p}_{\text{world}}), \\
L(\boldsymbol{p}_{\text{local}}) &= (0\ 0\ x_z), \\
P(\boldsymbol{p}_{\text{local}}) &= \vec{u} \cdot x_x + \vec{v} \cdot x_y + p(x_z).
\end{aligned}
$$

5.7.3 Surfaces

The third geometric type is the surface, which has a two-dimensional local coordinate system (Figure 5.8). Just as with lines, surfaces can use a variety of representations, from triangle and quadrilateral meshes to Bezier and NURBS patches. Triangle meshes do not have natural coordinate systems and, as such, are poorly suited as control geometry for our purposes. Quadrilaterals and higher-order surfaces do, however, have well-defined parametric coordinates, and each one may be used as an

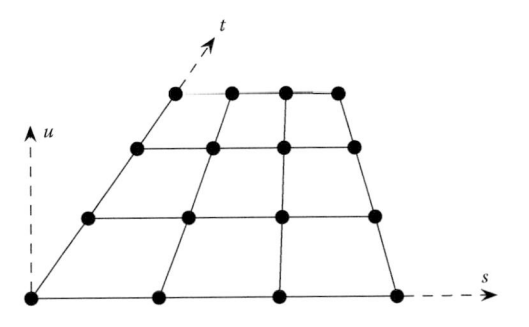

Figure 5.8. A surface's local coordinate system.

underlying geometric primitive for volume modeling, although PVR itself only uses linear quad meshes. Each surface patch is made up of
$M \times N$ vertices, and points on the surface can be parameterized using
the coordinate pair $(s\ t)$. To define the three-dimensional local coordinate system around the surface, we define the following conventions:

$$
\begin{aligned}
s \in [0,1] \quad &= \quad \text{position on surface along primary direction,} \\
t \in [0,1] \quad &= \quad \text{position on surface along secondaray direction,} \\
u \in [-1,1] \quad &= \quad \text{position behind/in front of surface, along normal,}
\end{aligned}
$$

$$
\begin{aligned}
p(s,t) \quad &= \quad \text{position in world space at parametric point } (s\ t), \\
T_s(s,t) \quad &= \quad \frac{\partial p(s,t)}{\partial s} \\
& \qquad \text{(tangent with respect to } s \text{ at parametric point } (s\ t)), \\
T_t(s,t) \quad &= \quad \frac{\partial p(s,t)}{\partial t} \\
& \qquad \text{(tangent with respect to } t \text{ at parametric point } (s\ t)),
\end{aligned}
$$

$$
\begin{aligned}
\vec{u} \quad &= \quad \frac{T_s(s,t)}{|T_s(s,t)|}, \\
\vec{v} \quad &= \quad \frac{T_t(s,t)}{|T_t(s,t)|}, \\
\vec{w} \quad &= \quad \vec{u} \times \vec{v}, \\
C(\boldsymbol{p}_{\text{world}}) \quad &= \quad \text{nearestPointQuery}(\boldsymbol{p}_{\text{world}}), \\
L(\boldsymbol{p}_{\text{local}}) \quad &= \quad (x_x\ x_y\ 0), \\
P(\boldsymbol{p}_{\text{local}}) \quad &= \quad p(x_x, x_y) + \vec{w} \cdot x_z.
\end{aligned}
$$

5.8   Procedural Noise and Fractal Functions

5.8.1   Making Noise Stick

By using each primitive type's local coordinate system when sampling
noise, it is simple to attach (so to speak) a noise function to the primitive,
even when samples are taken away from the surface of the primitive. And
because the basis vectors $\vec{u}$, $\vec{v}$, and $\vec{w}$ are defined everywhere in the space,
rotations and deformations performed on the underlying geometry are
transferred to the volumetric primitive as well.

5.8.2   Density Variation

The most common use of noise is to vary density across a volumetric
primitive. It is accomplished by sampling a scalar-valued fractal function
and modulating the primitive's density by the resulting value.

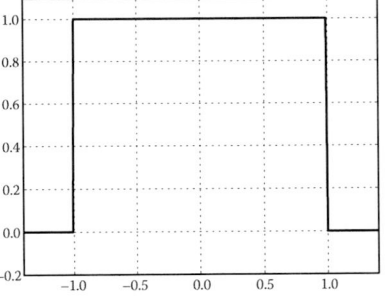
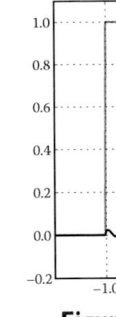
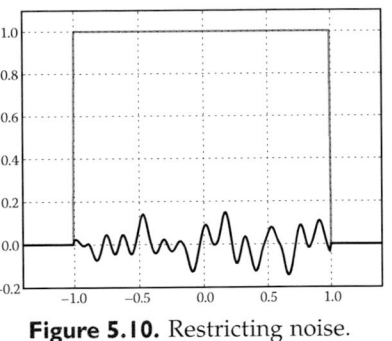

Figure 5.9. Sphere function.

Figure 5.10. Restricting noise.

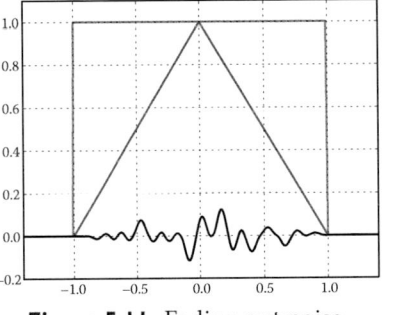
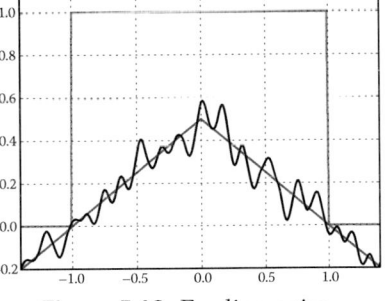

Figure 5.11. Fading out noise.

Figure 5.12. Eroding noise.

Because volumetric primitives are finite, it is important to ensure that the value of the fractal function goes to zero at the edge of the primitive. There are multiple ways to guarantee this, but as it turns out, the most intuitive way does not necessarily look the best.

If we consider a simple point with radius attribute, we can define a function that is one everywhere within the radius: $|x| < 1$ (Figure 5.9).

The sphere function (a step function in the one-dimensional illustration) can be used to restrict a noise function, limiting its effect to just the sphere: $(|x| < 1) \cdot \text{noise}(x)$. However, this has the unwanted effect of clamping the density value to zero at the boundary of the sphere (Figure 5.10).

To produce a less harsh transition at the edge, we need to ensure that the density value reaches zero before we reach the end of the primitive. The intuitive approach is to multiply the noise function by a function that goes to zero at the edge of the sphere. By taking $1 - |x|$, the noise can be gradually faded towards the edge, making for a smoother transition: $(1 - |x|) \cdot \text{noise}(x)$. However, this makes the relative amplitude variation of the noise smaller as we approach the edge, which reduces the detail of the noise (Figure 5.11).

A better solution is to *erode* the noise towards the edge of the sphere. Erosion of noise is accomplished by simply adding a value to the output of the noise function: $A \cdot (1 - |x|) + \text{noise}(x)$. The parameter A can be used to control the center value, making the core of the point more dense and the transition at the edge more abrupt. The erosion approach has the benefit of maintaining the amplitude of the noise, while still producing a value less than zero away from the edge of the sphere (Figure 5.12).

5.8.3   Impact on Primitive Bounds

In Figure 5.12, noise was eroded with a function that decreased constantly away from the center of the sphere. Although the resulting function is guaranteed to go to zero (or below) as the distance to the point increases, it does not necessarily do so at the radius of the sphere. Thus, if no displacement bound is added to the sphere, we may cut off nonzero density values that lie outside the radius.

Consider the following density function, where A and B are user-specified scaling parameters for the distance function and noise function, respectively:

$$A \cdot (1 - |x|) + B \cdot \text{noise}(x).$$

Because we know the range of the noise functions in PVR (**NoiseFunction** and **Fractal** objects have a **range()** call), we can write the following function as a worst case, letting us analyze for what x values the function is greater than zero. We let max(noise) represent the upper bound of the noise function, which gives us

$$A \cdot (1 - |x|) + B \cdot \text{max(noise)} > 0,$$
$$A + B \cdot \text{max(noise)} > A \cdot |x|.$$

If we assume $A = 1$, $B = 1$, and max(noise) $= 0.6$, we get

$$1 + 0.6 > |x|,$$
$$|x| < 1.6.$$

This shows how a simple analysis can help us define automatic displacement bounds, even for density functions that rely on user-supplied parameters.

6

PVR's Modeling Pipeline

PVR's modeling pipeline is a modular implementation of the concepts from the previous chapter. Volumetric primitives can be of both rasterization and instantiation types, and all the basic geometric types (points, lines, and meshes) can be used to drive them. A variety of user parameters and noise functions are available to alter the appearance of each primitive.

6.1   Overview

PVR's volume modeling pipeline is centered around the **Modeler** class. It serves two simple tasks: take volumetric modeling primitives as inputs and output a voxel buffer once all the inputs have been processed. Figure 6.1 illustrates the flow.

In practice, the modeling pipeline is accessed through the Python module, and a script that loads geometric primitives from disk, creates a volume-modeling primitive, and asks the **Modeler** to rasterize it can be as simple as the following:

Code 6.1. Example of volume modeling using Python API

```
geo = Geometry.read(filename)
prim = Prim.Rast.PyroclasticPoint()

input = ModelerInput()
input.setGeometry(geo)
input.setVolumePrimitive(prim)
```

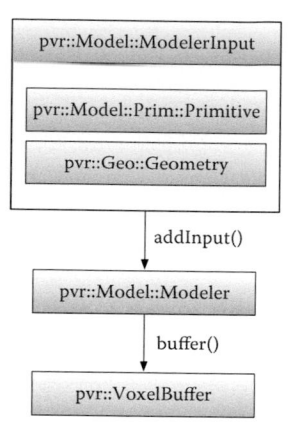

Figure 6.1. Overview of PVR's modeling pipeline.

```
modeler = Modeler()
modeler.addInput(input)
modeler.updateBounds()
modeler.setResolution(100, 100, 100)
modeler.execute()
modeler.saveBuffer(outputFilename)
```

6.2   The `Modeler` Class

The `Modeler`'s class interface in C++ consists of a main set of methods, which must be called in order to add inputs, update the domain of the voxel buffer, and then execute the modeling process.

Code 6.2. Main interface of the `Modeler` class

```
class Modeler
{
public:
...
  // Main methods
  void addInput(ModelerInput::Ptr modelerInput);
  void clearInputs();
  void updateBounds();
  void execute();
  void saveBuffer(const std::string &filename) const;
  VoxelBuffer::Ptr buffer() const;
```

```
private:
...
  // Protected data members
  Mapping                     m_mapping;
  DataStructure               m_dataStructure;
  SparseBlockSize             m_sparseBlockSize;
  std::vector<ModelerInput::Ptr>  m_inputs;
  VoxelBuffer::Ptr            m_buffer;
  Render::PerspectiveCamera::CPtr m_camera;
};
```

The **Modeler** class also provides some optional settings that can be called before using **execute()** to start the modeling process. They are used for setting properties of the generated voxel buffer, such as its resolution, its data structure, etc.

Code 6.3. The **Modeler** class's settings

```
class Modeler
{
public:
...
  // Settings
  void setResolution(const size_t x, const size_t y, const size_t z);
  void setResolution(const size_t res);
  void setVoxelSize(const Vector &size);
  void setMapping(const Mapping mapping);
  void setDataStructure(const DataStructure dataStructure);
  void setSparseBlockSize(const SparseBlockSize size);
  void setCamera(Render::PerspectiveCamera::CPtr camera);
...
private:
...};
```

Enumerators are used to specify which of the available mappings and voxel data structures to use during the modeling process.

Code 6.4. Enumerators in the **Modeler** class

```
class Modeler
{
public:
...
  // Enums
  enum Mapping {
    UniformMappingType,
    FrustumMappingType
  };
  enum DataStructure {
    DenseBufferType,
    SparseBufferType
  };
```

```
enum SparseBlockSize {
  SparseBlockSize8,
  SparseBlockSize16,
  SparseBlockSize32
};
...
private:
...};
```

6.2.1   Adding Inputs

The `Modeler::addInput()` call takes a `ModelerInput` (see Section 6.3) and adds it to the queue of inputs waiting to be written to the voxel buffer.

Inputs to the Modeler, 97

Code 6.5. The `Modeler` class's `addInput()` function.

```
void Modeler::addInput(ModelerInput::Ptr modelerInput)
{
  m_inputs.push_back(modelerInput);
}
```

Once one or more inputs have been added using `addInput()`, the `updateBounds()` call will create a voxel buffer domain (see Section 5.2) that encloses all the inputs by querying their `wsBounds()`. The union of all of the input primitives' bounds is then passed to `setupUniformMapping()` or `setupFrustumMapping()` to create the actual mapping instance that is assigned to the voxel buffer.

Defining the Voxel Buffer, 76

6.2.2   Building a Uniform Mapping

For uniform buffers, PVR uses the axis-aligned bounding box that `updateBounds()` computes in order to build a local-to-world transformation matrix. Given the bounds (min max), the matrix is constructed as

$$\mathbf{M} = \begin{pmatrix} \max_x - \min_x & 0 & 0 & 0 \\ 0 & \max_y - \min_y & 0 & 0 \\ 0 & 0 & \max_z - \min_z & 0 \\ 0 & 0 & 0 & 1 \end{pmatrix} \cdot \begin{pmatrix} 1 & 0 & 0 & 0 \\ 0 & 1 & 0 & 0 \\ 0 & 0 & 1 & 0 \\ \min_x & \min_y & \min_z & 1 \end{pmatrix} \cdot$$

Code 6.6. Setting up a uniform buffer

```
void Modeler::setupUniformMapping(const BBox &wsBounds) const
{
  MatrixFieldMapping::Ptr mapping(new MatrixFieldMapping);
  Matrix offset, scaling;
  offset.setTranslation(wsBounds.min);
  scaling.setScale(wsBounds.size());
```

```
    mapping->setLocalToWorld(scaling * offset);
    m_buffer->setMapping(mapping);
}
```

6.2.3   Building a Frustum Mapping

Frustum mappings are constructed by taking the existing render camera and re-defining its near and far planes to span the bounding box of the modeler's input primitives.

First, the camera is cloned so that properties can be altered without affecting the main render. Then, each corner vertex of the bounding box is transformed into camera space, which lets us find the near and far planes by looking at the csP_z component. A few corner cases need to be handled, such as ensuring that both the near and far planes lie in front of the camera. Finally, because the camera may be moving, each screen-to-world and camera-to-world time sample is copied from the camera into the **mapping** instance before assigning it to the buffer.

Code 6.7. Setting up a frustum buffer

```
void Modeler::setupFrustumMapping(const BBox &wsBounds) const
{
  using namespace Render;

  // Clone the camera so we can change the clip planes
  PerspectiveCamera::Ptr cam = m_camera->clone();
  // Check each corner vertex of the incoming bounds
  double near = std::numeric_limits<double>::max(), far = 0.0f;
  std::vector<Vector> wsCornerPoints = Math::cornerPoints(wsBounds);
  BOOST_FOREACH (const Vector &wsP, wsCornerPoints) {
    Vector csP = m_camera->worldToCamera(wsP, PTime(0.0));
    near = std::min(near, csP.z);
    far = std::max(far, csP.z);
  }
  // Clamp at zero
  near = std::max(near, 0.0);
  far = std::max(far, 0.0);
  // Set clip planes on cloned camera
  cam->setClipPlanes(near, far);
  // Copy the transforms from the camera
  FrustumFieldMapping::Ptr mapping(new FrustumFieldMapping);
  const Camera::MatrixVec& ssToWs = cam->screenToWorldMatrices();
  const Camera::MatrixVec& csToWs = cam->cameraToWorldMatrices();
  const size_t numSamples = ssToWs.size();
  for (size_t i = 0; i < numSamples; ++i) {
    float t = static_cast<float>(i) / (numSamples - 1);
    mapping->setTransforms(t, ssToWs[i], csToWs[i]);
  }
  m_buffer->setMapping(mapping);
}
```

6.2.4   Executing the Modeling Process

With a voxel buffer in place, the **execute()** call will go through the queue of **ModelerInput** instances, executing each in order. Instantiation primitives are asked to create a new **ModelerInput** (potentially recursively). Rasterization primitives are asked to directly write themselves to the voxel buffer through their **execute()** calls.

ModelerInput, 97

Code 6.8. Executing the **Modeler**

```
void Modeler::execute()
{
  BOOST_FOREACH (ModelerInput::Ptr i, m_inputs) {

    Prim::Primitive::CPtr prim = i->volumePrimitive();

    Prim::Inst::InstantiationPrim::CPtr instPrim =
      dynamic_pointer_cast<const Prim::Inst::InstantiationPrim>(prim);
    Prim::Rast::RasterizationPrim::CPtr rastPrim =
      dynamic_pointer_cast<const Prim::Rast::RasterizationPrim>(prim);

    if (instPrim) {
      // Handle instantiation primitives
      ModelerInput::Ptr newInput = instPrim->execute(i->geometry());
      Modeler::Ptr modeler = clone();
      modeler->clearInputs();
      modeler->addInput(newInput);
      modeler->execute();
    } else if (rastPrim) {
      // Handle rasterization primitives
      rastPrim->execute(i->geometry(), m_buffer);
    } else {
      throw InvalidPrimitiveException(prim->typeName());
    }

  }

  float mbUse = m_buffer->memSize() / (1024 * 1024);
  Log::print("Voxel buffer memory use: " + str(mbUse) + "MB");

  m_inputs.clear();
}
```

A **Modeler** object may be used a single time for multiple primitives (i.e., with multiple calls to **addInput()** and only a single call to **execute()**), or it may be used with multiple invocations of **execute()**, e.g., to force rasterization of one primitive before a second one is added. The final **VoxelBuffer** instance will be identical, assuming the same inputs were used in both cases.

6.2.5   Accessing the Voxel Buffer

Once the voxel buffer is filled, it may be written to disk using **saveBuffer()**.
The filename provided should have an **.f3d** suffix. The voxel buffer can
also be accessed directly with **buffer()**, in order to be passed to the rendering part of PVR.

6.3   Inputs to the Modeler

The **ModelerInput** class wraps up the two classes that cooperate in implementing the volume-modeling pipeline:

pvr::Model::Prim::Primitive The volumetric primitive. The primitive
will write an instance of itself for each underlying primitive in the
input geometry.

pvr::Geo::Geometry The underlying geometric primitives driving the volumetric primitive.

Code 6.9. Data members in **ModelerInput**

```
class ModelerInput
{
public:
...
protected:
  // Protected data members
  Geo::Geometry::CPtr   m_geometry;
  Prim::Primitive::CPtr m_primitive;
};
```

The public interface to **ModelerInput** is simple and only gives access to
getting and setting the data members.

Code 6.10. Main interface to **ModelerInput**

```
class ModelerInput
{
public:
...
  // Main methods
  void                  setGeometry(Geo::Geometry::CPtr geometry);
  Geo::Geometry::CPtr   geometry() const;
  void                  setVolumePrimitive(Prim::Primitive::CPtr primitive);
  Prim::Primitive::CPtr volumePrimitive() const;
protected:
...};
```

6.4   Handling User Parameters

The **ParamBase** class serves as the base for the **Primitive** class, along with many other base classes in PVR. For the **Primitive** class, **ParamBase** serves as an interface for specifying global attributes (i.e., affecting the entire set of underlying primitives in a **ModelerInput**). While most geometry-based volumetric primitives can use per-point or per-polygon attributes on the geometry to drive various aspects of their appearance, these attributes are often constant for the entire set of primitives, and it is cumbersome and unnecessary for the user to express those settings at the geometry level. Instead, it is more convenient to set these globally for the entire set of underlying primitives, and **ParamMap** is the way to accomplish this. For more details on geometry attributes in general and global attributes in particular, see Section 2.4.

Primitive, 99

ModelerInput, 97

ParamMap, 98

Geometry Attributes, 24

Code 6.11. The **ParamBase** base class

```
class ParamBase
{
public:
...
  // To be implemented by subclasses
  virtual std::string typeName() const = 0;
  virtual void setParams(const ParamMap &params)
  {
    // Default implementation does nothing.
  }
};
```

6.4.1   The **ParamMap** struct

The argument to **ParamBase::setParams()** is a **ParamMap**, which contains a set of **std::map** instances, each mapping attribute names (**std::string**) to integer, floating-point, vector, and string attributes. The types available in **ParamMap** match the ones in **AttrTable**.

AttrTable, 25

Code 6.12. The **ParamMap** struct

```
struct ParamMap
{
  // Typedefs
  typedef std::map<std::string, int>         IntMap;
  typedef std::map<std::string, float>       FloatMap;
  typedef std::map<std::string, Imath::V3f>  VectorMap;
  typedef std::map<std::string, std::string> StringMap;
  // Data members
  IntMap     intMap;
```

```
FloatMap  floatMap;
VectorMap vectorMap;
StringMap stringMap;
};
```

In the Python interface (described in more detail in Chapter 1), setting global attributes is especially easy because a Python **dict** instance can be translated automatically into a **ParamMap** once it crosses into the C++ side of the API.

Code 6.13. Using a Python dictionary as **ParamMap**

```
primParams = {
    "density"          : V3f(200.0),         // vector
    "thickness"        : 0.1,                // float
    "instance_radius"  : 0.002,             // float
    "num_points"       : 8000000,           // int
    "fill"             : 1,                  // int
    "noise_scale"      : V3f(0.2, 0.2, 0.4), // vector
    "noise_fade"       : V3f(0.5, 0.5, 0.5), // vector
    "noise_octaves"    : 8.0,                // float
    "noise_octave_gain": 0.75,              // float
    "noise_lacunarity" : 1.92,              // float
}
prim = Prim.Inst.Surface()
prim.setParams(primParams)
```

6.5   The **Primitive** Base Class

There are two basic tasks that any volume-modeling primitive needs to accomplish. The first is to bound itself, and the second is to write itself to a voxel buffer. The **Primitive** base class provides the interface for bounding of primitives, but it does not, however, provide the interface for writing a primitive to a voxel buffer because different primitives use different approaches for this. The different execution methods are instead added to subclasses that in turn inherit from **Primitive**.

With **wsBounds()**, each PVR primitive is given access to its input geometry, and is requested to return a world-space bounding box that encompasses all the space that it intends to write data to.

The **Primitive** base class also provides the **setParams()** specifying global attributes (i.e., attributes that are constant for all underlying geometric primitives) so that the primitive execution code can be implemented without explicitly checking if an attribute is being controlled from geometry attributes or from global attributes. When used together

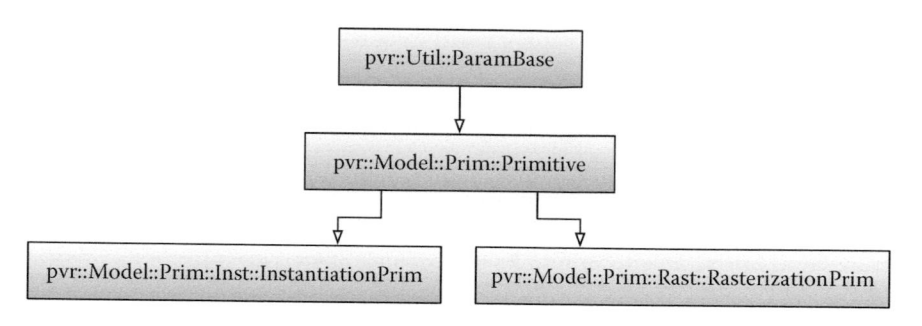

Figure 6.2. The hierarchy of primitive base classes.

with **AttrVisitor** and **Attr**, this design approach simplifies the code in the class implementations.

AttrVisitor, 29
Attr, 29

Figure 6.2 illustrates how **Primitive** and its hierarchy of primitive base classes are related.

Code 6.14. The **Primitive** base class

```
class Primitive : public Util::ParamBase
{
public:
...
  // Main methods
  virtual BBox wsBounds(Geo::Geometry::CPtr geometry) const = 0;
  void setParams(const Util::ParamMap &params)
  { m_params = params; }
protected:
  // Data members
  Util::ParamMap m_params;
};
```

6.5.1 Volumetric Primitive versus Underlying Primitive

The **Primitive** class represents a single *type* of volumetric-modeling primitive, but each instance of the class may produce any number of output instances during its execution phase. For example, a **Prim::Rast::Line** object may write hundreds or thousands of lines to a voxel buffer, based on its input **Geometry**. For this reason, we differentiate between *volumetric* primitives (of which there is only one per **ModelerInput**) and *underlying* primitives. A single volumetric primitive that is driven by geometry will take many geometric (underlying) primitives as its input. The underlying primitives are contained in the **pvr::Geo::Geometry** class.

Geometry, 20
ModelerInput, 97

Geometry, 20

6.6 Splatting Data to Voxel Buffers

Before we move on to the higher-level modeling primitives, we will look at how PVR writes data to voxel buffers because the splatting approach that is used to write samples is shared between all of the higher-level primitives.

6.6.1 Splatting a Point

The most straightforward way to splat a sample that does not line up with voxel centers is to simply round the coordinate to the closest integer. (See Figure 6.3.)

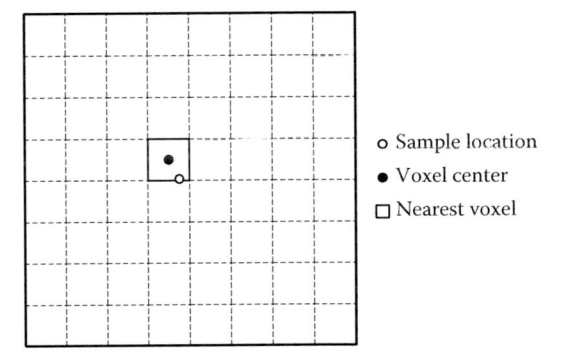

Figure 6.3. Non-antialiased splatting to a voxel buffer.

What Are the Coordinates of a Voxel?, 36

To implement the **writePoint()** function, the floating-point coordinates are given to **contToDisc** (see Section 3.1.4), which returns the integer voxel index containing the sample point. The sample's value is then added directly to the voxel buffer after checking that the coordinate is within the buffer's bounds.

Code 6.15. The **writePoint()** function

```
inline void writePoint(const Vector &vsP, const Imath::V3f &value,
                       VoxelBuffer::Ptr buffer)
{
  int i = contToDisc(vsP.x);
  int j = contToDisc(vsP.y);
  int k = contToDisc(vsP.z);

  if (buffer->isInBounds(i, j, k)) {
    buffer->lvalue(i, j, k) += value;
  }
}
```

Splatting to the nearest voxel has one inherent problem. If an animating point transitions from one voxel to the next over time, there will be a visible jump when the point crosses the voxel edge. For primitives where each individual point is clearly visible, this is likely to be a problem. However, for primitives that write a very large number of splats, many points likely overlap, and the resulting image can still appear smooth. It is usually up to the user to make this distinction.

6.6.2   Splatting an Antialiased Point

For points that need to be antialiased, PVR provides the `writeAntialiased Point()` function. It starts by offsetting the continuous floating-point voxel coordinate and offsetting it by -0.5. This shifts the coordinate into a space that is relative to voxel centers, rather than the pure voxel coordinates. (See Figure 6.4.)

Next, the fractional distance between the sample point and the upper-left neighbor voxel is found. This fraction goes to zero as the point approaches the neighbor but is actually used as a weight for the lower-left neighbor. (See Figure 6.5.)

To write the values to the voxel buffer, a loop traverses the eight neighbor voxels and adds the sample value weighted by $f_x \cdot f_y \cdot f_z$ to the current voxel. To avoid unnecessary calculations, rather than recomputing the weight for each voxel, the fractional distance is inverted after each loop step, giving the same result.

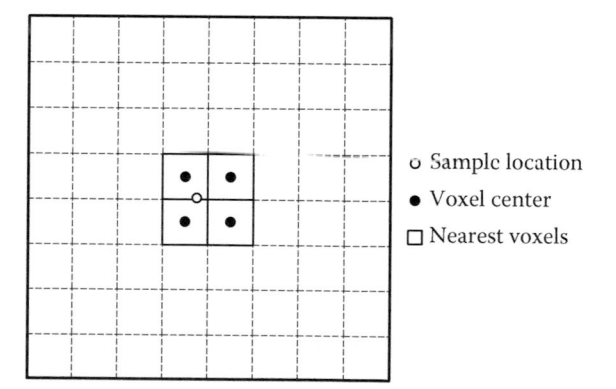

○ Sample location
● Voxel center
□ Nearest voxels

Figure 6.4. To antialias a point, the density is spread to the nearest eight voxels, weighted by the relative distance to each.

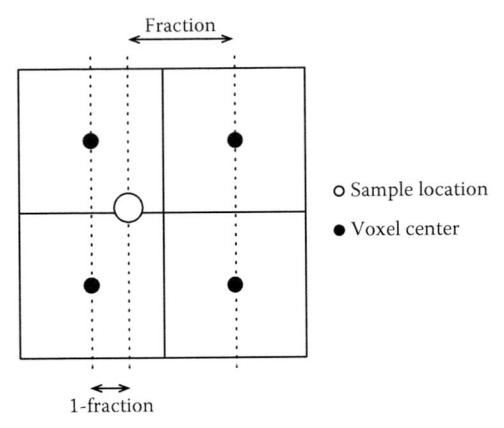

Figure 6.5. The weight is determined by factoring the distance to the neighboring voxels in each dimension.

Code 6.16. The `writeAntialiasedPoint()` function

```
inline void writeAntialiasedPoint(const Vector &vsP, const Imath::V3f &value,
                                  VoxelBuffer::Ptr buffer)
{
  // Offset the voxel-space position relative to voxel centers
  // The rest of the calculations will be done in this space
  Vector p(vsP.x - 0.5, vsP.y - 0.5, vsP.z - 0.5);
  // Find the lower-left corner of the cube of 8 voxels that
  // we need to access
  V3i corner(static_cast<int>(floor(p.x)),
             static_cast<int>(floor(p.y)),
             static_cast<int>(floor(p.z)));
  // Calculate P's fractional distance between voxels
  // We start out with weight = fraction, then each step in the loop
  // inverts the value.
  Vector fraction(static_cast<Vector>(corner + V3i(1)) - p);
  // Loop over the 8 voxels and distribute the value
  for (int k = 0; k < 2; k++) {
    for (int j = 0; j < 2; j++) {
      for (int i = 0; i < 2; i++) {
        double weight = fraction[0] * fraction[1] * fraction[2];
        if (buffer->isInBounds(corner.x + i, corner.y + j, corner.z + k)) {
          buffer->lvalue(corner.x + i,
                         corner.y + j,
                         corner.z + k) += value * weight;
        }
        fraction[0] = 1.0 - fraction[0];
      }
      fraction[1] = 1.0 - fraction[1];
    }
    fraction[2] = 1.0 - fraction[2];
  }
}
```

6.6.3   Splatting and Motion Blur

The most common way to handle motion blur in volume modeling is to
smear each sample into the voxel buffer. That is, with information about
how a given samples moves over the course of the current frame, the density values are distributed over all of the voxels that would be touched
by the moving sample. While the approach has some drawbacks, such
as losing temporal information about the motion of the sample, it is easily integrated into a volume-modeling system, and it provides accept-

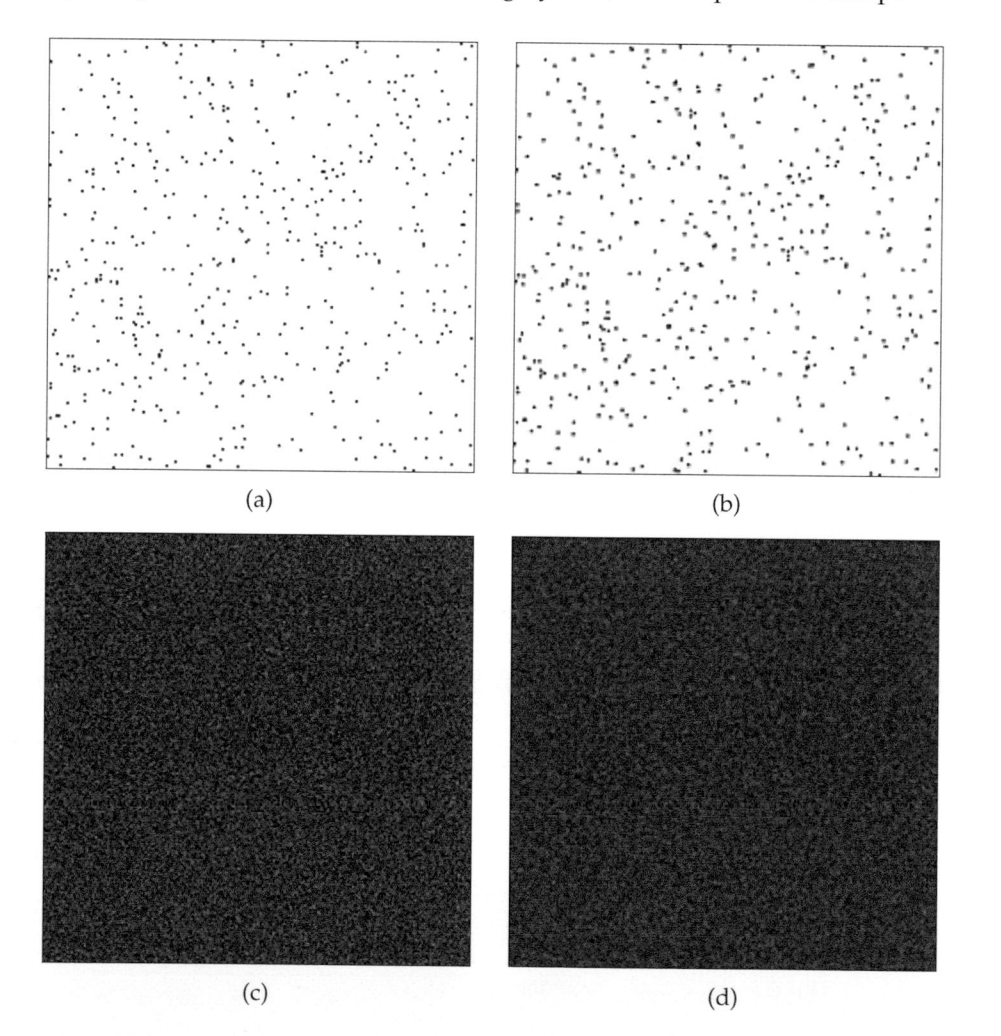

Figure 6.6. Splatting: (a) 200 non-antialiased points. (b) 200 antialiased points.
(c) 200,000 non-antialiased points. (d) 200,000 antialiased points.

Figure 6.7. Motion blur: 200 antialiased lines.

able image quality at a not-too-high computational cost. (See Figures 6.6 and 6.7.)

In PVR, the `writeLine<bool>()` function takes a start point, an endpoint, and a value to write to the buffer and then breaks down the motion path into a sequence of antialiased or non-antialiased splats, which together make for a smoothly streaked value. The template argument controls whether or not the line is antialiased.

The voxel space start point and endpoint are first used to compute the number of samples needed to cover the path of the motion vector. Then, each sample along the motion path is written either as a `writePoint()` or `writeAntialiasedPoint()` call, depending on the `Antialiased_T` template argument. Each splat is written with a density of $\frac{d}{N}$, so the total sum of all splats written to the buffer is equal to the value provided to the function.

Code 6.17. The `writeLine()` function

```
inline void writeLine(const Vector &vsStart, const Vector &vsEnd,
                      const Imath::V3f &value, VoxelBuffer::Ptr buffer)
{
  // Construct a line in voxel space
  Vector vsLine = (vsEnd - vsStart);
  // Determine number of splats based on length in voxel space
  size_t numSamples = static_cast<size_t>(std::ceil(vsLine.length()));
  numSamples = max(static_cast<size_t>(2), numSamples);
```

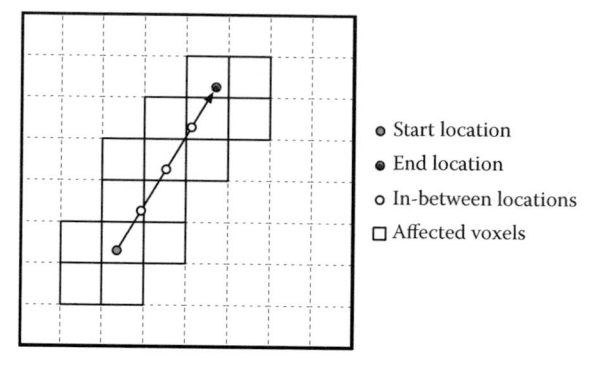

Figure 6.8. Writing a line to a voxel buffer by using multiple splats.

```
// Splat each sample
Imath::V3f sampleValue = value / static_cast<double>(numSamples);
for (size_t i = 0; i < numSamples; ++i) {
  // Find current point on line
  double fraction = static_cast<double>(i) /
    static_cast<double>(numSamples - 1);
  Vector vsP = Imath::lerp(vsStart, vsEnd, fraction);
  // Write antialiased or non-antialiased point based on template argument
  if (Antialiased_T) {
    writeAntialiasedPoint(vsP, sampleValue, buffer);
  } else {
    writePoint(vsP, sampleValue, buffer);
  }
}
}
```

Figure 6.8 illustrates how a smeared sample is written to a voxel buffer as a series of separate splats.

Rasterization Primitives in PVR

7.1 The RasterizationPrim Base Class

The rasterization primitives described in Section 5.4 are implemented in PVR as subclasses of the **pvr::Prim::Rast::RasterizationPrim** base class, which in turn is a subclass of **Primitive**. As we saw in Section 5.4, the basic rasterization loop is generic enough to support many different types of rasterization primitives, so **RasterizationPrim** provides an implementation that its subclasses can use.

The **RasterizationPrim** class does not implement any of the required virtual functions from **Primitive**, but it does specify the interface for which its subclasses write themselves to the **Modeler**'s voxel buffer, in the form of the virtual **execute()** function.

In action, the concrete subclasses of **RasterizationPrim** work in cooperation with the base class. The subclass is responsible for calling **rasterize()** from its implementation of **execute()**. This is normally done once for each underlying primitive. The rasterization loop in **Rasterization Prim** will then call the subclass's implementation of **getSample()**, which returns the density value of the current underlying primitive, for the given voxel. Figure 7.1 illustrates this collaboration.

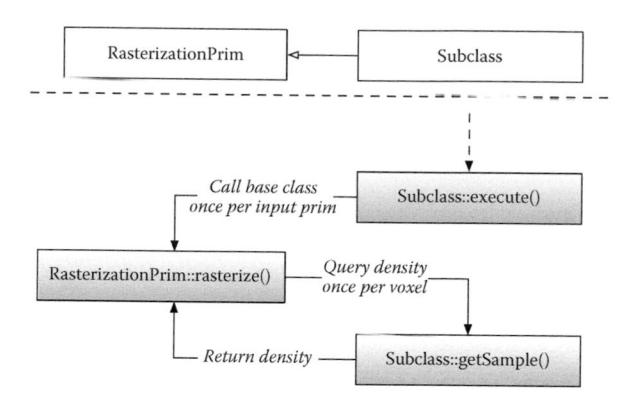

Figure 7.1. Collaboration diagram for `RasterizationPrim` and a subclass.

Code 7.1. The `RasterizationPrim` base class

```
class RasterizationPrim : public Primitive
{
public:
  // Typedefs
  PVR_TYPEDEF_SMART_PTRS(RasterizationPrim);
  // To be implemented by subclasses
  virtual void execute(Geo::Geometry::CPtr geometry,
                       VoxelBuffer::Ptr buffer) const = 0;
protected:
  // To be called from subclasses
  void rasterize(const BBox &vsBounds, VoxelBuffer::Ptr buffer) const;
  // To be implemented by subclasses
  virtual void getSample(const RasterizationState &state,
                         RasterizationSample &sample) const = 0;
};
```

7.1.1   The Rasterization Loop

The `rasterize()` call triggers a loop over the voxels in the buffer that overlap the bounding box provided to the function. Before calling `rasterize()`, the subclass's `execute()` function first sets up the state of the current primitive (attributes, point positions, etc.), then calls `rasterize()`, which in turn calls `getSample()` for each voxel.

Code 7.2. Example use of `rasterize()` (pseudocode)

```
for prim in prims:
  bounds = vsBounds(prim); // Computes bounds of current primitive
  setCurrentPrim(prim);    // Sets up the current state for getSample()
  rasterize(bounds);       // Calls getSample() for each voxel in bounds
```

The actual implementation of **rasterize()** does a little more work in order to provide the **getSample()** call with all the required information, but the loop is generic enough to work with all of PVR's rasterization primitives.

Code 7.3. The rasterization loop

```
// Iterate over voxels
for (VoxelBuffer::iterator i = buffer->begin(dvsBounds),
       end = buffer->end(dvsBounds); i != end; ++i, ++count) {
  RasterizationState rState;
  RasterizationSample rSample;
  // Get sampling derivatives/voxel size
  rState.wsVoxelSize = mapping->wsVoxelSize(i.x, i.y, i.z);
  // Transform voxel position to world space
  Vector vsP = discToCont(V3i(i.x, i.y, i.z));
  mapping->voxelToWorld(vsP, rState.wsP);
  // Sample the primitive
  this->getSample(rState, rSample);
  if (Math::max(rSample.value) > 0.0f) {
    if (rSample.wsVelocity.length2() == 0.0) {
      *i += rSample.value;
    } else {
      Vector vsEnd;
      Vector wsMotion = rSample.wsVelocity * RenderGlobals::dt();
      mapping->worldToVoxel(rState.wsP + wsMotion, vsEnd);
      writeLine<true>(vsP, vsEnd, rSample.value, buffer);
    }
  }
}
```

7.1.2 Sampling Density from the Subclass

The **getSample()** call is responsible for providing the **rasterize()** function with density samples at each voxel position that intersects the current primitive.

The **rasterize()** call communicates with **getSample()** through two structs: **RasterizationState** and **RasterizationSample**. The **Rasterization State** struct provides information about the position of the current point to sample and the voxel-to-voxel derivates, which are used for filtering the density function.

Code 7.4. The **RasterizationState** struct

```
struct RasterizationState
{
  // Data members
  Vector wsP;
  Vector wsVoxelSize;
```

```
  // Constructor
  RasterizationState()
    : wsP(Vector(0.0)), wsVoxelSize(Vector(0.0))
  { }
};
```

The **RasterizationSample** struct is used by **getSample()** to communicate its result back to the **rasterize()** call. It contains information about the sample point's *value*, as well as its *velocity*, which is used for motion blur.

Code 7.5. The **RasterizationSample** struct

```
struct RasterizationSample
{
  // Data members
  Imath::V3f value;
  Vector wsVelocity;
  // Constructor
  RasterizationSample()
    : value(Imath::V3f(0.0)), wsVelocity(Vector(0.0))
  { }
};
```

7.1.3   Optimal Bounds

Using a voxel-space bounding box can be a poor-fitting bound for many primitives. Consider a thin, diagonal line. The bounding box in voxel space will be large, but the actual number of voxels occupied by the line is small. Rather than trying to have **rasterize()** figure out the best way to traverse each primitive type, it is expected that the **getSample** call (as implemented by the subclass) quickly knows to return zero for any sample point that isn't near the primitive being rasterized. Volume primitive types that use points or particles as their underlying geometric primitives generally don't use this type of optimization, but ones that use poly lines, meshes, or other parametric surfaces tend to employ acceleration data structures to quickly rule out voxels that are far enough away from the geometry to not be influenced.

7.1.4   Rasterization and Motion Blur

The rasterization loop is assumed to be happening at time 0.0 and does not itself take into account the motion of the underlying geometry. Instead, a motion vector is returned from the **getSample()** call, indicating what the motion of the particular piece of primitive would be. If nonzero, the motion vector is then used to smear the sample into the voxel buffer, as implemented in Code 7.3.

7.2   Implementing Primitives

The simplest geometry-based volumetric primitive is a spherical point with constant density. It would be described as a position, a radius, and a density value. To convert that representation into voxel values in a buffer should be simple, but even so, a few questions need to be answered:

1. What are the voxel-space bounds of each sphere?

2. What is the density of a particular point in space around each volumetric sphere?

3. How should we antialias the edge of the sphere, if the edge falls between two voxels?

4. How should we antialias the sphere as a whole, if it is smaller than a single voxel?

5. Assuming that there are many points in the underlying geometry's particle system, how do we conveniently and efficiently iterate over all the points, finding not just the point positions but also traversing an arbitrary set of attributes associated with each point?

Each of these questions addresses a different aspect of what a volumetric primitive must do and how it is implemented.

7.2.1   Attributes

One of the most common tasks when using geometry to drive volumetric primitives is to use attributes on the geometry to control the look of the primitive.

Per-point attributes. For volumetric primitives driven by geometry that is particles or points, per-point attributes drive aspects that vary from one particle to the next. In this case, they are often referred to simply as attributes.

For primitives driven by line or surface geometry, where each geometric primitive is made up of more than one point, per-point attributes can control aspects of the primitive that vary across the underlying geometry, e.g., the density of the volume can be defined to vary across the surface used to model it.

Per-primitive attributes. In order to control aspects of volumetric primitives that change from one underlying geometric primitive to the next, per-primitive attributes are used. For example, the noise *seed* for a surface-based primitive could be made to vary from one primitive to the next. Per-primitive attributes only apply to primitives made up of more than one point. For a point cloud, each point is also a primitive, so per-point attributes serve the same purpose.

Global attributes. The **ParamBase** class (Section 6.4) is used to drive attributes that are constant for the entire volumetric primitive, i.e., attributes that are constant for all the underlying geometric primitives in the input geometry.

Handling User Parameters, 98

7.2.2   A Design Pattern for Handling Attributes

Let us take per-point attributes as an example. Base classes contain attributes in a struct called **Base::PointAttrState**. The struct is updated by a virtual function **Base::updatePointAttributes()**. The struct's constructor defines the attribute names as well as the default attribute values. Defaults are used if an attribute cannot be found either as a per-point attribute on geometry or in the **ParamMap** instance provided through **m_params**.

ParamMap, 98

    The subclass contains attributes in a separate struct **Sub::PointAttr State**, and it implements the same virtual function name: **Sub::update PointAttributes()**.

Code 7.6. Example of design pattern

```
class Base
{
public:
  // The virtual function used to update m_basePointAttrs;
  virtual void updatePointAttrs(Geo::AttrVisitor::const_iterator i) const
  {
    m_basePointAttrs.update(i);
  }
  // Updates the global attributes
  void setParams(const ParamMap &params)
  {
    m_params = params;
  }
protected:
  // The struct containing Geo::Attr instances for iterating
  struct PointAttrState
  {
    PointAttrState()
      : theInt ("the_int",   1),
        theFloat("the_float", 0.5f)
    { }
    void update(Geo::AttrVisitor::const_iterator i)
    {
```

```
      theInt.update(i);
      theFloat.update(i);
    }
    Geo::Attr<int>   theInt;
    Geo::Attr<float> theFloat;
  };
  // Instance of the struct
  PointAttrState m_basePointAttrs;
  // Global attributes
  ParamMap m_params;
};

class Sub {
public:
  // The virtual function used to update m_basePointAttrs;
  virtual void updatePointAttrs(Geo::AttrVisitor::const_iterator i) const
  {
    Base::updatePointAttrs(i);
    m_pointAttrs.update(i);
  }
protected:
  // The struct containing Geo::Attr instances for iterating
  struct PointAttrState
  {
    PointAttrState()
      : anInt  ("an_int",   1)
    { }
    void update(Geo::AttrVisitor::const_iterator i)
    {
      anInt.update(i);
    }
    Geo::Attr<int> anInt;
  };
  // Instance of the struct
  PointAttrState m_pointAttrs;
};
```

AttrVisitor, 29

To iterate over the points in the primitive, we use **AttrVisitor**.

```
void Sub::execute(Geo::Geometry::CPtr geometry, VoxelBuffer::Ptr buffer)
  const
{
  const AttrTable &points = geometry->particles()->pointAttrs();
  AttrVisitor visitor(points, m_params);
  for (AttrVisitor::const_iterator i = visitor.begin(), end = visitor.end();
       i != end; ++i, ++count) {
    updatePointAttrs(i);
    // Do work based on current point attribute settings
    int   theInt   = m_basePointAttrs.theInt;
    float theFloat = m_basePointAttrs.theFloat;
    int   theInt   = m_pointAttrs.anInt;
  }
}
```

The approach has several benefits. First, the name of each attribute and its default value is nicely encapsulated in the constructor of the struct that owns the attributes. This keeps us from inadvertently using attributes without proper defaults. Second, the **updatePointAttrs()** call takes care of setting the attribute value based first on the **AttrTable**, then the **ParamMap**, and finally the attribute's default value. This keeps us from introducing bugs such as forgetting to check the **ParamMap** before using an attribute's default value, etc. The third benefit comes from keeping the **execute()** call clean, since no elaborate checks need to be made in order to find attribute values, making the implementation of the volume-modeling algorithm clearer.

AttrTable, 25
ParamMap, 98

7.3   Sphere-Based Primitives

The first type of rasterization primitive we will look at are those that use points or spheres as their input geometry type. These types tend to see heavy use in production, as they are useful for everything from dust, mist, and clouds to explosions and other pyroclastic effects.

Before looking at the implementation of a concrete sphere-based rasterization primitive we will go through the base class that each of the sphere-based primitives inherits from. In order to keep us from reimplementing identical code in every subclass, the **PointBase** class takes care of part of the bounding process.

Although it does not itself provide any per-point attributes, the **PointBase** class is aware of the attribute design pattern from the previous section, and in implementing the basic bounding operation, it uses iterators into an **AttrVisitor** so that each subclass can update its own per-point attributes easily in the **pointWsBounds()** function.

Code 7.7. The **PointBase** base class

```
BBox PointBase::wsBounds(Geo::Geometry::CPtr geometry) const
{
  assert(geometry != NULL);
  assert(geometry->particles() != NULL);

  if (!geometry->particles()) {
    Log::warning("Rasterization primitive has no particles. "
                 "Skipping bounds generation.");
    return BBox();
  }

  BBox wsBBox;
  AttrVisitor visitor(geometry->particles()->pointAttrs(), m_params);
```

```
  for (AttrVisitor::const_iterator i = visitor.begin(), end = visitor.end();
       i != end; ++i) {
    BBox pointBounds = pointWsBounds(i);
    wsBBox.extendBy(pointBounds);
  }

  return wsBBox;
}
```

The **PointBase** class does not implement a default **execute()** call because the **Point** subclass implements both a rasterization primitive and a splatting primitive and chooses the approach based on the size of the primitive.

7.3.1   Bounding the Primitive

To simplify bounds calculations and avoid having each primitive implementation loop over all the input points, **PointBase** provides an implementation of the bounding of the primitive as a whole. This implementation also takes care of sanity checking the input geometry (making sure it exists, etc.). Internally, it loops over all points in the input geometry and calls **pointWsBounds()** (see below) once for each input point.

Code 7.8. The **PointBase::wsBounds()** member function

```
BBox PointBase::wsBounds(Geo::Geometry::CPtr geometry) const
{
  assert(geometry != NULL);
  assert(geometry->particles() != NULL);

  if (!geometry->particles()) {
    Log::warning("Rasterization primitive has no particles. "
                 "Skipping bounds generation.");
    return BBox();
  }

  BBox wsBBox;
  AttrVisitor visitor(geometry->particles()->pointAttrs(), m_params);

  for (AttrVisitor::const_iterator i = visitor.begin(), end = visitor.end();
       i != end; ++i) {
    BBox pointBounds = pointWsBounds(i);
    wsBBox.extendBy(pointBounds);
  }

  return wsBBox;
}
```

Subclasses of **PointBase** must implement **pointWsBounds()**, which is called for each point in the input, with the subclass expected to return a bounding box for the specified point.

7.4 The **Point** Primitive

Although the **Point** primitive is simple, it shows how a single primitive can adapt to user input and conditions and switch its behavior accordingly. The **Point** primitive represents all kinds of points, from large to small. (See Figure 7.2.) In Section 7.2 we brought up the question of proper antialiasing, and **Point** implements a solution for both antialiasing the edge of large points as well as correctly filtering points that are smaller than a voxel.

Implementing Primitives, 111

In implementing the antialiasing methods, **Point** effectively becomes two different modeling primitives. Small points, ones that are around the size of a single voxel, are turned into voxel data using splats (see Section 6.6), and points larger than a voxel use the rasterization method (Section 5.4).

Splatting Data to Voxel Buffers, 101

Rasterization Primitives, 79

As a rasterization primitive, **Point** implements the collaborative relationship with the **RasterizationPrim** previously described, where **execute()** processes one point at a time in the input geometry, calling **RasterizationPrim::rasterize()** for each one.

RasterizationPrim, 107

Figure 7.2. Single **Point** primitive.

Code 7.9. The **Point** class

```
class Point : public PointBase
{
public:
...
  // From RasterizationPrim
  virtual void execute(Geo::Geometry::CPtr geometry,
                       VoxelBuffer::Ptr buffer) const;
protected:
  // From RasterizationPrimitive
  virtual void getSample(const RasterizationState &state,
                         RasterizationSample &sample) const;
  // From PointRasterizationPrimitive
  virtual BBox pointWsBounds(const Geo::AttrVisitor::const_iterator &i) const;
  // Structs
  struct AttrState
  {
    // Constructor
    AttrState()
      : wsCenter   ("P"),
        wsVelocity ("v"),
        radius     ("radius",    0.1f),
        density    ("density",   Imath::V3f(1.0f)),
        antialiased("antialiased", 1)
    { }
    // Main methods
    void update(const Geo::AttrVisitor::const_iterator &i);
    // Data members
    Geo::Attr<Imath::V3f> wsCenter;
    Geo::Attr<Imath::V3f> wsVelocity;
    Geo::Attr<float>      radius;
    Geo::Attr<Imath::V3f> density;
    Geo::Attr<int>        antialiased;
    float                 densityFactor;
  };
  // Data members
  mutable AttrState m_attrs;
};
```

7.4.1   Executing the Primitive

The **execute()** call first performs basic sanity checks (ensuring that the **P** attribute exists) and then sets up an **AttrVisitor** instance to traverse the input points. A **Timer** and **ProgressReporter** are also set up to give the user feedback on how the modeling process is advancing and to give a final readout on the time spent rasterizing the primitive.

Code 7.10. execute(), with loop contents removed for brevity

```
void Point::execute(Geo::Geometry::CPtr geometry,
                    VoxelBuffer::Ptr buffer) const
{
  using namespace Field3D;
```

```
using namespace std;

const AttrTable &points = geometry->particles()->pointAttrs();

if (!points.vectorAttrRef("P").isValid()) {
  Log::warning("Point primitive - no P attribute in input");
  return;
}

Timer              timer;
size_t             count = 0;
ProgressReporter   progress(2.5f, "  ");
FieldMapping::Ptr  mapping(buffer->mapping());
AttrVisitor        visitor(points, m_params);

Log::print("Point primitive processing " + str(points.size()) +
           " input points");

for (AttrVisitor::const_iterator i = visitor.begin(), end = visitor.end();
     i != end; ++i, ++count) {

}

Log::print("  Time elapsed: " + str(timer.elapsed()));
}
```

For each point in the input, PVR first checks whether the user has aborted the render. Because even a single point can take a fair amount of time to rasterize if it is large, this check is performed once for every input point. The current progress is then updated, and the per-point attribute state is brought up to date for the current point. As a precaution against doing unnecessary work, we also check whether the current point's density is zero, in which case it won't contribute to the voxel buffer and can safely be ignored.

Code 7.11. execute(): Initial checks before starting rasterization process

```
// Check if user terminated
Sys::Interrupt::throwOnAbort();
// Print progress
progress.update(static_cast<float>(count) / points.size());
// Update attributes
m_attrs.update(i);
// Point attributes
const V3f      &density    = m_attrs.density;
const float    wsRadius    = m_attrs.radius;
const Vector   wsCenter    = m_attrs.wsCenter.as<Vector>();
const Vector   wsVelocity  = m_attrs.wsVelocity.as<Vector>();
const bool     antialiased = m_attrs.antialiased;
// Skip if density at or below zero
if (Math::max(density) <= 0.0) {
  continue;
}
```

Once we know that the point indeed needs to be rasterized, we transform its position from world space to voxel space. Because the voxel buffer's **Mapping** instance contains all the information about a buffer's position in space, we can use the same call regardless of the mapping type (i.e., regardless of whether the buffer is uniform or frustum shaped).

Code 7.12. execute( ): Transforming to voxel space

```
// Transform to voxel space
Vector vsP;
mapping->worldToVoxel(wsCenter, vsP);
```

With the voxel-space position known, we also need to query the voxel buffer's voxel size so that antialiasing can be performed. The **Point** call uses different forms of antialiasing based on the size of each point in relation to the voxel size.

Given the radius R and voxel size $\vec{S}$, the relative size of each point is measured as $R/\min(\vec{S})$. If the relative size is greater than one, indicating that it is large enough to be resolved, then the point is rasterized. If the point is smaller, it is written to the buffer as a splat.

Code 7.13. execute( ): Determining modeling approach

```
// Determine relative size of the point, compared to the shortest
// edge of a voxel.
Vector wsVoxelSize = pvr::Model::wsVoxelSize(mapping, vsP);
double relativeSize = wsRadius / Math::min(wsVoxelSize);

// Check relative size of point
if (relativeSize > 1.0) {

  // If we're larger than a voxel, rasterize the point as a sphere

} else {

  // If we are smaller than a voxel we splat the point,
  // compensating for pscale by varying density.

}
```

For large points, the rasterization process requires a bounding box in voxel space. The antialiasing approach is outlined below under the **getSample()** call, but the filter width used for antialiasing must also be taken into account when computing the primitive's bounds, since it causes each point to grow slightly. (See Figure 7.3.)

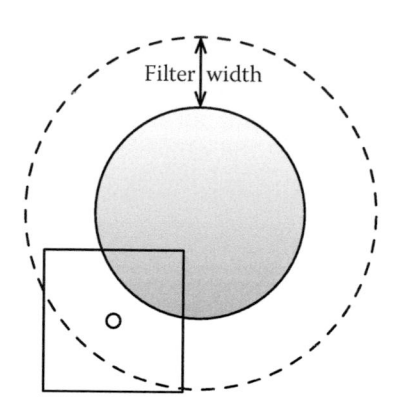

Figure 7.3. Illustrating the effect of enlarging the **Point** by the filter width.

The **vsSphereBounds** is a utility function that computes the voxel-space bounds for a given point/radius combination. Because it uses the **Mapping** of the current voxel buffer, it automatically adapts to both uniform and frustum-shaped buffers.

Code 7.14. execute( ): Rasterizing large points

```
// Calculate filter width
float filterWidth = wsVoxelSize.length();
// Calculate rasterization bounds
BBox vsBounds =
  vsSphereBounds(mapping, wsCenter, wsRadius + filterWidth * 0.5);
// Call rasterize(), which will query getSample() for values
rasterize(vsBounds, buffer);
```

Smaller points don't require edge antialiasing. Instead, they need to be appropriately filtered, since a direct point sample at the center of a voxel most likely would miss the small point. Using the splatting approach for small points has two benefits: it is faster than performing a full rasterization, and it is easy to filter. Splatting in PVR does not use an explicit filter kernel, but the non-antialiased version is implicitly a box filter and the antialiased version a triangle filter. Both versions compute a final density based on the fractional size of the point versus the voxel size.

Non-antialiased splats can be very useful when instancing large numbers of points, where the stochastic distribution itself averages out sharp edges.

Code 7.15. execute(): Splatting small points

```
// Account for voxel size
V3f voxelVolume = V3f(wsVoxelSize.x * wsVoxelSize.y * wsVoxelSize.z);
V3f voxelDensity =
  density / voxelVolume * sphereVolume(wsRadius);
// Write points
if (wsVelocity.length() == 0) {
  if (antialiased) {
    writeAntialiasedPoint(vsP, voxelDensity, buffer);
  } else {
    writePoint(vsP, voxelDensity, buffer);
  }
} else {
  Vector wsEnd = wsCenter + wsVelocity * RenderGlobals::dt();
  Vector vsEnd;
  mapping->worldToVoxel(wsEnd, vsEnd);
  if (antialiased) {
    writeLine<true>(vsP, vsEnd, voxelDensity, buffer);
  } else {
    writeLine<false>(vsP, vsEnd, voxelDensity, buffer);
  }
}
```

7.4.2 Density Function

RasterizationPrim, 107

In the cases where a point is being rasterized rather than splatted, the **RasterizationPrim** will call **getSample()** to find the density of a given voxel. The **Point** class's density function is computed by looking at the distance from the sample point (**state.wsP**) to the point center (**m_attrs. wsCenter**). If no antialiasing is to be performed, the distance could simply be compared against the point radius (**m_attrs.radius**). Using this approach, there would be a chance that a voxel that partially overlaps the point would sample a distance outside the point's radius, giving it zero density and introducing an *aliasing artifact*.

To solve this problem, the point radius is padded by half the size of a voxel, which ensures that a point that partially overlaps the voxel will have a nonzero influence at the voxel center. Because the point is artificially enlarged to cover at least the center of the voxel, the overall density is reduced so that the total amount of density added by the primitive stays constant, regardless of the filter width.

Code 7.16. Point::getSample()

```
void Point::getSample(const RasterizationState &state,
                      RasterizationSample &sample) const
{
  float filterWidth = state.wsVoxelSize.length();
```

```
float halfWidth = 0.5 * filterWidth;
float factor = 1.0 / (1.0 + pow(halfWidth / m_attrs.radius, 3.0f));
sample.value = evaluateSphere(state.wsP, m_attrs.wsCenter.as<Vector>(),
                       m_attrs.radius + halfWidth,
                       m_attrs.density.value() * factor,
                       (m_attrs.radius - halfWidth) / m_attrs.radius);
sample.wsVelocity = m_attrs.wsVelocity.as<Vector>();
}
```

7.4.3   Bounding a Single Point

The bounds of the **Point** are computed by taking the position, radius, and velocity into account. An **AttrVisitor::const_iterator** referring to the current point is provided to the function and can be used to update the **m_attrs** member variable with the current per-point attributes.

AttrVisitor, 29

Code 7.17. Point::pointWsBounds()

```
BBox Point::pointWsBounds(const Geo::AttrVisitor::const_iterator &i) const
{
  BBox wsBBox;
  // Update point attrs
  m_attrs.update(i);
  // Pad to account for radius and motion
  Vector wsStart = m_attrs.wsCenter.value();
  Vector wsEnd = m_attrs.wsCenter.value() +
    m_attrs.wsVelocity.value() * RenderGlobals::dt();
  wsBBox.extendBy(wsStart + m_attrs.radius.as<Vector>());
  wsBBox.extendBy(wsStart - m_attrs.radius.as<Vector>());
  wsBBox.extendBy(wsEnd + m_attrs.radius.as<Vector>());
  wsBBox.extendBy(wsEnd - m_attrs.radius.as<Vector>());
  return wsBBox;
}
```

7.5   The **PyroclasticPoint** Primitive

Although the **Point** primitive was instructive, showing how a basic volume-modeling primitive is implemented, it is not until we start to introduce noise functions that we can produce interesting-looking results. To this end, **PyroclasticPoint** implements a staple primitive in volume modeling: a simple point with a pyroclastic fractal function attached. This type of primitive is often used to create effects such as billowing smoke, as well as cumulus-type cloud formations. PVR's implementation also offers user parameters that make the point "nonpyroclastic,"

Rast::Point, 116

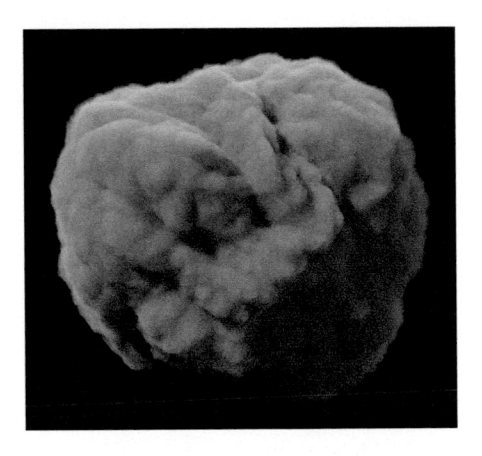

Figure 7.4. Single **PyroclasticPoint** primitive.

essentially making it a simple eroded noise puff. However, the name of the class reflects its primary use.

The **PyroclasticPoint** has the same basic class structure as **Point** but uses many more attributes to control the look of its fractal function. (See Figure 7.4.)

Code 7.18. The **PyroclasticPoint** class

```
class PyroclasticPoint : public PointBase
{
public:
...
  // From RasterizationPrim
  virtual void execute(Geo::Geometry::CPtr geometry,
                       VoxelBuffer::Ptr buffer) const;
protected:
  // From RasterizationPrimitive
  virtual void getSample(const RasterizationState &state,
                         RasterizationSample &sample) const;
  // From PointRasterizationPrimitive
  virtual BBox pointWsBounds(const Geo::AttrVisitor::const_iterator &i) const;
  // Structs
  struct AttrState
  {
    // Constructor
    AttrState()
      : wsCenter    ("P"),
        wsVelocity  ("v"),
        orientation("orientation"),
        radius      ("radius",      1.0f),
        density     ("density",     Imath::V3f(1.0f)),
        seed        ("seed",        1),
        scale       ("scale",       1.0f),
```

```
       octaves     ("octaves",       8.0f),
       octaveGain ("octave_gain",    0.5f),
       lacunarity ("lacunarity",     1.92f),
       amplitude  ("amplitude",      1.0f),
       gamma       ("gamma",         1.0f),
       pyroclastic("pyroclastic",    1),
       pyro2D      ("pyroclastic_2d", 1),
       absNoise    ("absolute_noise", 1),
       antialiased("antialiased",    1)
    { }
    // Main methods
    void update(const Geo::AttrVisitor::const_iterator &i);
    // Data members
    Geo::Attr<Imath::V3f> wsCenter;
    Geo::Attr<Imath::V3f> wsVelocity;
    Geo::Attr<Imath::V3f> orientation;
    Geo::Attr<float>       radius;
    Geo::Attr<Imath::V3f> density;
    Geo::Attr<int>         seed;
    Geo::Attr<float>       scale;
    Geo::Attr<float>       octaves;
    Geo::Attr<float>       octaveGain;
    Geo::Attr<float>       lacunarity;
    Geo::Attr<float>       amplitude;
    Geo::Attr<float>       gamma;
    Geo::Attr<int>         pyroclastic;
    Geo::Attr<int>         pyro2D;
    Geo::Attr<int>         absNoise;
    Geo::Attr<int>         antialiased;
    Matrix                 rotation;
    Noise::Fractal::CPtr   fractal;
  };
  // Data members
  mutable AttrState m_attrs;
};
```

7.5.1   Executing the Primitive

The **PyroclasticPoint::execute()** call is similar to that of the **Point** class, although it does not implement a splatting approach for points smaller than a voxel, as the overall density is dependent on fractal functions that make the final density difficult to predict. One notable addition is that the fractal function's range is taken into account when computing the voxel-space bounds.

Rast::Point, 116

Code 7.19. PyroclasticPoint::execute()

```
void PyroclasticPoint::execute(Geo::Geometry::CPtr geometry,
                               VoxelBuffer::Ptr buffer) const
{
  const AttrTable &points = geometry->particles()->pointAttrs();
```

```
AttrVisitor      visitor(points, m_params);
FieldMapping::Ptr mapping(buffer->mapping());

for (AttrVisitor::const_iterator i = visitor.begin(), end = visitor.end();
     i != end; ++i, ++count) {
  // Update attributes
  m_attrs.update(i);
  // Transform to voxel space
  Vector vsP;
  mapping->worldToVoxel(m_attrs.wsCenter.as<Vector>(), vsP);
  // Check fractal range
  Fractal::Range range = m_attrs.fractal->range();
  // Calculate rasterization bounds
  float totalRadius = m_attrs.radius +
    m_attrs.radius * m_attrs.amplitude * range.second;
  BBox vsBounds = vsSphereBounds(mapping, m_attrs.wsCenter.as<Vector>(),
                                 totalRadius);
  // Call rasterize(), which will come back and query getSample() for
  // values
  rasterize(vsBounds, buffer);
}
}
```

7.5.2 Density Function

When sampling the density function of each underlying point through
getSample(), the first thing that needs to be done is to transform the
RasterizationState::wsP coordinate into the local space of the point.

The noise coordinate system is equal to the local coordinate system,
except in the case of so-called *two-dimensional displacement*. Two-dim
ensional displacement effectively turns the noise coordinate space into
a flat texture map on the surface of the sphere. This type of displacement
is accomplished by projecting the noise space coordinate to a unit sphere,
effectively giving all points along the normal of a sphere the same noise
space coordinate. Pyroclastic-type points use this to prevent overhangs,
but it is an artistic control that can be useful to disable in many circum-
stances. (See Figures 7.5 and 7.6.)

Code 7.20. PyroclasticPoint::getSample()

```
// Transform to the point's local coordinate system
Vector lsP, lsPUnrot = (state.wsP - wsCenter) / wsRadius;
rotation.multVecMatrix(lsPUnrot, lsP);
Vector nsP = lsP;

// Normalize noise coordinate if '2D' displacement is desired
if (isPyroclastic && isPyro2D) {
  nsP.normalize();
}
```

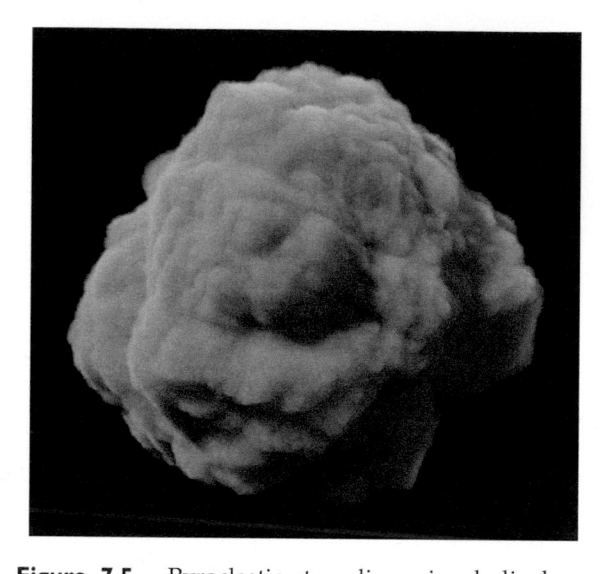

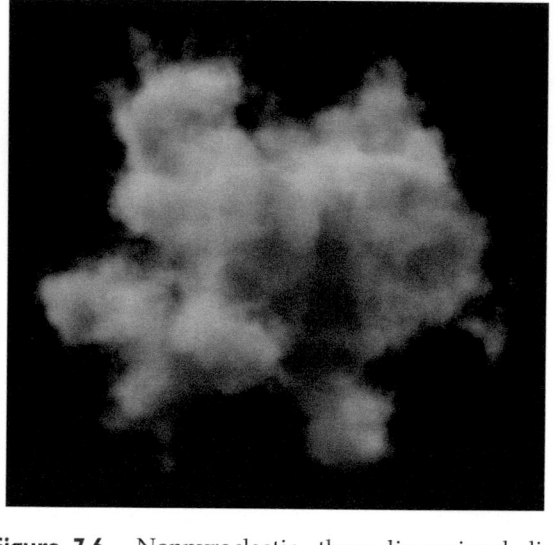

Figure 7.5. Pyroclastic, two-dimensional displacement, absolute noise function.

Figure 7.6. Nonpyroclastic, three-dimensional displacement, signed noise function.

In order to make each input point look different, the noise space is *offset* by a random vector, based on the per-point attribute **m_attrs.seed**. Without this offset, each modeled point would have the same noise pattern.

Code 7.21. PyroclasticPoint::getSample()

```
// Offset by seed
nsP += Math::offsetVector<double>(seed);
```

Regardless of whether the point is evaluated in a pyroclastic or nonpyroclastic state, the fractal function is computed the same way. A gamma function is also applied, allowing the user to shift the density value higher or lower in order to achieve different artistic goals. The final fractal value is also scaled by the **m_attrs.amplitude** attribute, giving control over the amount of noise-based displacement that takes place.

Code 7.22. PyroclasticPoint::getSample()

```
// Compute fractal function
double fractalVal = fractal->eval(nsP);
fractalVal = Math::gamma(fractalVal, gamma);
fractalVal *= amplitude;
```

Because the pyroclastic (thresholded) and nonpyroclastic density functions are quite different, an **if** statement separates the two.

Code 7.23. PyroclasticPoint::getSample()

```
// Calculate sample value
if (isPyroclastic) {
  // Pyroclastic mode
} else {
  // Non-pyroclastic mode
}
```

The pyroclastic density function is based on thresholding a distance function with noise added. By thresholding, the transition from zero density to full density is sudden, making the primitive appear almost surface-like.

Rast::Point, 116

Similar to how the **Point** class was antialiased, **PyroclasticPoint** fits the modulated distance function in a segment whose width is determined by the voxel size. The **pyroclastic()** function performs the thresholding, as it's shared by several pyroclastic primitive types.

Code 7.24. pyroclastic()

```
float pyroclastic(const float distance, const float noise,
                  const float filterWidth)
{
  float width     = filterWidth * 0.5;
  float pyroValue = Math::fit(distance - noise, -width, width, 1.0, 0.0);
  return Imath::clamp(pyroValue, 0.0f, 1.0f);
}
```

Code 7.25. PyroclasticPoint::getSample()

```
// Pyroclastic mode
double sphereFunc  = lsP.length() - 1.0;
float  filterWidth = state.wsVoxelSize.length() / wsRadius;
float  pyro        = pyroclastic(sphereFunc, fractalVal, filterWidth);
sample.value       = density * pyro;
```

The nonpyroclastic version simply adds an erosion density function to the fractal value. It needs no further antialiasing, so the code is simpler.

Code 7.26. PyroclasticPoint::getSample()

```
// Non-pyroclastic mode
double distanceFunc = 1.0 - lsP.length();
float  noise        = std::max(0.0, distanceFunc + fractalVal);
sample.value        = density * noise;
```

7.5.3   Bounding a Single Pyroclastic Point

Computing the bounds of **PyroclasticPoint** is similar to computing **Point ::pointWsBounds()**, with the exception that the fractal function's value range is taken into account.

Code 7.27. pointWsBounds()

```
BBox PyroclasticPoint::pointWsBounds
(const Geo::AttrVisitor::const_iterator &i) const
{
  BBox wsBBox;
  m_attrs.update(i);

  // Check fractal range
  Fractal::Range range = m_attrs.fractal->range();

  // Compute start and end of motion
  Vector wsStart = m_attrs.wsCenter.value();
  Vector wsEnd = m_attrs.wsCenter.value() +
    m_attrs.wsVelocity.value() * RenderGlobals::dt();

  // Pad to account for displacement
  Vector padding = Vector(m_attrs.radius.value() +
                          range.second * m_attrs.amplitude * m_attrs.radius);
  wsBBox.extendBy(wsStart + padding);
  wsBBox.extendBy(wsStart - padding);
  wsBBox.extendBy(wsEnd + padding);
  wsBBox.extendBy(wsEnd - padding);

  return wsBBox;
}
```

7.6   Line-Based Primitives

The second basic class of volumetric primitives are those based on polygonal lines. Just as with the sphere-based rasterization primitives, there is a base class that provides some operations that are common to all kinds of line-based primitives. And although **PointBase** didn't implement **execute**, the base class for line primitives does.

Just as in **PointBase**, **LineBase** primitives maintain state during their rasterization. But where **PointBase** only used per-point attributes, **Line Base** uses both per-point and per-primitive attributes. In order to keep the two separate, **PointAttrState** holds information about all per-point attributes that drive an individual line (N per line), and **PolyAttrState** holds information that is common for each line (one per line). Each struct holds the attributes that are common to all types of line primitives, and

PointBase, 114

PointBase, 114

subclasses use their own separate structs to hold any additional per-point or per-poly attributes.

The two attribute structs are data members in the primitive, and **updatePolyAttrs()** and **updatePointAttrs()** are used to set the current state. Many of the available **LineBase** methods assume that this state has been set up and will read from **m_basePointAttrs** and **m_basePolyAttrs**.

Code 7.28. The **LineBase** base class

```
class LineBase : public RasterizationPrim
{
public:
...
  // From Primitive
  virtual BBox wsBounds(Geo::Geometry::CPtr geometry) const;
  // From RasterizationPrim
  virtual void execute(Geo::Geometry::CPtr geometry,
                       VoxelBuffer::Ptr buffer) const;
protected:
  // Structs
  struct PointAttrState
  {
    PointAttrState()
      : wsCenter   ("P"),
        wsVelocity ("v"),
        density    ("density", Imath::V3f(1.0f)),
        radius     ("radius",  0.1f)
    { }
    void update(const Geo::AttrVisitor::const_iterator &i);
    Geo::Attr<Imath::V3f> wsCenter;
    Geo::Attr<Imath::V3f> wsVelocity;
    Geo::Attr<Imath::V3f> density;
    Geo::Attr<float>      radius;
  };
  struct PolyAttrState
  {
    PolyAttrState()
      : antialiased("antialiased", 1)
    { }
    void update(const Geo::AttrVisitor::const_iterator &i);
    Geo::Attr<int> antialiased;
  };
  struct SegmentInfo
  {
    SegmentInfo()
      : index(0), t(0.0), distance(std::numeric_limits<double>::max()),
        radius(0.0)
    { }
    size_t index;
    double t;
    double distance;
    double radius;
  };
```

```
  // To be implemented by subclasses
  virtual void updatePolyAttrs(Geo::AttrVisitor::const_iterator i) const;
  virtual void updatePointAttrs(Geo::AttrVisitor::const_iterator i,
                                const size_t numPoints) const;
  virtual float displacementBounds(const size_t) const
  { return 0.0f; }
  // Utility methods
  void updateAccelStruct() const;
  bool findClosestSegment(const RasterizationState &state,
                          SegmentInfo &info) const;
  // Data members
  mutable std::vector<PointAttrState> m_basePointAttrs;
  mutable PolyAttrState m_basePolyAttrs;
  mutable pvr::Accel::UniformGrid<size_t> m_gridAccel;
};
```

7.6.1   Bounding a Line

The **LineBase** implementation of **Primitive::wsBounds()** traverses each polygon in the input geometry, and for each polygon it then traverses the points that make up each line. For each point, it checks the position, radius, velocity, and displacement bounds to arrive at a bounding box that encloses the point. The final bounds of the primitive is the union of each point's bounding box.

This bounds calculation is generic enough that line-type subclasses only need to implement **displacementBounds()** (see below).

Code 7.29. LineBase::wsBounds()

```
BBox LineBase::wsBounds(Geo::Geometry::CPtr geometry) const
{
  typedef AttrVisitor::const_iterator AttrIter;

  assert(geometry != NULL);
  assert(geometry->polygons() != NULL);

  if (!geometry->polygons()) {
    Log::warning("Line primitive(s) have no polygons. "
                 "Skipping bounds generation.");
    return BBox();
  }

  // Iteration variables
  BBox            wsBBox;
  Polygons::CPtr polys = geometry->polygons();
  AttrVisitor     polyVisitor(polys->polyAttrs(), m_params);
  AttrVisitor     pointVisitor(polys->pointAttrs(), m_params);

  for (AttrIter iPoly = polyVisitor.begin(), endPoly = polyVisitor.end();
       iPoly != endPoly; ++iPoly) {
```

```
        // Update poly attributes
        updatePolyAttrs(iPoly);
        // Update point attribute
        size_t first = polys->pointForVertex(iPoly.index(), 0);
        size_t numPoints = polys->numVertices(iPoly.index());
        updatePointAttrs(pointVisitor.begin(first), numPoints);
        // Compute world-space bounds
        size_t index = 0;
        for (std::vector<PointAttrState>::const_iterator i
                                      = m_basePointAttrs.begin(),
            end = m_basePointAttrs.end(); i != end; ++i, ++index) {
          Vector radius       = Vector(i->radius.value());
          float displacement = displacementBounds(index);
          Vector wsV          = i->wsVelocity.value();
          Vector wsP          = i->wsCenter.value();
          Vector wsEnd        = wsP + wsV * RenderGlobals::dt();
          wsBBox = extendBounds(wsBBox, wsP, radius * (1.0 + displacement));
          wsBBox = extendBounds(wsBBox, wsEnd, radius * (1.0 + displacement));
        }
      }

    return wsBBox;
  }
```

7.6.2   Executing the Primitive

Similar to **wsBounds()**, **execute()** loops over each polygon and updates the current per-point and per-poly attributes. Since **updatePointAttrs()** and **updatePolyAttrs()** are virtual, this updates the attributes for both the base class and the subclass. With the current state up to date, it then computes the voxel-space bounds of each polygon (including displacement bounds).

After updating the current state, **execute()** calls **updateAccelStruct()**, which sets up the acceleration data structure so that calls to **getSample()** can find the closest line segment quickly.

Once the acceleration structure is in place, **rasterize()** is called, using the voxel-space bounding box as its domain specification.

Code 7.30. LineBase::execute()

```
void LineBase::execute(Geo::Geometry::CPtr geometry,
                                     VoxelBuffer::Ptr buffer) const
{
  typedef AttrVisitor::const_iterator AttrIter;

  Polygons::CPtr    polys  = geometry->polygons();
  const AttrTable &points = polys->pointAttrs();
```

```
// Iteration variables
AttrVisitor      polyVisitor(polys->polyAttrs(), m_params);
AttrVisitor      pointVisitor(polys->pointAttrs(), m_params);

for (AttrIter iPoly = polyVisitor.begin(), endPoly = polyVisitor.end();
      iPoly != endPoly; ++iPoly, ++count) {
  // Update attributes
  updatePolyAttrs(iPoly);
  size_t first = polys->pointForVertex(iPoly.index(), 0);
  size_t numPoints = polys->numVertices(iPoly.index());
  updatePointAttrs(pointVisitor.begin(first), numPoints);
  // Compute voxel-space bounds
  BBox vsBounds;
  // Loop over each point
  size_t ptIndex = 0;
  for (std::vector<PointAttrState>::const_iterator i =
                              m_basePointAttrs.begin(),
        end = m_basePointAttrs.end(); i != end; ++i, ++ptIndex) {
    float displ = displacementBounds(ptIndex);
    vsBounds.extendBy(vsSphereBounds(buffer->mapping(),
                              i->wsCenter.value(),
                              i->radius.value() * (1.0 + displ)));
  }
  // Update acceleration structure
  updateAccelStruct();
  // Finally rasterize
  rasterize(vsBounds, buffer);
  }
}
```

7.6.3   Updating the Acceleration Data Structure

The **LineBase** class uses the **pvr::Accel::UniformGrid** class in order to quickly perform closest-point queries on a single line.

Because the line-rasterization process treats one poly line at a time, the acceleration structure is updated once per polygon. For lines with very few points, this does incur some overhead, but in production scenes where each line segment often has tens or hundreds of points, the acceleration structure is a good time investment.

We first compute the bounds of the poly line, as well as the average radius (since the radius may vary per point). Because the acceleration structure gets used only to find closest points, there is no need to take displacement bounds into account. The average radius is used to set the cell size of the acceleration grid.

Once the acceleration structure is initialized, each line segment is added using **UniformGrid::addLine()**.

Code 7.31. LineBase::updateAccelStruct()

```
void LineBase::updateAccelStruct() const
```

```
{
  // Compute bounds and average radius
  BBox wsBounds;
  double sumRadius = 0.0;
  for (size_t i = 0, size = m_basePointAttrs.size() - 1; i < size; ++i) {
    float radius = m_basePointAttrs[i].radius;
    wsBounds = extendBounds(wsBounds, m_basePointAttrs[i].wsCenter.value(),
                            radius);
    sumRadius += radius;
  }
  double avgRadius = sumRadius / m_basePointAttrs.size();
  // Update acceleration structure domain
  Vector origin = wsBounds.min;
  size_t res = 32;
  Vector voxelSize = wsBounds.size() / static_cast<double>(res);
  float cellSize = max(voxelSize);
  if (cellSize < avgRadius) {
    res = std::ceil(max(wsBounds.size()) / avgRadius);
    cellSize = avgRadius;
  }
  m_gridAccel.clear(cellSize, res, origin);
  // Add line segments to hash
  for (size_t i = 0, size = m_basePointAttrs.size() - 1; i < size; ++i) {
    Vector p0(m_basePointAttrs[i].wsCenter.value());
    Vector p1(m_basePointAttrs[i + 1].wsCenter.value());
    float displ = std::max(displacementBounds(i), displacementBounds(i + 1));
    float radius = std::max(m_basePointAttrs[i].radius.value(),
                            m_basePointAttrs[i + 1].radius.value());
    m_gridAccel.addLine(p0, p1, radius * (1.0 + displ) + cellSize, i);
  }
}
```

7.6.4 Finding the Closest Point on a Line

When **LineBase** subclasses implement the function **RasterizationPrim::getValue()**, they will need to find the index of the closest line segment, as well as the parametric coordinate along that segment that is closest to the sample point. The **SegmentInfo** struct wraps up the relevant data: index, parametric coordinate, as well as the radius of the line at the closest point and the distance from the sample point to the closest point.

To find the closest line segment, we simply iterate over the contents of the appropriate grid cell (returned by **UniformGrid::get()**).

Code 7.32. LineBase::findClosestSegment()

```
bool LineBase::findClosestSegment(const RasterizationState &state,
                                  SegmentInfo &info) const
{
  typedef Accel::UniformGrid<size_t>::HashVec HashVec;
```

```
  double minRelDist   = std::numeric_limits<double>::max();
  double t            = 0.0;
  double lExtend      = 0.0;
  double displacement = 0.0;
  const HashVec &vec  = m_gridAccel.get(state.wsP);

  if (vec.size() == 0) {
    return false;
  }

  for (HashVec::const_iterator iIdx = vec.begin(), end = vec.end();
       iIdx != end; ++iIdx) {
    // Segment index
    const size_t i = *iIdx;
    // Find closest point on Line
    Vector p0(m_basePointAttrs[i].wsCenter.value());
    Vector p1(m_basePointAttrs[i + 1].wsCenter.value());
    Vector pOnLine = Math::closestPointOnLineSegment(p0, p1, state.wsP,
                                                     t, tExtend);
    // Compare distance to radius
    double radius = Math::fit01(t, m_basePointAttrs[i].radius.value(),
                                m_basePointAttrs[i + 1].radius.value());
    double dist = (state.wsP - pOnLine).length();
    double relDist = dist / radius;
    // If within radius, update info
    if (relDist < minRelDist) {
      minRelDist = relDist;
      displacement = std::max(displacementBounds(i),
                    displacementBounds(i + 1));
      info.radius = radius;
      info.distance = dist;
      info.index = i;
      if (i == 0 && t == 0.0 || i == (m_basePointAttrs.size() - 2) &&
                    t == 1.0) {
        info.t = tExtend;
      } else {
        info.t = t;
      }
    }
  }

  double maxDist = (info.radius * (1.0 + displacement) +
                   state.wsVoxelSize.length() * 0.5);

  return info.distance < maxDist;
}
```

7.6.5 Displacement Bounds

The **displacementBounds()** call lets subclasses report how much padding is required around a given point on the current polygonal line. It is assumed that **updatePointAttrs()** has been called and that the index provided is within the valid range of **numPoints** for the current polygon.

7.6.6   Interpolating Attributes along the Line

The **LINE_INTERP** macro is used to interpolate per point from the **m_base PointAttrs** struct. It takes a variable name, and a **SegmentInfo** struct that provides the segment index, as well as the interpolation point. For example:

Code 7.33. Interpolating velocity along the line

```
Imath::V3f v = LINE_INTERP(wsVelocity, info);}
```

7.7   The Line Primitive

Rast::LineBase, 128

The **Rast::Line** class is the simplest implementation of **LineBase** and only handles simple lines, without any noise or other embellishments. (See Figure 7.7.) It is mostly intended to show a stripped-down line-primitive implementation, but can also be useful for drawing lots of thin lines where the lack of additional detail is acceptable.

The class is much simpler than **LineBase** and implements nothing more than the required **getSample()** call from **RasterizationPrim**. It maintains no per-point or per-poly state beyond what **LineBase** provides.

Code 7.34. The Line class

```
class Line : public LineBase
{
public:
...
protected:
  // From RasterizationPrimitive
  virtual void getSample(const RasterizationState &state,
                         RasterizationSample &sample) const;
};
```

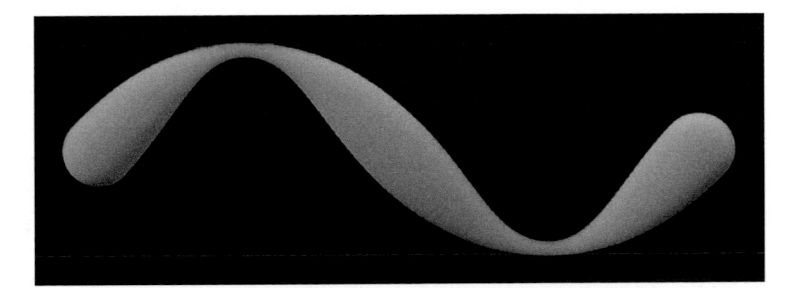

Figure 7.7. Line primitive with varying radii.

7.7.1   Density Function

The **Rast::Line** primitive's **getSample()** call is very simple: it finds the closest line segment, computes a density falloff value depending on whether antialiasing is to be used, and then returns interpolated density and velocity to the rasterization loop.

Code 7.35. Line::getSample()

```
void Line::getSample(const RasterizationState &state,
                     RasterizationSample &sample) const
{
  if (m_basePointAttrs.size() < 2) {
    return;
  }

  SegmentInfo info;

  if (findClosestSegment(state, info)) {

    // Compute falloff depending on whether we want antialiasing
    float falloff;
    if (m_basePolyAttrs.antialiased.value()) {
      float halfWidth = state.wsVoxelSize.length() * 0.5;
      falloff = 1.0 - Math::smoothStep(info.distance,
                                       info.radius - halfWidth,
                                       info.radius + halfWidth);
    } else {
      falloff = info.distance < info.radius ? 1.0 : 0.0;
    }

    // Set values in RasterizationSample
    sample.value     = falloff * LINE_INTERP(density, info);
    sample.wsVelocity = LINE_INTERP(wsVelocity, info);

  }
}
```

7.8   The **PyroclasticLine** Primitive

Whereas **Rast::Line** implemented the simplest possible line primitive, **PyroclasticLine** implements a more fully featured one, with a well-defined local noise coordinate system and fractal function controls. (See Figure 7.8.)

Rast::Line, 135

The **PyroclasticLine** primitive uses several per-polygon and per-point attributes, which are contained in the **PolyAttrState** and **PointAttrState** structs. Although they are named the same as their counterparts in **LineBase**, there is no name clash, since they are nested within each class.

Figure 7.8. PyroclasticLine primitive with varying noise amplitude.

Code 7.36. The **PyroclasticLine** class

```
class PyroclasticLine : public LineBase
{
public:
...
protected:
  // From RasterizationPrimitive
  virtual void getSample(const RasterizationState &state,
                         RasterizationSample &sample) const;
  // From LineRasterizationPrimitive
  virtual void updatePolyAttrs(Geo::AttrVisitor::const_iterator i) const;
  virtual void updatePointAttrs(Geo::AttrVisitor::const_iterator i,
                                const size_t numPoints) const;
  virtual float displacementBounds(const size_t index) const;
  // Structs
  struct PolyAttrState
  {
    PolyAttrState()
      : scale      ("scale",          Imath::V3f(1.0f)),
        octaves    ("octaves",        8.0f),
        octaveGain ("octave_gain",    0.5f),
        lacunarity ("lacunarity",     1.92f),
        absNoise   ("absolute_noise", 1),
        pyroclastic ("pyroclastic",   1),
        pyro2D     ("pyroclastic_2d", 1)
    { }
    void update(const Geo::AttrVisitor::const_iterator &i);
    Geo::Attr<Imath::V3f> scale;
    Geo::Attr<float>      octaves;
    Geo::Attr<float>      octaveGain;
    Geo::Attr<float>      lacunarity;
    Geo::Attr<int>        absNoise;
    Geo::Attr<int>        pyroclastic;
    Geo::Attr<int>        pyro2D;
```

```
    Noise::Fractal::CPtr  fractal;
  };
  struct PointAttrState
  {
    PointAttrState()
      : wsNormal   ("N",            Imath::V3f(0.0, 1.0, 0.0)),
        wsTangent  ("T",            Imath::V3f(0.0, 0.0, 1.0)),
        u          ("u",            0.0f),
        amplitude  ("amplitude",    1.0f),
        gamma      ("gamma",        1.0f)
    { }
    void update(const Geo::AttrVisitor::const_iterator &i);
    Geo::Attr<Imath::V3f> wsNormal;
    Geo::Attr<Imath::V3f> wsTangent;
    Geo::Attr<float>      u;
    Geo::Attr<float>      amplitude;
    Geo::Attr<float>      gamma;
  };
  // Data members
  mutable std::vector<PointAttrState> m_pointAttrs;
  mutable PolyAttrState m_polyAttrs;
};
```

7.8.1   Density Function

The **getSample()** call is a little more involved than the simple **Line::get Sample()**. The first step, however, is still to find the closest segment and point using **findClosestSegment()**.

Code 7.37. Finding the closest point on the line

```
void PyroclasticLine::getSample(const RasterizationState &state,
                                RasterizationSample &sample) const
{
  if (m_basePointAttrs.size() < 2) {
    return;
  }

  // Per-Polygon attribute
  const bool      isPyroclastic = m_polyAttrs.pyroclastic;
  const bool      isPyro2D      = m_polyAttrs.pyro2D;
  const V3f       scale         = m_polyAttrs.scale;
  Fractal::CPtr fractal         = m_polyAttrs.fractal;

  SegmentInfo info;

  if (findClosestSegment(state, info)) {
    }

  }
}
```

LineBase, ??

Once the closest point has been determined, all per-point attributes are interpolated to the closest point on the line. Two macros are used for the lookup, depending on whether the attribute is handled by **LineBase** (**LINE_INTERP**) or by **PyroclasticLine** (**PYRO_LINE_INTERP**).

Code 7.38. Interpolating per-point attributes

```
// Interpolate values along line
sample.wsVelocity      = LINE_INTERP(wsVelocity, info);
Imath::V3f wsCenter    = LINE_INTERP(wsCenter, info);
Imath::V3f density     = LINE_INTERP(density, info);
Imath::V3f N           = PYRO_LINE_INTERP(wsNormal, info);
Imath::V3f T           = PYRO_LINE_INTERP(wsTangent, info);
float      u           = PYRO_LINE_INTERP(u, info);
float      gamma       = PYRO_LINE_INTERP(gamma, info);
float      amplitude   = PYRO_LINE_INTERP(amplitude, info);
```

Transforming from World to Local Space, 141

Given the normal and tangent vectors, and the closest point on the line, the world-space sample point is transformed to local space (see Section 7.8.2). Local space is defined as $[-1, 1]$ in the x- and y-dimensions, where the local-space coordinates $|(p_x \ p_y)| = 1.0$ fall on the radius of the cylinder. The z-dimension has the range $[0, 1]$, corresponding to the first and last vertex of the line.

Code 7.39. Transforming to local space

```
// Transform to local space
Vector lsP = lineWsToLs(state.wsP, N.cross(T), N, T,
                        wsCenter, u, info.radius);
```

Similar to **PyroclasticPoint**, **PyroclasticLine** has an **isPyro2D** option, which projects noise-space coordinates to unit length, giving all points along the same normal the same noise-space coordinate. The projection is slightly modified since only the x- and y-dimensions span the cylinder.

Code 7.40. Normalizing the x, y-components

```
// Normalize the length of the vector in the XY plane
// if user wants "2D" style displacement.
if (isPyroclastic && isPyro2D) {
  lsP = Math::normalizeXY(lsP);
}
```

The noise space is conveniently defined to be the same as the local space of the line. In addition, a scaling factor is specified by the per-poly attribute **scale**. This scaling factor lets the user squash and stretch the noise across the primitive to achieve different artistic results.

Code 7.41. Scaling local space to form noise space

```
// Transform to noise space
Vector nsP = lsP / scale;
```

With the noise coordinate defined, the fractal function is sampled at the noise-space position. Gamma is applied to the resulting value using **Math::gamma()**, which takes extra care to handle negative values appropriately. The attributes that control the look of the noise are all per polygon and are assigned in **updatePolyAttrs()**. Therefore, the only per-point attribute that needs to be considered is **amplitude**.

Code 7.42. Evaluating the fractal function

```
// Evaluate fractal
double fractalVal = fractal->eval(nsP);
fractalVal = Math::gamma(fractalVal, gamma);
fractalVal *= amplitude;
```

By default, **PyroclasticLine** applies a pyroclastic-type look to the primitive using the fractal function. As was previously discussed, the pyroclastic look is achieved by thresholding the density function. The **Pyro clasticLine** class looks at the **pyroclastic** per-primitive attribute to determine whether the thresholding and special distance function should be used.

Although pyroclastic noise uses a threshold (i.e., step) function, it is filtered to prevent aliasing artifacts. The filter width used is length of the diagonal of one voxel in the output frustum buffer.

The pyroclastic function uses the fractal value and a spherical, signed distance function. The pyroclastic density value is found by thresholding the sum of the fractal function and the signed distance function, using the **pyroclastic()** function.

The nonpyroclastic look is simpler to compute and is identical to the eroded noise approach in Section 5.8.2. The distance function is defined as 1.0 at the center of the line, 0.0 at the radius, and linearly decreasing past the radius. The final density value is found by summing the distance function and the fractal value.

Density Variation, 88

Code 7.43. Evaluating the pyroclastic and nonpyroclastic functions

```
// Calculate sample value
if (isPyroclastic) {
  float  filterWidth = state.wsVoxelSize.length() / info.radius;
  double distanceFunc = info.distance / info.radius - 1.0;
  float  pyro        = pyroclastic(distanceFunc, fractalVal,
```

```
                                                    filterWidth);
      sample.value       = pyro * density;
    } else {
      double distanceFunc = 1.0 - info.distance / info.radius;
      float  noise        = std::max(0.0, distanceFunc + fractalVal);
      sample.value        = noise * density;
    }

  }
}
```

7.8.2   Transforming from World to Local Space

The **lineWsToLs()** function helps transform a point into the local space
of the line. First, a coordinate system is built at the line's center point,
with vectors $(N \times T, N, T)$. This represents the geometric local to world
transform. Distances are preserved in the transform, as the basis vectors
are normalized.

The final geometric local space coordinate is defined in x and y as
$\frac{p_{geo}}{radius}$ and in z as the interpolated t-coordinate.

Code 7.44. Transforming from world space to local space

```
Vector lineWsToLs(const Vector &wsP, const Vector &wsE1, const Vector &wsE2,
                  const Vector &wsE3, const Vector &wsCenter,
                  const float u, const float radius)
{
  // Build transform
  Matrix lsToWs = Math::coordinateSystem(wsE1, wsE2, wsE3, wsCenter);
  Matrix wsToLs = lsToWs.inverse();
  // Compute coordinate
  Vector lsP = wsP * wsToLs;
  return Vector(lsP.x / radius, lsP.y / radius, u);
}
```

7.8.3   Updating Per-Polygon Attributes

Because the only per-point varying parameter to the fractal function is
the amplitude, we create the fractal function once in **updatePolyAttrs()**
and then reuse the same instance with each call to **getSample()**.

Code 7.45. updatePolyAttrs()

```
void PyroclasticLine::updatePolyAttrs(Geo::AttrVisitor::const_iterator i)
  const
{
```

```
    // Update base class
    LineBase::updatePolyAttrs(i);
    // Update this class
    m_polyAttrs.update(i);
    // Update fractal
    NoiseFunction::CPtr noise;
    if (m_polyAttrs.absNoise) {
      noise = NoiseFunction::CPtr(new AbsPerlinNoise);
    } else {
      noise = NoiseFunction::CPtr(new PerlinNoise);
    }
    m_polyAttrs.fractal.reset(new fBm(noise, 1.0, m_polyAttrs.octaves,
                                     m_polyAttrs.octaveGain,
                                     m_polyAttrs.lacunarity));
}
```

7.8.4 Updating Per-Point Attributes

Since each **PyroclasticLine** has more than just one point, **updatePoint Attrs()** first resizes and then updates each of the elements in a **std:: vector<PointAttrState>** when called.

Code 7.46. updatePointAttrs()

```
void PyroclasticLine::updatePointAttrs(Geo::AttrVisitor::const_iterator
                                       iPoint, const size_t numPoints) const
{
  // Update base class
  LineBase::updatePointAttrs(iPoint, numPoints);
  // Update this class
  m_pointAttrs.resize(numPoints);
  for (size_t i = 0; i < numPoints; ++i, ++iPoint) {
    m_pointAttrs[i].update(iPoint);
  }
}
```

7.8.5 Displacement Bounds

To compute the displacement bounds for each underlying line vertex, we need to construct the **Fractal** instance and query its **range()** in order to determine the maximal value. The bounds of the function are the same for both the pyroclastic and nonpyroclastic looks, as they both use a normalized distance function with slope $k = 1.0$ in local space.

Fractal, 64

Code 7.47. displacementBounds()

```
float PyroclasticLine::displacementBounds(const size_t index) const
```

```
{
  float amplitude  = m_pointAttrs[index].amplitude;
  float scale      = Math::max(m_polyAttrs.scale.value());
  float lacunarity = m_polyAttrs.lacunarity;

  NoiseFunction::CPtr noise;
  if (m_polyAttrs.absNoise) {
    noise = NoiseFunction::CPtr(new AbsPerlinNoise);
  } else {
    noise = NoiseFunction::CPtr(new PerlinNoise);
  }

  Fractal::CPtr fractal(new fBm(noise, scale, m_polyAttrs.octaves,
                               m_polyAttrs.octaveGain, lacunarity));

  return fractal->range().second * amplitude;
}
```

Instantiation Primitives in PVR

PVR's implementations of instantiation primitives are in many ways simpler than its rasterization primitives. Many of the features that make instantiation primitives more efficient than rasterization primitives also make them simpler to implement.

8.1 The **InstantiationPrim** Base Class

Instantiation primitives (Section 5.5) inherit from the **InstantiationPrim** base class. It requires nothing from its subclasses apart from the **execute()** call, which generates new input to the **Modeler**, based on the instantiation primitive's inputs and parameters.

Code 8.1. The **InstantiationPrim** base class

```
class InstantiationPrim : public Primitive
{
public:
  // Typedefs
  PVR_TYPEDEF_SMART_PTRS(InstantiationPrim);
  // Main methods
  virtual ModelerInput::Ptr execute(const Geo::Geometry::CPtr geo) const = 0;
};
```

When the **Modeler** (described in Section 6.2) finds an instantiation primitive, it calls **execute()** to allow the instantiation primitive to return its result in the form of a new **ModelerInput**. It should be noted that because the output of **execute()** is a full **ModelerInput** object, complete with **Geometry** and **Primitive** instances, the **InstantiationPrim** can return volumetric primitives of different types than itself.

8.2   Common Strategies

8.2.1   Number of Points to Instance

One of the first operations is to traverse all the input geometry to decide the number of points that will be instanced. Precomputing the number of points that will be generated saves us from repeated reallocation of memory in order to fit the growing number of output points.

8.2.2   Local Coordinate Space

Each instantiation primitive uses a local coordinate space not only for distribution of instance points but also as the base for the noise coordinate space. The domain of the local coordinate space is normally $[0, 1]$, but for primitives with symmetric dimensions (i.e., all dimensions of a sphere, or the radial dimensions of a cylinder), it is often defined as $[-1, 1]$.

8.2.3   Output from Point-Based Instantiation Primitives

The output of PVR's point-based instantiation primitives is always made up of two parts: a **Particles** instance, containing the positions and per-point varying attributes for each instance, and a **Prim::Rast::Point** instance, which tells the PVR how to turn the points in the **Particles** instance into volumetric data. The per-point attributes set on the **Particles** instance are

- **P** (position),
- **v** (velocity),
- **density**,
- **radius**.

8.3   The **Sphere** Instantiation Primitive

Although it may seem like a repeat of the **Point** primitive, the **Sphere** instantiation primitive is able to produce much more interesting results,

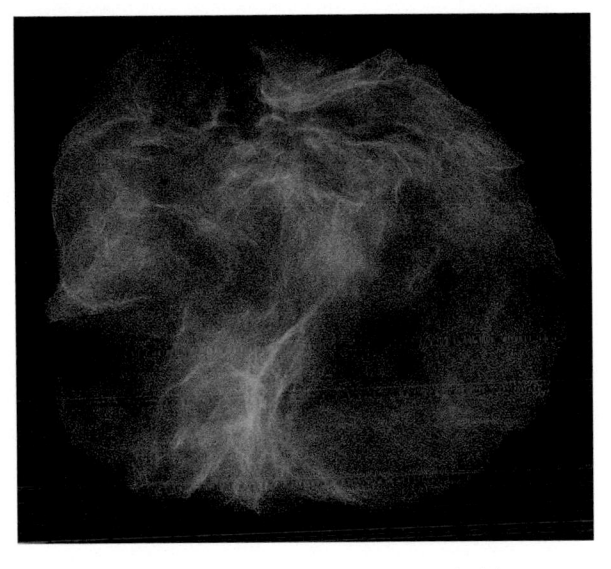

Figure 8.1. Sphere instantiation primitive.

despite being a basic sphere-based primitive. Where the **Point** just implemented a simple sphere, the sphere instances have several types of noise available to achieve different looks. (See Figure 8.1.)

Code 8.2. The **Sphere** instancer class

```
class Sphere : public InstantiationPrim
{
public:
...
  // From ParamBase
  PVR_DEFINE_TYPENAME(SphereInstancer);
  // From Primitive
  virtual BBox wsBounds(Geo::Geometry::CPtr geometry) const;
  // From InstantiationPrimitive
  virtual ModelerInput::Ptr execute(const Geo::Geometry::CPtr geo) const;
protected:
  // Structs
  struct AttrState
  {
...
    // Main methods
    void update(const Geo::AttrVisitor::const_iterator &i);
    // Data members
    Geo::Attr<Imath::V3f> wsCenter;
    Geo::Attr<Imath::V3f> wsVelocity;
    Geo::Attr<float>      radius;
    Geo::Attr<float>      instanceRadius;
```

```
  Geo::Attr<Imath::V3f> density;
  Geo::Attr<int>        numPoints;
  Geo::Attr<int>        doFill;
  Geo::Attr<int>        seed;
  Geo::Attr<float>      densScale;
  Geo::Attr<float>      densOctaves;
  Geo::Attr<float>      densOctaveGain;
  Geo::Attr<float>      densLacunarity;
  Geo::Attr<float>      dispScale;
  Geo::Attr<float>      dispOctaves;
  Geo::Attr<float>      dispOctaveGain;
  Geo::Attr<float>      dispLacunarity;
  Geo::Attr<float>      dispAmplitude;
  Geo::Attr<int>        doDensNoise;
  Geo::Attr<int>        doDispNoise;
  Noise::Fractal::CPtr  densFractal;
  Noise::Fractal::CPtr  dispFractal;
  };
  // Utility functions
  size_t numOutputPoints(const Geo::Geometry::CPtr geo) const;
  // Data members
  mutable AttrState m_attrs;
};
```

8.3.1   Executing the Primitive

The **execute()** call first performs some sanity checks, such as ensuring that geometry was indeed passed in and that the geometry contains particles.

Code 8.3. Sphere::execute()

```
ModelerInput::Ptr Sphere::execute(const Geo::Geometry::CPtr geo) const
{
  assert(geo != NULL);
  assert(geo->particles() != NULL);

  if (!geo->particles()) {
    Log::warning("Instantiation primitive has no particles. "
                 "Skipping execution.");
    return ModelerInput::Ptr();
  }
```

Before any instancing is performed, the output data structures are set up. A **Geometry** instance is created to hold the **Particles** object, which in turn holds the instanced points. Since the volumetric primitive used to model points is **Prim::Rast::Point**, we create an instance of that and add it to the **ModelerInput** along with the **Geometry**, which will drive the **Point** primitive.

Geometry, 20
Particles, 21
Rast::Point, 116
ModelerInput, 97

Code 8.4. **Sphere::execute()**

```
// Set up output geometry ---

size_t numPoints                    = numOutputPoints(geo);

Geometry::Ptr          outGeo    = Geometry::create();
Particles::Ptr         particles = Particles::create();
ModelerInput::Ptr      result    = ModelerInput::create();
Prim::Rast::Point::Ptr pointPrim = Prim::Rast::Point::create();

particles->add(numPoints);
outGeo->setParticles(particles);
result->setGeometry(outGeo);
result->setVolumePrimitive(pointPrim);
```

Once the data structures are in place, the necessary per-point attributes are added. The **radius** attribute here is the radius of each *instance*
point, not the radius of the **Sphere**'s input geometry points, and likewise
for the **density** attribute.

Code 8.5. **Sphere::execute()**

```
AttrTable &points  = particles->pointAttrs();
AttrRef    wsV     = points.addVectorAttr("v", Vector(0.0));
AttrRef    radius  = points.addFloatAttr("radius", 1,
                                          vector<float>(1, 1.0));
AttrRef    density = points.addVectorAttr("density", Vector(1.0)),
```

AttrVisitor, 29

After setting up the output data structures, we traverse each input
geometry point in turn, using the **AttrVisitor**. Similar to the **Point** rasterization primitive, we perform a user abort check once for each point.

Code 8.6. **Sphere::execute()**

```
// Loop over input points ---

size_t idx = 0;
ProgressReporter progress(2.5f, "   ");
AttrVisitor visitor(geo->particles()->pointAttrs(), m_params);

Log::print("Sphere processing " + str(geo->particles()->size()) +
           " input points");
Log::print("  Output: " + str(numPoints) + " points");

for (AttrVisitor::const_iterator i = visitor.begin(), end = visitor.end();
     i != end; ++i) {
  // Check if user terminated
  Sys::Interrupt::throwOnAbort();
```

The current attribute state is then updated so that attribute values can be accessed conveniently through the **AttrState** struct. Some aspects of the instancing are constant for all the instanced points generated from a single input geometry point. The **Fractal** instances for density and displacement noise are both updated inside **AttrState::update()**, and the noise offset is randomized based on the input point's **seed** attribute.

Fractal, 64

Code 8.7. Sphere::execute()

```
// Update attributes
m_attrs.update(i);
// Seed random number generator
Imath::Rand48 rng(m_attrs.seed);
// Noise offset by seed
Vector nsOffset;
nsOffset.x = rng.nextf(-100, 100);
nsOffset.y = rng.nextf(-100, 100);
nsOffset.z = rng.nextf(-100, 100);
```

Because there is no limit as to how many instances can be created from a single input point, we also check for user termination inside the per-instance for loop. This is done to prevent the renderer from appearing "hung" to the user. We also update the **ProgressReporter** instance once for each instanced point.

Code 8.8. Sphere::execute()

```
// For each instance
for (int i = 0; i < m_attrs.numPoints; ++i, ++idx) {
  // Check if user terminated
  Sys::Interrupt::throwOnAbort();
  // Print progress
  progress.update(static_cast<float>(idx) / numPoints);
```

To compute the instance position, we start with a random position in a unit sphere. Depending on whether we want a solid sphere or just a thin shell, we either scatter points using **Imath::solidSphereRand()**, which produces a uniform distribution with the property $|p| < 1$, or, to instead produce a thin shell, we use **Imath::hollowSphereRand()**, which produces a uniform distribution with the property $|p| = 1$.

Code 8.9. Sphere::execute()

```
// Randomize local space position
Vector lsP(0.0);
if (m_attrs.doFill) {
```

```
    lsP = solidSphereRand<V3f>(rng);
  } else {
    lsP = hollowSphereRand<V3f>(rng);
  }
```

The noise space is defined as identical to the local space. We also add in the noise offset vector to ensure that each set of instances (i.e., all the instances generated from a single input particle) has a continuous, but unique, noise pattern.

Code 8.10. Sphere::execute()

```
// Define noise space
V3f nsP = lsP;
nsP += nsOffset;
```

The world-space position of the instance is computed by offsetting from the input point's position by the local-space instance coordinate times the radius.

Code 8.11. Sphere::execute()

```
// Set instance position
V3f instanceWsP = m_attrs.wsCenter;
instanceWsP += lsP * m_attrs.radius;
```

Because the process of instancing points is a "forwards" modeling approach, it is easy to apply a noise function to displace each point's position. The displacement noise value is weighted by the **displacement_amplitude** attribute and scaled by the point radius.[1]

Code 8.12. Sphere::execute()

```
// Apply displacement noise
if (m_attrs.doDispNoise) {
  V3f noise = m_attrs.dispFractal->evalVec(nsP);
  instanceWsP += noise * (m_attrs.dispAmplitude / m_attrs.radius);
}
```

A second fractal function (**AttrState::densFractal**) is used to modulate the **density** of each instanced point.

---

[1]This ensures that the noise is coherent if a point is scaled up or down in size using the radius attribute.

Code 8.13. `Sphere::execute()`

```
// Set instance density
V3f instanceDensity = m_attrs.density;
// Apply density noise
if (m_attrs.doDensNoise) {
  float noise = m_attrs.densFractal->eval(nsP);
  instanceDensity *= noise;
}
```

Once the position and density of each point are known, we update the **AttrTable** of the output geometry to reflect these new values. The velocity of the input geometry point is forwarded as is to each instance.

Code 8.14. `Sphere::execute()`

```
// Set instance attributes
particles->setPosition(idx, instanceWsP);
points.setVectorAttr(wsV, idx, m_attrs.wsVelocity.value());
points.setVectorAttr(density, idx, instanceDensity);
points.setFloatAttr(radius, idx, 0, m_attrs.instanceRadius);
```

Once the loop over each input point is complete, the **ModelerInput** variable **result** is returned.

ModelerInput, 97

8.4   The **Line** Instantiation Primitive

The **Line** primitive implements a similar instantiation primitive as **Sphere**, but uses polygonal lines rather than point clouds as its underlying primitive. (See Figure 8.2.)

Inst::Sphere, 146

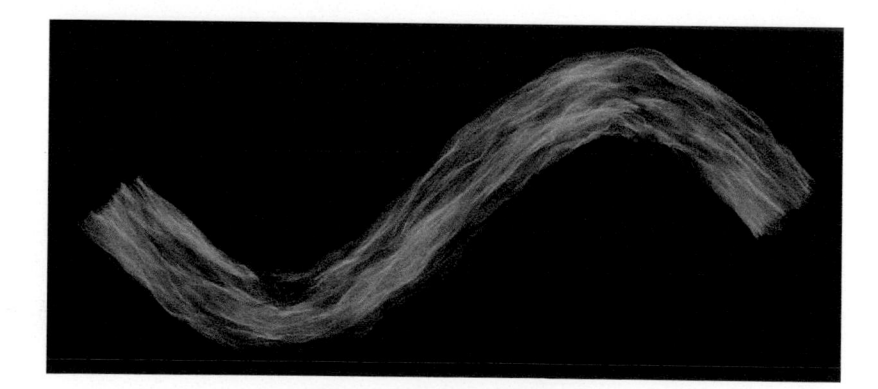

Figure 8.2. Line primitive.

Code 8.15. The **Line** instancer class

```
class Line : public InstantiationPrim
{
public:
...
  // From ParamBase
  PVR_DEFINE_TYPENAME(LineInstancer);
  // From Primitive
  virtual BBox wsBounds(Geo::Geometry::CPtr geometry) const;
  // From InstantiationPrimitive
  virtual ModelerInput::Ptr execute(const Geo::Geometry::CPtr geo) const;
protected:
  // Structs
  struct PolyAttrState
  {
    PolyAttrState()
      : seed          ("seed",                         1),
        instanceRadius("instance_radius",              0.01f),
        numPoints     ("num_points",                   1000),
        doFill        ("fill",                         0),
        densScale     ("density_noise_scale",          Imath::V3f(1.0f)),
        densOctaves   ("density_noise_octaves",        8.0f),
        densOctaveGain("density_noise_octave_gain",    0.5f),
        densLacunarity("density_noise_lacunarity",     1.92f),
        dispScale     ("displacement_noise_scale",     Imath::V3f(1.0f)),
        dispOctaves   ("displacement_noise_octaves",   8.0f),
        dispOctaveGain("displacement_noise_octave_gain", 0.5f),
        dispLacunarity("displacement_noise_lacunarity", 1.92f),
        dispAmplitude ("displacement_noise_amplitude", 1.0f),
        doDensNoise   ("density_noise",                0),
        doDispNoise   ("displacement_noise",           0)
    { }
    void update(const Geo::AttrVisitor::const_iterator &i);
    Geo::Attr<int>         seed;
    Geo::Attr<float>       instanceRadius;
    Geo::Attr<int>         numPoints;
    Geo::Attr<int>         doFill;
    Geo::Attr<Imath::V3f>  densScale;
    Geo::Attr<float>       densOctaves;
    Geo::Attr<float>       densOctaveGain;
    Geo::Attr<float>       densLacunarity;
    Geo::Attr<Imath::V3f>  dispScale;
    Geo::Attr<float>       dispOctaves;
    Geo::Attr<float>       dispOctaveGain;
    Geo::Attr<float>       dispLacunarity;
    Geo::Attr<float>       dispAmplitude;
    Geo::Attr<int>         doDensNoise;
    Geo::Attr<int>         doDispNoise;
    Noise::Fractal::CPtr   densFractal;
    Noise::Fractal::CPtr   dispFractal;
  };
  struct PointAttrState
  {
...
    // Main methods
    void update(const Geo::AttrVisitor::const_iterator &i);
```

```
  // Data members
  Geo::Attr<Imath::V3f> wsP;
  Geo::Attr<Imath::V3f> wsNormal;
  Geo::Attr<Imath::V3f> wsTangent;
  Geo::Attr<Imath::V3f> wsVelocity;
  Geo::Attr<float>      radius;
  Geo::Attr<Imath::V3f> density;
};
// Utility functions
size_t numOutputPoints(const Geo::Geometry::CPtr geo) const;
virtual void updatePolyAttrs(Geo::AttrVisitor::const_iterator i) const;
virtual void updatePointAttrs(Geo::AttrVisitor::const_iterator i,
                              const size_t numPoints) const;
// Data members
mutable PolyAttrState m_polyAttrs;
mutable std::vector<PointAttrState> m_pointAttrs;
};
```

8.4.1   Executing the Primitive

The implementation of the **Line** primitive is very similar to the **Sphere**. The output geometry is set up in the same way, with the same **v**, **radius**, and **density** attributes. But because polygons are involved, the loop over input geometry is slightly different.

Code 8.16. Line::execute()

```
// Iteration variables
Polygons::CPtr polys = geo->polygons();
AttrVisitor    polyVisitor(polys->polyAttrs(), m_params);
AttrVisitor    pointVisitor(polys->pointAttrs(), m_params);

for (AttrIter iPoly = polyVisitor.begin(), endPoly = polyVisitor.end();
     iPoly != endPoly; ++iPoly) {
```

The **AttrVisitor** class can be used to iterate over both the per-polygon attributes and their corresponding per-point attributes. The **Line** primitive assumes that processing happens polygon for polygon, so the instance's state must be set up to contain all the information about a single line. This is handled by the **PolyAttrState** and **PointAttrState** structs. Since only one polygon is processed at a time, a single instance of **Poly AttrState** is enough, but for **PointAttrState** it is necessary to keep a resizable array, so that all per-point attributes for the current polygon are available at once. Each state-keeping attribute variable has its own update function (see above). First, **updatePolyAttrs()** is called to set up per-polygon attributes, and that information (first point index and number of points in polygon) is then used to update the per-point attributes.

Code 8.17. Line::execute()

```
// Update poly attributes
updatePolyAttrs(iPoly);
// Update point attributes
size_t first = polys->pointForVertex(iPoly.index(), 0);
size_t numPoints = polys->numVertices(iPoly.index());
updatePointAttrs(pointVisitor.begin(first), numPoints);
```

With all the required attribute information in place, the loop over output points is started, similar to **Sphere::execute()**.

Code 8.18. Line::execute()

```
// Seed random number generator
Imath::Rand48 rng(m_polyAttrs.seed);
// For each instance
for (int i = 0; i < m_polyAttrs.numPoints; ++i, ++idx) {
```

The local space for a **Line** is a cylinder stretching along z, circular in the x, y-plane. To create a random position in this local space, the x, y-components are randomized using the same **Imath::solidSphereRand** and **Imath::hollowSphereRand** functions as **Sphere::execute()**, but templated on **V2f**. While this sounds counter-intuitive, a *sphere* in two dimensions is really a *disk* (if filled) or *circle* (if hollow). The z-component in local space is simply a random one-dimensional variable (provided by **Rand48::nextf()**).

It is important to maintain the local-space z-coordinate in the range $[0, 1]$. A user will often resample a polygonal line so that the vertices make an appropriately smooth curve. Changing the local-space coordinates based on the number of points that define a polygon would change the look of the primitive with each point count update, which would be undesirable.

An interpolation variable t is also computed, which simply maps $lsP_z \in [0, 1]$ to $t \in [0, N - 1]$.

Code 8.19. Line::execute()

```
// Randomize local space position
V2f disk;
if (m_polyAttrs.doFill) {
  disk = solidSphereRand<V2f>(rng);
} else {
  disk = hollowSphereRand<V2f>(rng);
}
V3f lsP(disk.x, disk.y, rng.nextf());
// Let t be floating-point index
float t = lsP.z * (m_pointAttrs.size() - 1);
```

The **LINE_INST_INTERP** macro (see above) is used to conveniently interpolate any variable in **m_pointAttrs** to the in-between position t (based on lsP_z).

The **N** and **T** attributes are especially important, and to make their definitions as being in world space obvious, they are labeled **wsN** and **wsT**, respectively.

Code 8.20. Line::execute()

```
// Interpolate instance attributes
V3f instanceDensity = LINE_INST_INTERP(density, t);
V3f instanceWsP     = LINE_INST_INTERP(wsP, t);
V3f instanceWsV     = LINE_INST_INTERP(wsVelocity, t);
V3f wsN             = LINE_INST_INTERP(wsNormal, t).normalized();
V3f wsT             = LINE_INST_INTERP(wsTangent, t).normalized();
float radius        = LINE_INST_INTERP(radius, t);
```

In order to form the local coordinate system basis vectors we use $\hat{v} = \vec{N}$ and $\hat{w} = \vec{T}$ as the second and third bases, with the first basis derived from the other two as $\hat{u} = \vec{N} \times \vec{T}$.

Code 8.21. Line::execute()

```
// Compute third basis vector from N and T
V3f wsNxT = wsN.cross(wsT);
```

Although it would possible to transform the local-space position to world space using a matrix multiplication, it is more efficient to just offset the instance position in world space by each of the basis vectors.

We already found the world-space position taking the local-space w-coordinate into account by interpolating the **wsP** attribute along the curve to the instance point position. To find the final world-space position, we simply offset the instance by $\hat{u} \cdot u \cdot r + \hat{v} \cdot v \cdot r$.

Code 8.22. Line::execute()

```
// Offset instance position based on local space coordinate
instanceWsP += lsP.x * wsNxT * radius;
instanceWsP += lsP.y * wsN * radius;
```

Just as with **Sphere::execute()**, the noise space is defined directly from the local space. And similarly, **Line** uses both a density modulation and a displacement fractal function. The density modulation function is straightforward: the noise lookup point is computed from the noise coordinate times a scaling factor, which lets the user control the feature size of the fractal. The density value that was interpolated along the line is then multiplied directly against the result of the fractal function.

The displacement calculation is a little more involved than in **Sphere:: execute()**, since the coordinate system basis vectors vary along the line. The simple solution is to use each vector component of the result of the displacement fractal function as a coordinate along each of the coordinate system bases. We also scale this offset by **radius** and the noise amplitude, in order to make the effect independent of the size of the primitive. Thus, if the displacement magnitude is of length one, the resulting displacement will be the same as the size of the line. This makes our primitive easier to control for a potential user.

Code 8.23. Line::execute()

```
// Apply noises
V3f nsP = lsP;
if (m_polyAttrs.doDensNoise) {
  V3f nsLookupP = nsP / m_polyAttrs.densScale.value();
  instanceDensity *= m_polyAttrs.densFractal->eval(nsLookupP);
}
if (m_polyAttrs.doDispNoise) {
  V3f nsLookupP = nsP / m_polyAttrs.dispScale.value();
  V3f disp = m_polyAttrs.dispFractal->evalVec(nsLookupP);
  instanceWsP += disp.x * wsNxT * radius *
    m_polyAttrs.dispAmplitude.value();
  instanceWsP += disp.y * wsN * radius *
    m_polyAttrs.dispAmplitude.value();
  instanceWsP += disp.z * wsT * radius *
    m_polyAttrs.dispAmplitude.value();
}
```

With all properties of the instance point computed, we update the **particles** instance with the point position and the relevant attributes and proceed to the next loop iteration.

Code 8.24. Line::execute()

```
// Set instance attributes
particles->setPosition(idx, instanceWsP);
points.setVectorAttr(vRef, idx, instanceWsV);
points.setVectorAttr(densityRef, idx, instanceDensity);
points.setFloatAttr(radiusRef, idx, 0, m_polyAttrs.instanceRadius);
```

Figure 8.3. Surface primitive.

8.5 The **Surface** Instantiation Primitive

The last instantiation primitive in PVR is the **Surface** class. It extends
the same concepts used in **Sphere** and **Line**, but applies it to meshes of
quadrilaterals. The control attributes are largely the same as for the other
two primitive types, with separate density and distortion noises. (See
Figure 8.3.)

Inst::Sphere, 146
Inst::Line, 152

Code 8.25. The **Surface** instancer class

```
class Surface : public InstantiationPrim
{
public:
...
  // From ParamBase
  PVR_DEFINE_TYPENAME(SurfaceInstancer);
```

```
                // From Primitive
                virtual BBox wsBounds(Geo::Geometry::CPtr geometry) const;
                // From InstantiationPrimitive
                virtual ModelerInput::Ptr execute(const Geo::Geometry::CPtr geo) const;
            protected:
                // Structs
                struct SurfAttrState
                {
                  SurfAttrState()
                    : seed            ("seed",                             1),
                      instanceRadius("instance_radius",                    0.01f),
                      numPoints      ("num_points",                        1000),
                      doFill         ("fill",                              1),
                      densScale      ("density_noise_scale",               Imath::V3f(1.0f)),
                      densFade       ("density_noise_fade",                Imath::V3f(0.0)),
                      densOctaves    ("density_noise_octaves",             8.0f),
                      densOctaveGain("density_noise_octave_gain",          0.5f),
                      densLacunarity("density_noise_lacunarity",           1.92f),
                      dispScale      ("displacement_noise_scale",          Imath::V3f(1.0f)),
                      dispOctaves    ("displacement_noise_octaves",        8.0f),
                      dispOctaveGain("displacement_noise_octave_gain",     0.5f),
                      dispLacunarity("displacement_noise_lacunarity",      1.92f),
                      dispAmplitude ("displacement_noise_amplitude",       1.0f),
                      doDensNoise    ("density_noise",                     0),
                      doDispNoise    ("displacement_noise",                0)
                  { }
                  void update(const Geo::AttrVisitor::const_iterator &i);
                  Geo::Attr<int>        seed;
                  Geo::Attr<float>      instanceRadius;
                  Geo::Attr<int>        numPoints;
                  Geo::Attr<int>        doFill;
                  Geo::Attr<Imath::V3f> densScale;
                  Geo::Attr<Imath::V3f> densFade;
                  Geo::Attr<float>      densOctaves;
                  Geo::Attr<float>      densOctaveGain;
                  Geo::Attr<float>      densLacunarity;
                  Geo::Attr<Imath::V3f> dispScale;
                  Geo::Attr<float>      dispOctaves;
                  Geo::Attr<float>      dispOctaveGain;
                  Geo::Attr<float>      dispLacunarity;
                  Geo::Attr<float>      dispAmplitude;
                  Geo::Attr<int>        doDensNoise;
                  Geo::Attr<int>        doDispNoise;
                  Noise::Fractal::CPtr  densFractal;
                  Noise::Fractal::CPtr  dispFractal;
                };
                struct PointAttrState
                {
            ...
                  // Main methods
                  void update(const Geo::AttrVisitor::const_iterator &i);
                  // Data members
                  Geo::Attr<Imath::V3f> wsP;
                  Geo::Attr<Imath::V3f> wsNormal;
                  Geo::Attr<Imath::V3f> wsDPds;
```

```
    Geo::Attr<Imath::V3f> wsDPdt;
    Geo::Attr<Imath::V3f> wsVelocity;
    Gco::Attr<float>      thickness;
    Geo::Attr<Imath::V3f> density;
  };
  // Utility functions
  size_t pointIdx(const float s, const float t,
                  const size_t numCols, const size_t numRows,
                  const int xOff, const int yOff) const;
  float edgeFade(float x, float y, float z) const;
  size_t numOutputPoints(const Geo::Geometry::CPtr geo) const;
  virtual void updateSurfAttrs(Geo::AttrVisitor::const_iterator i) const;
  virtual void updatePointAttrs(Geo::AttrVisitor::const_iterator i,
                                const size_t numPoints) const;
  // Data members
  mutable SurfAttrState m_surfAttrs;
  mutable std::vector<PointAttrState> m_pointAttrs;
};
```

8.5.1   Executing the Primitive

The **Surface** instantiation primitive is conceptually very similar to **Line**. The main difference is that where **Line** iterates over the contents of a **Polygons** instance, **Surface** traverses the contents of a **Meshes** object, turning each one into a slab of density. As far as the iteration loop goes, the only difference is that the **AttrVisitor** traverses per-mesh attributes (`meshes->meshAttrs()`) instead of per-polygon attributes.

Inst::Line, 152

Polygons, 22
Meshes, 23
AttrVisitor, 29

Code 8.26. `Surface::execute()`

```
  // Iteration variables
  Meshes::CPtr meshes       (geo->meshes());
  AttrVisitor  meshVisitor (meshes->meshAttrs(), m_params);
  AttrVisitor  pointVisitor(meshes->pointAttrs(), m_params);

  for (AttrIter iMesh = meshVisitor.begin(), endMesh = meshVisitor.end();
       iMesh != endMesh; ++iMesh) {
```

The per-mesh attributes are updated directly using **updateSurfAttrs()**, but to find all the per-point attributes for the current mesh, we first need to calculate the number of points that make it up. By passing (*numCols* · *numRows*) to **updatePointAttrs()**, the appropriate number of array slots are allocated, and the per-point attributes are read into each **PointAttrState** instance.

Code 8.27. Surface::execute()

```
// Update mesh attributes
updateSurfAttrs(iMesh);
// Update point attribute
size_t first    = meshes->startPoint(iMesh.index());
size_t numCols  = meshes->numCols(iMesh.index());
size_t numRows  = meshes->numRows(iMesh.index());
size_t numPoints = numCols * numRows;
updatePointAttrs(pointVisitor.begin(first), numPoints);
// Seed random number generator
Imath::Rand48 rng(m_surfAttrs.seed);
// For each instance
for (int i = 0; i < m_surfAttrs.numPoints; ++i, ++idx) {
```

Inst::Sphere, 146
Inst::Line, 152

While **Sphere** and **Line** had to deal with round primitives, the space filled around each mesh is a simple slab, and so the coordinate range for the local space is $[0, 1]$ in each dimension, which is easily created using the **Rand48::nextf()** call.

It is important to be aware of certain compiler aspects when writing code that uses random-number generators. In our case, **Imath::Rand48** and **Imath::Rand32** both guarantee a predictable sequence of random numbers, given a certain seed value. It would thus be tempting to create a vector of random values using

```
V3f lsP(rng.nextf(), rng.nextf(), rng.nextf());
```

However, for a function that takes multiple arguments, the C++ standard provides no specification of what *order* the arguments should be evaluated in. Thus, the code above could return a vector $(0.124\ 0.6124\ 0.44)$ on one architecture, but $(0.44\ 0.6124\ 0.124)$ on another. This type of undefined behavior across different compilers and platforms can lead to hard-to-find bugs, and so we avoid the problem by initializing each component randomly on a separate line of code.

Code 8.28. Surface::execute()

```
// Randomize local space position
V3f lsP;
lsP.x = rng.nextf();
lsP.y = rng.nextf();
lsP.z = rng.nextf();
```

Once we have a well-defined local-space coordinate for the instance point, we interpolate all per-point attributes on the mesh at the current $(s\ t)$-coordinate.

Code 8.29. Surface::execute()

```
// Let s,t be floating point index
float s = lsP.x * (numCols - 1);
float t = lsP.y * (numRows - 1);
// Interpolate instance attributes
V3f instanceDensity = SURFACE_INST_INTERP(density, s, t);
V3f instanceWsP    = SURFACE_INST_INTERP(wsP, s, t);
V3f instanceWsV    = SURFACE_INST_INTERP(wsVelocity, s, t);
V3f wsN            = SURFACE_INST_INTERP(wsNormal, s, t).normalized();
V3f wsDPds         = SURFACE_INST_INTERP(wsDPds, s, t).normalized();
V3f wsDPdt         = SURFACE_INST_INTERP(wsDPdt, s, t).normalized();
float thickness    = SURFACE_INST_INTERP(thickness, s, t);
```

To find the final world-space position of the instance, we only need to apply an offset along the normal of the mesh, since lsP_x and lsP_y have already been used to interpolate wsP at the surface of the mesh.

Code 8.30. Surface::execute()

```
// Offset along normal
instanceWsP += Math::fit01(lsP.z, -1.0f, 1.0f) * wsN * thickness;
```

Density is modulated using the fractal function that was created in **updateSurfAttrs()**. The problems that were discussed in Section 5.8.2 on how to ramp out noise values towards the edge of the primitive applies to meshes, and we use the erosion technique described there to ensure that values at the edge of the primitive are all nonpositive.

Density Variation, 88

The **edgeFade** function returns the erosion value, and the fractal function's value range is queried to determine the largest possible value that it may return.

Code 8.31. Surface::execute()

```
// Apply noises
V3f nsP = lsP;
if (m_surfAttrs.doDensNoise) {
  V3f nsLookupP = nsP / m_surfAttrs.densScale.value();
  float noise = m_surfAttrs.densFractal->eval(nsLookupP);
  float fade = edgeFade(lsP.x, lsP.y, lsP.z);
  instanceDensity *= noise + fade;
}
```

Displacement noise is applied along each of the basis vectors $\hat{u}$, $\hat{v}$ and $\hat{w}$, scaling by the thickness of the primitive and by the amplitude of the displacement.

Code 8.32. Surface::execute()

```
if (m_surfAttrs.doDispNoise) {
  V3f nsLookupP = nsP / m_surfAttrs.dispScale.value();
  V3f disp = m_surfAttrs.dispFractal->evalVec(nsLookupP);
  instanceWsP += disp.x * wsDPds * thickness *
    m_surfAttrs.dispAmplitude.value();
  instanceWsP += disp.y * wsDPdt * thickness *
    m_surfAttrs.dispAmplitude.value();
  instanceWsP += disp.z * wsN * thickness *
    m_surfAttrs.dispAmplitude.value();
}
```

The final set of attributes that need to be set are identical to the other two instantiation primitive types and update the **particles** and **points** variables accordingly.

Code 8.33. Surface::execute()

```
// Set instance attributes
particles->setPosition(idx, instanceWsP);
points.setVectorAttr(vRef, idx, instanceWsV);
points.setVectorAttr(densityRef, idx, instanceDensity);
points.setFloatAttr(radiusRef, idx, 0, m_surfAttrs.instanceRadius);
```

8.5.2 Eroding the Edges

The **edgeFade()** call is responsible for computing an erosion value that, when added to the fractal function, guarantees that the final sum is less than or equal to zero. It does so by checking the **range** parameter and computing a function that is zero at the center of the local coordinate system, starts falling off at **fit**, and reaches −*range* at each edge of the primitive (i.e., near each end of the $[0, 1]$ interval).

Code 8.34. Surface::edgeFade()

```
float Surface::edgeFade(float x, float y, float z) const
{
  // Mirror at 0.5 for each dimension
  x = std::min(x, 1.0f - x);
  y = std::min(y, 1.0f - y);
  z = std::min(z, 1.0f - z);

  // Get fit param
  V3f fit = m_surfAttrs.densFade.value();

  // Re-fit according to param
  if (fit.x > 0.0f) {
```

```
    x = Math::fit(x, 0.0f, fit.x, -1.0f, 1.0f);
  } else {
    x = 0.0f;
  }
  if (fit.y > 0.0f) {
    y = Math::fit(y, 0.0f, fit.y, -1.0f, 1.0f);
  } else {
    y = 0.0f;
  }
  if (fit.z > 0.0f) {
    z = Math::fit(z, 0.0f, fit.z, -1.0f, 1.0f);
  } else {
    z = 0.0f;
  }

  // Clamp
  x = Imath::clamp(x, -1.0f, 1.0f);
  y = Imath::clamp(y, -1.0f, 1.0f);
  z = Imath::clamp(z, -1.0f, 1.0f);

  // Return min
  return std::min(std::min(x, y), z);
}
```

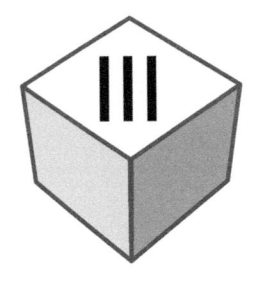

Volume Rendering

9

Volumetric Lighting

So far, we have focused on the modeling of volumetric data, but in order to turn the data into an image, we also need to explore how volume rendering works. In this chapter, we will look at the mathematical foundation behind volume rendering and see how a very simple model allows us to replicate the majority of the different appearances that we come across in nature.

9.1 Lighting Fundamentals

To explore how light interacts with a volume, we will begin with a simplified mathematical model. If we consider a viewer (a person or a camera) looking along a given direction ω, we are interested in finding out what the incoming radiance L is. To study how light behaves during its interaction with the medium along the ray, we also consider a differential cylinder dV, with cross section $d\sigma$ and length ds. Figure 9.1 illustrates the arrangement.

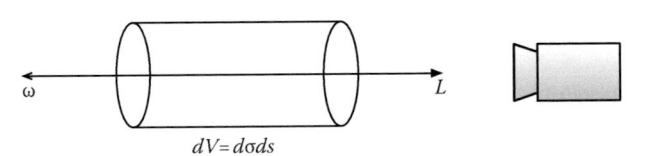

Figure 9.1. Differential volume along view ray.

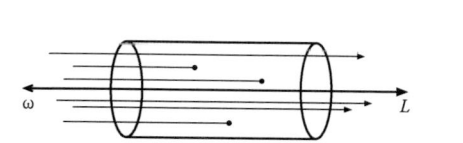

Figure 9.2. Absorption along a ray.

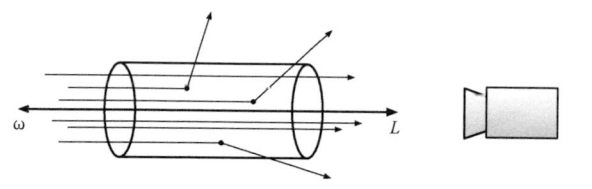

Figure 9.3. Out-scattering along a ray.

If we first consider a photon that travels in the direction ω, for example, light that has bounced off of a surface and is now traveling in the direction of the camera, as it passes through dV, it will interact with the medium, unless the differential cylinder is completely empty. One possible outcome is that the photon is absorbed by the medium, in which case it can be considered, for our rendering purposes, to be gone. Figure 9.2 illustrates this interaction, which we refer to as *absorption*.

A second possibility is that a photon hits a particle that reflects it to some direction other than ω. This happens in media such as water vapor, which absorbs very little energy but reflects a great deal. We refer to these interactions as *out-scattering*, and also include interactions where the light refracts inside a particle before leaving. From the volume-rendering standpoint, the refraction and reflection interactions are indistinguishable. Figure 9.3 shows an example. Although it is possible that a photon continues along the same direction after a scattering event, the probability is vanishingly small, and we consider any scattering event where a photon enters from direction ω to continue along some other direction, no longer contributing to L.

Conversely, for a photon traveling in some direction ω' through the differential volume, there is a nonzero probability that it is reflected in the direction of the camera. We refer to this event as *in-scattering*, and when this happens, the radiance along the ray is increased. Figure 9.4 illustrates these events. The probability distribution for scattering events is called a *phase function*, and it is discussed in Section 9.5.

Phase Functions, 172

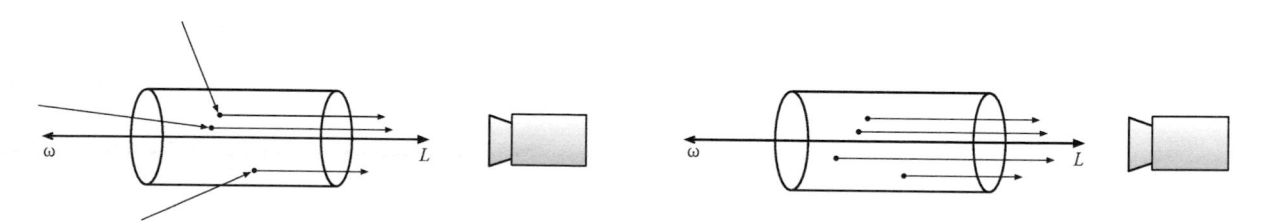

Figure 9.4. In-scattering into the viewing ray.

Figure 9.5. Emission in differential volume.

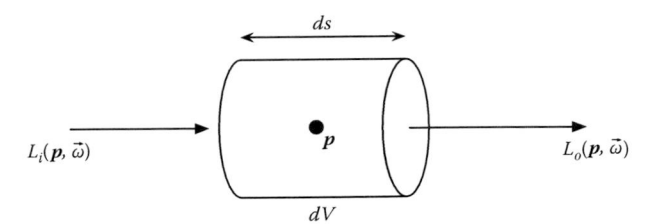

Figure 9.6. Incoming luminance L_i and outgoing luminance L_o, for a differential volume dV.

The probability of in-scattering and out-scattering are identical; in fact, we can only distinguish between the two when considering the view direction of the observer. Without an observer, there are only *scattering* events.

The final process we need to study is *emission*, which occurs in media such as fire, where molecules are hot enough to excite electrons that then emit photons in all directions. For the viewer in our case, only light emitted in the direction $-\omega$ is of interest (Figure 9.5).

These three physical processes are all we need to model in order to reproduce just about every type of appearance that one comes across in nature. In the following sections, we will look at each one in more detail.

To sum things up, we can express the change in luminance dL along ds to be the difference between the incoming luminance L_i and the outgoing luminance L_o at point p along the direction vector $\vec{\omega}$. The change in luminance is also equal to the sum of the effect of scattering, absorption, and emission (see also Figure 9.6.):

$$dL(\boldsymbol{p},\vec{\omega}) = L_i(\boldsymbol{p},\vec{\omega}) - L_o(\boldsymbol{p},\vec{\omega})$$
$$= \text{emission} + \text{scattering}_{\text{in}} - \text{scattering}_{\text{out}} - \text{absorption}.$$

9.2   Absorption

In discussing the light-scattering properties of volumes, we will draw some parallels to surfaces and their bidirectional reflectance distribution functions (BRDFs). A dark surface is dark because of its low reflectivity. The laws of physics dictate that the incident radiant energy that does not get reflected away from the surface must be absorbed and converted into some other form of energy. Volumes share this property, but where a volume can be described by a reflectivity factor (the surface color, essentially), volumetric absorption needs to express what fraction of light is

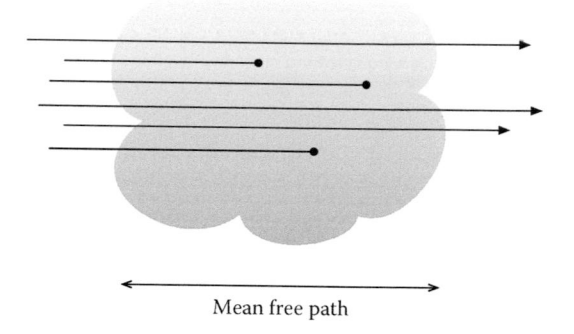

Mean free path

Figure 9.7. The mean free path is the average distance traveled between two events.

absorbed over a nonzero distance ds (the same ds as above). The amount by which a medium absorbs light is called the *absorption coefficient* or *absorption cross section* and is usually labeled σ_a.

The unit of the absorption coefficient is a *reciprocal distance* (i.e., m^{-1}), which can be interpreted several ways. One way to think of it is the probability density[1] that a ray of light is absorbed as it travels through one length unit of the medium.

The inverse of σ_a, which is an actual distance, is referred to as the *mean free path*. The mean free path is often easier to visualize, as it describes the average distance that a photon will travel through the medium before interacting, i.e., the average distance between interaction events. And because of the linear relationship, we can see that doubling the absorption coefficient σ_a halves the mean free path, indicating that light on average will travel half as far before interacting with the medium. (See Figure 9.7.)

It is also important to consider that the absorption coefficient can assume any positive noninfinite value; it can be infinitely large. One interpretation of this value range is that no volume can extinguish light completely if one considers a sufficiently short distance. And conversely, the model predicts that light never gets entirely extinguished, even over a large distance. This is a result of the continuous approximation of the absorption event. In reality, there is a finite number of particles of finite size interacting with the light, and at some point even the last photon is absorbed.

To put this into an equation, we are interested in finding out what the exitant luminance L_o is, given an incoming luminance L_i and our

---

[1]A probability density describes the likelihood that a random event occurs at a given point.

absorption coefficient σ_a:

$$L_o(\boldsymbol{p},\vec{\omega}) = L_i(\boldsymbol{p},\vec{\omega}) + dL_a,$$

$$dL_a = -\sigma_a L_i(\boldsymbol{p},\vec{\omega})ds. \qquad (9.1)$$

It is important to note that the effect of absorption is independent of the incoming radiance (luminance). The same fraction of light is absorbed, regardless of how much light enters the segment ds, indicating that there is a linear relationship. We also see that the absorption cross section and the differential length affect the change equally. This implies the same linear relationship: absorption increases equally whether we double the density of the medium or double the distance that light travels.

9.3 Emission

When it comes to production volume rendering, the most common cases of emissive media tend to be fire and energy effects. Fire is emissive due to the chemical reactions that occur, and energy effects are emissive mostly because it looks cool.

If we consider a medium that is purely emissive, we find the following formula, where L_e is the emitted light at a point $\boldsymbol{p}$ in the direction $\vec{\omega}$. The unit is radiance per unit length:

$$L_o(\boldsymbol{p},\vec{\omega}) = L_i(\boldsymbol{p},\vec{\omega}) + dL_e,$$

$$dL_e = L_e(\boldsymbol{p},\vec{\omega})ds.$$

9.4 Scattering

We mentioned in the previous section that in-scattering and out-scattering are equally probable, and we describe the likelihood of a scattering event with a single coefficient as the *scattering coefficient*. The coefficient is normally written as σ_s, and similar to the absorption coefficient, it is expressed as a reciprocal distance. Before we look at how this coefficient is used in our equations, we first look at how in-scattering and out-scattering change the exitant radiance L_o:

$$L_o(\boldsymbol{p},\vec{\omega}) = L_i + dL_{\text{in}}(\boldsymbol{p},\vec{\omega}) + dL_{\text{out}}(\boldsymbol{p},\vec{\omega}).$$

If we consider the change in luminance along the differential cylinder, out-scattering is indistinguishable from absorption. As far as the observer is concerned, a certain amount of light disappeared, whether it was reflected or absorbed. Because of this, we can use the same basic equation as for absorption:

$$dL_{out}(\boldsymbol{p}, \vec{\omega}) = -\sigma_s L_i(\boldsymbol{p}, \vec{\omega})ds. \tag{9.2}$$

When treated together, out-scattering and absorption are referred to as *extinction* or *attenuation*, and it uses the symbol σ_e. This is useful when tracing a ray only to determine transmittance, without caring about radiance.

The light sources in the scene become relevant once we try to compute the effects of in-scattering. In the following equations, the incoming radiance from a light source S is a function of a point $\boldsymbol{p}$ and the direction to the light source $\vec{\omega}'$. The scattering coefficient σ_s tells us how much of the light is likely to scatter over a given length, but we also need to know how much of the light actually scatters towards the observer, as compared to all of the other possible directions. The function that describes the relationship is called the phase function. The phase function is denoted $p(\vec{\omega}, \vec{\omega}')$, and it tells us how much light traveling in the direction $\vec{\omega}'$ will be reflected in the direction $\vec{\omega}$:

$$dL_{in}(\boldsymbol{p}, \vec{\omega}) = \sigma_s p(\vec{\omega}, \vec{\omega}')S(\boldsymbol{p}, \vec{\omega}')ds. \tag{9.3}$$

That is, the change in luminance due to in-scattering is equal to the scattering coefficient times the result of the phase function for the viewing direction $\vec{\omega}$ and the vector between the sample point $\boldsymbol{p}$ and the light source $\vec{\omega}'$, times the incoming light at $\boldsymbol{p}$ from $\vec{\omega}'$, multiplied by the differential length ds.[2]

9.5   Phase Functions

The closest parallel to a volume's phase function is the BRDF of a surface. A BRDF defines how much of light hitting a surface while traveling in direction $\vec{\omega}_{in}$ will scatter to direction $\vec{\omega}_{out}$, and similarly, the phase function determines how much light traveling through a medium in direction $\vec{\omega}'$ will, upon scattering, reflect to direction $\vec{\omega}$. (See Figure 9.8.) This relationship can be expressed as a probability $p(\vec{\omega}, \vec{\omega}')$.

Phase functions have a few important properties. First, they are reciprocal, so $p(\vec{\omega}, \vec{\omega}') = p(\vec{\omega}', \vec{\omega})$. Second, they are rotationally invariant, and only the relative angle between $\vec{\omega}$ and $\vec{\omega}'$ needs to be considered,

---

[2]The differential length ds becomes important once we try to solve the integral using raymarching. There, ds is the size of the raymarch step.

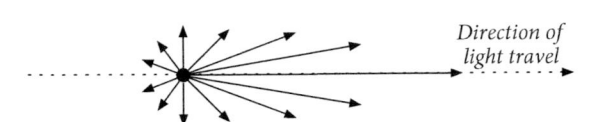

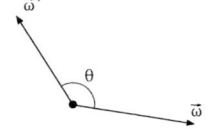

Figure 9.8. For light traveling in a given direction, the likelihood that it scatters in each of the other directions is indicated by the length of each vector.

Figure 9.9. A phase function depends only upon the angle θ between the two vectors $\vec{\omega}$ and $\vec{\omega}'$.

thus we can write $p(\vec{\omega}, \vec{\omega}') = p(\theta)$. Third, they are normalized such that integrating across all angles for $\vec{\omega}$ while holding $\vec{\omega}'$ constant gives exactly one. (See Figure 9.9.)

Phase functions come in two flavors: isotropic and anisotropic. An isotropic phase function scatters light equally in all directions. Anisotropic phase functions on the other hand are biased either forward or backward, as seen from the direction of light travel before the scattering event.

Isotropic phase functions are perfectly sufficient when rendering low-albedo media, such as ash clouds, dust, etc., but for media such as clouds and atmospheres, anisotropy is an important element to include in lighting calculations. Anisotropic behavior in participating media can be thought of as the parallel to specular BRDFs, while isotropic behavior is similar to diffuse/lambertian BRDFs. In everyday life, anisotropy is responsible for the silver lining in clouds, where the edge of a cloud becomes increasingly bright as the sun reaches a grazing angle. Figure 9.10 illustrates different forms of anisotropic phase functions.

Phase functions are well researched, and the two most common ones are the Rayleigh model (which describes atmospheric scattering, the interaction of light with particles the size of molecules) and the Mie model (which is more general and can handle much larger particle sizes, for example, water vapor and droplets suspended in the atmosphere). In production rendering, we often use a few other, simpler models, since Rayleigh and particularly Mie are expensive to evaluate. Henyey-Greenstein is a simple model that can handle both isotropic and aniso-

Phase Functions in PVR, 300

tropic media, and Section 14.7 discusses how PVR implements it.

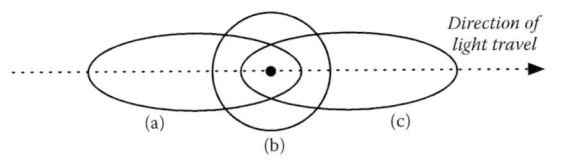

Figure 9.10. Isotropic and anisotropic phase functions: (a) back-scattering, (b) isotropic, and (c) forward-scattering.

9.6   Optical Thickness and Transmittance

Now that we are familiar with the behavior of light as it passes through a short, homogeneous cylinder, we need to look at how it behaves as we consider an entire ray. We mentioned that we can study out-scattering and absorption together, something we called extinction. When we consider an entire ray, extinction is directly related to how far the observer can see along the ray.

Let's first consider a slab of dark (i.e., nonscattering, $\sigma_s = 0$) smoke. If the slab is thin, an observer would likely be able to see through it. However, if we keep the smoke's density constant while increasing the thickness of the slab, we reach a point where it's no longer possible to easily see through the entire volume. (See Figure 9.11.) When it's possible to mostly see through a volume, it is called *optically thin*, and when there is enough substance to mostly block our view, it is called *optically thick*. Both terms refer to a measure of transparency called *optical thickness* or *optical depth*.

If we again consider the differential equations describing the effects of out-scattering and absorption (Equations (9.2) and (9.1)), we can see how it's possible to define the fraction of light that remains as the light travels through the medium by integrating and rearranging the expression for $L(s)$, where s is a measure of how far into volume the light has traveled. We note that the first line is a first order linear ODE (ordinary differential equation), which can be solved as:

Scattering, 172

Absorption, 171

$$dL(s) = -\sigma L(s)ds,$$
$$\frac{dL(s)}{L(s)ds} = -\sigma,$$
$$\int \frac{dL(s)}{L(s)ds}ds = \int -\sigma ds,$$
$$ln(L(s)) = -\sigma s + C.$$

Using the final form, we can find a relationship between $L(s)$ at a given depth s, compared to $L(0)$:

$$ln(L(s)) = -\sigma s + C,$$
$$ln(L(s)) - ln(L(0)) = (-\sigma s + C) - (-\sigma 0 + C)$$
$$= -\sigma s,$$
$$e^{ln(L(s)) - ln(L(0))} = e^{-\sigma s},$$
$$\frac{L(s)}{L(0)} = e^{-\sigma s}.$$

(a)

(b)

(c)

(d)

Figure 9.11. Changing the optical thickness of a slab of density that is 2 units wide. The light source is positioned immediately to the volume's right side. The scattering coefficient σ_s was set to (a) 2, (b) 4, (c) 8, and (d) 16.

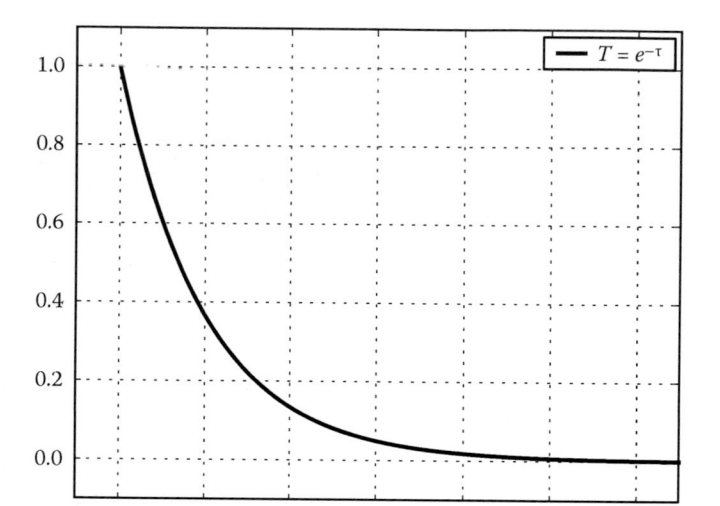

Figure 9.12. Beer's law.

The relationship $\frac{L(s)}{L(0)}$ is called *transmittance*, and it is the definition of how much light can pass between two points in the medium. For out-scattering, the equation is the same, so we can combine σ_s and σ_a into the following formula, which defines transmittance in a medium that both scatters and absorbs:

$$T = e^{-(\sigma_s+\sigma_a)s}.$$

With that, we have arrived at the solution to our initial thought experiment. The incoming and outgoing radiance measures are directly related by transmittance, and the relationship is called *Beer's law*, where T is the transmittance and τ is the optical thickness measure (see Figure 9.12):

$$T = e^{-\tau},$$
$$\tau = (\sigma_s + \sigma_a)s.$$

So far, we have assumed the medium that light passes through to be homogeneous, in which case Beer's law is trivial to compute. However, once we consider a volume where density varies, we need to extend our formulation. First, we look at the optical thickness and find that we need to integrate $\sigma_e = \sigma_s + \sigma_a$ along the ray, such that

$$\tau = \int_0^d \sigma_e(\boldsymbol{p})ds.$$

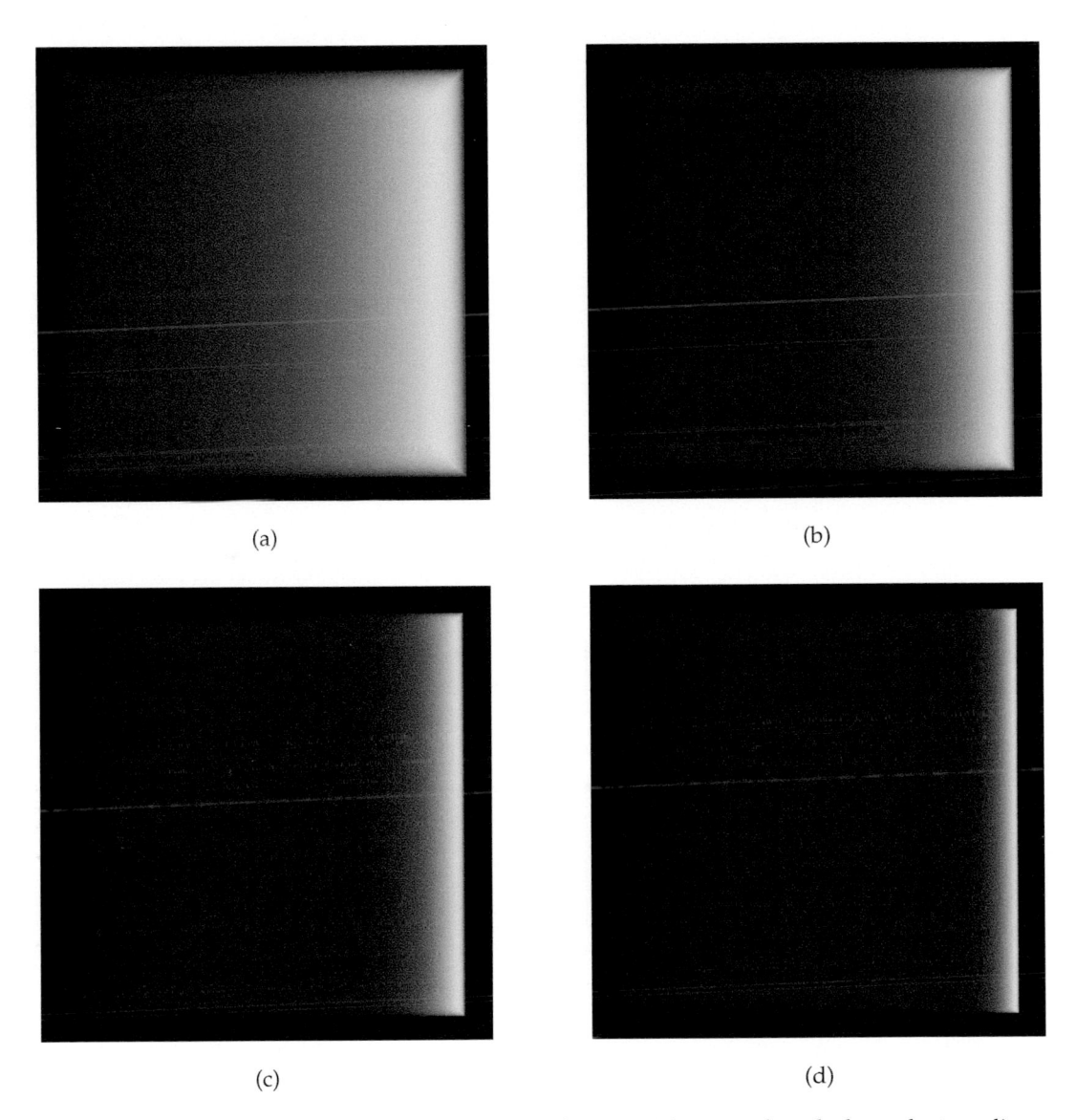

(a)

(b)

(c)

(d)

Figure 9.13. Illustrating the effects of increasing density with a wavelength-dependent medium. Here, the scattering coefficient σ_s was set to (a) (1 2 4), (b) (2 4 8), (c) (4 8 16), and (d) (8 16 32).

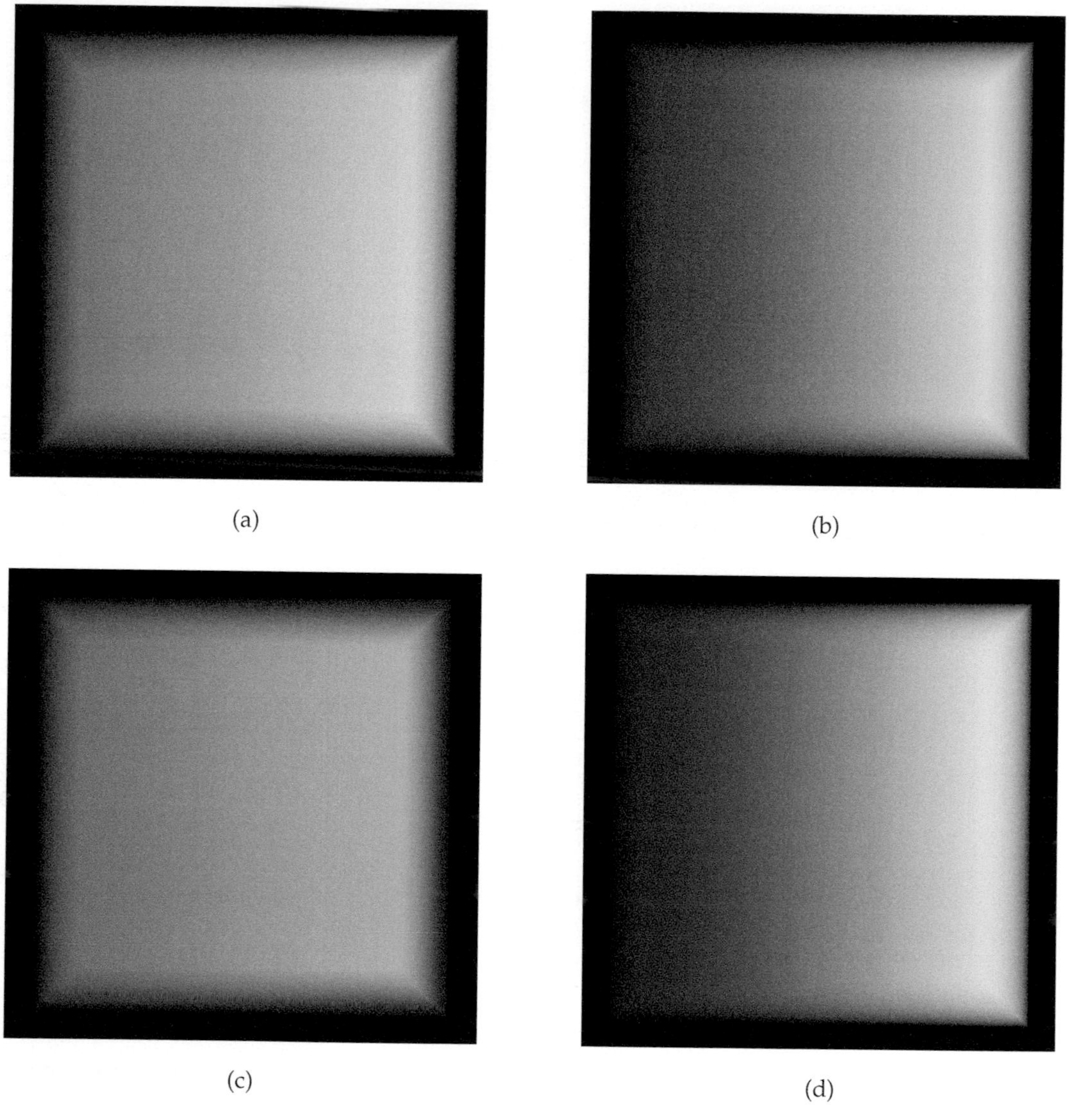

Figure 9.14. With a spectrally varying scattering coefficient, colors shift to the complement. (a) A wavelength-independent σ_s of (1.0 1.0 1.0). (b) With $\sigma_s = $ (0.25 1.0 1.0) the first reflected light is cyan and light then shifts towards red as it gets deeper into the volume. (c) With $\sigma_s = $ (1.0 0.25 1.0) light shifts from magenta to green. (d) And finally, with $\sigma_s = $ (1.0 1.0 0.25) light shifts from yellow to blue. In practice, much more subtle color variations would be used.

Fortunately, once we have a measure of optical thickness, Beer's law still holds; so for a heterogeneous volume, we can find $T(d)$ as

$$T(d) = e^{\int_0^d \sigma_e(\boldsymbol{p})ds}. \tag{9.4}$$

9.7 Wavelength Dependency

So far, we have not mentioned whether the σ_s, σ_a, and L_e coefficients assume scalar or spectral values. Although most volumes scatter and/or absorb light equally at all wavelengths, some have different behavior at different wavelengths. For example, the earth's atmosphere scatters blue light more than red.[3] Smog, smoke, and other aerosols in the air also tend to both absorb and scatter light unevenly across the visible light spectrum.

To implement the effects in a rendering system, we simply let σ_s and the other volume properties be represented as an RGB triplet rather than a scalar property. Figure 9.13 illustrates the appearance of continuously increasing the overall density of a wavelength-dependent scattering medium. Figure 9.14 shows how the color of light shifts to the complement as it passes through a scattering medium.

9.8 Other Approaches to Volume Rendering

The physically based approach is not the only way to render volumes. In fact, many of the in-house solutions used in visual effects production use other approaches. One of the most common ones is to let the user provide separate density and color buffers instead of directly specifying scattering, absorption and emission coefficients. In this case, density is used to control opacity accumulation, and color controls the luminance along the ray. If density is 1.0 and color is (0.0 0.0 0.0), the final result is the same as for a purely absorbing medium. If density is 1.0 and color is (1.0 1.0 1.0), then the material is both absorbing and emissive.

Lighting in PVR, 285

In Chapter 14, we will look at both physically based and nonphysical ways to integrate volumetric properties.

---

[3]This type of scattering is called *Rayleigh scattering*.

Raymarching

10.1   An Introduction to Raymarching

In the previous chapter, we studied light interactions in controlled environments, either in a very short and thin cylinder or in slabs. However, to render interesting images, we need to find an approach that computes the luminance for an entire ray and for all the ray directions that the camera can see (i.e., one luminance value per pixel in the image). Fortunately, being able to compute the behavior of light in a small segment of volume will prove to be quite useful in this case as well because the problem we will be solving is an *integration* and integrals can be computed as sums.

We begin with emission and absorption and imagine a spatially varying function $L_e(p, \vec{\omega})$ that describes the emission at a point in space along a given direction. For simplicity, we ignore the directional variation of L_e and assume the function only changes with the position p, so we have $L_e(p)$. For absorption, we will let σ_a be the absorption coefficient, and using Beer's law from the previous chapter, we know that transmittance between two points can be computed as $T = e^{-\sigma_a dt}$.

The integral we want to solve is one where we accumulate the emitted light along the ray, taking into account how much of it can actually reach the camera. The value $L_e(p)$ is the measure of emitted light, and we can use $T(p', p)$, which is the transmittance between two points in the scene. Putting the two together and integrating along the parametric coordinate t of the ray, we get an expression for $L(p, \vec{\omega})$, which is the luminance arriving at a point p (the position of the camera) along direction $\vec{\omega}$ (the

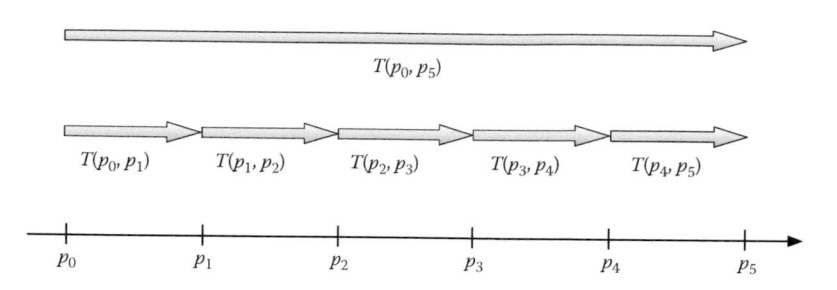

Figure 10.1. Transmittance down a long path can be broken into a sequence of shorter calculations.

direction a given pixel projects to):

$$L(\boldsymbol{p}, \vec{\omega}) = \int_0^\infty T(\boldsymbol{p}', \boldsymbol{p}) L_e(\boldsymbol{p}') dt, \qquad (10.1)$$
$$\boldsymbol{p}' = \boldsymbol{p} + \vec{\omega} t.$$

Because $L_e(\boldsymbol{p})$ can vary arbitrarily, it is not possible to find a closed-form solution to the integral. Instead, it needs to be solved numerically. If we study the two components of the integral, we find that $L_e(\boldsymbol{p}')$ can be sampled directly, while $T(\boldsymbol{p}', \boldsymbol{p})$ cannot. The problem with $T(\boldsymbol{p}', \boldsymbol{p})$ is that it depends on yet another integral (see Equation 9.4) that describes the transmittance between two points. Because we will solve the integral numerically, computing a second integral at each point in the first integral would be expensive. Fortunately, $T(\boldsymbol{p}', \boldsymbol{p})$ has a property that we can take advantage of: it can be broken down into smaller factors that can then be multiplied to find the final answer:

Optical Thickness and Transmittance, 179

$$T(\boldsymbol{p}'', \boldsymbol{p}) = T(\boldsymbol{p}'', \boldsymbol{p}') T(\boldsymbol{p}', \boldsymbol{p}).$$

Here, the transmittance between two points $\boldsymbol{p}''$ and $\boldsymbol{p}$ can be broken into two computations: one from $\boldsymbol{p}''$ to some point $\boldsymbol{p}'$ and a second computation from $\boldsymbol{p}'$ to $\boldsymbol{p}$. We can take advantage of this property when solving our integral by keeping track of the previous T value and simply appending the change in transmittance for the current integration step to the accumulated value. Figure 10.1 illustrates this.

Now that we know how to efficiently compute T for an arbitrary position along the ray, we can break down the numerical integration to a simple sum (see also Figure 10.2):

$$L(\boldsymbol{p}_0) = \sum_{i=0}^{N} L_e(\boldsymbol{p}_i) T(\boldsymbol{p}_0, \boldsymbol{p}_i) |\boldsymbol{p}_i - \boldsymbol{p}_{i-1}|. \qquad (10.2)$$

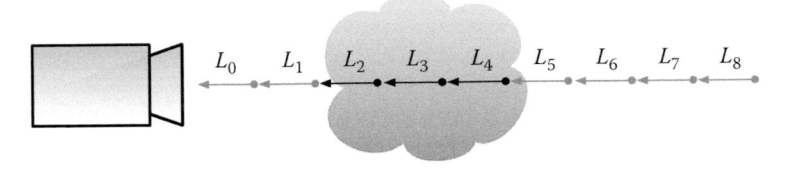

Figure 10.2. Summing up the luminance of each step in Equation (10.2). Gray segments indicate zero luminance due to L_e being zero.

That is, the luminance arriving at p_0 is the sum of the luminance at each point p_i, weighted by the transmittance from p_0 to p_i and the distance between each pair of sample points, $|p_i \quad p_{i\ 1}|$. The technique for computing luminance and transmittance in this way, by stepping along the ray in small increments, is called *raymarching*. (See Figures 10.3 and 10.4.)

Next we look at how we can implement the raymarching technique in code form. In our first attempt, we assume that the integral needs to be computed for the range $[0, 10]$. We define the following integration variables:

- L – the accumulated luminance,
- T – the accumulated transmittance.

Code 10.1. Raymarching emission and absorption

```
Color integrateEmission(Volume vol, Vector p, Vector w)
{
  // Integration bounds
  float current = 0.0;
  float end = 10.0;
  float stepSize = 1.0;
  // Integration variables
  float T = 1.0;
  Color L = 0.0;
  // Integration loop
  while (current < end) {
    // Determine sample position
    Vector p_i = p + w * current;
    // Sample volume properties
    Color Le = vol->emission(p_i);
    float sigma_a = vol->absorption(p_i);
    // Compute change in transmittance
    float T_i = std::exp(-sigma_a * stepSize);
    // Update accumulated transmittance
    T *= T_i;
    // Update accumulated luminance
    L += T * Le;
```

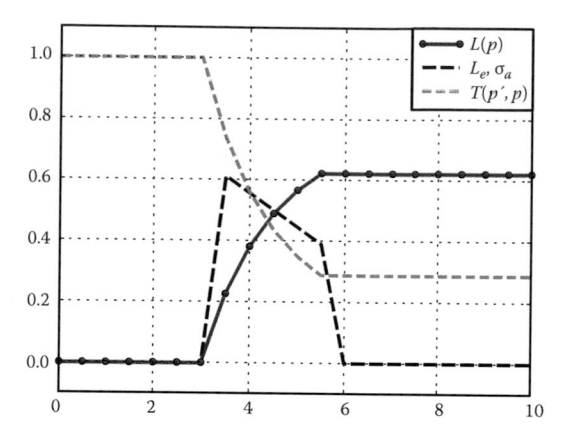

Figure 10.3. Result of integrating Equation (10.1) with step length set to 0.5.

```
    // Increment sample position
    current += stepSize;
  }
  // Integration done.
  return L;
}
```

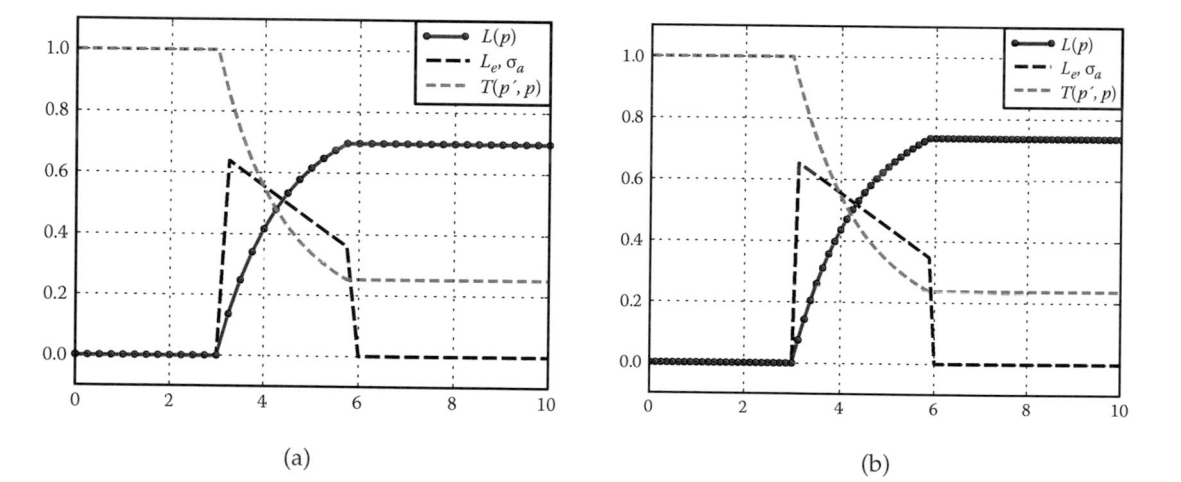

(a)   (b)

Figure 10.4. Decreasing the integration step size results in a more accurate result: (a) step length = 0.25 and (b) step length = 0.125. Note that the final luminosity increases and transmittance decreases as we converge to the solution.

10.2   Lighting and Raymarching

Volumetric Lighting, 167

With a basic understanding of how we can solve the volume-rendering problem using raymarching, we continue on to the last volumetric property: scattering. If we consider the scattering equations from Chapter 9, they differed from the treatment of emission and absorption.

Out-scattering is handled identically to absorption, so we can simply replace σ_a with $\sigma_s + \sigma_a$ in our existing code. In-scattering, however, depended on light coming from light sources in the scene, not just the light traveling in the direction of the view ray.

In order to compute how much light scatters into the view direction, we need to know a few things. First, the scattering probability, which is the scattering coefficient σ_s. Second, we need to know the phase function $p(\vec{\omega}, \vec{\omega}')$ in order to find out how much light is reflected into the view direction ω. But most importantly, we need to know how much light actually arrives at the current point from the light source. In Equation (9.3), we labeled this function $S(p, \vec{\omega}')$, but here we will break that function into multiple components to better make sense of how we can compute it.

The function $S(p, \vec{\omega}')$ is conceptually very similar to $L(p, \vec{\omega})$, which is the integral we solve to render the pixel itself. If we consider the light source in a space with no participating media, the light arriving at a point p would only be relative to the light source's position p_{light} and the light source's intensity I. Because the position of the light source is known, we can remove $\vec{\omega}'$ from S, and we get

$$S(p) = I_{\text{light}} |p_{\text{light}} - p|^2.$$

Once we involve a participating medium, we need to consider the transmittance between the light source and p, as some of the light will be extinguished between the two points. The equation instead becomes

$$S(p) = \frac{T(p, p_{\text{light}}) I_{\text{light}}}{|p_{\text{light}} - p|^2}.$$

If we add the scattering components to Equation (10.1), the full $L(p, \vec{\omega})$ integral now becomes

$$L(p, \vec{\omega}) = \int_0^\infty T(p', p) \left(L_e(p') + \sum_{i=0}^N \sigma_s p(\vec{\omega}, \vec{\omega}_i') S_i(p') T(p', p_i) \right) dt.$$

For brevity, we will sometimes write the integral in a shorter form when considering all the lights in the scene as a whole:

$$L(p, \vec{\omega}) = \int_0^\infty T(p', p) \left(L_e(p') + L_s(p') \right) dt.$$

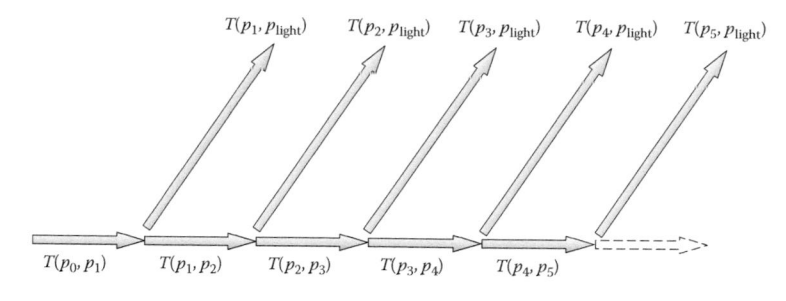

Figure 10.5. Although the view transmittance can be computed iteratively along the primary ray, transmittance for shadow rays cannot.

Solving $T(p, p_i)$ requires integration of transmittance, just as in the previous section, but with one important difference: we cannot build the transmittance function cumulatively the way it's done for the main raymarch. Figure 10.5 illustrates the difference.

Because each transmittance calculation for in-scattering happens between independent points, we must compute the full integral, which implies a secondary raymarch calculation.

Using a second raymarch loop at each sample point in the primary raymarch loop should hopefully set off some alarm bells; if the primary raymarch is linear in complexity ($O(n)$), we have effectively made the new algorithm $O(n^2)$ by introducing in-scattering. Speeding up this transmittance function computation is a major part of any volume renderer, and Chapter 15 describes in detail how PVR implements several different solutions. In the meantime, we assume that the transmittance function between the sample point and the light source can be computed independently of the primary ray, which gives us the following pseudocode:

Precomputed Occlusion, 315

Code 10.2. Raymarching scattering

```
Color integrateScattering(Volume vol, Vector p, Vector w)
{
  // Integration bounds
  float current = 0.0;
  float end = 10.0;
  float stepSize = 1.0;
  // Integration variables
  float T = 1.0;
  Color L = 0.0;
  // Integration loop
  while (current < end) {
    // Determine sample position
    Vector p_i = p + w * current;
```

```
    // Sample volume properties
    float sigma_s = vol->scattering(p_i);
    // Compute change in transmittance
    float T_i = std::exp(-sigma_s * stepSize);
    // Update accumulated transmittance
    T *= T_i;
    // Sample each light source
    for (int l = 0; l < nLights; l++) {
      // Find light direction, intensity and visibility
      Vector w_light = lightDirection(l, p_i);
      Color L_light = lightIntensity(l, p_i);
      L_light *= lightVisibility(l, p_i);
      // Accumulate reflected light
      L += T * sigma_s * phaseFunction(w, w_light) * L_Light;
    }
    // Increment sample position
    current += stepSize;
  }
  // Integration done.
  return L;
}
```

10.3   Integration Intervals

When we write the continuous form of the raymarch integral (Equation (10.3)), we integrate the interval $[0, \infty]$. Of course, when integrating numerically, infinity is not a good bound, and in the example code above, we chose an arbitrary interval $[0, 10]$ to limit the number of loop iterations needed. The problem we face is that we cannot choose a good interval to integrate over at compile time, so we need to find a way to decide both what a reasonable integration interval should be for a given ray and also how many integration steps need to be taken in order to find a good estimate to the integral.

There are two main paths to take. We could require the user to input the start and the end of the integration interval, either implicitly through the camera clipping-plane settings or explicitly as two world-space distances. The second option is to automatically figure out some reasonable integration bounds based on the scene the user wants to render. While the first option may seem tempting—tying integration bounds to the clipping planes would have the expected effect of cutting parts of the scene out—it is rarely a good idea, and users shouldn't be required to set tight clipping planes in order to render a scene efficiently.

One way to find a reasonable integration interval is to intersect the view ray $\vec{\omega}$ against the scene's bounding box, as illustrated in Figure 10.6. The raymarch loop can then be changed to only take the distance between

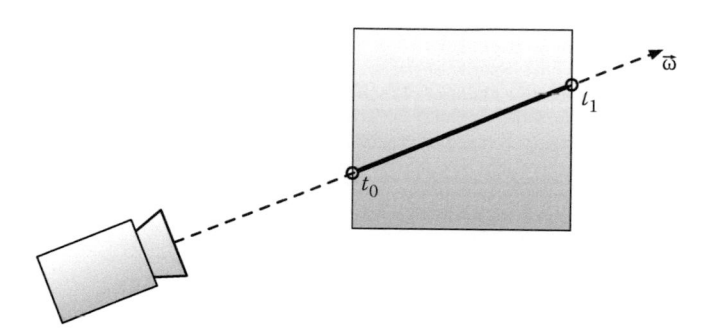

Figure 10.6. Finding t_0 and t_1 as intersection with scene.

the entry and exit points into account. This solution works well since we only exclude parts of the interval that are known to be zero:

$$L(\boldsymbol{p}, \vec{\omega}) = \int_{t_0}^{t_1} T(\boldsymbol{p}', \boldsymbol{p}) \ \left(L_e(\boldsymbol{p}') + L_s(\boldsymbol{p}') \right) dt, \qquad (10.3)$$

$$t_0 = \text{intersect}_{\text{in}}(\vec{\omega}, scene),$$

$$t_1 = \text{intersect}_{\text{out}}(\vec{\omega}, scene).$$

Our pseudocode raymarcher could then be updated to find its start point and endpoint from the intersection between the ray and the `Volume`.

Code 10.3. Raymarching only the portion of the ray that intersects the scene

```
Color integrate(Scene scene, Vector p, Vector w)
{
  // Integration bounds
  std::pair<float, float> isect = intersect(w, scene.bounds());
  float current = isect.first;
  float end = isect.second;
  float stepSize = 1.0;
  while (current < end) {
    // ...
  }
}
```

10.4   Integration Intervals for Multiple Volumes

For more complicated scenes, for example ones where multiple volumes are involved, intersecting against the bounds of the scene can still be inefficient. Figure 10.7 shows the reported integration interval for two

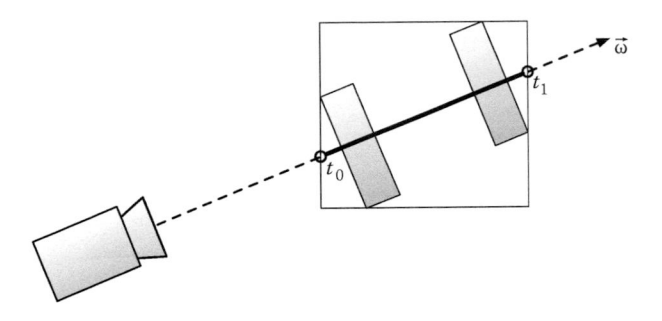

Figure 10.7. For a scene with multiple volumes, intersecting against the global bounds often results in empty space being included in the integration interval.

shallow volumes. In this case, most of the interval is empty, and any time spent calculating the integral in empty areas will be wasted.

Fortunately, it is quite simple to fix the problem. Instead of intersecting against the bounds of the scene, we simply intersect $\vec{\omega}$ against the bounds of each volume. In this case, each intersection gives us a tighter bound on the part of the ray that requires sampling, but we also end up with multiple disjoint intervals. (See Figure 10.8.) To handle this in our pseudocode, we need to create an outer loop that traverses each volume in the scene.

Code 10.4. Raymarching multiple intervals

```
Color integrate(Scene scene, Vector p, Vector w)
{
  // Intersect each volume independently
  for (int i = 0; i < scene.numVolumes(); i++) {
    // Integration bounds
    std::pair<float, float> isect = intersect(w, scene.volume(i).bounds());
```

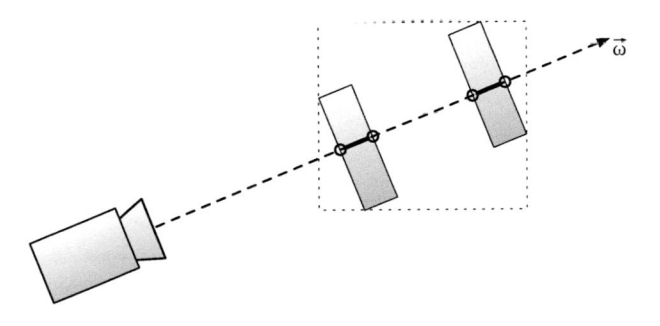

Figure 10.8. Intersecting against each volume in the scene gives multiple integration intervals and ignores the empty space between the volumes.

```
  float current = isect.first;
  float end = isect.second;
  float stepSize = 1.0;
  // Raymarch loop
  while (current < end) {
    // ...
  }
 }
}
```

10.5 Integration Intervals for Overlapping Volumes

Although it's possible to optimize the raymarcher by computing the integral for each volume individually, this approach breaks in some cases. If we consider Figure 10.9, we can see that the two integration intervals that need to be computed overlap. If we simply integrate one volume at a time, our integration variable t no longer moves monotonically down the ray. Instead, once the first interval is computed, it steps backwards along the ray and recomputes the portion where the two volumes overlap. This behavior is incorrect, so we need to handle the case of overlapping volumes differently.

To solve the problem, we could either merge overlapping segments into one, or we could split the segments into disjoint parts that can then be treated individually. Merging may seem like the most efficient solution, but as we'll see in the next section, splitting the segments has an advantage when dealing with volumes that can benefit from different sampling step lengths. (See Figure 10.10.)

Adding the code for handling overlapping volumes to our pseudocode raymarcher we get the following:

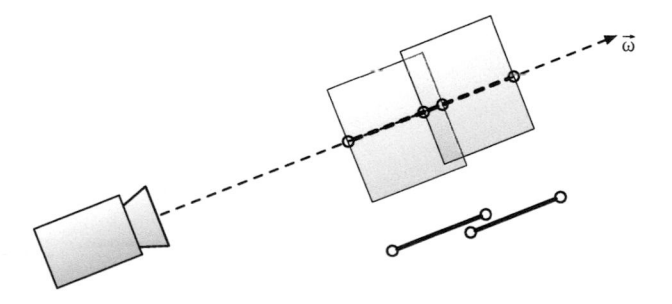

Figure 10.9. When volumes overlap, it is no longer possible to raymarch each volume separately.

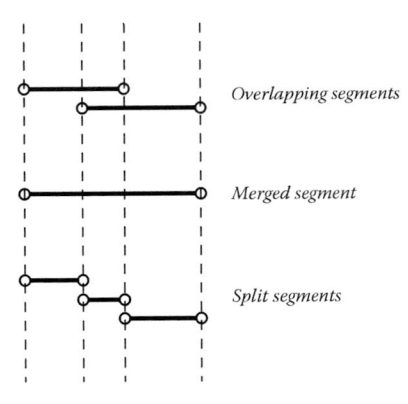

Figure 10.10. Using merging and splitting to turn overlapping segments into nonoverlapping ones.

Code 10.5. Raymarching multiple disjoint intervals

```
Color integrate(Scene scene, Vector p, Vector w)
{
  // Integration bounds
  typedef std::pair<float, float> Interval;
  std::vector<Interval> overlappingIsects = intersect(w, scene.volumes());
  std::vector<Interval> isects = splitIntervals(overlappingIsects);
  // Handle each disjoint interval
  for (int i = 0, end = isects.size(); i < end; i++) {
    float current = isects[i].first;
    float end = isects[i].second;
    float stepSize = 1.0;
    // Raymarch loop
    while (current < end) {
      // ...
    }
  }
}
```

10.6   Sampling Strategies

In the previous sections, we explored how we can determine which segments along a ray need to be raymarched, but we glossed over the question of where, or how densely, to sample. In all the examples, we found the start and the end of the integration bounds from the intersection between the ray and the volume, but the *step length* was hardcoded to 1.0.

There are a few things we need to keep in mind when choosing the step length. First, we want to make sure that we capture all of the features

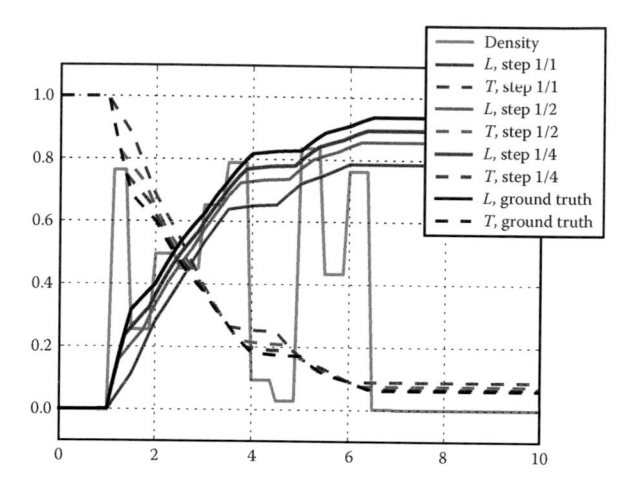

Figure 10.11. Sampling a 5^3 voxel buffer at the Nyquist limit and successively smaller step lengths. The plotted functions are $T(\boldsymbol{p}', \boldsymbol{p})$ and $L(\boldsymbol{p}, \vec{\omega})$.

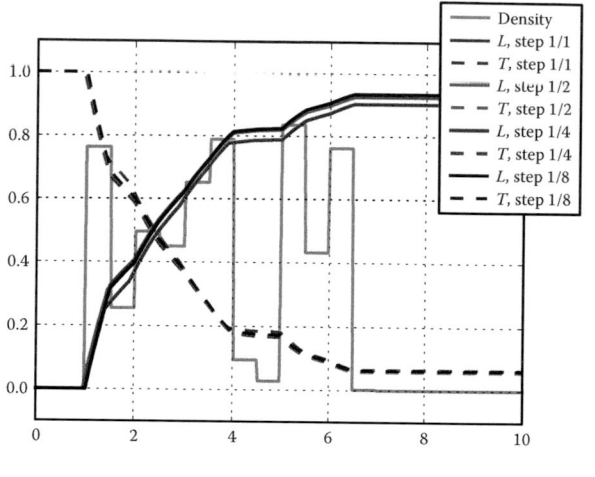

Figure 10.12. Sampling a 25^3 voxel buffer at the Nyquist limit and successively smaller step lengths. The error is much smaller than in Figure 10.11.

in the volume. If we used a very large step, some small features may fall in the space between two sample points and be missed altogether. This problem is a sampling problem and relates to the Nyquist limit.

The second problem relates to the accuracy of the integral that we are solving. If we consider a very low-resolution volume, perhaps only 5^3, it would be tempting to set a step length such that we take only ten samples through it. Although that would satisfy the Nyquist limit, it would result in a poor approximation of the integral. Figure 10.11 illustrates the problem.

We can see that because of the large step size, both T and L differ significantly from the result we get at short step lengths. Running the same test for a higher-resolution voxel buffer gives a much smaller error, even when sampling at the Nyquist limit. (See Figure 10.12.) We can assume that the limiting factor in this case is the numerical integration rather than the Nyquist limit.

10.7   Empty-Space Optimization

In Section 10.3 we looked at ways of narrowing down the parts of the ray that needed to be raymarched, and we saw that intersecting each volume individually rather than the scene as a whole gave us much tighter-fitting

Integration Intervals, 187

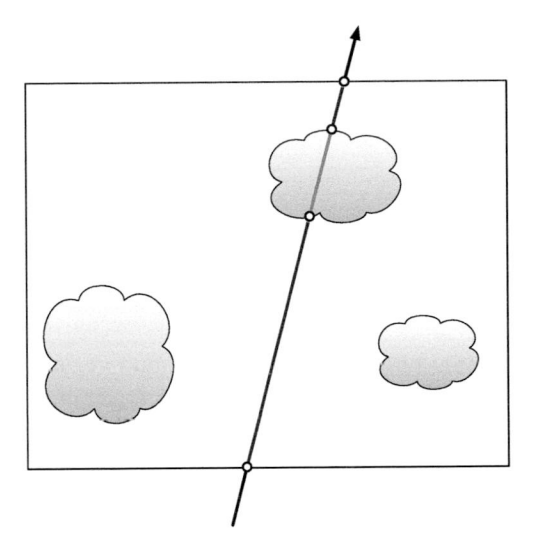

Figure 10.13. In the ideal case, the raymarcher would only need to integrate the part of the ray where density is present (in green), skipping the space in the buffer that is empty (red).

integration bounds. The next step in speeding up the integral is to apply the same idea to the contents of each volume.

Let's first consider a voxel buffer that is sparsely populated. Ideally, we would want to tell the raymarcher that only certain parts were interesting and that some could be skipped entirely. The problem lies in finding a way to do so that is cheap, so that the cost of analyzing which parts of a ray can be skipped isn't greater than the cost of raymarching it. (See Figure 10.13.)

If we had no knowledge of the structure of the voxel buffer, one way to solve the problem would be to check the value of each voxel along the ray. Unfortunately, this involves a number of operations on the same order as the raymarch itself, so the benefit would be negligible.

There are, however, ways of determining which parts of a volume are empty that are much cheaper. Some volumes have analytic solutions, but the factor that is easiest to take advantage of is the volume's data structure.

If we consider a sparse voxel buffer with only 10% or so of the blocks active, we see that a lot of the raymarch samples will fall in areas with zero density. Fortunately, the sparse buffer's block structure provides us with a high-level culling mechanism, where a large number of voxels can be skipped (depending on the size of the sparse block) simply by checking if a given block is in use. (See Figure 10.14.)

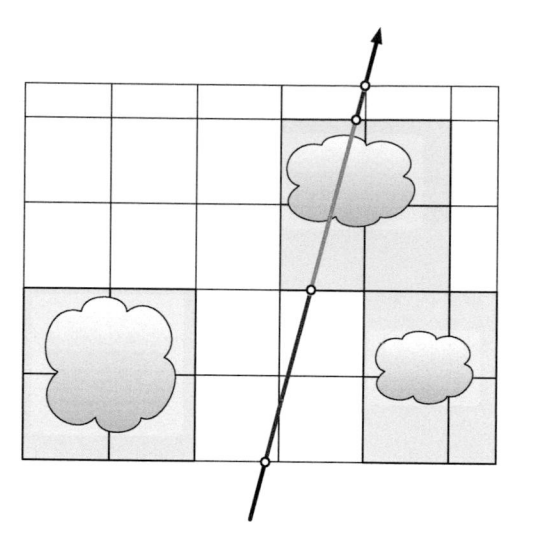

Figure 10.14. Using the blocks of a sparse voxel buffer gives us an efficient way of determining which regions are populated and which can be skipped. We note that the resulting integration interval is less tight than we would like. There is always a trade-off between fast evaluation and optimal bounds.

The efficiency of an empty-space optimization algorithm can vary; in the worst case, it does nothing (or worse, slows down rendering), and in the best case, it tells the raymarcher exactly which areas can be skipped. But there is always a dependency on how sparse the actual volume is: if a volume is nonzero inside its entire domain, an empty-space optimization algorithm can't help.

10.8   Holdouts

Volumetric elements rarely exist in isolation, and in almost any shot there are other elements that the volumetric must integrate with in the final composite. For example, when inserting a computer-graphics smoke element into a scene, it may be partially occluded by other parts of the scene, either real objects that were in the photographed image or other computer-graphics objects that are also being added into the frame. The most brute-force solution to the problem would be for the compositor to rotoscope the smoke element to remove the parts that should not be visible. Although it works, it can be a tedious and difficult process. Ideally, we would want the renderer to figure out what is hidden and what is visible.

Fortunately, because this is a very common problem in production rendering, there is a technique called *holdouts* that solves it. A holdout is an object in the scene that occludes and shadows other objects but that does not itself show up in the final frame or its alpha channel. Intuitively, it may seem strange to render objects that have no effect on the final image other than to block other objects from being visible, but the purpose is to remove parts from a rendered image that are visible elsewhere, either in the photographed plate or in a second computer-graphics element.

To see how we can incorporate holdouts in our raymarcher, we will look at three aspects of transmittance. Up until now, we have assumed that alpha is directly proportional to the transmittance returned by the raymarcher according to the equation

$$\alpha = 1 - T.$$

Once we introduce holdouts, this assumption no longer holds. In fact, we need to be a bit more precise about what T represents. When no holdouts were present, it was the integrated extinction[1] along the ray. Holdouts also occlude what's behind them, so it may at first be tempting to simply integrate the holdout-based extinction along with scattering and absorption:

$$T = T \cdot e^{-(\sigma_s + \sigma_a + \sigma_h)dt}.$$

The problem with this approach is that the alpha value of the final image increases as the holdout becomes more prominent, which is the opposite of what we want. For the equation $\alpha = 1 - T$, we actually want T to be larger, so that α is smaller, if a holdout object is present.

We can solve the problem by keeping track of three different types of transmittance:

- T_e, which is the transmittance along the ray accounting for ordinary extinction effects (scattering and absorption),
- T_h, which is the transmittance accounting for holdout extinction,
- T_α, which is the transmittance that is used as the basis for α.

The transmittance T_e is the same property that we integrated earlier and called T, but here we use the T_e symbol to be more specific. The equation for updating it will be the same as before, i.e.,

$$T_e = T_e \cdot e^{-\sigma_e dt}.$$

The transmittance T_h is computed the same way as T_e but using a different coefficient. If we consider what a holdout needs to represent,

---

[1] I.e., $\sigma_s + \sigma_a$.

we find that the coefficient is both familiar and intuitive. A common-use case for holdouts is when two different volumetric elements overlap but need to be rendered separately and later composited.[2] The amount by which element A occludes element B should be the same whether or not element A is rendered as a holdout. This leads us to the conclusion that we can define a new extinction-like coefficient called σ_h, which, for an object tagged as a holdout, is found through the simple relationship

$$\sigma_h = \sigma_e = \sigma_s + \sigma_a.$$

The corresponding transmittance value T_h is computed the same way as T_e, but uses σ_h rather than σ_e:

$$T_h = T_h \cdot e^{-\sigma_h dt}.$$

Sometimes the holdout is not a volume element but a deep shadow map coming either from a separate render pass or even from a different renderer. In these cases, the transmittance function doesn't need to be integrated, but can be point sampled directly from the deep shadow map. If we call the shadow map M and the function that samples it $M(p)$, then we can find T_h at any point in space through the relationship

$$T_h(p) = M(p).$$

Because T_e and T_h are kept separate, we need to change the basic raymarching equation (Equation (10.3)) into a form that includes the transmittance due to holdout effects. This is done by multiplying in T_h into the raymarch equation along with T_e (which was T in the original equation):

$$L(p,\vec{\omega}) = \int_0^\infty T_e(p',p)T_h(p',p)\left(L_e(p') + \sum_{i=0}^N \sigma_s p(\vec{\omega},\vec{\omega}_i')S_i(p')T(p',p_i)\right)dt.$$

The final property that we need to track is T_α. We start with a thought experiment, illustrated in Figure 10.15. Two volumes, A and B are oriented along the ray so that A occludes B. The intersection between the ray and each volume is the same length, so $a = b = 1$. Both volumes are purely scattering, with $\sigma_s = \ln(0.5)$. Although it may seem like a peculiar choice of scattering coefficient, it results in changes to the transmittance functions that are exactly 0.5:

$$T_e(p_1,p_2) = T_e(p_3,p_4) = e^{\ln(0.5)} = 0.5.$$

---

[2]This is common in visual effects production, where the compositing artist has more control if elements are broken out into separate passes.

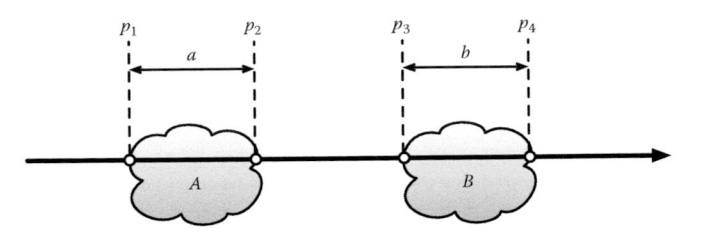

Figure 10.15. Volume A occludes Volume B, but the two volumes are disjoint.

If A and B were both ordinary volumes, we would expect the integrated transmittance and alpha value to be

$$T = T_e(p_1, p_2)T_e(p_3, p_4) = 0.5 \times 0.5 = 0.25,$$
$$\alpha = 1 - T = 0.75.$$

For the sake of illustration, we assume that the in-scattered radiance along a and b each add up to 1.0. Of course, B is occluded by A by the factor $T_e(p_1, p_2) = 0.5$, cutting its contribution to the final pixel in half. Thus, for luminance, the values would be

$$L = 1.0 + 0.5 = 1.5.$$

We will refer to this combined render of A and B as R. Now, if we wanted to separate the two elements,[3] we would need to render the scene twice. The first render R_a would mark volume B as a holdout object and produce a luminance value L_a and an alpha value α_a. The second render R_b would produce a corresponding L_b and α_b. (See Figure 10.16.) Once rendered, the two images would be composited using an additive operation, both for luminance and alpha, and the result should ideally look identical to R:

$$L = L_a + L_b,$$
$$\alpha = \alpha_a + \alpha_b.$$

The properties of R_a are fairly trivial to find. B does not occlude or intersect A, so the luminance is (as was shown before) simply $L_a = 1.0$ and the alpha $\alpha_a = 1 - T_e(p_1, p_2) = 0.5$. The reason these are simple is because $T_h = 1$ over the span of a.

For R_b, things get a bit more complicated. Here, T_h is no longer one, but rather equal to the transmittance found in R_a, i.e., $T_h = T_a = 0.5$.

---

[3]Of course, this is unnecessary since A and B don't overlap. Please bear with us as we make this point.

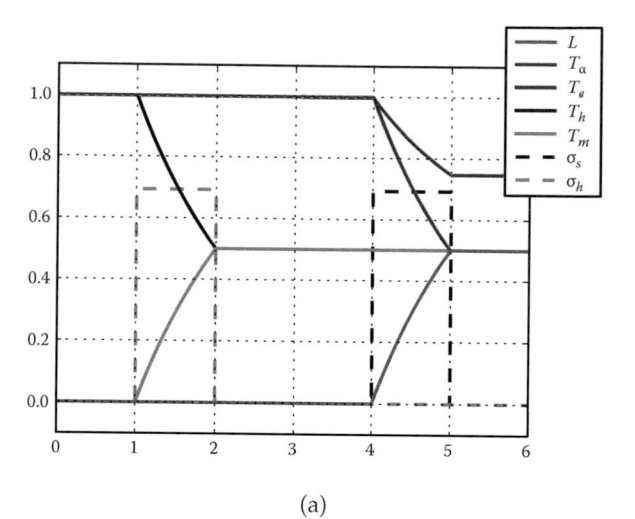

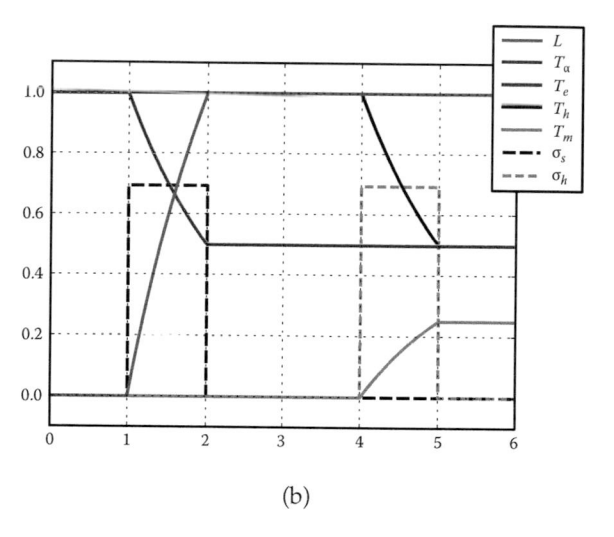

(a)   (b)

Figure 10.16. Plotting the accumulation variables for (a) R_a and (b) R_b.

Above, we saw that we could integrate T_h into the luminance calculation by multiplying it into the same equation as the usual T transmittance value. The next step will be to look at how we can produce an alpha value that satisfies $\alpha = \alpha_a + \alpha_b$. Intuitively, what we want is half as much alpha as was found in the first render, since the element is now occluded by a factor $T_h = 0.5$.

Looking at the results of R_a and R_b, we see that the sum of the two indeed add up exactly to the result of R:

$$L_a + L_b = 1.0 + 0.5 = 1.5,$$
$$\alpha_a + \alpha_b = 0.5 + 0.25 = 0.75.$$

Holdouts are simple to handle in cases where the holdout region does not overlap the visible volumes, but when we look at cases where the holdout occupies the same space as the visible volume, the problem becomes more complicated. In this case, we need to account for the fact not only that the holdout affects the transmittance and luminance of the visible volumes but also that the visible volume affects how much influence the holdout has. If we modify our previous example such that A and B overlap, it becomes very difficult to answer the question about what the luminance and alpha should be once each volume is considered a holdout to the other; A may not be opaque enough to obscure B completely, and B's density will influence how much of A is visible in the areas where they overlap. Figure 10.17 illustrates this case.

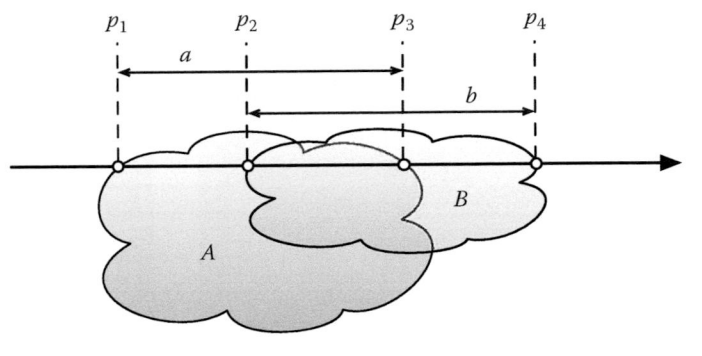

Figure 10.17. Volume A occludes and also overlaps volume B.

Before we look at how we can solve the problem, we will revisit the standard integration update for transmittance, $T = T \cdot e^{-\sigma_e dt}$. The integral is guaranteed to be monotonically decreasing, approaching zero as σ_e or dt get larger, or as an increasing number of iterations are computed. Without holdouts, this is exactly the behavior we want, because as T approaches 0, α approaches 1. But of course, with holdouts in a scene, we no longer want α to go all the way to 1.

We begin with re-formulating the transmittance update to tend toward a specific value T_t, rather than 0:

$$T = t \cdot T + (1 - t) \cdot T_t,$$
$$t = e^{-\sigma_e dt}.$$

Next, we introduce two new integration variables: T_α, which is a transmittance value that will be used only for the purpose of producing the pixel's final alpha value, and T_m, which is the minimum transmittance for the ray. The value T_α is monotonically decreasing just like T_e and T_h, whereas T_m is monotonically *increasing*. Further, T_α decreases based on $e^{-\sigma_e dt}$, just like T_e, and T_m increases based on $e^{-\sigma_h dt}$. The big difference between the two new variables and the old T_e and T_h is that they tend toward each other rather than toward zero.

The logic behind the variable choice is as follows: as we step through a holdout, the lowest possible transmittance for the visible volume will no longer be zero, but rather it will tend to a higher value based on the integral of the holdout property, T_h. To complicate things further, we must consider that as we step through a visible volume, any subsequent effects from holdouts will also be attenuated, since less of the holdout is visible. (See Figures 10.18 and 10.19.)

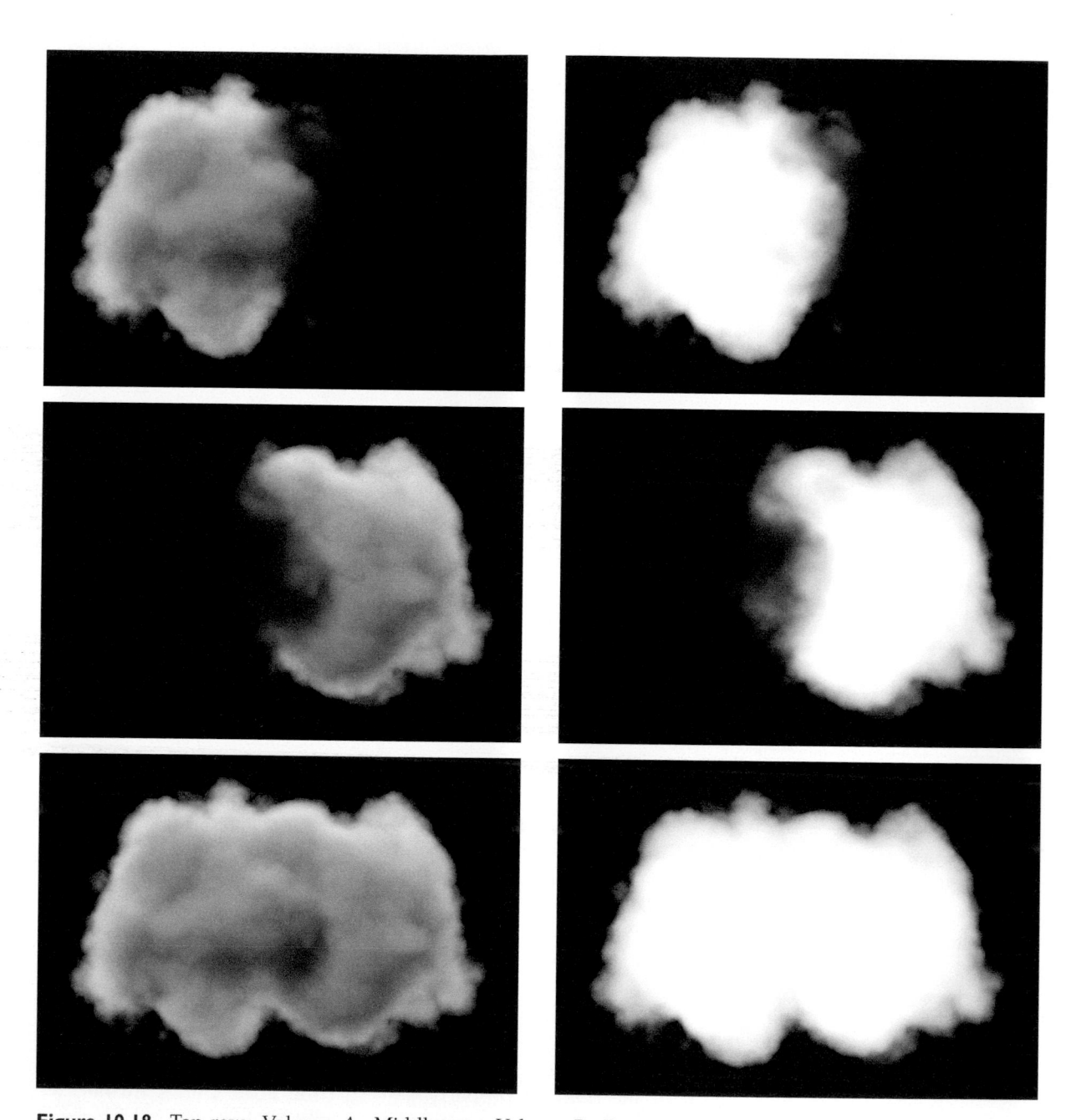

Figure 10.18. Top row: Volume A. Middle row: Volume B. Bottom row: Additive composite of volumes A and B. Each row shows RGB and alpha layers.

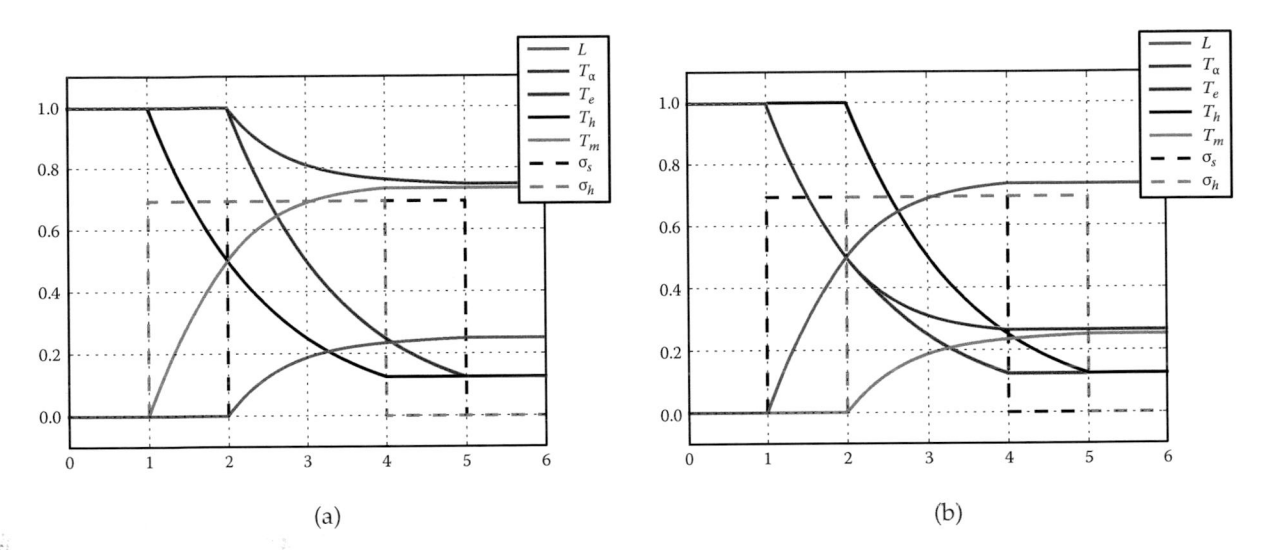

Figure 10.19. Plotting the accumulation variables for two overlapping volumes. Dashed lines show volumes A and B as scattering and holdout coefficients (a) Integration with volume A as holdout and volume B visible. (b) Integration with volume A visible and volume B as holdout.

We can express these codependent variables as follows:

$$T_m = t_m \cdot T_m + (1 - t_m) \cdot T_\alpha,$$
$$t_m = e^{-\sigma_h dt},$$
$$T_\alpha = t_\alpha \cdot T_\alpha + (1 - t_\alpha) \cdot T_m,$$
$$t_\alpha = e^{-\sigma_e dt}.$$

Expressed in code, we get the following:

Code 10.6. Raymarching scattering with holdouts

```
Color integrateScatteringWithHoldouts(Volume vol, Vector p, Vector w)
{
    // Integration bounds
    float current = 0.0;
    float end = 10.0;
    float stepSize = 1.0;
    // Integration variables
    Color L = 0.0;
    float T_e = 1.0;
    float T_h = 1.0;
    float T_alpha = 1.0;
    float T_m = 0.0;
```

```
// Integration loop
while (current < end) {
  // Determine sample position
  Vector p_i = p + w * current;
  // Sample volume properties
  float sigma_s = vol->scattering(p_i);
  float sigma_h = vol->holdout(p_i);
  // Compute change in transmittance
  float expSigmaS = std::exp(-sigma_s * stepSize);
  float expSigmaH = std::exp(-sigma_h * stepSize);
  // Update accumulated transmittance
  T_e *= expSigmaS;
  T_h *= expSigmaH;
  T_m     = Imath::lerp(T_alpha, T_m, expSigmaH);
  T_alpha = Imath::lerp(T_m, T_alpha, expSigmaE);
  // Sample each light source
  for (int l = 0; l < nLights; l++) {
    // Find light direction, intensity and visibility
    Vector w_light = lightDirection(l, p_i);
    Color L_light = lightIntensity(l, p_i);
    L_light *= lightVisibility(l, p_i);
    // Accumulate reflected light
    L += T_e * T_h * sigma_s * phaseFunction(w, w_light) * L_Light;
  }
  // Increment sample position
  current += stepSize;
}
// Integration done.
return Result(L, T_alpha);
}
```

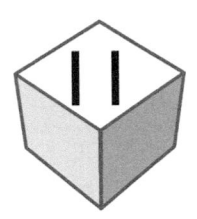

PVR's Rendering Pipeline

11.1 The Scene Class

Volume, 233

To render a scene in PVR, a few different types of objects must be used. Most importantly, we need a **Volume** to represent the volume data that should be rendered, and for scenes that are not completely self-illuminated,[1] we also need one or more light sources. The **Scene** class wraps up these two types of objects and holds them in memory from the time they are first added (through **Renderer::addLight()** and **Renderer:: addVolume()**) until rendering is done and the **Renderer** goes out of scope.

Renderer, 204

Code 11.1. The **Scene** class

```
class Scene
{
public:
  // Typedefs
  PVR_TYPEDEF_SMART_PTRS(Scene);
  typedef Util::SPtr<const Volume>::type VolumePtr;
  typedef Util::SPtr<const Light>::type  LightPtr;
  typedef std::vector<LightPtr>          LightVec;
  // Ctor, dtor, cloning
  Ptr clone() const;
  // Data members
  VolumePtr volume;
  LightVec  lights;
};
```

---

[1]Fire is one example of volumes that require no light sources.

A PVR scene can contain both multiple volumes and multiple lights, but the way the **Scene** stores them is a little bit different. Volumes often have a hierarchy, and the **CompositeVolume** acts as a container for all the underlying volumes in the scene if there is more than one. That way, the **Scene** class can be ignorant of what type of hierarchy is built and how it is structured. On the other hand, **Light** instances are not evaluated hierarchically in PVR, so the **Scene** simply keeps a list of lights that are active for a given scene setup.

CompositeVolume, 262

Light, 292

11.2   The **Renderer** Class

The center point of all the rendering-related tasks in PVR is the **Renderer** class. It holds the **Scene** instance (which contains lights and volumes), the render camera, as well as the raymarcher used for integrating the luminance value of each pixel in the camera's view. The interface is divided into a few sections. First, we have the calls related to setup of the scene and the renderer instance. These calls all take **const** pointers to their respective classes, since the **Renderer** never needs to alter their state.

Scene, 203

Code 11.2. Renderer: Setup-related methods

```
class Renderer
{
public:
...
  // Setup
  void setCamera     (Camera::CPtr camera);
  void setRaymarcher(Raymarcher::CPtr raymarcher);
  void addVolume     (Volume::CPtr volume);
  void addLight      (Light::CPtr light);
...
private:
...};
```

The second group of functions are related to rendering options. These let us control whether the render should produce both luminance and transmittance or transmittance only (**setPrimaryEnabled()**), whether deep images are requested for luminance and transmittance (see Section 15.6), as well as controls over the number of rays to fire for each pixel (**setNum PixelSamples()**).

The **DeepImage** Class, 323

Code 11.3. Renderer: Options-related methods

```
class Renderer
{
```

```
public:
...
   // Options
   void setPrimaryEnabled          (const bool enabled);
   void setTransmittanceMapEnabled(const bool enabled);
   void setLuminanceMapEnabled     (const bool enabled);
   void setDoRandomizePixelSamples(const bool enabled);
   void setNumPixelSamples         (const size_t numSamples);
   void setNumDeepSamples          (const size_t numSamples);
...
private:
...};
```

Camera, 213

Raymarcher, 268

Finally, once the **Renderer** is configured, the user calls **Renderer::exe cute()**, which fires one or more rays for each pixel in the **Camera**'s view and lets the **Raymarcher** integrate the luminance and transmittance for that pixel.

Once rendering is completed, the resulting transmittance and luminance map can be accessed, and the image can be written to disk.

Code 11.4. Executing the **Renderer** and retrieving results

```
class Renderer
{
public:
...
   // Execution
   void printSceneInfo() const;
   void execute();
...
   // Results
   DeepImage::Ptr transmittanceMap() const;
   DeepImage::Ptr luminanceMap() const;
   void            saveImage(const std::string &filename) const;
private:
...};
```

11.2.1   Setting Up Rays

Scene, 203

Camera, 213

To fire a ray into the **Scene**, we first need to find the ray's *origin* and *direction*. The origin is always the position of the render camera, and by calling **Camera::position()**, we get the position at the current time.

PVR uses the Imath library's **Line3<T>** class to represent rays,[2] and an instance is created by providing two points. The first will be considered the origin, and the vector from the first to the second becomes the

---

[2]**pvr::Ray** is a typedef of **Imath::Line3<double>**.

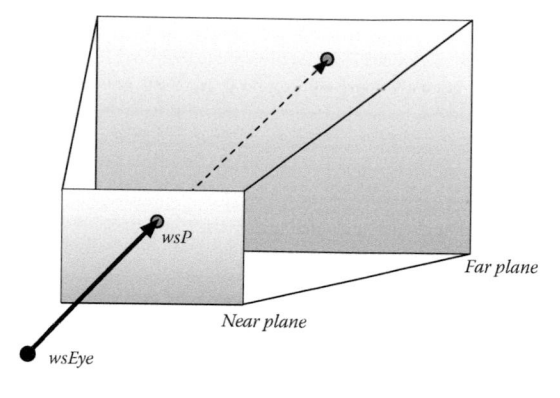

Figure 11.1. Building a **Ray** from the camera's position and a point on the near clipping plane.

direction. To find the second point, we transform a point at the current pixel position in raster space to world space. (See Figure 11.1.)

Code 11.5. setupRay()

```
Ray setupRay(Camera::CPtr camera, const float x, const float y,
             const PTime time)
{
  // Find camera position at current time. This will serve as the Ray's origin
  const Vector wsEye = camera->position(time);
  // Compute direction by transforming pixel position in raster space to
  // world space
  const Vector rsP(x, y, 1.0);
  Vector wsP = camera->rasterToWorld(rsP, time);

  return Ray(wsEye, wsP);
}
```

Although it is not immediately obvious, **setupRay** is the place where *camera motion blur* is handled in PVR, by distributing rays in time [Cook et al. 84] [Cook 86]. Depending on the current **time** variable, the **Ray** is created with a different origin point and a different direction, based on the configuration of the camera at that point. Figure 11.2 illustrates how a **PerspectiveCamera** with only two time samples still provides a continuum of possible ray directions. Furthermore, because most of the **PerspectiveCamera**'s parameters are driven by **Curve** instances, curved motion blur can be achieved by simply adding more samples to those curves. The cost of creating rays is independent of the number of time samples in the **Camera**.

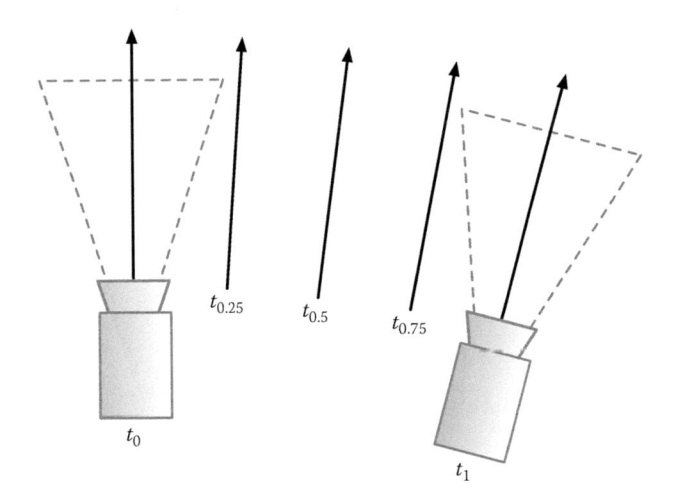

Figure 11.2. Constructing a **Ray** at various time values. The camera has time samples defined at t_0 and t_1.

11.2.2   Firing and Integrating Rays

RayState, 210
Raymarcher, 268

The **integrateRay()** call is responsible for constructing a **Ray** (using **setupRay()**) and for constructing the current pixel's **RayState**. The **Ray State** wraps up all the information that the **Raymarcher** needs in order to integrate the luminance and transmittance for a pixel.

Code 11.6. Renderer::integrateRay()

```
IntegrationResult Renderer::integrateRay(const float x, const float y,
                                         const PTime time) const
{
  // Create default RayState. Rely on its constructor to set reasonable
  // defaults
  RayState state;
  // Update the values that are non-default
  state.wsRay = setupRay(m_camera, x, y, time);
  state.time = time;
  if (!m_params.doPrimary) {
    state.rayType = RayState::TransmittanceOnly;
    state.rayDepth = 1;
  }
  state.doOutputDeepT = m_params.doTransmittanceMap;
  state.doOutputDeepL = m_params.doLuminanceMap;
  // Let the Raymarcher do the integration work
  return m_raymarcher->integrate(state);
}
```

11.2.3 Executing the Render

Apart from some general error-checking code, the most important part
of **Renderer::execute()** is a loop over each pixel in the image. In each
loop step, we start by initializing the luminance and alpha values that
will be the result of the render. We also create a list of deep transmittance
and luminance functions (the **tf** and **lf** variables). Because the renderer
is able to fire multiple rays per pixel, the final deep transmittance and
luminance functions will be computed as an average of each subpixel's
function.

Code 11.7. Renderer::execute()

```
void Renderer::execute()
{
  // Initialization ---

  RenderGlobals::setCamera(m_camera);

  m_rng.init(0);

  // For each pixel ---

  for (Image::pixel_iterator i = m_primary->begin(), end = m_primary->end();
       i != end; ++i) {
    // Pixel result
    Color luminance = Colors::zero();
    Color alpha = Colors::zero();
    // Transmittance functions to be averaged
    std::vector<ColorCurve::CPtr> tf, lf;
```

Each pixel in the final image is built from a number of *subpixels*. The
number of subpixels is always the same in both the x- and y-dimensions,
so the value that the user selects actually gives N^2 pixel samples. Although a clever distribution could be used for the pixel samples, PVR
just picks a random position on the pixel, which keeps the code simple.
The setup of the sample position is handled by **setupSample()**.

Code 11.8. Renderer::setupSample()

```
void Renderer::setupSample(const float xCenter, const float yCenter,
                           const size_t xSubpixel, const size_t ySubpixel,
                           float &xSample, float &ySample, PTime &pTime) const
{
  const size_t numSamples = m_params.numPixelSamples;

  xSample = xCenter;
  ySample = yCenter;
  if (m_params.doRandomizePixelSamples) {
```

```
    xSample += m_rng.nextf() - 0.5f;
    ySample += m_rng.nextf() - 0.5f;
  }
  pTime = PTime((xSubpixel + ySubpixel * numSamples + m_rng.nextf()) /
                (numSamples * numSamples));
}
```

PTime, 15

Each subpixel has an associated **PTime** instance. The time samples do use a stratified distribution because PVR is more dependent on good sample distributions in time to produce motion blur than it is on nice sampling across the pixel for antialiasing purposes. For each subpixel sample, time is chosen according to the formula

$$t = \frac{i + \zeta}{N},$$

where $\zeta \in [0, 1]$ is the random variable, i is the current subpixel number, and N is the total number of subpixels.

Code 11.9. Renderer::execute()

```
// For each pixel sample (in x/y)
for (size_t iX = 0; iX < numSamples; iX++) {
  for (size_t iY = 0; iY < numSamples; iY++) {
    // Set up the next sample
    float xSample, ySample;
    PTime pTime(0.0);
    setupSample(i.rsX(), i.rsY(), iX, iY, xSample, ySample, pTime);
```

Once the pixel and time samples have been set up, the ray is integrated using **integrateRay()**, and the **luminance** and **alpha** variables are updated to accumulate the values from the result.

Code 11.10. Renderer::execute()

```
// Render pixel
IntegrationResult result = integrateRay(xSample, ySample, pTime);
// Update accumulated result
luminance += result.luminance;
alpha     += Colors::one() - result.transmittance;
if (result.transmittanceFunction) {
  tf.push_back(result.transmittanceFunction);
}
if (result.luminanceFunction) {
  lf.push_back(result.luminanceFunction);
}
    }
  }
}
```

After each subpixel has been integrated and the value recorded, the **luminance** and **alpha** variables are divided by the total number of pixel samples that was taken. Those values are then set directly in the output image.

The deep luminance and transmittance functions can't be normalized as easily. Each one contains a fixed number of samples, but the sample locations vary. To produce a single resulting pixel function, the **Curve<T>::average()** function is used.

Code 11.11. Renderer::execute()

```
// Normalize luminance and transmittance
luminance *= 1.0 / std::pow(m_params.numPixelSamples, 2.0);
alpha     *= 1.0 / std::pow(m_params.numPixelSamples, 2.0);
// Update resulting image and transmittance/luminance maps
i.setPixel(luminance);
i.setPixelAlpha((alpha.x + alpha.y + alpha.z) / 3.0f);
if (tf.size() > 0) {
  m_deepTransmittance->setPixel(i.x, i.y, ColorCurve::average(tf));
}
if (lf.size() > 0) {
  m_deepLuminance->setPixel(i.x, i.y, ColorCurve::average(lf));
}
  }
}
```

The **average()** function is used to turn N number of **Curve** instances into a single one.

Curve, 16

11.2.4   The **RayState** Struct

One of the most important utility classes in PVR is the **RayState**. It holds all the information about the current ray.

RayState, 210

wsRay   The current ray, defined in world space. For a primary/ camera ray, this has its origin at the camera position and direction towards the pixel being rendered. See Section 11.2.1 for details. For secondary/shadow rays, the origin is at the point along the primary ray that is currently being shaded, and the direction aims towards the current light source.

Setting Up Rays, 205

tMin   The parametric distance to start raymarching at. This will generally be 0.0.

tMax   The parametric distance to stop raymarching at. For a camera ray, this will be a large value, such as **std::numeric_limits <double>::max()**. When a **Raymarcher** intersects the current

Raymarcher, 268

ray against the scene, it checks *tMin* and *tMax* to potentially shorten the segment of the ray that gets raymarched; *tMax* is primarily used for shadow rays, when it gets set to the distance between the ray origin and the light source.

rayDepth   The current ray depth: 0 for a camera ray and 1+ for secondary rays. In general, PVR never uses rays with depth greater than 1.

rayType   Specifies what type of raymarch calculation is required. By default, the value is **FullRaymarch**, which asks the **Raymarcher** instance to compute both luminance and transmittance for the ray. When firing a secondary ray, however, *rayType* is set to **TransmittanceOnly**, which allows the raymarcher to do less work, only computing transmittance along the ray.

time   The current time of the ray. This is a **PTime** and determines the time in a $[0, 1]$ interval, between shutter open and shutter close

times. Section 2.1 describes **PTime** in more detail.

doOutputDeepL   Tells the **Raymarcher** whether deep luminance is requested. In PVR, this is mostly used for debugging, but in a production environment, these data would be valid to use for deep compositing.

doOutputDeepT   Tells the **Raymarcher** to output deep transmittance data. The deep data are used in PVR for creating transmittance maps, but it would also be useable for deep compositing.

Code 11.12. The **RayState** struct

```
struct RayState
{
  enum RayType {
    FullRaymarch,
    TransmittanceOnly,
  };
  RayState()
    : tMin(0.0),
      tMax(std::numeric_limits<double>::max()),
      rayDepth(0),
      rayType(FullRaymarch),
      time(0.0f),
      doOutputDeepL(false),
      doOutputDeepT(false)
  { }
  Ray     wsRay;
  double  tMin;
```

```
  double   tMax;
  size_t   rayDepth;
  RayType  rayType;
  PTime    time;
  bool     doOutputDeepL;
  bool     doOutputDeepT;
};
```

11.2.5 The RenderGlobals Class

In contrast to the **RayState** struct, which stores information about the *current* state of the renderer, the **RenderGlobals** class stores information about the renderer that doesn't change during execution.

RayState, 210

fps() Returns the current setting for frames per second. This is used when converting velocity in m/s into *motion*, which tells us how far something moves from one frame to the next.

shutter() The shutter length, or the duration that the camera shutter stays open for. The value is in the $[0,1]$ range, corresponding to a shutter angle of $0°$ and $360°$, respectively.

dt() Returns the length of the current render frame. This is short-hand for 1.0 * **shutter() / fps()**.

setupMotionBlur() Sets the frame rate and shutter angle to use for rendering. This is called explicitly in the rendering script. If the user never calls it, PVR's defaults for motion blur are 24 frames per second and 0.0 shutter length.

setScene() Sets the scene pointer so that all parts of the renderer can access it during rendering by calling **RenderGlobals::scene()**.

setCamera() Sets the camera pointer, making it available through the **RenderGlobals::camera()** function.

Code 11.13. The **RenderGlobals** class

```
class RenderGlobals
{
public:
  // Typedefs
  typedef boost::shared_ptr<const pvr::Render::Scene> SceneCPtr;
  typedef boost::shared_ptr<const pvr::Render::Camera> CameraCPtr;
```

```
   // Exceptions
   DECLARE_PVR_RT_EXC(BadFpsException, "Bad frames per second value:");
   DECLARE_PVR_RT_EXC(BadShutterException, "Bad shutter value:");
   // Main methods
   static void        setupMotionBlur(const float fps, const float shutter);
   static void        setScene(SceneCPtr scene);
   static void        setCamera(CameraCPtr camera);
   // Accessors
   static float       fps();
   static float       shutter();
   static float       dt();
   static SceneCPtr   scene();
   static CameraCPtr  camera();
private:
   // Data members
   static float       ms_fps;
   static float       ms_shutter;
   static float       ms_dt;
   static SceneCPtr   ms_scene;
   static CameraCPtr  ms_camera;
};
```

11.3   The **Camera** Base Class

The **Camera** class is the base class for the included camera types in PVR.
Although the concrete camera types are very different, some using non-
linear transforms, a few properties are common between the various
types: all cameras have a position, an orientation, and an image resolution. The resolution is assumed to be fixed over the course of a single
render frame, but both the position and orientation may change, which
introduces camera motion blur. Time-dependent properties are handled
using the **pvr::Util::Curve<T>** class, with position expressed as a vector
and the orientation as a quaternion.

Curve, 16

Cameras, 18
Camera Coordinate Spaces, 19

For a general overview of PVR's cameras and coordinate spaces, see
Sections 2.2 and 2.2.1.

Code 11.14. The **Camera** class

```
class Camera
{
public:
...
  // Constructor, destructor, factory
  Camera();
  virtual ~Camera();
...
protected:
...
```

```
  // Protected data members
  Util::VectorCurve m_position;
  Util::QuatCurve m_orientation;
  Imath::V2i m_resolution;
  uint m_numSamples;
  MatrixVec m_cameraToWorld;
  MatrixVec m_worldToCamera;
};
```

Using time-varying properties is so fundamental to PVR that the only way to set the position and orientation attributes is to pass in a **Curve**. And conversely, in order to query the attributes of the camera, a time argument must be specified. Time is always specified using the **PTime** class, and the time scale assumed in the function curves is also presumed to be aligned according to the **PTime** definition from Section 2.1.

Curve, 16

PTime, 15

Time and Motion Blur, 13

Code 11.15. The **Camera** class

```
class Camera
{
public:
...
  // Placement
  void setPosition(const Util::VectorCurve &curve);
  Vector position(const PTime time) const;
  void setOrientation(const Util::QuatCurve &curve);
  Quat orientation(const PTime time) const;
...
protected:
...};
```

By default, cameras in PVR have a resolution of 640×480. If the resolution needs to be changed, it is done using the **setResolution()** member function. Although it is common for production renderers to specify a crop region or overscan area to render, PVR supports only a basic resolution control, for purposes of simplicity.

Code 11.16. The **Camera** class

```
class Camera
{
public:
...
  // Resolution
  void setResolution(const Imath::V2i &resolution);
  const Imath::V2i& resolution() const;
...
protected:
...};
```

The external interface to the camera permits each attribute to have an arbitrary number of samples, which can be arbitrarily spaced in time. Internally, however, the **Camera** classes use a fixed set of time samples that get spaced evenly over the $[0, 1]$ **PTime** interval. By default, two time samples are used: one at the start of the frame, at shutter open time, and the second at the end of the frame, at shutter close time. Whenever the camera needs to transform a point at a time in between the two time samples, a linear interpolation of the motion is used. If the user desires, the number of time samples can be increased by calling the member function **setNumTimeSamples()**.

Code 11.17. The **Camera** class

```
class Camera
{
public:
...
  // Motion blur settings
  void setNumTimeSamples(const uint numSamples);
  uint numTimeSamples() const ;
...
protected:
...};
```

The only transform that the **Camera** class itself implements goes from world space to camera space and vice versa and requires a **PTime** argument, as the transforms are assumed to be time varying.

In the function **computeCameraToWorld** below, we will look at how the camera's position and orientation attributes are used to build the set of transformation matrices used for these transforms. Once built, the full set of transformation matrices can be accessed through **worldToCameraMatri ces()** and **cameraToWorldMatrices()**.

Code 11.18. The **Camera** class

```
class Camera
{
public:
...
  // Transforms
  Vector worldToCamera(const Vector &wsP, const PTime time) const;
  Vector cameraToWorld(const Vector &csP, const PTime time) const;
  const MatrixVec& worldToCameraMatrices() const;
  const MatrixVec& cameraToWorldMatrices() const;
...
protected:
...};
```

Besides the world/camera transforms, the **Camera** base class requires **Camera**, 213
that subclasses provide a set of member functions that transform to and
from screen and raster space. And although the world-to-camera transforms are implemented as transformation matrices, there is no assumption that subclasses implement their screen- and raster-space transformations the same way.

Subclasses also need to implement **canTransformNegativeCamZ()**, which
tells PVR whether points behind the camera are part of the camera's
screen space.

Code 11.19. The **Camera** class

```
class Camera
{
public:
...
  // To be implemented by subclasses
  virtual Vector worldToScreen(const Vector &wsP, const PTime time) const = 0;
  virtual Vector screenToWorld(const Vector &ssP, const PTime time) const = 0;
  virtual Vector worldToRaster(const Vector &wsP, const PTime time) const = 0;
  virtual Vector rasterToWorld(const Vector &rsP, const PTime time) const = 0;
  virtual bool canTransformNegativeCamZ() const = 0;
...
protected:
...};
```

11.3.1 Camera Transformations

Whenever the user changes the position, orientation, resolution, or time
sample settings of a **Camera**, the internal camera-to-world and world-to-
camera matrices must be recomputed. As we mentioned, multiple matrices are used, one for each time sample. The first step is therefore to
resize the **m_cameraToWorld** and **m_worldToCamera** vectors to fit the appropriate number of time samples.

Code 11.20. The **Camera::recomputeTransforms()** method

```
void Camera::recomputeTransforms()
{
  m_cameraToWorld.resize(m_numSamples);
  m_worldToCamera.resize(m_numSamples);
```

Then, for each time sample, we first find the **PTime** using the utility **PTime**, 15
function **parametric()**, which returns a value suitable for **PTime** use, ac-

cording to the formula

$$t = \frac{i}{N-1}.$$

The **time** variable given by **parametric** is passed to **computeCameraToWorld()**, which builds the given time sample's transformation matrix. The world-to-camera transform is simply taken as the the inverse.

Code 11.21. The **Camera::recomputeTransforms()** method

```
for (uint i = 0; i < m_numSamples; ++i) {
  // Compute position in open/close parametric shutter time
  PTime time(Math::parametric(i, m_numSamples));
  // Compute transformation matrix at given time
  m_cameraToWorld[i] = computeCameraToWorld(time);
  m_worldToCamera[i] = m_cameraToWorld[i].inverse();
}
}
```

To find the camera-to-world transform, we first interpolate values from the position and orientation curves at the current **time**.

Code 11.22. The **Camera::computeCameraToWorld()** method

```
Matrix Camera::computeCameraToWorld(const PTime time) const
{
  // Interpolate current position and orientation
  Vector position    = m_position.interpolate(time);
  Quat   orientation = m_orientation.interpolate(time);
```

The camera-to-world transform can now be found by first flipping the z-axis,[3] applying rotations, and finally translating the camera into its position:

$$\mathbf{M}_{\text{camera}} = \mathbf{M}_z \cdot \mathbf{M}_{\text{rotate}} \cdot \mathbf{M}_{\text{translate}}.$$

The translation matrix is found using the **Imath::Matrix44** member function **setTranslation()**, which builds a matrix along the form

$$\mathbf{M}_{\text{translate}} = \begin{pmatrix} 1 & 0 & 0 & 0 \\ 0 & 1 & 0 & 0 \\ 0 & 0 & 1 & 0 \\ x & y & z & 1 \end{pmatrix}.$$

---

[3]As we mentioned earlier, the camera space is left-handed, with positive camera-space z-coordinates corresponding to negative world-space z-coordinates.

The rotation matrix is computed by taking the coefficients of the orientation quaternion $(x \; y \; z \; w)$ and building a matrix according to

$$\mathbf{M}_{\text{rotate}} = \begin{pmatrix} 1 - 2y^2 - 2z^2 & 2xy - 2zw & 2xz + 2yw & 0 \\ 2xy + 2zq & 1 - 2x^2 - 2z^2 & 2yz - 2xw & 0 \\ 2xz - 2yw & 2yz + 2xw & 1 - 2x^2 - 2y^2 & 0 \\ 0 & 0 & 0 & 1 \end{pmatrix}.$$

The matrix that flips the z-axis is a simple scaling matrix, with the z-component set to -1:

$$\mathbf{M}_z = \begin{pmatrix} 1 & 0 & 0 & 0 \\ 0 & 1 & 0 & 0 \\ 0 & 0 & -1 & 0 \\ 0 & 0 & 0 & 1 \end{pmatrix}.$$

Code 11.23. The `Camera::computeCameraToWorld()` method

```
// Compute transformation components
Matrix translation, rotation, flipZ;
translation.setTranslation(position);
rotation = orientation.toMatrix44();
flipZ.setScale(Vector(1.0, 1.0, -1.0));
return flipZ * rotation * translation;
}
```

11.3.2 Transforming Points

When the camera is asked to transform a point either from camera to world space or vice versa, both functions use the internal utility function `transformPoint()` to do the work.

Code 11.24. The `Camera::worldToCamera()` method

```
Vector Camera::worldToCamera(const Vector &wsP, const PTime time) const
{
  return transformPoint(wsP, m_worldToCamera, time);
}
```

The `transformPoint()` function takes a point, an array of transformation matrices, and a point in time. The transformation matrices are assumed to be spaced evenly in time, with the first and last falling at PTime 0.0 and 1.0, respectively. Figure 11.3 illustrates the configuration.

PTime, 15

When transforming a point, we first find the two neighboring matrices as well as the relative distance to them. We let t be a position in the

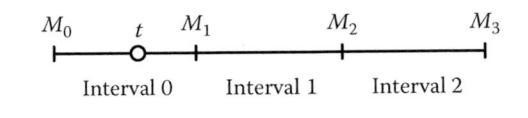

Figure 11.3. Illustration of time sample matrices.

interval $[0, N-1]$, based on the incoming **time**. The lowest nearest-matrix index is i, and the position of the time sample t between i and $i+1$ is l:

$$t = \frac{\text{time}}{1/(N-1)},$$
$$i = \lfloor t \rfloor,$$
$$l = t - i.$$

Code 11.25. The **Camera::transformPoint()** method

```
Vector Camera::transformPoint(const Vector &p,
                              const std::vector<Matrix> &matrices,
                              const PTime time) const
{
  // Calculate which interval to interpolate in
  double stepSize     = 1.0 / static_cast<float>(m_numSamples - 1);
  double t            = time / stepSize;
  uint   first        = static_cast<uint>(std::floor(t));
  uint   second       = first + 1;
  second              = std::min(second, m_numSamples - 1);
  double lerpFactor = t - static_cast<double>(first);
```

Once we know i and l, we can transform the point p using the two nearest matrices and then interpolate the result based on l. The interpolation gives us a linearly varying transform over time. The cost of the transform, however, is independent of how many time samples are used, so curved motion blur can be achieved simply by increasing the number of time samples, if the position and/or orientation curves contain curved motion.

Code 11.26. The **Camera::transformPoint()** method

```
  // Transform point twice
  Vector t0         = p * matrices[first];
  Vector t1         = p * matrices[second];
  // Interpolate transformed positions
  return lerp(t0, t1, lerpFactor);
}
```

11.4   The `PerspectiveCamera` Class

The most commonly used camera type in production rendering tends to be a standard perspective projection camera. In PVR, this is implemented in the `PerspectiveCamera` class. The perspective transform does not require many parameters on top of what the `Camera` base class uses, but two are very important: the clipping planes of the projection and the field of view. (See Figure 11.4.)

Camera, 213

In many types of surface rendering, the clipping planes are an integral part of the rendering system, and only geometry between the two can be transformed correctly into view and rendered. In PVR, and in most production volume rendering systems, cameras are used mostly to spawn rays in appropriate directions, and clipping planes do not actually need to clip what is being rendered. So the near and far planes only define how the z-component of the screen space and raster space maps into world space.

The field of view of the perspective camera controls how wide the projection is. It is essentially the same as changing the focal length of a physical camera: a large field of view corresponds to a wide angle lens. While it would be possible to specify the projection as a focal length rather than an angle, there are some drawbacks to that approach. An angle always has a well-defined projection, whereas the projection of a given focal length also depends on the size of the receiving medium (i.e., a film frame or a CCD/CMOS sensor). For example, a 50-mm lens mounted on a normal 35-mm film camera projects a much more narrow field of view onto the capturing film than if a lens of the same focal length was mounted on a 60-mm medium format camera.

The `PerspectiveCamera` implements all of the virtual member functions required by `Camera` and also offers control over the clip planes and the field of view. (See Figure 11.5.) The clip planes are presumed to be

Camera, 213

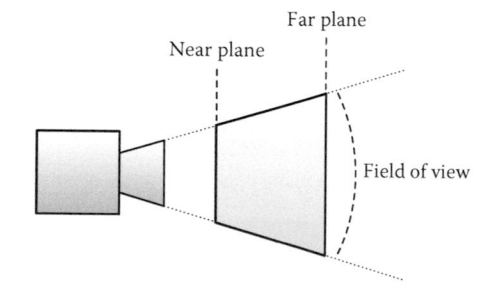

Figure 11.4. A perspective projection has a near plane, a far plane, and a field of view.

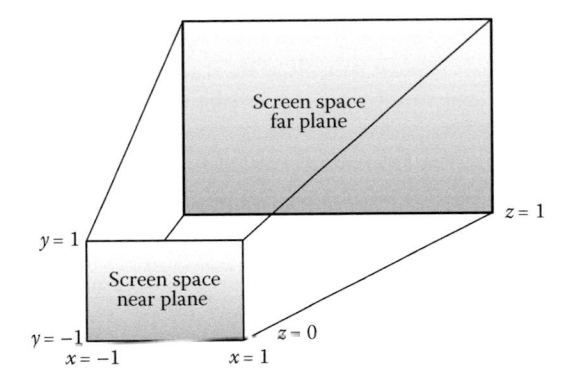

Figure 11.5. PVR's convention for the screen space coordinate system.

constant over the duration of each rendered frame, but the field of view is allowed to change, making it possible to account for motion blur due to zooming.

Code 11.27. The **PerspectiveCamera** class

```
class PerspectiveCamera : public Camera
{
public:
...
  // Main methods
  void setClipPlanes(const double near, const double far);
  void setVerticalFOV(const Util::FloatCurve &curve);
...
  // From Camera
  PVR_DEFINE_STATIC_CLONE_FUNC(PerspectiveCamera);
  virtual Vector worldToScreen(const Vector &wsP, const PTime time) const;
  virtual Vector screenToWorld(const Vector &ssP, const PTime time) const;
  virtual Vector worldToRaster(const Vector &wsP, const PTime time) const;
  virtual Vector rasterToWorld(const Vector &rsP, const PTime time) const;
  virtual bool canTransformNegativeCamZ() const;
...
protected:
  // From Camera
  virtual void recomputeTransforms();
...
private:
...};
```

The **PerspectiveCamera** class also implements **recomputeTransforms()** to respond to changes to the camera's user parameters. When using a virtual function that is implemented in several classes in the inheritance hierarchy, only the lowest-level function is called. Of course, we still want the **Camera** base class to initialize its transformation matrices, so the first thing the subclass must do is to explicitly call the base class. Once the base class has recomputed its transforms, we proceed to resizing the **PerspectiveCamera**'s own transform matrices.

Camera, 213

Code 11.28. The `PerspectiveCamera::recomputeTransforms()` method

```
void PerspectiveCamera::recomputeTransforms()
{
  Camera::recomputeTransforms();

  m_worldToScreen.resize(m_numSamples);
  m_screenToWorld.resize(m_numSamples);
  m_worldToRaster.resize(m_numSamples);
  m_rasterToWorld.resize(m_numSamples);
```

The structure of the function is very similar to the base class's version. We loop over each time sample, create the respective **PTime**, and then build transform matrices that are stored in the appropriate vectors. The only real difference is that while the **Camera** base class used **computeCameraToWorld**, the perspective camera has **getTransforms()**, which builds a camera-to-screen and screen-to-raster transformation matrix.

Camera, 213

Code 11.29. The `PerspectiveCamera::recomputeTransforms()` method

```
  Matrix cameraToScreen, screenToRaster;

  for (uint i = 0; i < m_numSamples; ++i) {
    // Compute position in open/close parametric shutter time
    PTime time(Math::parametric(i, m_numSamples));
    // Compute matrices
    getTransforms(time, cameraToScreen, screenToRaster);
    m_worldToScreen[i] = m_worldToCamera[i] * camcraToScreen;
    m_screenToWorld[i] = m_worldToScreen[i].inverse();
    m_worldToRaster[i] = m_worldToScreen[i] * screenToRaster;
    m_rasterToWorld[i] = m_worldToRaster[i].inverse();
  }
}
```

The most interesting part of the **PerspectiveCamera** is implemented in the **getTransforms()** method. It is responsible for computing transformation matrices that go from camera to screen space and then from screen space to raster space.

The first step is to create the perspective projection matrix $\mathbf{M}_{\text{perspective}}$ based on the near plane n and far plane f:

$$\mathbf{M}_{\text{perspective}} = \begin{pmatrix} 1 & 0 & 0 & 0 \\ 0 & 1 & 0 & 0 \\ 0 & 0 & f/(f-n) & 1 \\ 0 & 0 & -f \cdot n/(f-n) & 0 \end{pmatrix}.$$

Code 11.30. The **PerspectiveCamera::getTransforms()** method

```
void PerspectiveCamera::getTransforms(const PTime time,
                                      Matrix &cameraToScreen,
                                      Matrix &screenToRaster) const
{
  // Standard projection matrix
  Matrix perspective(1, 0, 0, 0,
                     0, 1, 0, 0,
                     0, 0, (m_far) / (m_far - m_near),                1,
                     0, 0, (-m_far * m_near) / (m_far - m_near), 0);
```

The perspective projection has a natural field of view of $90°$ in both the x- and y-dimensions. In order to adapt this to the field of view selected by the user, and also to the aspect ratio of the image, we will scale the projection in the x,y-plane accordingly.

The scaling factor can be found by studying Figure 11.6. We want to find the length of b, given a user-specified field of view f. This scaling factor can then be used to multiply the projection matrix so that the appropriate field of view is achieved.

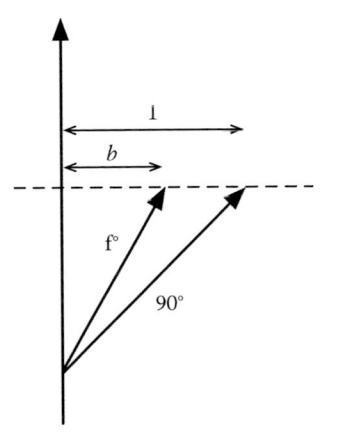

Figure 11.6. The scaling factor b can be found using the expression $b = \tan^{-1}\frac{f}{2}$.

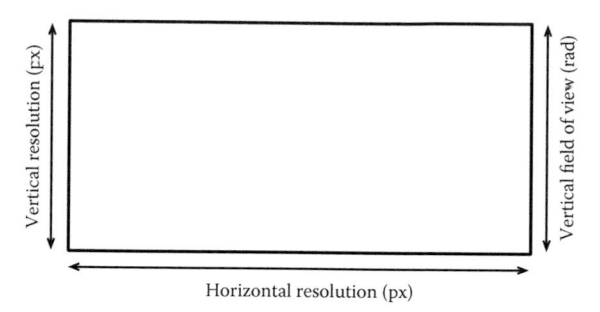

Figure 11.7. The relationship between vertical and horizontal field of view is the same as between vertical and horizontal image resolution.

In PVR, the user only specifies the field of view along the vertical dimension. Technically, we could let the user specify both a vertical and horizontal field of view, but that would force the user to manually calculate values that matched the relative dimensions of the image. Instead, we find the horizontal field of view by looking at the vertical value and scaling by the aspect ratio of the image. (See Figure 11.7.)

The matrix that scales the perspective projection matrix to the appropriate field of view can then be found as

$$b_v = \tan^{-1} \frac{f_v}{2},$$

$$b_h = b_v \cdot \frac{r_x}{r_y},$$

$$\mathbf{M}_{\text{fov}} = \begin{pmatrix} b_h & 0 & 0 & 0 \\ 0 & b_v & 0 & 0 \\ 0 & 0 & 1 & 0 \\ 0 & 0 & 0 & 1 \end{pmatrix}.$$

Code 11.31. The `PerspectiveCamera::getTransforms()` method

```
// Field of view
double fovDegrees       = m_verticalFOV.interpolate(0.0);
double fovRadians       = fovDegrees * M_PI / 180.0;
double invTan           = 1.0f / std::tan(fovRadians / 2.0f);
double imageAspectRatio = static_cast<double>(m_resolution.x) /
  static_cast<double>(m_resolution.y);
Matrix fov;
fov.setScale(Vector(invTan / imageAspectRatio, invTan, 1.0));
```

Finally, we build the matrix $\mathbf{M}_{\text{screen}}$ from $\mathbf{M}_{\text{perspective}}$ and $\mathbf{M}_{\text{fov}}$.

Code 11.32. The **PerspectiveCamera::getTransforms()** method

```
// Build camera to screen matrix
cameraToScreen = perspective * fov;
```

The transformation from screen space to NDC space is more straight-forward than the perspective transform, since all that's needed is to scale and translate the $[-1, 1]$ range of screen space to the $[0, 1]$ range of NDC space. Likewise, the transform from NDC space to raster space is just a scaling from $[0, 1]$ to $[0, r]$:

$$\mathbf{N}_{\text{translate}} = \begin{pmatrix} 1 & 0 & 0 & 0 \\ 0 & 1 & 0 & 0 \\ 0 & 0 & 1 & 0 \\ 1 & 1 & 0 & 1 \end{pmatrix},$$

$$\mathbf{N}_{\text{scale}} = \begin{pmatrix} 0.5 & 0 & 0 & 0 \\ 0 & 0.5 & 0 & 0 \\ 0 & 0 & 1 & 0 \\ 0 & 0 & 0 & 1 \end{pmatrix},$$

$$\mathbf{M}_{\text{ndc}} = \mathbf{N}_{\text{translate}} \cdot \mathbf{N}_{\text{scale}}.$$

Code 11.33. The **PerspectiveCamera::getTransforms()** method

```
// NDC to screen space
Matrix ndcTranslate, ndcScale;
ndcTranslate.setTranslation(Vector(1.0, 1.0, 0.0));
ndcScale.setScale(Vector(0.5, 0.5, 1.0));
Matrix screenToNdc = ndcTranslate * ndcScale;
```

$$\mathbf{M}_{\text{res}} = \begin{pmatrix} r_x & 0 & 0 & 0 \\ 0 & r_y & 0 & 0 \\ 0 & 0 & 1 & 0 \\ 0 & 0 & 0 & 1 \end{pmatrix}.$$

Code 11.34. The `PerspectiveCamera::getTransforms()` method

```
// Raster to NDC space
Matrix rasterToNdc, ndcToRaster;
ndcToRaster.setScale(Vector(m_resolution.x, m_resolution.y, 1.0));
rasterToNdc = ndcToRaster.inverse();
```

The screen-to-raster matrix $\mathbf{M}_{\mathrm{raster}}$ is finally computed from $\mathbf{M}_{\mathrm{ndc}}$ and $\mathbf{M}_{\mathrm{res}}$.

Code 11.35. The `PerspectiveCamera::getTransforms()` method

```
// Build screen to raster matrix
screenToRaster = screenToNdc * ndcToRaster;
```

11.5   The `SphericalCamera` Class

Besides the perspective projection camera, PVR also supports a spherical projection camera. The spherical camera has one especially important feature. Whereas a perspective camera at most is able to see $f < 180°$, the spherical camera can see in all directions. The two main uses for the spherical camera is to produce environment map renders and to act as a shadow map projection for point lights.

When it comes to spherical coordinates, there is a variety of conventions. Mathematicians tend to use a coordinate system where the z-axis

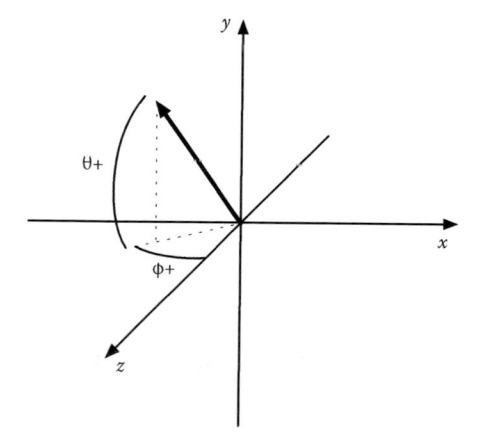

Figure 11.8. PVR's spherical coordinate system

faces up, but in computer graphics, we prefer a coordinate space where the y-axis is up (see Figure 11.8). Likewise, the symbols used to label the elevation (latitude, declination) and azimuthal (longitude, right ascension) angles sometime get exchanged, although ϕ and θ tend to be the two symbols used.

In PVR, the radial dimension is referred to as r, the latitude as θ, and the longitude dimension as ϕ: r is the Euclidian distance from origin to the point, and it can assume any non-negative value; θ is defined to lie in the range $\left[-\frac{\pi}{2}, \frac{\pi}{2}\right]$, and its zero value lies exactly in the x, z-plane of the Cartesian coordinate system; and ϕ has a range of $[-\pi, \pi]$, and its zero value corresponds to the heading of the z-axis in the Cartesian coordinate space.

For convenience's sake, PVR provides the **SphericalCoords** struct for storing spherical coordinates.

Code 11.36. The SphericalCoords struct

```
struct SphericalCoords
{
  float radius;
  float latitude;
  float longitude;
  SphericalCoords()
    : radius(0.0f), latitude(0.0f), longitude(0.0f)
  { }
};
```

Camera, 213

Since the **SphericalCamera** class sees in all directions, there is no need for any user parameters apart from what the **Camera** provides. The only added member functions are **cartToSphere()**, which transforms a point in Cartesian coordinates to spherical coordinates, and **sphereToCart()**, which performs the inverse transformation.

Code 11.37. The SphericalCamera class

```
class SphericalCamera : public Camera
{
public:
...
protected:
...
  // Utility methods
  SphericalCoords cartToSphere(const Vector &cs) const;
  Vector sphereToCart(const SphericalCoords &ss) const;
...
private:
...};
```

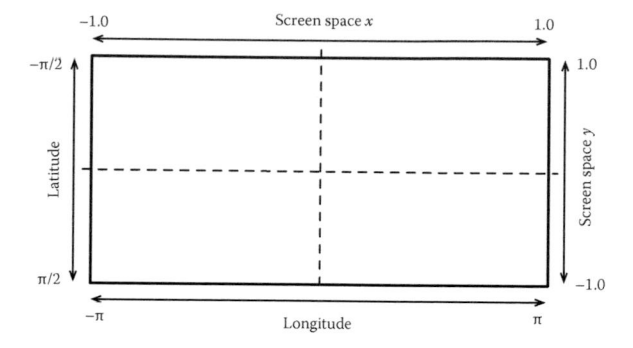

Figure 11.9. Mapping spherical coordinates to the camera's screen space.

The basic premise of the spherical camera is that world space and camera space remain Cartesian, but screen space and raster space use the spherical projection. It is also important to remember that we are interested in spherical coordinates that are centered on the position of the camera, not on the world-space origin.

In order to transform a point p_w from world space to screen space, we first transform it into camera space. This centers the point around the camera, setting it up for the transformation to spherical coordinates performed by **cartToSphere()**. Once the spherical coordinates are found, they need to be remapped into the valid range of the screen-space coordinate system. (See Figure 11.9.) This is done simply by dividing by the range limits of the spherical coordinate system:

$$p_{\text{screen}} = \left(\frac{\phi}{\pi}, \frac{\theta}{\pi/2}, \rho \right).$$

We note that the radial coordinate ρ is left unchanged. It contains the distance from the point to the camera position, and as such, is perfectly suited to be stored in the image as the z-dimension, or *depth*.

Code 11.38. The **SphericalCamera::worldToScreen()** method

```
Vector SphericalCamera::worldToScreen(const Vector &wsP, const PTime time)
    const
{
  Vector csP = worldToCamera(wsP, time);
  SphericalCoords sc = cartToSphere(csP);
  return Vector(sc.longitude / M_PI, sc.latitude / (M_PI * 0.5), sc.radius);
}
```

The `cartToSphere()` function follows the standard textbook equations for transforming from Cartesian to spherical coordinates, although the axes of the Cartesian space are adapted to suit PVR's y-up convention, and the range of θ is made to be $\left[\frac{\pi}{2}, -\frac{\pi}{2}\right]$ rather than the standard $[0, \pi]$:

$$\rho = \sqrt{x^2 + y^2 + z^2},$$

$$\theta = \frac{\pi}{2} - \arccos\left(\frac{y}{\rho}\right),$$

$$\phi = \arctan\left(\frac{x}{z}\right).$$

Code 11.39. The `SphericalCamera::cartToSphere()` method

```
SphericalCoords SphericalCamera::cartToSphere(const Vector &cc) const
{
  SphericalCoords sc;

  sc.radius = std::sqrt(cc.x * cc.x + cc.y * cc.y + cc.z * cc.z);

  if (sc.radius == 0.0) {
    return SphericalCoords();
  }

  sc.longitude = atan2(cc.x, cc.z);
  sc.latitude  = M_PI * 0.5 - acos(cc.y / sc.radius);

  return sc;
}
```

When we transform from screen space to world space, we simply do the inverse calculation. First, the screen-space coordinate is remapped to spherical coordinates, which is the direct inverse of the division that was done above to go from spherical coordinates to screen-space coordinates. The Cartesian coordinates that **spereToCart()** returns are in camera space, so to get back to world space, we can call **cameraToWorld()**.

Code 11.40. The `SphericalCamera::screenToWorld()` method

```
Vector SphericalCamera::screenToWorld(const Vector &ssP, const PTime time)
    const
{
  SphericalCoords sc;
  sc.longitude = ssP.x * M_PI;
  sc.latitude  = ssP.y * (M_PI * 0.5);
  sc.radius    = ssP.z;
```

```
  Vector csP = sphereToCart(sc);
  return cameraToWorld(csP, time);
}
```

The transformation from spherical to Cartesian coordinates also follows the standard literature, with the exception of adapting to PVR's coordinate system conventions:

$$x = \rho \sin\phi \sin\theta,$$
$$y = \rho \cos\theta,$$
$$z = \rho \cos\phi \sin\theta.$$

Code 11.41. The `SphericalCamera::sphereToCart()` method

```
Vector SphericalCamera::sphereToCart(const SphericalCoords &sc) const
{
  const float rho   = sc.radius;
  const float theta = 0.5 * M_PI - sc.latitude;
  const float phi   = sc.longitude;

  return Vector(rho * std::sin(phi) * std::sin(theta),
                rho * std::cos(theta),
                rho * std::cos(phi) * std::sin(theta));
}
```

11.6   Image Output

When it comes to image storage, PVR has quite simple requirements. The **Image** class is used only to store the resulting luminance and alpha for each pixel and to write those data to disk.

The RGB channels are set separately from the alpha component of the image, since luminance and transmittance are handled as separate variables in PVR. Likewise, when an image is written to disk, the **Channels** enum is used to specify whether alpha should be included or not by calling **Image::write(filename, Image::RGB)** or **Image::write(filename, Image::RGBA)**.

Internally, the **Image** class uses OpenImageIO, so a large number of file formats are supported, such as JPEG, PNG, TIFF, and OpenEXR.

Code 11.42. The **Image** class

```
class Image
{
```

```
public:
  PVR_TYPEDEF_SMART_PTRS(Image);
  // Enums
  enum Channels {
    RGB,
    RGBA
  };
  // Structs
  struct pixel_iterator;
  // Constructor, destructor, factory
  static Ptr create();
  Ptr        clone();
  // Main methods
  void       setSize(const size_t width, const size_t height);
  void       setPixel(const size_t x, const size_t y, const Color &value);
  void       setPixelAlpha(const size_t x, const size_t y, const float value);
  Imath::V2i size() const;
  Color      pixel(const size_t x, const size_t y) const;
  float      pixelAlpha(const size_t x, const size_t y) const;
  void       write(const std::string &filename, Channels channels) const;
  // Iteration
  pixel_iterator begin();
  pixel_iterator end();
private:
  // Private data members
  OpenImageIO::ImageBuf m_buf;
};
```

PVR Volume Types

12.1 Volumes in PVR

Every renderable object in PVR is a subclass of the **per::Render::Volume** class.

Volumes can be of two basic types: *source volumes* and *shader volumes*. Source volumes are able to act alone, with no inputs other than user parameters and possibly data files on disk. An example of a source volume would be a voxel buffer or a procedural volume such as a noise bank. Shader volumes, on the other hand, use other volumes (along with user parameters) as their inputs and alter their appearance in some way.

Integration Intervals, 187

Section 10.3 introduced the concept of integration intervals, which were found by intersecting the camera ray against the bounds of a volume in order to find portions of the ray that were worth raymarching. In PVR, this functionality is handled by the **Volume** class through the **intersect()** method. The function generally looks at the current **RayState**, determines

RayState, 210

the portion or portions along the ray that intersect the volume, and returns a list of intervals to the raymarcher. Because the returned list of intervals can be arbitrarily long, there is no limitation on the complexity of a **Volume**.

When a **Volume** returns an interval from the **intersect()** method, it does so using the **Interval** struct, more specifically as a **std::vector <Interval>**, which is typedef'ed for convenience as **IntervalVec**.

Code 12.1. The `Interval` struct

```
struct Interval
{
  // Constructor
  Interval(double start, double end, double step)
    : t0(start), t1(end), stepLength(step)
  { }
  // Public data members
  double t0;
  double t1;
  double stepLength;
};
```

In order to be renderable, each `Volume` must also be able to answer queries about its contents. In Chapter 13, this was done in the pseudocode by calling `vol->absorption()` and `vol->scattering()`. But hardcoding each attribute name in this way puts a limit on what properties a volume can provide, which is the opposite of what we are trying to accomplish with a flexible shading system. Rather than using the hardcoded approach, PVR uses a weaker tie between volumes, where properties are queried by name. The `Volume` class provides the `sample()` call, which takes a `VolumeSampleState`, containing information about the point being sampled, and a `VolumeAttr`, which specifies the attribute that the caller is interested in. This approach gives more flexibility, in that a volume can choose to expose any number of attributes, each with an arbitrarily selected name.

One important point to make is that volumes provide volumetric properties but never actually perform any lighting calculations, which is the domain of the `RaymarchSampler` classes.

Raymarching in PVR, 267

VolumeSampleState, 237
VolumeAttr, 235

RaymarchSampler, 285

Code 12.2. The `Volume` base class

```
class Volume : public Util::ParamBase
{
public:
  // Typedefs
  PVR_TYPEDEF_SMART_PTRS(Volume);
  typedef std::vector<std::string>  AttrNameVec;
  typedef std::vector<std::string>  StringVec;
  typedef std::vector<Volume::CPtr> CVec;
  // Constructors and destructor
  Volume();
  virtual ~Volume();
  // Main methods
  void                     setPhaseFunction(Phase::PhaseFunction::CPtr p);
  Phase::PhaseFunction::CPtr phaseFunction() const;
  // To be implemented by subclasses
  virtual AttrNameVec      attributeNames() const = 0;
  virtual VolumeSample     sample(const VolumeSampleState &state,
```

```
                                       const VolumeAttr &attribute) const = 0;
  virtual BBox              wsBounds() const = 0;
  virtual IntervalVec       intersect(const RayState &state) const = 0;
  // Optionally implemented by subclasses
  virtual StringVec         info() const;
  virtual CVec              inputs() const;
protected:
  // Data members
  Phase::PhaseFunction::CPtr m_phaseFunction;
};
```

The only nonvirtual member functions provided by **Volume** are set **PhaseFunction()** and **phaseFunction()**, which give access to each volume's phase function instance. Phase functions were introduced in Section 9.5, and PVR's implementations are outlined in Section 14.7.

The virtual **wsBounds()** function reports the world-space bounds of the volume. Although the **intersect()** function is related, the bounds are more generic, reporting on the full size of the volume rather than the intersection with a ray.

The last of the virtual calls that the **Volume** class provides is **attribute Names()**, which simply returns a list of the attributes that the volume exposes. This can be used by other volumes (especially shader volumes)

or by the **RaymarchSampler** to query what attributes a volume exposes.

12.1.1   Volume Properties and Attributes

As we mentioned in the previous section, volumetric properties are queried by name, rather than using specific member functions on a volume. This satisfies the need to expose arbitrary attributes, rather than some fixed set that is pre-determined by the renderer. And while the **Volume::sample()** call could take a **std::string** or **const char***, that would require the volume to perform string comparisons each time it was sampled in order to determine which attribute it was being queried for. Needless to say, this would be an expensive operation to perform, as well as being wasteful, since volumes tend to get sampled thousands or hundreds of thousands of times with the same attribute name.

A faster way to specify which attribute was requested by the caller would be to use an index that could be checked cheaply, but a convention for which indices to use would have to be maintained, which would be a source of error and most likely hard to debug.

PVR's solution is the **VolumeAttr** class, which combines both a string attribute name and an index in one. (See Figure 12.1.) The string representation is used the first time the object is used and requires a string comparison to be executed. But once the attribute name has been determined, an index is stored in the **VolumeAttr** that can then be used for

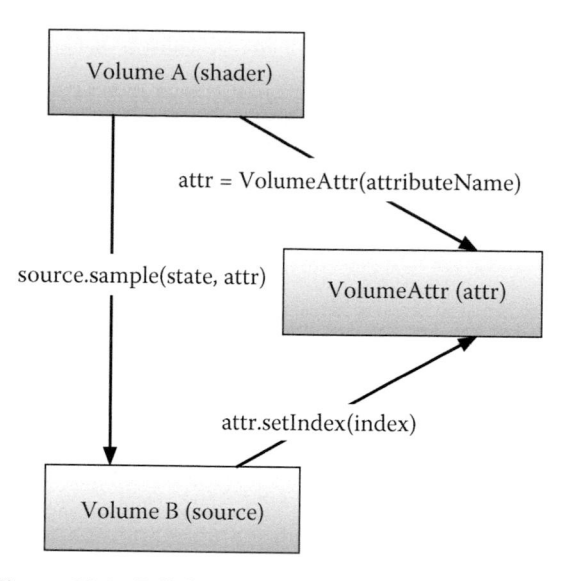

Figure 12.1. Collaboration diagram for **VolumeAttr**.

further comparisons. That way, the cost of the string comparison is amortized over a very large number of calls, essentially making it free.

It's important to consider that the **VolumeAttr** class has two clients: the caller, which specifies the attribute to be sampled using the string representation, and the callee, which is responsible for interpreting the string and assigning an integer index that will be meaningful to the callee the next time **sample()** is called. It follows that a **VolumeAttr** cannot be shared between two volumes, as each one is allowed to assign an arbitrary index to represent the given attribute name.

Code 12.3. The **VolumeAttr** class

```
class VolumeAttr
{
public:
  // Enums
  static const int IndexNotSet  = -1;
  static const int IndexInvalid = -2;
...
  // Constructors
  VolumeAttr(const std::string &name);
  // Main methods
  const std::string& name() const;
  int                index() const;
  void               setIndex(const int index) const;
  void               setIndexInvalid() const;
private:
```

```
// Data members
std::string m_name;
mutable int m_index;
};
```

12.1.2   The `VolumeSampleState` Struct

The `VolumeSampleState` struct wraps up the information needed when sampling a volume. It contains a reference to the current **RayState** as well as the world-space sample position.

Code 12.4. The `VolumeSampleState` struct

```
struct VolumeSampleState
{
  VolumeSampleState(const RayState &rState)
    : rayState(rState)
  { }
  const RayState &rayState;
  Vector wsP;
};
```

12.1.3   The `VolumeSample` Struct

The `VolumeSample` struct holds the result of a call to `Volume::sample()`, which is the value of the attribute requested, but also a pointer to the phase function that can answer what the scattering probability is at the given point.

We will return to the use of this phase function when we study the raymarch samplers in Section 14.1 and PVR's implementation of phase functions in Section 14.7.

Code 12.5. The `VolumeSample` struct

```
struct VolumeSample
{
  // Constructors
  VolumeSample(const Color &v, Phase::PhaseFunction::CPtr p)
    : value(v), phaseFunction(p)
  { }
  // Public data members
  Color value;
  Phase::PhaseFunction::CPtr phaseFunction;
};
```

Figure 12.2. A single **ConstantVolume**.

12.2 The **ConstantVolume** Class

To introduce PVR's various **Volume** subclasses, we will start with **Constant Volume**. As the name indicates, it is a source volume whose value is constant throughout its domain. Although simple, it illustrates well the steps we need to go through in order to make it possible to bound, intersect, and sample a volume. (See Figure 12.2.)

Volume, 233

Code 12.6. The **ConstantVolume** class

```
class ConstantVolume : public Volume
{
public:
...
  // Main methods
  void addAttribute(const std::string &attrName, const Imath::V3f &value);
...
```

```
     // From Volume
     virtual AttrNameVec        attributeNames() const;
     virtual VolumeSample       sample(const VolumeSampleState &state,
                                       const VolumeAttr &attribute) const;
     virtual BBox               wsBounds() const;
     virtual IntervalVec        intersect(const RayState &state) const;
     virtual Volume::StringVec info() const;
  protected:
     ...
     // Data members
     Util::MatrixCurve        m_localToWorld;
     Util::MatrixCurve        m_worldToLocal;
     BBox                     m_wsBounds;
     AttrNameVec              m_attrNames;
     std::vector<Imath::V3f> m_attrValues;
     float                    m_maxAttrValue;
  };
```

Each **ConstantVolume** instance is constructed with a transform matrix, indicating how the local space of the volume is transformed to world space. By convention, only the unity interval (i.e., $[0, 1]$) in the local space is considered to be within the volume.

Code 12.7. The **ConstantVolume** constructor

```
ConstantVolume::ConstantVolume(const Util::MatrixCurve &localToWorld)
  : m_localToWorld(localToWorld),
    m_maxAttrValue(0.0f)
{
  for (size_t i = 0, size = localToWorld.numSamples(); i < size; ++i) {
    float t = localToWorld.samplePoints()[i];
    Matrix m = localToWorld.sampleValues()[i].inverse();
    m_worldToLocal.addSample(t, m);
  }
}
```

DensitySampler, 286
PhysicalSampler, 288

To make the volume work with any number of attributes (for example, density when working with the **DensitySampler** and scattering when working with the **PhysicalSampler**), the constant volume provides the **addAttribute()** call. This lets the user specify an attribute name as well as a value, which is then used by the volume during sampling. Since the **ConstantVolume** is a good tool for debugging and analyzing the behavior of the renderer, having control over which attribute names and values are used makes this class very useful.

When an attribute value is added to the volume, the largest component is recorded in **m_maxAttrValue**. This value is later used to determine a step length for the raymarcher.

Code 12.8. The `ConstantVolume::addAttribute` call

```
void ConstantVolume::addAttribute(const std::string &attrName,
                                  const Imath::V3f &value)
{
  // No need to add an attribute whose value is zero.
  if (Math::max(value) == 0.0) {
    return;
  }

  m_attrNames.push_back(attrName);
  m_attrValues.push_back(value);
  m_maxAttrValue = std::max(m_maxAttrValue, Math::max(value));
}
```

Every **Volume** must also be able to return a list of the attributes that it exposes. For **ConstantVolume**, this is as simple as returning the list of attributes in **m_attrNames**, which is already in the appropriate format.

Code 12.9. The `ConstantVolume::attributeNames()` call

```
Volume::AttrNameVec ConstantVolume::attributeNames() const
{
  return m_attrNames;
}
```

During rendering, every volume must be able to report to the renderer what its *bounds* are. For **ConstantVolume**, it is as simple as transforming a [0, 1] bounding box from local space to world space. For volumes whose local-to-world transform only involves translation and scaling components, the bounding box in world space will be a perfectly tight-fitting bound on the volume. However, if rotations are involved, the world-space bounds will be loosely fitted, in order to cover the extremes of the rotated volume (see Figure 12.3). Although this may seem wasteful, the **intersect()** call performs its intersection test against the oriented volume, producing the optimal result.

Code 12.10. The `ConstantVolume::wsBounds` call

```
BBox ConstantVolume::wsBounds() const
{
  BBox bounds;
  for (size_t i = 0, size = m_localToWorld.numSamples(); i < size; ++i) {
    Matrix m = m_localToWorld.sampleValues()[i];
    BBox b = Imath::transform(Bounds::zeroOne(), m);
    bounds.extendBy(b);
  }
  return bounds;
}
```

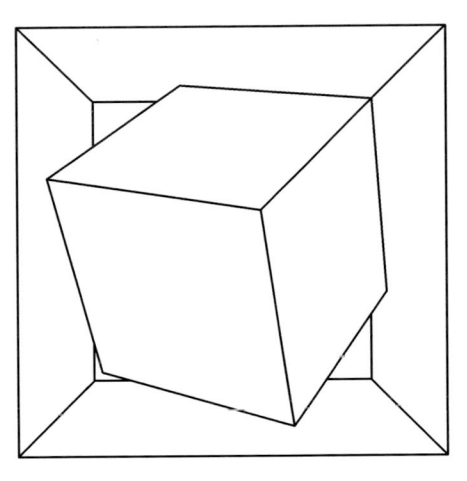

Figure 12.3. The axis-aligned bounding box around an oriented box.

The **ConstantVolume** can determine its intersection with the raymarcher's ray by simply transforming it into local space and then performing the intersection with an oriented bounding box positioned with corners at $(0\ 0\ 0)$ and $(1\ 1\ 1)$.

Interval, 234

If an intersection is found to have occurred, a new **Interval** is created based on the intersection points t_0 and t_1. Since each interval is defined not only by its endpoints but also its step length, the **ConstantVolume** uses the largest attribute value to compute a reasonable value. The assumption for this is that a thinner volume makes the transmittance and luminance integral vary less abruptly, and thus allows for a larger step size.

Code 12.11. The **ConstantVolume::intersect** call

```
IntervalVec ConstantVolume::intersect(const RayState &state) const
{
  // Transform ray to local space
  Ray lsRay;
  const Matrix wsToLs = m_worldToLocal.interpolate(state.time);
  wsToLs.multVecMatrix(state.wsRay.pos, lsRay.pos);
  wsToLs.multDirMatrix(state.wsRay.dir, lsRay.dir);
  // Intersect against unity bounds
  double t0, t1;
  if (Math::intersect(lsRay, Bounds::zeroOne(), t0, t1)) {
    return IntervalVec(1, Interval(t0, t1, (t1 - t0) /
                                  (std::sqrt(m_maxAttrValue) * 20.0)));
  } else {
    return IntervalVec();
  }
}
```

Once the appropriate integration interval has been found, the ray-march sampler returns to query the volume's attribute values. The first thing all volumes must do once their **sample()** function is called is to check if the attribute being requested has been initialized. If not, **Constant Volume** uses the **setIndexForName()** utility function from Volume.h, which looks for the attribute's name in the supplied list of names and sets the appropriate index if found. If the attribute name cannot be found, the attribute is marked as invalid.

Code 12.12. The **setIndexForName()** function

```
void setIndexForName(const VolumeAttr &attr, const Volume::StringVec &v)
{
  Volume::AttrNameVec::const_iterator i =
    std::find(v.begin(), v.end(), attr.name());
  if (i != v.end()) {
    attr.setIndex(std::distance(i, v.begin()));
  } else {
    attr.setIndexInvalid();
  }
}
```

Once the attribute index has been determined, we need to check if the sample's position falls within the domain of the volume. By transforming the sample point from world space to local space and testing if it falls within the $[0,1]$ bounding box, we can determine whether we should return the attribute's value or zero, based on the outcome of the test.

Code 12.13. The **ConstantVolume::sample** call

```
VolumeSample ConstantVolume::sample(const VolumeSampleState &state,
                                    const VolumeAttr &attribute) const
{
  if (attribute.index() == VolumeAttr::IndexNotSet) {
    setIndexForName(attribute, m_attrNames);
  }
  if (attribute.index() == VolumeAttr::IndexInvalid) {
    return VolumeSample(Colors::zero(), m_phaseFunction);
  }

  // Check if sample falls within volume
  Vector lsP;
  m_worldToLocal.interpolate(state.rayState.time).multVecMatrix(state.wsP,
                                                               lsP);
  if (Bounds::zeroOne().intersects(lsP)) {
    return VolumeSample(m_attrValues[attribute.index()], m_phaseFunction);
  } else {
    return VolumeSample(Colors::zero(), m_phaseFunction);
  }
}
```

12.3 The VoxelVolume Class

Volume, 233

One of the most important **Volume** subclasses in PVR is **VoxelVolume**. It acts as a wrapper around a **VoxelBuffer**, which by itself is not directly renderable. Voxel buffers make up the majority of rendering done in production, and PVR's implementation tries to show in extra detail the various parts that are required in a typical production context. As with other **Volume** subclasses, the two main functions it needs to implement are intersection testing and sampling. We will look first at intersection testing.

Because voxel buffers support more than one mapping type, the intersection test needs to change depending on which mapping is used. The **VoxelVolume** class handles this by delegating the task of intersecting

BufferIntersection, 244

the current ray against the volume to a **BufferIntersection** subclass that knows how to deal with a particular mapping type. This approach would also let us extend the intersection testing to new mapping types, should a new one become available. The **BufferIntersection** class, as well as the uniform and frustum-mapping implementations, are described below.

The second task, sampling, is more straightforward. The only option available to the user is to choose an interpolation scheme.

Because **VoxelVolume** really only wraps and exposes a **VoxelBuffer** to the rendering system, it also provides functions for assigning an existing voxel buffer or for loading a voxel buffer from disk.

Code 12.14. The VoxelVolume class

```
class VoxelVolume : public Volume
{
public:
...
  // From Volume
  virtual AttrNameVec   attributeNames() const;
  virtual VolumeSample  sample(const VolumeSampleState &state,
                           const VolumeAttr &attribute) const;
  virtual BBox          wsBounds() const;
  virtual IntervalVec   intersect(const RayState &state) const;
  virtual StringVec     info() const;
  // Main methods
  void                  load(const std::string &filename);
  void                  setBuffer(VoxelBuffer::Ptr buffer);
  void                  addAttribute(const std::string &attrName,
                           const Imath::V3f &value);
  void                  setInterpolation(const InterpType interpType);
  void                  setUseEmptySpaceOptimization(const bool enabled);
protected:
...
  // Utility methods
  void                  updateIntersectionHandler();
  // Protected data members
```

```
VoxelBuffer::Ptr          m_buffer;
BBox                      m_wsBounds;
AttrNameVec               m_attrNames;
std::vector<Imath::V3f>   m_attrValues;
BufferIntersection::CPtr  m_intersectionHandler;
InterpType                m_interpType;
LinearInterpType          m_linearInterp;
CubicInterpType           m_cubicInterp;
MonotonicCubicInterpType  m_monotonicCubicInterp;
GaussianInterpType        m_gaussInterp;
MitchellInterpType        m_mitchellInterp;
EmptySpaceOptimizer::CPtr m_eso;
bool                      m_useEmptySpaceOptimization;
};
```

12.3.1 Attribute Handling

The **VoxelVolume** behaves similarly to the **ConstantVolume** when it comes
to exposed attributes. The user provides an attribute name and a scaling
value, which is later used to multiply the value looked up from the voxel
buffer.

ConstantVolume, 238

Code 12.15. The **VoxelVolume::addAttribute** call

```
void VoxelVolume::addAttribute(const std::string &attrName,
                               const Imath::V3f &value)
{
  m_attrNames.push_back(attrName);
  m_attrValues.push_back(value);
}
```

12.3.2 Ray Intersection Testing

The **VoxelVolume**'s ray intersection test is divided into two steps. First, a
test is performed to find the intersection points between the ray and the
the bounds of the volume. After the intersection points are found, the
voxel volume tries to see if the integration interval may be shortened, in
order to skip over parts of the volume that are known to be empty. The
first part is handled by an *intersection handler* and the second by an *empty-
space optimizer*. Each of the two concepts are implemented as delegate
classes, which are called upon from the **VoxelVolume** as required.

Because the **VoxelVolume** supports multiple types of transforms (both
uniform and frustum), the ray intersection test is different depending on
the transform used for the current voxel buffer. In order to keep the different intersection logics separate from the rest of the voxel volume, the

delegate is implemented as two separate subclasses of the **BufferIntersec tion** class.

Code 12.16. The VoxelVolume intersection test

```
IntervalVec VoxelVolume::intersect(const RayState &state) const
{
  assert (m_intersectionHandler && "Missing intersection handler");
  if (m_eso && m_useEmptySpaceOptimization) {
    IntervalVec i = m_intersectionHandler->intersect(state.wsRay,
                                                     state.time);
    return m_eso->optimize(state, i);
  } else {
    return m_intersectionHandler->intersect(state.wsRay, state.time);
  }
}
```

The **BufferIntersection** base class provides only a single virtual function, which is the **intersect()** call. It takes a **Ray** as well as a **time** at which to perform the intersection. The ray is assumed to already have been transformed to the appropriate time, but since the buffer itself could be moving, the **time** variable can be used to adjust the position accordingly.

The task of the subclass is to provide a set (zero or more) of integration intervals the need to be raymarched.

When implementing a subclass, we need to remember that the instance will be created once for each voxel buffer but that there will be a large number of calls to **intersect()**. It is therefore worthwhile to perform any relevant precomputations that could speed up the actual intersection test in the constructor.

Code 12.17. The BufferIntersection class

```
class BufferIntersection
{
public:
  // Typedefs
  PVR_TYPEDEF_SMART_PTRS(BufferIntersection);
  // To be implemented by subclasses
  virtual IntervalVec intersect(const Ray &wsRay, const PTime time) const =
                                                                        0;
};
```

12.3.3   Intersecting Uniform Buffers

For voxel buffers that use **Field3D::MatrixFieldMapping**, the **VoxelVolume** class uses a **UniformBufferIntersection** instance.

Code 12.18. The `UniformMappingIntersection` class

```
class UniformMappingIntersection : public BufferIntersection
{
public:
  ...
  // Ctor
  UniformMappingIntersection(Field3D::MatrixFieldMapping::Ptr mapping);
  // From BufferIntersection
  virtual IntervalVec intersect(const Ray &wsRay, const PTime time) const;
private:
  // Data members
  // Matrix m_worldToLocal, m_worldToVoxel;
  Field3D::MatrixFieldMapping::Ptr m_mapping;
};
```

The intersection test itself is handled by transforming the ray's origin and direction into the local space of the voxel buffer. The bounds of the voxel buffer in local space is, per definition, $[0, 1]$ along each axis. The intersection test is performed by `Math::intersect(ray, box, t0, t1)`. Once the intersection has been found, the intersection points are used to determine the length of the segment (by computing distance in world space), as well as the number of voxels (distance in voxel space) the segment crosses, which is then used to find a step length.

Code 12.19. The `UniformMappingIntersection` intersection test

```
IntervalVec UniformMappingIntersection::intersect(const Ray &wsRay,
                                                  const PTime time) const
{
  // Transform ray to local space for intersection test
  Ray lsRay;
  m_mapping->worldToLocal(wsRay.pos, lsRay.pos, time);
  m_mapping->worldToLocalDir(wsRay.dir, lsRay.dir);
  // Use unit bounding box to intersect against
  BBox lsBBox = Bounds::zeroOne();
  // Calculate intersection points
  double t0, t1;
  if (Math::intersect(lsRay, lsBBox, t0, t1)) {
    return IntervalVec(1, makeInterval(wsRay, t0, t1, m_mapping));
  } else {
    return IntervalVec();
  }
}
```

Code 12.20. The `makeInterval()` utility function

```
  return makeInterval(wsRay, intT0, intT1, m_sparse->mapping());
}
```

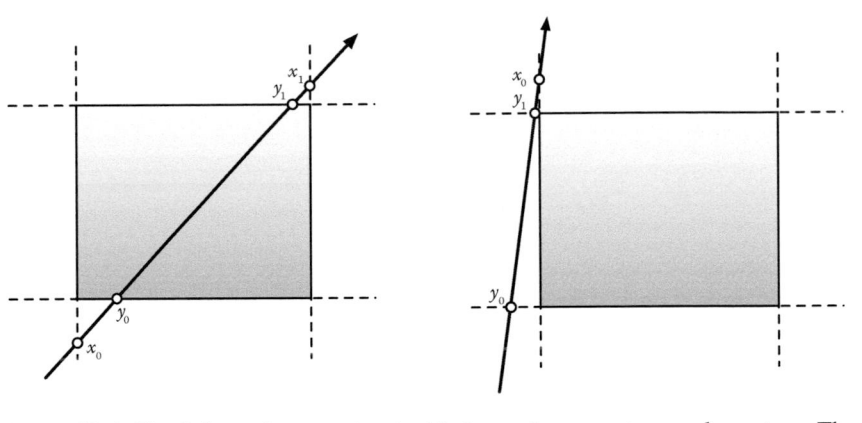

Figure 12.4. The left ray intersection test is true, since $x_0 < y_1$ and $y_0 < x_1$. The right test is false, as $x_0 > y_1$.

The bounding-box intersection test works by considering each pair of parallel planes defining the box and intersecting the ray against those. The logic goes that if the closest point on a pair of planes is farther away than the farthest point on another pair, there can be no intersection for a box defined by all the planes taken together. (See Figure 12.4.)

Code 12.21. pvr::Math::intersect() for bounding boxes

```
bool intersect(const Ray &ray, const BBox &box, double &outT0, double &outT1)
{
  double tNear = -std::numeric_limits<double>::max();
  double tFar = std::numeric_limits<double>::max();
  const double epsilon = 1.0e-6;

  for (size_t dim = 0; dim < 3; ++dim) {
    double t0, t1;
    if (std::abs(ray.dir[dim]) < epsilon) {
      // Ray is parallel, check if inside slab
      if (ray.pos[dim] < box.min[dim] || ray.pos[dim] > box.max[dim]) {
        return false;
      }
    }
    t0 = (box.min[dim] - ray.pos[dim]) / ray.dir[dim];
    t1 = (box.max[dim] - ray.pos[dim]) / ray.dir[dim];
    if (t0 > t1) {
      std::swap(t0, t1);
    }
    tNear = std::max(tNear, t0);
    tFar = std::min(tFar, t1);
    if (tNear > tFar) {
      return false;
    }
    if (tFar < 0.0) {
```

```
      return false;
    }
  }
  outT0 = tNear;
  outT1 = tFar;
  return true;
}
```

12.3.4   Intersecting Frustum Buffers

For voxel buffers that use **Field3D::FrustumFieldMapping**, the voxel volume creates a **FrustumBufferIntersection** to use for intersection tests. While the uniform version was able to directly use the transforms available in the **Mapping**, the frustum intersection test constructs six planes, corresponding to each face of the frustum. The intersection testing is then performed on those planes in the **intersect()** call.

Code 12.22. The **FrustumMappingIntersection** class

```
class FrustumMappingIntersection : public BufferIntersection
{
public:
...
  // Ctor
  FrustumMappingIntersection(Field3D::FrustumFieldMapping::Ptr mapping);
  // From BufferIntersection
  virtual IntervalVec intersect(const Ray &wsRay, const PTime time) const;
private:
  // Data members
  Field3D::FrustumFieldMapping::Ptr m_mapping;
};
```

The intersection test builds the frustum face planes by first transforming each of the local-space corner points to world space. With the corner points in place, the planes are built in the order X_{min}, X_{max}, Y_{min}, Y_{max}, Z_{min}, Z_{max}. The convention used for the point order creates planes whose normal faces outward from the frustum (see Figure 12.5).

Code 12.23. The **FrustumMappingIntersection** intersection test

```
IntervalVec FrustumMappingIntersection::intersect(const Ray &wsRay,
                                                  const PTime time) const
{
  typedef std::vector<Vector> PointVec;

  // Get the eight corners of the local space bounding box
  BBox lsBounds = Bounds::zeroOne();
```

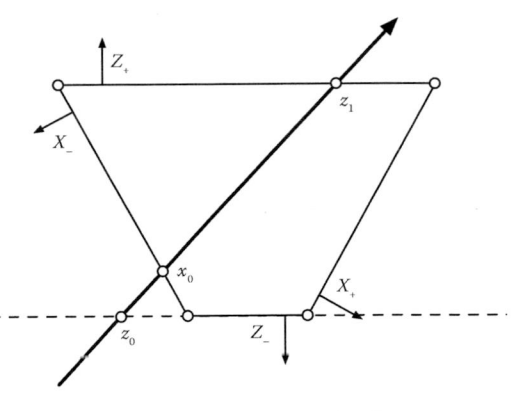

Figure 12.5. Point-order convention for a frustum.

Figure 12.6. Intersection test for frustums.

```
PointVec lsCorners = Math::cornerPoints(lsBounds);
// Get the world space positions of the eight corners of the frustum
PointVec wsCorners(lsCorners.size());
for (PointVec::iterator lsP = lsCorners.begin(), wsP = wsCorners.begin(),
        end = lsCorners.end(); lsP != end; ++lsP, ++wsP) {
  m_mapping->localToWorld(*lsP, *wsP, time);
}

// Construct plane for each face of frustum
Plane planes[6];
planes[0] = Plane(wsCorners[4], wsCorners[0], wsCorners[6]);
planes[1] = Plane(wsCorners[1], wsCorners[5], wsCorners[3]);
planes[2] = Plane(wsCorners[4], wsCorners[5], wsCorners[0]);
planes[3] = Plane(wsCorners[2], wsCorners[3], wsCorners[6]);
planes[4] = Plane(wsCorners[0], wsCorners[1], wsCorners[2]);
planes[5] = Plane(wsCorners[5], wsCorners[4], wsCorners[7]);
```

The actual intersection test is performed by testing the ray against each plane in turn. The normal is used to decide whether the plane should be used as the near point or the far point. If the dot product of the ray direction and the plane's normal is positive, the plane faces away from the camera and is thus a far point, and vice versa. The intersection test is true if the farthest opposing plane intersection is closer than the nearest nonopposing one. (See Figure 12.6.)

To determine the step length of the interval, we call the same **make Interval()** function as **UniformMappingIntersection**.

Code 12.24. The **FrustumMappingIntersection** intersection test

```
// Intersect ray against planes
double t0 = -std::numeric_limits<double>::max();
double t1 = std::numeric_limits<double>::max();
```

```
for (int i = 0; i < 6; ++i) {
  double t;
  const Plane &p - planes[i];
  if (p.intersectT(wsRay, t)) {
    if (wsRay.dir.dot(p.normal) > 0.0) {
      // Non-opposing plane
      t1 = std::min(t1, t);
    } else {
      // Opposing plane
      t0 = std::max(t0, t);
    }
  }
}
if (t0 < t1) {
  t0 = std::max(t0, 0.0);
  return IntervalVec(1, makeInterval(wsRay, t0, t1, m_mapping));
} else {
  return IntervalVec();
}
}
```

12.3.5   Empty-Space Optimization

As we discussed in Chapter 13 on raymarching, optimizing the integration bounds is done in two steps. First, each **Volume** in the scene intersects itself against the current ray. This takes care of excluding parts of the scene where no volume data exist, and for **VoxelVolume** instances, that task was delegated to the **BufferIntersection** classes.

Raymarching in PVR, 267
Volume, 233

VoxelVolume, 243
BufferIntersection, 244

The second level of optimization, where empty space inside each individual volume is removed, is handled by a second set of delegate classes, called *empty-space optimizers*. The base class is called **EmptySpaceOptimizer**, and it requires only that the virtual **optimize()** function is implemented. The **VoxelVolume** calls on the optimizer right after the **BufferIntersection** has produced the initial intersection points. It is then up to the optimizer to try and further shorten the **Interval** instances, or even to split and remove parts of them.

VoxelVolume, 243

Interval, 234

Code 12.25. The **EmptySpaceOptimizer** base class

```
class EmptySpaceOptimizer : public Util::ParamBase
{
public:
  // Typedefs
  PVR_TYPEDEF_SMART_PTRS(EmptySpaceOptimizer);
  // To be implemented by subclasses
  virtual IntervalVec optimize(const RayState &state,
                               const IntervalVec &intervals) const = 0;
};
```

12.3.6 Optimizing Sparse Uniform Buffers

We will first look at a technique for optimizing integration intervals for sparse voxel buffers with a uniform mapping.

Code 12.26. The **SparseUniformOptimizer** base class

```
class SparseUniformOptimizer : public EmptySpaceOptimizer
{
public:
...
  // Ctor, factory
  PVR_DEFINE_CREATE_FUNC_2_ARG(SparseUniformOptimizer, SparseBuffer::Ptr,
                               Field3D::MatrixFieldMapping::Ptr);
  SparseUniformOptimizer(SparseBuffer::Ptr sparse,
                         Field3D::MatrixFieldMapping::Ptr mapping);
...
  // From EmptySpaceOptimizer
  virtual IntervalVec optimize(const RayState &state,
                               const IntervalVec &intervals) const;
private:
  // Utility methods
  Interval          intervalForRun(const Ray &wsRay, const PTime time,
                                   const Imath::V3i &start,
                                   const Imath::V3i &end) const;
  void              intersect(const Ray &wsRay, const PTime time,
                              const Imath::V3i block,
                              double &t0, double &t1) const;
  // Private data members
  SparseBuffer::Ptr m_sparse;
  Field3D::MatrixFieldMapping::Ptr m_mapping;
};
```

Interval, 234

    Before any actual work is done, we check that the optimizer has been called in the correct context. The **BufferIntersection** should return either zero or one **Interval** instances. If we get zero intervals, we can return immediately, and if the count is larger than one, something unexpected has happened.

Code 12.27. The **SparseUniformOptimizer::optimize** call

```
IntervalVec
SparseUniformOptimizer::optimize(const RayState &state,
                                 const IntervalVec &intervals) const
{
  if (intervals.size() != 1) {
    return intervals;
  }
```

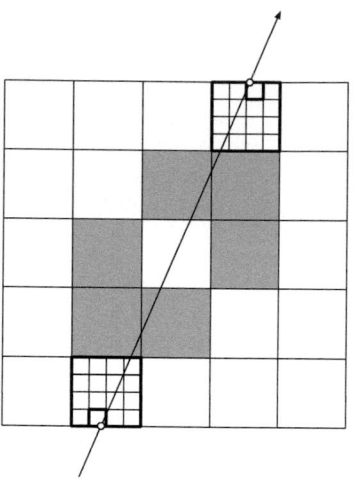

Figure 12.7. Start and end voxels (small, bold) and start and end blocks (large, bold).

To efficiently traverse all of the blocks, we use a voxel-traversal algorithm. This works because the sparse blocks themselves make up a sort of coarse voxel grid. The voxel-traversal algorithm that PVR uses is based on a paper by John Amanatides and Andrew Woo, "A Fast Voxel Traversal Algorithm for Ray Tracing" [Amanatides and Woo 87].

The first step is to find the first voxel that the incoming ray hit, so that we can start the traversal of sparse blocks from that point. The exact point in the block is unimportant, as each step to the next neighboring voxel will be determined by intersecting each neighbor block against the current ray. (See Figure 12.7.)

When finding the first voxel, we use the buffer's `worldToVoxel()` transform. Because of numerical imprecision, the point found by `wsRay(interval[0].t0)` may lie slightly inside or outside the voxel buffer. To ensure that we start with a voxel that lies within the valid extents, we use `Imath::clip()` to clamp the voxel coordinates.

Once the first voxel has been found, the containing `SparseBlock` can be found using the `SparseField::getBlockCoord()` call.

Code 12.28. The `SparseUniformOptimizer::optimize` call

```
IntervalVec result;

const Ray &wsRay = state.wsRay;
const PTime &time = state.time;
```

```
// Find start voxel
Vector wsStart = wsRay(intervals[0].t0), vsStart;
m_sparse->mapping()->worldToVoxel(wsStart, vsStart, time);
V3i in = Imath::clip(V3i(vsStart), m_sparse->extents());

// Find start block
V3i bStart;
m_sparse->getBlockCoord(in.x, in.y, in.z, bStart.x, bStart.y, bStart.z);
```

The voxel-traversal algorithm requires that the ray used to walk the buffer is in the same coordinate space as the voxels. In our case, that means it must be transformed into the space of the blocks, which we will refer to as *block space*.

Code 12.29. The SparseUniformOptimizer::optimize call

```
// Transform ray to block space
Ray bsRay;
worldToBlock(m_mapping, m_sparse->blockSize(), wsRay, bsRay);
```

The transformation from world space to block space is straightforward. The **MatrixFieldMapping** class provides **worldToVoxel()** and **worldToVoxelDir()**, which together can transform the ray into voxel space. The transformation from voxel to block space can then be performed by dividing out the block size.

Code 12.30. The worldToBlock() call

```
void worldToBlock(Field3D::MatrixFieldMapping::Ptr mapping,
                  const int blockSize, const pvr::Ray &wsRay,
                  pvr::Ray &bsRay)
{
  mapping->worldToVoxel(wsRay.pos, bsRay.pos);
  mapping->worldToVoxelDir(wsRay.dir, bsRay.dir);
  bsRay.pos /= static_cast<double>(blockSize);
  bsRay.dir /= static_cast<double>(blockSize);
}
```

Next, we set up the iteration variables that will walk us through the block array in the same order as the ray intersects each block.

Code 12.31. The SparseUniformOptimizer::optimize call

```
// Current block
int x = bStart.x, y = bStart.y, z = bStart.z;
// Direction to step
V3i sgn(sign(bsRay.dir.x), sign(bsRay.dir.y), sign(bsRay.dir.z));
```

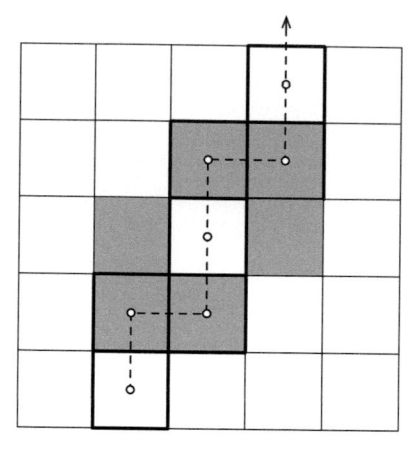

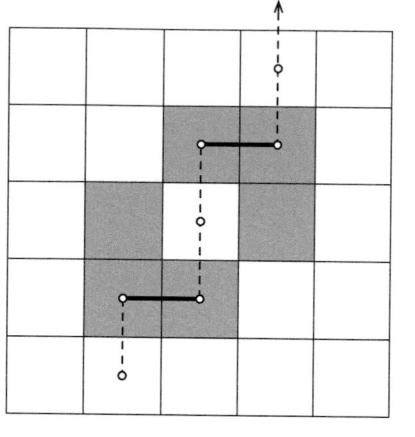

Figure 12.8. Block-traversal order.

Figure 12.9. Two runs found along a block-traversal path.

```
// Whether to look at positive or negative side of block
Vector cell(x + (sgn.x > 0 ? 1 : 0),
            y + (sgn.y > 0 ? 1 : 0),
            z + (sgn.z > 0 ? 1 : 0));
// Distance we could step in each direction, at most
Vector tMax((cell - bsRay.pos) / bsRay.dir);
// Size of one step in each dimension
Vector tDelta(sgn.x / bsRay.dir.x, sgn.y / bsRay.dir.y, sgn.z /
            bsRay.dir.z);
// Ensure there are no inf's or nan's
handleNaN(tMax);
handleNaN(tDelta);
// Check if first block starts a run
bool run = m_sparse->blockIsAllocated(x, y, z);
// Keep track of start-of-run and last visited block
V3i last(bStart), startRun(bStart);
```

The block-traversal loop is guaranteed to step through the blocks that the ray hits in order. (See Figure 12.8.) Thus, by keeping track of contiguous active blocks, we can easily produce an optimal list of intervals that the raymarcher needs to sample.

In each loop iteration, we check if the current block is active or not. If it's active and we are currently in the middle of a *run*, we do nothing. If there is no run, we start one and mark the start to be the current voxel. If the current block is inactive, we need to see if there was a run in progress, in which case we need to add a new interval to the output set of intervals. (See Figure 12.9.)

Once the run-length logic has been executed, we mark the current block as the last visited and proceed to the next block.

Code 12.32. The `SparseUniformOptimizer::optimize` call

```
// Traverse blocks
while (m_sparse->blockIndexIsValid(x, y, z)) {
  if (m_sparse->blockIsAllocated(x, y, z)) {
    if (!run) {
      startRun = V3i(x, y, z);
      run = true;
    }
  } else {
    if (run) {
      result.push_back(intervalForRun(wsRay, time, startRun, last));
      run = false;
    }
  }
  last = V3i(x, y, z);
  stepToNextBlock(tDelta, sgn, tMax, x, y, z);
}

if (run) {
  result.push_back(intervalForRun(wsRay, time, startRun, last));
}

return result;
}
```

The logic for stepping to the next block goes as follows: find the dimension to step in, based on the components of **tMax**, and then increment the current block coordinate, as well as **tMax** in the given dimension. This ensures that the closest next block is chosen.

Code 12.33. The `stepToNextBlock()` call

```
void stepToNextBlock(const pvr::Vector &tDelta, const Imath::V3i &sgn,
                     pvr::Vector &tMax, int &x, int &y, int &z)
{
  if (tMax.x < tMax.y && tMax.x < tMax.z) {
    x += sgn.x;
    tMax.x += tDelta.x;
  } else if (tMax.y < tMax.z) {
    y += sgn.y;
    tMax.y += tDelta.y;
  } else {
    z += sgn.z;
    tMax.z += tDelta.z;
  }
}
```

Once a run is found and completed, either because an inactive block was found or because we came to the end of the buffer, a new integration interval must be constructed and added to the list of output intervals.

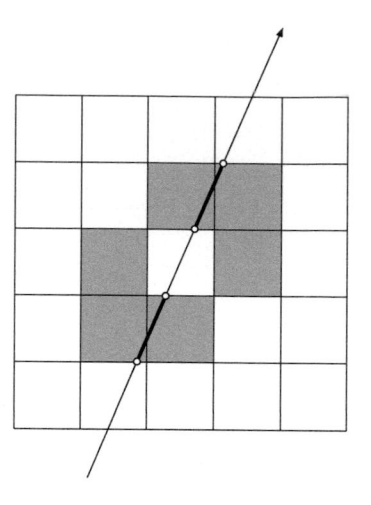

Figure 12.10. Final integration intervals found after intersecting the ray against the start and end blocks.

First, the start block is intersected against the block-space ray. Because of the nature of transformations of rays, the parametric distance t found in the intersection test is valid for all coordinate spaces. We can thus find the intersection in a convenient space (in this case, local space) and then apply that distance along the ray in world space. Once the closest intersection t_0 has been found, the ray is again intersected, this time against the ending block. The far intersection point t_1 is then used to determine the endpoint of the interval. (See Figure 12.10.)

Code 12.34. The `SparseUniformOptimizer::intervalForRun()` call

```
Interval
SparseUniformOptimizer::intervalForRun(const Ray &wsRay, const PTime time,
                                       const Imath::V3i &start,
                                       const Imath::V3i &end) const
{
  double t0, t1, intT0, intT1;
  intersect(wsRay, time, start, t0, t1);
  intT0 = std::min(t0, t1);
  intersect(wsRay, time, end, t0, t1);
  intT1 = std::max(t0, t1);
  return makeInterval(wsRay, intT0, intT1, m_sparse->mapping());
}
```

The intersection test itself is done by transforming both the ray and the block bounds to local space and then using PVR's `Math::intersect(ray, box, t0, t1)` call to find the precise intersection points.

Code 12.35. The `SparseUniformOptimizer::intersect()` call

```
void
SparseUniformOptimizer::intersect(const Ray &wsRay, const PTime time,
                                  const Imath::V3i block,
                                  double &t0, double &t1) const
{
  // Transform to local space
  Ray lsRay;
  m_mapping->worldToLocal(wsRay.pos, lsRay.pos, time);
  m_mapping->worldToLocalDir(wsRay.dir, lsRay.dir);
  // Intersect in local space
  Imath::Box3i box;
  int blockSz = m_sparse->blockSize();
  box.min = V3i(block.x * blockSz, block.y * blockSz, block.z * blockSz);
  box.max = box.min + V3i(blockSz - 1, blockSz - 1, blockSz - 1);
  BBox vsBox(box.min, box.max + V3i(1)), lsBox;
  m_mapping->voxelToLocal(vsBox.min, lsBox.min);
  m_mapping->voxelToLocal(vsBox.max, lsBox.max);
  Math::intersect(lsRay, lsBox, t0, t1);
}
```

The `SparseUniformOptimizer` works for rays regardless of origin and direction, which means it can optimize integration intervals for both camera and shadow rays.

12.3.7   Optimizing Sparse Frustum Buffers

For sparse buffers using a frustum mapping, it is also possible to improve the integration interval past what the `BufferIntersection` provides. The `SparseFrustumOptimizer` handles this case, and it implements the same interface as `SparseUniformOptimizer`.

Code 12.36. The `SparseFrustumOptimizer` base class

```
class SparseFrustumOptimizer : public EmptySpaceOptimizer
{
public:
...
  // Ctor, factory
  PVR_DEFINE_CREATE_FUNC_2_ARG(SparseFrustumOptimizer, SparseBuffer::Ptr,
                               Field3D::FrustumFieldMapping::Ptr);
  SparseFrustumOptimizer(SparseBuffer::Ptr sparse,
                         Field3D::FrustumFieldMapping::Ptr mapping);
...
  // From EmptySpaceOptimizer
  virtual IntervalVec optimize(const RayState &state,
                               const IntervalVec &intervals) const;
private:
  // Utility methods
  Interval              intervalForRun(const Ray &wsRay, const PTime time,
                                       const Vector &vsFirst,
                                       const int start, const int end) const;
```

```
// Private data members
SparseBuffer::Ptr m_sparse;
Field3D::FrustumFieldMapping::Ptr m_mapping;
};
```

The **SparseFrustumOptimizer** takes advantage of the fact that both voxels and sparse blocks are oriented in a straight line following the projection of each camera pixel. Thus, any camera ray is guaranteed to follow a straight line of blocks along the z-axis. Using this knowledge, we can implement a sparse frustum optimizer based on a simpler version of the uniform optimizer. Because of this assumption that rays will travel straight down the z-axis, we have to check not only that there is exactly one incoming interval but also that the ray depth is zero and the ray type is **FullRaymarch**.

Code 12.37. The **SparseFrustumOptimizer::optimize** call

```
IntervalVec
SparseFrustumOptimizer::optimize(const RayState &state,
                                 const IntervalVec &intervals) const
{
  if (intervals.size() != 1) {
    return intervals;
  }

  if (state.rayType != RayState::FullRaymarch ||
      state.rayDepth != 0) {
    return intervals;
  }
```

Once we are sure that the ray is "optimizable," we proceed to transform the start and end voxels from world space to voxel space. Just as in the uniform buffer case, we need to clip the voxel coordinate to the buffer's extents. Then, from the voxel-space coordinates, we find the blocks that hold the start and end voxels.

Code 12.38. The **SparseFrustumOptimizer::optimize** call

```
  IntervalVec result;
  const Ray &wsRay = state.wsRay;
  const PTime &time = state.time;

  // Find start and end voxel
  Vector vsStart, vsEnd;
  m_sparse->mapping()->worldToVoxel(wsRay(intervals[0].t0), vsStart);
  m_sparse->mapping()->worldToVoxel(wsRay(intervals[0].t1), vsEnd);
  V3i in = Imath::clip(V3i(vsStart), m_sparse->extents());
  V3i out = Imath::clip(V3i(vsEnd), m_sparse->extents());
```

```
// Find start and end block
V3i bStart, bEnd;
m_sparse->getBlockCoord(in.x, in.y, in.z, bStart.x, bStart.y, bStart.z);
m_sparse->getBlockCoord(out.x, out.y, out.z, bEnd.x, bEnd.y, bEnd.z);
```

As a precautionary measure, we check that the start and end blocks that were found indeed lie in the same row of blocks. This could occur if the frustum buffer was generated from a different camera than the one used for rendering.

Code 12.39. The `SparseFrustumOptimizer::optimize` call

```
// Ensure ray travels down z axis
if (bStart.x != bEnd.x || bStart.y != bEnd.y) {
  return intervals;
}
```

SparseUniformOptimizer, 251

Similar to the block-walking loop in **SparseUniformOptimizer**, the frustum version performs its own traversal of the sparse blocks in order to find runs of allocated and nonallocated blocks. In the frustum case, the loop is simpler, so quite few iteration variables are required.

Code 12.40. The `SparseFrustumOptimizer::optimize` call

```
// Current block
int x = bStart.x, y = bStart.y, z = bStart.z;
// Check if first block starts a run
bool run = m_sparse->blockIsAllocated(x, y, z);
// Keep track of start-of-run and last visited block
int startRun = z, last = z;
```

The logic for finding runs along the block structure is the same as in the uniform case. Each block is checked and a run is recorded whenever a nonallocated block is found.

Code 12.41. The `SparseFrustumOptimizer::optimize` call

```
// Traverse row of blocks
for (; z <= bEnd.z; z++) {
  if (m_sparse->blockIsAllocated(x, y, z)) {
    if (!run) {
      startRun = z;
      run = true;
    }
  } else {
```

```
    if (run) {
      result.push_back(intervalForRun(wsRay, time, vsStart, startRun,
                                      last));
      run = false;
    }
  }
  last = z;
}

if (run) {
  result.push_back(intervalForRun(wsRay, time, vsStart, startRun, last));
}

return result;
}
```

12.3.8   Sampling the Buffer

When a request is made to sample a value in the voxel buffer, we first
have to check if the attribute index has been set or if the **sample()** call
received an uninitialized **VolumeAttr** (see Section 12.1.1). If the index has
not yet been set, we set it if (and only if) the attribute name matches the
name of one of the contained voxel buffer attributes.

    Once the check is made for an uninitialized **VolumeAttr**, we also have
to check if the attribute is invalid, indicating that the current voxel buffer
has a different attribute name than what is being requested. In this case,
the **sample()** call should return a zero intensity color.

VolumeAttr, 235

Volume Properties and Attributes, 235

Code 12.42. VoxelVolume::sample()

```
VolumeSample VoxelVolume::sample(const VolumeSampleState &state,
                                const VolumeAttr &attribute) const
{
  // Check (and set up) attribute index ---

  if (attribute.index() == VolumeAttr::IndexNotSet) {
    setIndexForName(attribute, m_attrNames);
  }
  if (attribute.index() == VolumeAttr::IndexInvalid) {
    return VolumeSample(Colors::zero(), m_phaseFunction);
  }
}
```

    When we know that the attribute requested is indeed one that the
voxel buffer provides, we first transform the world-space sample point
in the **RenderState** to voxel space. With knowledge of the voxel-space
position, the voxel volume first checks if it falls within the valid bounds.
If not, the attribute value is known to be zero and the function returns
zero luminance.

Code 12.43. VoxelVolume::sample()

```
// Transform to voxel space for sampling ---

Vector vsP;
m_buffer->mapping()->worldToVoxel(state.wsP, vsP, state.rayState.time);

if (!Math::isInBounds(vsP, m_buffer->dataWindow())) {
  return VolumeSample(Colors::zero(), m_phaseFunction);
}
```

After ruling out cases where the value is known to be zero, we use one of the voxel volume's interpolation schemes to sample the volume. By default, linear interpolation is used. There is also a noninterpolating mode (**NoInterp**), where the continuous voxel-space position is rounded to the closest voxel and the value read directly. See Section 3.5 for more details on interpolating values from voxel buffers.

Interpolating Voxel Data, 45

Code 12.44. VoxelVolume::sample()

```
// Interpolate voxel value ---

V3f value(0.0);

switch (m_interpType) {
case NoInterp:
  {
    V3i dvsP = contToDisc(vsP);
    value = m_buffer->value(dvsP.x, dvsP.y, dvsP.z);
    break;
  }
case CubicInterp:
  value = m_cubicInterp.sample(*m_buffer, vsP);
  break;
case MonotonicCubicInterp:
  value = m_monotonicCubicInterp.sample(*m_buffer, vsP);
  break;
case GaussianInterp:
  value = m_gaussInterp.sample(*m_buffer, vsP);
  break;
case MitchellInterp:
  value = m_mitchellInterp.sample(*m_buffer, vsP);
  break;
case LinearInterp:
default:
  value = m_linearInterp.sample(*m_buffer, vsP);
  break;
}

return VolumeSample(m_attrValues[attribute.index()] * value,
                    m_phaseFunction);
}
```

12.4   The `CompositeVolume` Class

Because of the way PVR's rendering pipeline is structured, the **Scene** only holds a single **Volume** instance, which the **RaymarchSampler** then queries to find the properties of the medium at a given point. Although this might seem to imply that only one volume at a time may be rendered, the intent is instead to leave it to the **Volume** classes themselves to determine how they are combined in a scene with multiple instances. Using this approach, the raymarching and raymarch-sampling code can be written without having to consider cases of single volumes versus multiple volumes.

Scene, 203
Volume, 233
RaymarchSampler, 285

The class that is responsible for holding multiple **Volume** instances and exposing them as if they were a single one is the **CompositeVolume**. When setting up the composite volume, the caller uses **CompositeVolume::add()** to indicate which volumes should be contained in the composite. These volumes are then referred to as the *child volumes* in the composite.

Volume, 233

Code 12.45. The `CompositeVolume` class

```
class CompositeVolume : public Volume
{
public:
  // Structs
  struct ChildAttrs
  {
    std::string            name;
    std::vector<VolumeAttr> attrs;
  };
  ...
  // From Volume
  virtual AttrNameVec  attributeNames() const;
  virtual VolumeSample sample(const VolumeSampleState &state,
                             const VolumeAttr &attribute) const;
  virtual BBox         wsBounds() const;
  virtual IntervalVec  intersect(const RayState &state) const;
  virtual CVec         inputs() const;
  // Main methods
  void                 add(Volume::CPtr child);
protected:
  ...
  // Protected data members
  std::vector<Volume::CPtr> m_volumes;
  mutable ChildAttrsVec     m_childAttrs;
  Phase::Composite::Ptr     m_compositePhaseFunction;
};
```

When the **CompositeVolume** is asked to intersect the current ray, it passes the request to each child volume in order and combines the resulting intervals into a single array, which is then returned to the caller.

Code 12.46. CompositeVolume::intersect()

```
IntervalVec CompositeVolume::intersect(const RayState &state) const
{
  IntervalVec intervals;
  BOOST_FOREACH (Volume::CPtr child, m_volumes) {
    IntervalVec childIntervals = child->intersect(state);
    intervals.insert(intervals.begin(),
                      childIntervals.begin(), childIntervals.end());
  }
  return intervals;
}
```

Attribute handling is a little more complicated than **VoxelVolume**'s as the composite volume has to hide from the caller the fact that there are multiple volumes contained internally. Although it may at first seem reasonable to simply forward the **VolumeAttr** instance to each child volume, this violates the rule that **VolumeAttr** instances not be shared (see Section 12.1.1). If we imagine a composite volume with two child volumes, the first with attributes "scattering" and "emission" and the second with "absorption" and "scattering," then the first volume would set the index for "scattering" to be 0, and the second volume would then see that the index had already been set and proceed to return its attribute at index 0, which is really "absorption."

To solve this problem, we introduce a level of indirection. Instead of having the **VolumeAttr** that gets passed to **sample()** point directly to attributes in the child volumes, we let it refer to an array of other **VolumeAttr** instances. The array is **CompositeVolume::m_childAttrs**, and it grows in size by one for each unique attribute name that is requested of **sample()**. Each array item in **m_childAttrs** is an instance of the **CompositeVolume:: ChildAttr** struct, which contains a name indicating the attribute it represents, as well as a vector of **VolumeAttr** instances, which will be used to sample the attribute from each child volume. Figure 12.11 illustrates the data layout for a composite with three child volumes.

The **setupAttribute()** call is used to configure the incoming **Volume Attr**, if its **VolumeAttr::index()** value indicates that it has not yet been set up. First, we search the **m_childAttrs** array's **name** instances to see if the attribute name being sampled already has the auxiliary struct in place. If it does, we simply assign its index to the **VolumeAttr** and continue. If the attribute name does not yet exist, it means this is the first request for it. The first step is to check if any of the child volumes have the attribute. If none of them do, we mark the attribute as invalid. Marking the attribute as invalid means that each consecutive call to **sample()** will return immediately, which saves us from passing invalid requests to each one.

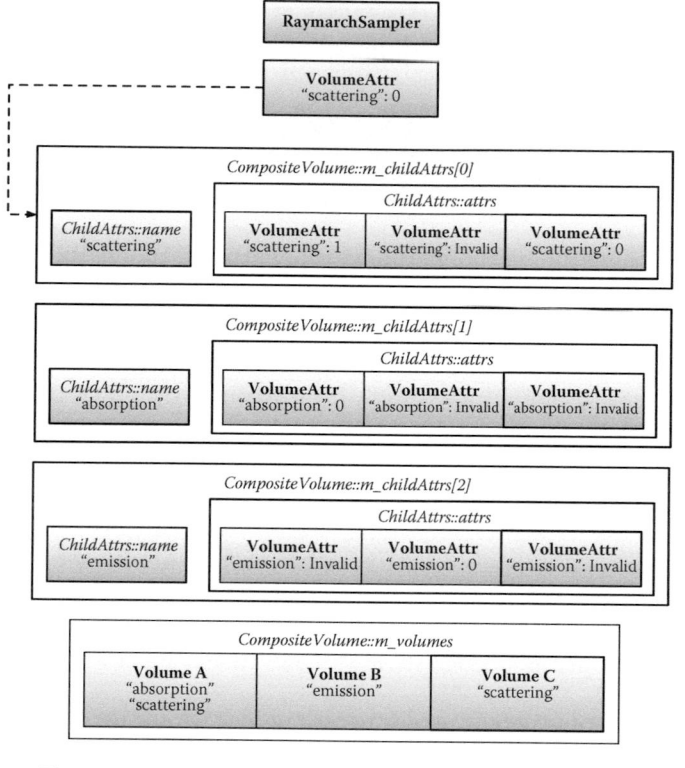

Figure 12.11. Attribute handling in `CompositeVolume`.

The last case to handle is if at least one of the child volumes provides the given attribute name. In that case, we set up a new `ChildAttrs` struct containing the name of the attribute as well as an array of `VolumeAttr` instances, equal in size to the number of child volumes in the composite. The new struct is added to the `m_childAttrs` array, and the index of the attribute is updated to point to the last entry in the array.

Code 12.47. `CompositeVolume::setupAttribute()`

```
void CompositeVolume::setupAttribute(const VolumeAttr &attribute) const
{
  ChildAttrsVec::const_iterator i =
    find_if(m_childAttrs.begin(), m_childAttrs.end(),
        MatchName(attribute.name()));

  if (i != m_childAttrs.end()) {
    // Attribute already exists in m_childAttrs, so set index directly
    attribute.setIndex(i - m_childAttrs.begin());
  } else {
```

```
      // Attribute does not yet exist, look for it among children
      AttrNameVec attrs = attributeNames();
      if (find(attrs.begin(), attrs.end(), attribute.name()) != attrs.end()) {
        // One or more children have the attribute
        ChildAttrs newAttr;
        newAttr.name = attribute.name();
        newAttr.attrs.resize(m_volumes.size(), VolumeAttr(attribute.name()));
        m_childAttrs.push_back(newAttr);
        attribute.setIndex(m_childAttrs.size() - 1);
      } else {
        // No child has the attribute. Mark as invalid
        attribute.setIndexInvalid();
      }
    }
  }
}
```

Once a **VolumeAttr** is set up and marked as valid, we proceed to sampling each child volume in turn. Because **setupAttribute()** created a set of unique **VolumeAttr** instances to be used with each attribute/volume combination, we first look up the attribute index in the **m_childAttrs** array, which gives us the **VolumeAttr** instance to use for that particular child volume. The composite value is then incremented by the value returned by **m_volumes[i]->sample()**.

VolumeAttr, 235

Code 12.48. CompositeVolume::sample()

```
VolumeSample CompositeVolume::sample(const VolumeSampleState &state,
                                     const VolumeAttr &attribute) const
{
  if (attribute.index() == VolumeAttr::IndexNotSet) {
    setupAttribute(attribute);
  }
  if (attribute.index() == VolumeAttr::IndexInvalid) {
    return VolumeSample(Colors::zero(), m_phaseFunction);
  }

  Color value = Colors::zero();
  int attrIndex = attribute.index();

  for (size_t i = 0, size = m_volumes.size(); i < size; ++i) {
    const VolumeAttr &childAttr = m_childAttrs[attrIndex].attrs[i];
    const Color sampleValue = m_volumes[i]->sample(state, childAttr).value;
    value += sampleValue;
    if (state.rayState.rayType == RayState::FullRaymarch) {
      m_compositePhaseFunction->setWeight(i, Math::max(sampleValue));
    }
  }

  return VolumeSample(value, m_phaseFunction);
}
```

Raymarching in PVR

13.1   Introduction

In PVR, there are three major modules that work together in order to produce a final rendered image. First of all, the **Renderer** is responsible for firing rays into the scene, corresponding to each pixel in the final image. Once the ray start point and direction have been determined, it is up to one of the **Raymarcher** subclasses to step along the ray and incrementally compute the luminance and transmittance for the given ray. It does not, however, compute the luminance directly; rather, it delegates

that task to one of the **RaymarchSampler** subclasses. The sampler classes do the work of sampling volumetric properties from the scene's **Volume** instances and turn those into luminance and transmittance measures that the **Raymarcher** is then able to integrate. This chapter will discuss the

Raymarcher base class and its only subclass, the **UniformRaymarcher**. Chapter 14 will discuss the **RaymarchSampler** classes.

Conceptually, the **Raymarcher** classes only interact with **Volume** objects in their spatial representation, i.e., by performing intersection tests and finding integration intervals. All of the interaction with the actual volu-

metric properties are left to the **RaymarchSampler**. Thus, the raymarcher is responsible for *integration*, and the sampler is responsible for *sampling* and potential *light integration*. Figure 13.1 illustrates the relationship.

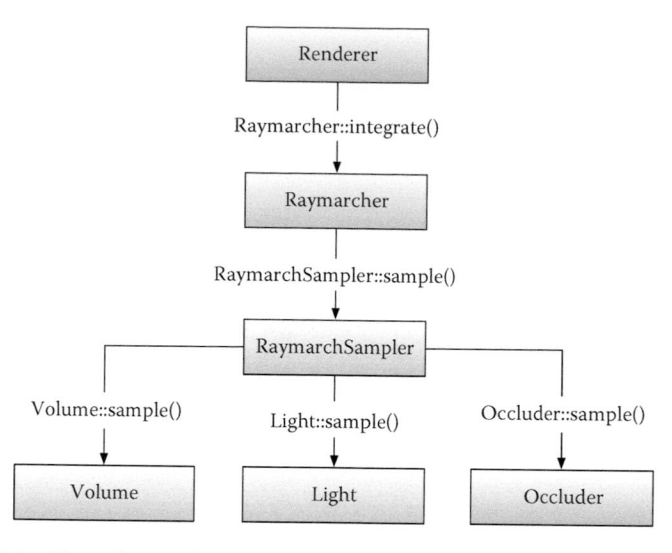

Figure 13.1. The relationship between the **Renderer**, the **Raymarcher**, and the **RaymarchSampler**. Only the **RaymarchSampler** interacts with the scene's volumes, lights, and occluders.

13.2   The **Raymarcher** Base Class

The **Raymarcher** base class is very simple. It holds a pointer to the **Raymarch Sampler**, which is used at each raymarch step to compute luminance and transmittance. The sampler can be changed by calling **Raymarcher::set RaymarchSampler()**.

The only virtual function that subclasses need to implement is **inte grate()**, which takes a **RayState**, holding information about the ray that should be integrated, and returns an **IntegrationResult**, containing the final luminance and transmittance for the ray.

The reason for separating the raymarcher from the scene sampling and potential light integration is that they deal with two separate integrals. The raymarcher is concerned with the line integral $L(p, \vec{\omega})$, which includes the integration of transmittance, $T(p', p)$. The calculation of $L_i(p')$, however, is independent of the line integral, and to the extent that it does involve integration, for example, to compute incoming radiance, it is a separate problem that is best dealt with independently from the line integral. Equation (13.1) illustrates the difference:

$$L(p, \vec{\omega}) = \overbrace{\int_0^\infty T(p', p)\, \overbrace{L_i(p')}^{\text{light}}\, dt}^{\text{line integral}}. \tag{13.1}$$

Code 13.1. The **Raymarcher** class

```
class Raymarcher : public Util::ParamBase
{
public:
  // Typedefs
  PVR_TYPEDEF_SMART_PTRS(Raymarcher);
  // Main methods
  void setRaymarchSampler(RaymarchSampler::CPtr sampler)
  { m_raymarchSampler = sampler; }
  // To be implemented by subclasses
  virtual IntegrationResult integrate(const RayState &state) const = 0;
protected:
  // Protected data members
  RaymarchSampler::CPtr m_raymarchSampler;
};
```

13.2.1   The **IntegrationResult** Struct

As mentioned above, the **IntegrationResult** contains the resulting luminance and transmittance that the raymarcher computes. The two values
map directly to the RGB and alpha outputs of the renderer, respectively.
The **IntegrationResult** also contains two **ColorCurve** pointers. Depending on whether **RayState::doOutputDeepL** and **RayState::doOutputDeepT**
are set, the **Raymarcher** subclass is responsible for allocating and filling in
the two **Curve** instances with deep data. Chapter 15 will show the use of
these functions in more detail.

Code 13.2. The **IntegrationResult** struct

```
struct IntegrationResult
{
  IntegrationResult()
    : luminance(0.0), transmittance(1.0)
  { }
  IntegrationResult(const Color &L, const Color &T)
    : luminance(L), transmittance(T)
  { }
  IntegrationResult(const Color &L, Util::ColorCurve::CPtr Lf,
                    const Color &T, Util::ColorCurve::CPtr Tf)
    : luminance(L), transmittance(T),
      luminanceFunction(Lf), transmittanceFunction(Tf)
  { }
  Color luminance;
  Color transmittance;
  Util::ColorCurve::CPtr luminanceFunction;
  Util::ColorCurve::CPtr transmittanceFunction;
};
```

13.3   The `UniformRaymarcher` Class

PVR's only raymarcher class is the **UniformRaymarcher**. Though it may seem superfluous to use a base class/subclass separation for a single class, the intent of PVR is to make it simple to extend the included feature set, and the raymarcher types are no exception.

The **UniformRaymarcher** class takes a number of user parameters, and it implements the virtual **ParamBase::setParams()** function to pick them up. The parameters are stored in a struct **UniformRaymarcher::Params** for purposes of modularity.

ParamBase, 98

Code 13.3. The `UniformRaymarcher::Params` struct

```
struct Params
{
  Params();
  double stepLength;
  int    useVolumeStepLength;
  double volumeStepLengthMult;
  int    doEarlyTermination;
  double earlyTerminationThreshold;
};
```

The **Params** struct is updated in **UniformRaymarcher::setParams()**, where the **getValue()** call from pvr/StlUtil.h is used to check a **ParamMap** for a given attribute and assigning a default if it does not exist.

ParamMap, 98

Code 13.4. The `UniformRaymarcher::setParams()` function

```
void UniformRaymarcher::setParams(const Util::ParamMap &params)
{
  getValue(params.floatMap, k_strStepLength,
           m_params.stepLength);
  getValue(params.intMap, k_strUseVolumeStepLength,
           m_params.useVolumeStepLength);
  getValue(params.floatMap, k_strVolumeStepLengthMult,
           m_params.volumeStepLengthMult);
  getValue(params.intMap, k_strDoEarlyTerm,
           m_params.doEarlyTermination);
  getValue(params.floatMap, k_strEarlyTermThresh,
           m_params.earlyTerminationThreshold);
}
```

13.3.1   Ray Integration

Once the user parameters have been set, most of the raymarcher's logic is in the **integrate()** function. The first step, common to all raymarchers, is to intersect the world-space ray found in **RayState::wsRay** against the scene's root volume. Because the list of intervals returned by **Volume:: intersect()** may contain an arbitrary number of potentially overlapping parts, the **splitIntervals()** utility function is used to turn them into a list of intervals that are guaranteed to be nonoverlapping. The **split Intervals()** function is described in more detail in Section 13.4.1.

If the returned list of intervals is empty, the function returns before doing any more work.

Code 13.5. The `UniformRaymarcher::integrate()` function

```
IntegrationResult
UniformRaymarcher::integrate(const RayState &state) const
{
  // Integration intervals ---

  IntervalVec rawIntervals = RenderGlobals::scene()->volume->intersect(state);
  IntervalVec intervals = splitIntervals(rawIntervals);

  if (intervals.size() == 0) {
    return IntegrationResult();
  }
```

When the **Renderer** spawns a ray for integration, it can specify whether the raymarcher should output the luminance and transmittance values for each step along the ray, in the form of a **Curve<Color>**, which PVR refers to as luminance and transmittance functions. The transmittance function is used by the **Renderer** to build *transmittance maps*, which are used to precompute light occlusion. Chapter 15 will describe these in more detail. Because all raymarchers need to support the same basic functionality, the setup of the deep pixel data is implemented in the functions **setupDeepLCurve()** and **setupDeepTCurve()**.

Code 13.6. The `setupDeepLCurve()` function

```
Util::ColorCurve::Ptr setupDeepLCurve(const RayState &state,
                                      const float first)
{
  Util::ColorCurve::Ptr lf;

  if (state.doOutputDeepL) {
    lf = Util::ColorCurve::create();
    lf->addSample(first, Colors::zero());
  }

  return lf;
}
```

Code 13.7. The **setupDeepTCurve()** function

```
Util::ColorCurve::Ptr setupDeepTCurve(const RayState &state,
                                      const float first)
{
  Util::ColorCurve::Ptr tf;

  if (state.doOutputDeepT) {
    tf = Util::ColorCurve::create();
    tf->addSample(first, Colors::one());
  }

  return tf;
}
```

The two functions return an allocated **ColorCurve** pointer, or a null pointer, depending on the value of **RayState::doOutputDeepL** and **RayState::do OutputDeepT**. Each deep pixel is initialized to zero (for luminance) and one (for transmittance), with the first sample point at the depth of the start of the first integration interval.

Code 13.8. The **UniformRaymarcher::integrate()** function

```
// Set up transmittance function and luminance function ---

ColorCurve::Ptr lf = setupDeepLCurve(state, intervals[0].t0);
ColorCurve::Ptr tf = setupDeepTCurve(state, intervals[0].t0);
```

Once the deep pixel data are initialized, the ray-integration variables are set up. Each time the **RaymarchSampler** is called, it will need to be passed a **VolumeSampleState**, but only the sample position will change from one raymarch step to the next. Because of this, it is allocated outside the raymarch loop itself. The accumulation variables for luminance and transmittance are also initialized at this point.

Code 13.9. The **UniformRaymarcher::integrate()** function

```
// Ray integration variables ---

VolumeSampleState sampleState(state);
Color             L       = Colors::zero();
Color             T_e     = Colors::one();
Color             T_h     = Colors::one();
Color             T_alpha = Colors::one();
Color             T_m     = Colors::zero();
```

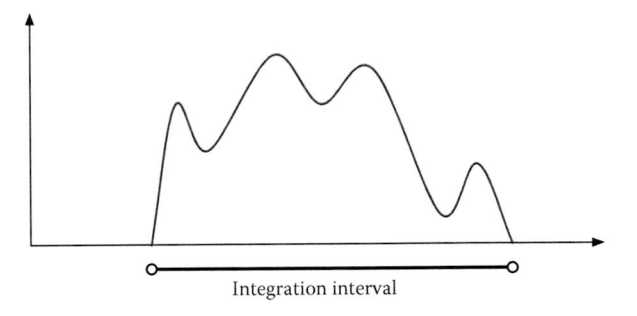

Figure 13.2. The integration interval is the shortest segment along a ray that needs to be sampled in order to fully capture the volumetric data in the scene.

With the accumulation variable in place, we start the outer raymarch loop, which iterates over each integration interval. Its job is to determine the range that needs integrating and which step length to use.

The first step is to set the start and end of the interval that will be raymarched. For this, the raymarcher looks not only at the start and end of the interval that was provided but also at the min and max clipping distances that the **Renderer** set when it spawned the ray. Usually, the near clipping distance is 0.0 and the far clipping distance is infinity, but in some cases, they may be shortened, to render only a specific depth of the scene. (See Figure 13.2.)

Code 13.10. The UniformRaymarcher::integrate() function

```
// Interval loop ---

BOOST_FOREACH (const Interval &interval, intervals) {

  // Interval integration variables
  const double tStart = std::max(interval.t0, state.tMin);
  const double tEnd   = std::min(interval.t1, state.tMax);
```

Once the start point and endpoint of the interval have been found, the step length needs to be determined. (See Figure 13.3.) The **UniformRay marcher** has several ways of choosing this. Depending on user preference, either an explicitly chosen step length is used or the step length is chosen based on what the **Volume** specified in the **Interval** returned from **Volume::intersect()**.

One of the corner cases that must be handled here is where a very short portion of the volume is being raymarched. If the volume's suggested step length is longer than the integration interval itself, then the

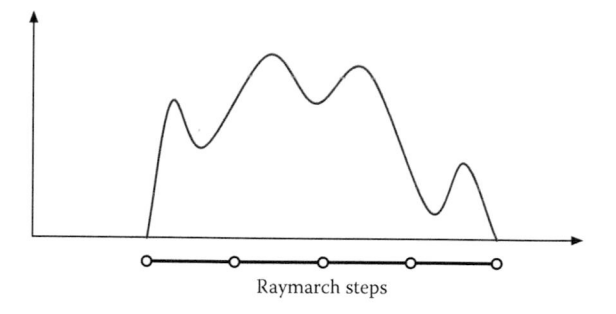

Figure 13.3. Dividing the integration interval into raymarch steps.

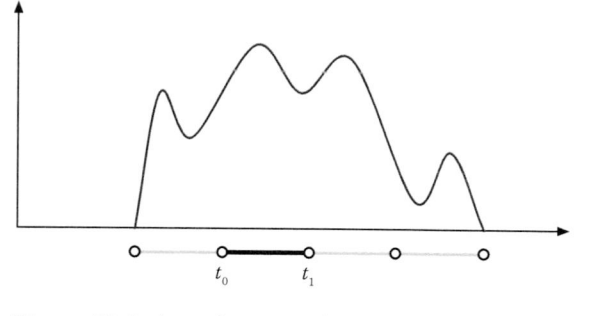

Figure 13.4. At each raymarch step, the start (t_0) and end (t_1) of the step interval are tracked.

step length of the raymarcher must be adjusted. Taking this into account, the final step length is stored in the **baseStepLength** variable.

Code 13.11. The `UniformRaymarcher::integrate()` function

```
// Pick step length
const double stepLengthToUse =
  m_params.useVolumeStepLength ?
  interval.stepLength * m_params.volumeStepLengthMult :
  m_params.stepLength;
const double baseStepLength = std::min(stepLengthToUse, tEnd - tStart);
```

The **UniformRaymarcher** uses an approach to the inner raymarch loop that is different from most common raymarch code. Instead of incrementing the current sample position t explicitly, it tracks the start and end of each raymarch step. The **stepT0** variable indicates the start of the current raymarch step, and **stepT1** refers to the end. Figure 13.4 illustrates the concept.

Again, a corner case arises when a very short interval is being raymarched. Due to floating-point precision issues, the base step length may be small enough that even a nonzero step length still produces a zero-length interval. This occurs when **tStart + baseStepLength == tStart**. The **UniformRaymarcher** simply checks if the start and end of the integration interval is identical and, if so, skips the raymarch loop entirely.

Code 13.12. The `UniformRaymarcher::integrate()` function

```
// Set up first raymarch step
double stepT0 = tStart;
double stepT1 = tStart + baseStepLength;
```

```
// Prevent infinite loops
if (stepT0 == stepT1) {
  continue;
}
```

With the integration interval decided, the raymarch loop is started. The loop continues as long as the start of the current raymarch step is less than the end of the integration interval, i.e., **stepT0 < tEnd**. The **doTerminate** variable is used inside the loop to allow for *early termination* if the ray transmittance drops below a certain threshold.

Code 13.13. The `UniformRaymarcher::integrate()` function

```
// Raymarch loop ---

bool doTerminate = false;

while (stepT0 < tEnd) {
```

Although the step length was initially determined and stored in **base StepLength**, a fresh step length is computed based on **stepT1 - stepT0**. This ensures that we get a reasonable value in cases where numeric precision is an issue.

We also need to determine where along the current raymarch step the volume should be sampled. The **UniformRaymarcher** uses the midpoint rule for integration and selects the middle of the interval. With the parametric distance t found, the world-space sample point is found by evaluating the current ray at distance t. The result is stored in the **VolumeSampleState**.

VolumeSampleState, 237

Code 13.14. The `UniformRaymarcher::integrate()` function

```
// Information about current step
const double stepLength = stepT1 - stepT0;
const double t          = (stepT0 + stepT1) * 0.5;
sampleState.wsP         = state.wsRay(t);
```

VolumeSampleState, 237

With the **VolumeSampleState** configured, it is time to sample the volumetric properties of the scene and integrate them into a luminance measure and extinction measure, which the raymarcher can use to update its accumulated luminance and transmittance. Because the conversion of volumetric properties into a luminance measure can be somewhat arbitrary, this task is handled by the **RaymarchSampler** classes. It is assumed that the

RaymarchSampler, 285

sampler has already been configured, so the **UniformRaymarcher** simply
calls **RaymarchSampler::sample()** to request a new **RaymarchSample**.

RaymarchSample, 286

Code 13.15. The `UniformRaymarcher::integrate()` function

```
// Get holdout, luminance and extinction from the scene
VolumeSample hoSample =
  RenderGlobals::scene()->volume->sample(sampleState, m_holdoutAttr);
RaymarchSample sample = m_raymarchSampler->sample(sampleState);
```

13.3.2 Updating Transmittance and Luminance

The **RaymarchSample** struct contains a measure of luminance (radiance
per unit length) and extinction (inverse extinction distance), and our
first task is to update the transmittance value based on the extinction.
This is where Beer's law from Section 9.6 comes into play. The update to the transmittance variables is a little less straightforward since
UniformRaymarcher handles *holdout objects*, but the logic is isolated to **up
dateTransmittance()**.

RaymarchSample, 286

Optical Thickness and
Transmittance, 174

Code 13.16. The `UniformRaymarcher::integrate()` function

```
// Update transmittance
updateTransmittance(state, stepLength, sample.extinction,
                    hoSample.value, T_e, T_h, T_alpha, T_m);
```

Section 10.8 described how holdouts could be implemented in a raymarching framework, and **UniformRaymarcher** follows the approach directly. The **updateTransmittance()** function is called at each raymarch
step, so if possible, we want to avoid evaluating **std::exp()** in cases where
σ_e or σ_h are zero. Initializing **expSigmaE** and **expSigmaH** to 1.0 means we
can skip the computation if either of the coefficients are zero.

Holdouts, 194

Code 13.17. The `updateTransmittance()` function

```
void updateTransmittance(const Render::RayState &state,
                         const double stepLength,
                         Color &sigma_e, const Color &sigma_h,
                         Color &T_e, Color &T_h, Color &T_alpha,
                         Color &T_m)
{
  Color expSigmaE = Colors::one();
  Color expSigmaH = Colors::one();
```

Depending on the context in which the raymarcher was called, we may or may not need to track the holdout variables **T_h**, **T_alpha**, and **T_m**. For shadow rays, holdouts are treated as any other type of extinction, so we simply add σ_h to σ_e and proceed without touching the holdout variables. For camera rays, we do need to compute **T_h**, which is done according to the equation

$$T_h = T_h \cdot e^{\sigma_h dt}.$$

Code 13.18. The `updateTransmittance()` function

```
// Update holdout transmittance
if (state.rayDepth > 0) {
  sigma_e += sigma_h;
} else {
  // Update accumulated holdout
  if (Math::max(sigma_h) > 0.0f) {
    expSigmaH = exp(-sigma_h * stepLength);
    T_h *= expSigmaH;
  }
}
```

The main transmittance variable, **T_e**, is updated using the same formula but looking at σ_e.

Code 13.19. The `updateTransmittance()` function

```
// Update transmittance
if (Math::max(sigma_e) > 0.0f) {
  expSigmaE = exp(-sigma_e * stepLength);
  T_e *= expSigmaE;
}
```

The last step in updating transmittance is to produce the correct T_α and T_m. This is also done according to the approach outlined in Section 10.8.

Holdouts, 194

Code 13.20. The `updateTransmittance()` function

```
// Update output transmittance
if (state.rayDepth == 0) {
  T_m     = Math::lerp(T_alpha, T_m, expSigmaH);
  T_alpha = Math::lerp(T_m, T_alpha, expSigmaE);
}
```

The luminance variable **L** is updated by the sample's luminance value, scaled by the current step length as well as the current accumulated transmittance due to extinction (**T_e**) and holdouts (**T_h**).

Code 13.21. The `UniformRaymarcher::integrate()` function

```
// Update luminance
L += sample.luminance * T_e * T_h * stepLength;
```

Because the expression $e^{-x} > 0$ is guaranteed to hold for any $x > 0$, we know that our accumulation variable **T_e** will be nonzero no matter how much density we pass through. In practice, however, there is a certain point where it no longer makes sense to track the exact value of **T_e**; we instead assume that it has gone all the way to zero.

Setting **T_e** to zero at a given threshold value helps speed up renders, and we refer to this as *early termination*. Whether or not to use early termination is a user preference, and the termination threshold is also specified by the user through the **Params** struct.

The **UniformRaymarcher** looks at the maximum value of **T_e**, since **T_e** is a **Color** property, and checks if the value is smaller than the early-termination threshold. If it is, **T_e** is set to zero, but rather than abort the current raymarch loop, the **doTerminate** flag is set to **true**. This is done to allow for updating of the deep pixel data structures before returning from the raymarch function.

Code 13.22. The `UniformRaymarcher::integrate()` function

```
if (m_params.doEarlyTermination &&
    Math::max(T_e) < m_params.earlyTerminationThreshold) {
  T_e         = Colors::zero();
  T_alpha     = Colors::zero();
  doTerminate = true;
}
```

The deep pixel data are updated after ray termination is decided, so that the value recorded can reflect whether **T_e** was set to zero.

It is important to store the transmittance value at the end of the current raymarch step, rather than at the midpoint where the raymarch sampler was executed because the integral has computed the change in transmittance all the way to the end of the raymarch step (see Figure 13.5). The midpoint is only used for sampling purposes. These subtle yet important distinctions are another reason why **UniformRaymarcher** tracks the actual raymarch step start point and endpoint, rather than just a sample point.

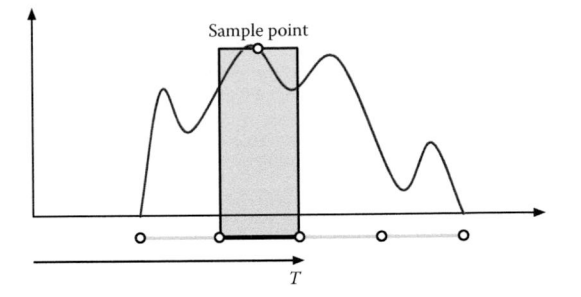

Figure 13.5. Although the sample point is placed at the midpoint of the interval, the computed transmittance reflects the state of the ray at the end of the raymarch step.

Code 13.23. The `UniformRaymarcher::integrate()` function

```
// Update transmittance and luminance functions
updateDeepFunctions(stepT1, L, T_e, lf, tf);
```

The `updateDeepFunctions()` call is used mainly to hide the multiple **if** checks, helping to keep the raymarch code a little simpler.

Code 13.24. The `updateDeepFunctions()` function

```
void updateDeepFunctions(const float t, const Color &L, const Color &T,
                         Util::ColorCurve::Ptr lf, Util::ColorCurve::Ptr tf)
{
  if (tf) {
    tf->addSample(t, T);
  }
  if (lf) {
    lf->addSample(t, L);
  }
}
```

Once the raymarch step is computed and recorded, we need to prepare for the next step in the loop. As the integral is currently solved up to the point **stepT1**, we want that to be the start of the next integration step, so we assign **stepT0 = stepT1**.

The end of the next integration step should intuitively be **stepT1 + baseStepLength**, but we have to consider that the length of the interval $[t_{start}, t_{end}]$ is unlikely to be an exact multiplier of the step length. (See Figure 13.6.) Thus, when we arrive at the final raymarch step, we must clamp the end of the integration step so that it ends at t_{end}. Failing to do so would mean integrating over a longer distance than actually exists, overestimating the integral.

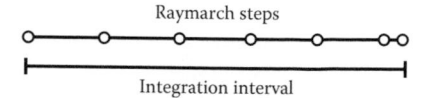

Figure 13.6. The integration interval may not be evenly divisible by the step size.

Code 13.25. The `UniformRaymarcher::integrate()` function

```
// Set up next raymarch step
stepT0 = stepT1;
stepT1 = min(tEnd, stepT1 + baseStepLength);
```

With the update of the deep pixel data performed, it is safe to terminate the ray if the value of T_e has been determined to be below the termination threshold. Calling **break** at this point in the code will break the **while** loop, so a second **break** is added outside, which forces the **for** loop over all the intervals to terminate as well.

Code 13.26. The `UniformRaymarcher::integrate()` function

```
// Terminate if requested
if (doTerminate) {
  break;
}

} // end raymarch of single interval

if (doTerminate) {
  break;
}
```

To reduce the memory overhead associated with the deep pixel data, any duplicated transmittance or luminance values are removed from the **Curve** instances. More advanced compression could be used, but for the purpose of simplicity, PVR simply throws out duplicates.

Code 13.27. The `UniformRaymarcher::integrate()` function

```
if (tf) {
  tf->removeDuplicates();
}

if (lf) {
  lf->removeDuplicates();
}
```

The result of the raymarch is then returned, including both the final luminance and transmittance values as well as the deep pixel data (**lf** and **tf**). We also use a check of the ray depth to see if holdouts were computed for the ray. If they were, we need to return **T_alpha** rather than **T_e**, since **T_e** doesn't incorporate the effects of holdouts.

Code 13.28. The `UniformRaymarcher::integrate()` function

```
  if (state.rayDepth == 0) {
    return IntegrationResult(L, lf, T_alpha, tf);
  } else {
    return IntegrationResult(L, lf, T_e, tf);
  }
}
```

13.4   Integration Intervals

As we saw in the previous section, one of the first things a raymarcher needs to do is to intersect the ray against the scene's volume or volumes, to determine which parts need raymarching. The result of the intersection test is referred to in PVR as the *integration bounds* or *integration interval*. The first step, finding the raw intervals, is up to each **Volume** subclass. Once the (potentially overlapping) intervals have been found, they need to be split into a set of nonoverlapping intervals, suitable for raymarching. This was discussed in Section 10.3, but it was not implemented in detail.

13.4.1   Splitting Intervals

In PVR, **splitIntervals()** is the function that handles splitting of overlapping intervals into disjoint intervals, and both its input and output are **IntervalVec** instances.

The stages of the algorithm are shown in Figure 13.7. The first step is to take the endpoints of each interval and store them in a separate list. In the second step, a new interval is temporarily constructed between each of the individual endpoints. In the third step, each of the new intervals is checked against the input intervals to determine whether they can be removed, and if not, what the smallest step length is for all the input intervals that overlap it.

Because the function is called for all interval sets after they are returned from the **Volume::intersect()** routine, regardless of the number of intervals in the set and regardless of whether any of the intervals actually overlap, the function must be robust enough to handle all

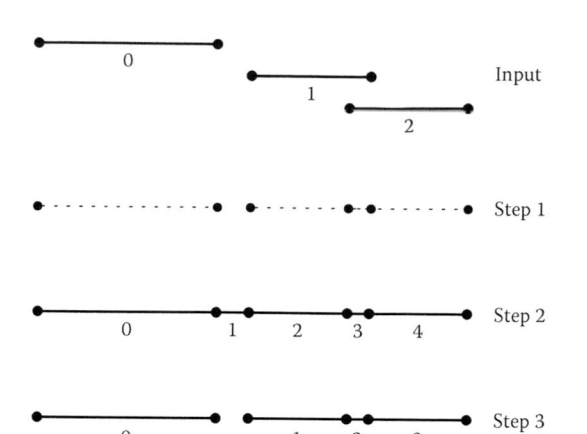

Figure 13.7. Visual representation of the **splitIntervals()** algorithm.

configurations. The first thing **splitInterval()** does is to see if the input
was a single **Interval**. In this case, no work needs to be done and it is
safe to return the input directly.

Interval, 234

Code 13.29. The **splitIntervals()** function

```
IntervalVec splitIntervals(const IntervalVec &intervals)
{
  // If we have zero or one intervals we do nothing
  if (intervals.size() < 2) {
    return intervals;
  }
}
```

Next, **splitIntervals()** builds a temporary **std::vector<double>** to hold
each of the input interval's endpoints. The **std::vector** is preallocated to
the appropriate size to prevent any reallocation from happening during
the **for** loop.

Code 13.30. The **splitIntervals()** function

```
vector<double> points;
points.reserve(intervals.size() * 2);
BOOST_FOREACH (const Interval &i, intervals) {
  points.push_back(i.t0);
  points.push_back(i.t1);
}
```

Once the endpoints have been collected, they are sorted and any duplicates are removed. Duplicates occur when the start point and endpoint of two input intervals are identical. The **std::unique** function takes a sorted container of points and moves all of the duplicates to the end. The end can then be trimmed off using **resize()** to permanently delete the duplicates.

Code 13.31. The **splitIntervals()** function

```
// Sort and unique start/end points
sort(points.begin(), points.end());
vector<double>::iterator newEnd = unique(points.begin(), points.end());
points.resize(newEnd - points.begin());
```

Interval, 234

The final step is to take the sorted list of points, construct a temporary **Interval**, and then to find all of the input intervals that overlap it. An input is considered to overlap the current interval if **input.t0 < newInterval.t1 && input.t1 > newInterval.t0**. If a matching interval is found, the current interval is marked as being valid. Because multiple input intervals may overlap the current one, the minimum step length (i.e., the most conservative and accurate) is selected.

Code 13.32. The **splitIntervals()** function

```
// For each endpoint pair, find the incoming interval(s) that overlap it
IntervalVec outIntervals;
for (size_t i = 0, size = points.size() - 1; i < size; ++i) {
  Interval newInterval(points[i], points[i + 1],
                       std::numeric_limits<float>::max());
  bool foundInterval = false;
  BOOST_FOREACH (const Interval &interval, intervals) {
    if (interval.t0 < newInterval.t1 && interval.t1 > newInterval.t0) {
      newInterval.stepLength = std::min(interval.stepLength,
                                        newInterval.stepLength);
      foundInterval = true;
    }
  }
  if (foundInterval) {
    outIntervals.push_back(newInterval);
  }
}

return outIntervals;
```

Lighting in PVR

In the previous chapter, we used the **Raymarcher** classes to integrate luminance along a ray. At each raymarch step, we found luminance in the **RaymarchSample** struct, and the integral of all the luminance values then became the result of the raymarch and later the final pixel value. We did not, however, specify how the luminance value at each raymarch step was found, except that it was returned from the **RaymarchSampler**. In this chapter, we will look at the implementation of PVR's **RaymarchSampler** classes, which are responsible for sampling values from the **Scene** object's **Volume** and **Light** instances and turning them into a single measure of luminance. We will also look at PVR's light sources, phase functions, and occlusion handling.

14.1 Raymarch Samplers

While the **Raymarcher** classes were responsible for integrating the luminance along a ray, we also need to integrate all of the incoming light at each sample point on that ray. PVR does not dictate how this calculation of luminance should happen; instead, it just specifies that the result of the calculation be presented as a measure of luminance, indicating how much light is added at the given sample point, and a measure of extinction, which tells the raymarcher how transmittance along the ray changes at the point. The computation takes place in **sample()**, which is the only virtual function that subclasses are required to implement.

Code 14.1. The **RaymarchSampler** class

```
class RaymarchSampler : public Util::ParamBase
{
public:
...
  // To be implemented by subclasses
  virtual RaymarchSample sample(const VolumeSampleState &state) const = 0;
};
```

14.1.1   The **RaymarchSample** Struct

The result of the light integration step is returned as a **RaymarchSample**, which contains a luminance and an extinction value. The struct is just a convenient holder for both values and provides reasonable defaults so that a sampler can return an empty result by using return Raymarch Sample().

Code 14.2. The **RaymarchSample** struct

```
struct RaymarchSample
{
  // Constructors
  RaymarchSample()
    : luminance(Colors::zero()), extinction(Colors::zero())
  { }
  RaymarchSample(const Color &L, const Color &A)
    : luminance(L), extinction(A)
  { }
  // Public data members
  Color luminance;
  Color extinction;
};
```

14.2   The **DensitySampler** Class

To illustrate how simple a **RaymarchSampler** can be, we first look at the **DensitySampler** class. Instead of attempting any kind of volumetric lighting, it only looks up the density property in the scene and uses that value as a measure of both luminance and extinction. The sampler produces nothing more than an image indicating how much volume is present in various parts of the image. (See Figure 14.1.)

RaymarchSampler, 285

Figure 14.1. A pyroclastic point rendered using the **DensitySampler**.

Code 14.3. The **DensitySampler** class

```
class DensitySampler : public RaymarchSampler
{
public:
...
  // From ParamBase
  PVR_DEFINE_TYPENAME(DensitySampler);
  // From RaymarchSampler
  virtual RaymarchSample sample(const VolumeSampleState &state) const;
private:
  // Private data members
  VolumeAttr m_densityAttr;
};
```

VolumeAttr, 235

The only work done by the **DensitySampler**'s constructor is to first initialize the **VolumeAttr** with the density attribute name. With the **VolumeAttr** initialized, it samples the scene and returns the density value directly to the raymarcher as a measure of both luminance and transmittance.

Code 14.4. The `DensitySampler` constructor

```
DensitySampler::DensitySampler()
  : m_densityAttr("density")
{

}
```

Code 14.5. The `DensitySampler::sample` function

```
RaymarchSample
DensitySampler::sample(const VolumeSampleState &state) const
{
  VolumeSample sample =
    RenderGlobals::scene()->volume->sample(state, m_densityAttr);
  return RaymarchSample(sample.value, sample.value);
}
```

14.3   The `PhysicalSampler` Class

The most commonly used raymarch sampler in PVR is the `PhysicalSam pler`, which implements a lighting model based on the approach presented in Chapter 9. The attributes it samples from the scene are direct representations of the physical properties of a volume, and to compute the luminance for each sample it looks at the scene's lights, occluders, and phase functions. (See Figure 14.2.)

Volumetric Lighting, 167

     The `PhysicalSampler`'s constructor is similar to `DensitySampler`'s. The only difference is the names of the attributes that we will be sampling from the scene, which are the physically based volumetric properties.

Code 14.6. The `PhysicalSampler` constructor

```
PhysicalSampler::PhysicalSampler()
  : m_scatteringAttr("scattering"),
    m_absorptionAttr("absorption"),
    m_emissionAttr("emission")
{

}
```

     The `sample()` implementation is more involved than the `DensitySam pler`, for obvious reasons, but the process is still easy to follow. First, the sampler sets up the sample states that will be required for sampling

DensitySampler, 286

Figure 14.2. A pyroclastic point rendered using the **PhysicalSampler**.

the lights and occluders in the scene. Also, because it is constant for all the lights in the scene, the outgoing ray direction $\vec{\omega}$ is recorded in the **wo** variable.

Code 14.7. The **PhysicalSampler::sample** function

```
RaymarchSample PhysicalSampler::sample(const VolumeSampleState &state) const
{
    const Scene::CPtr    scene        = RenderGlobals::scene();
    const Volume::CPtr   volume       = scene->volume;

    LightSampleState     lightState   (state.rayState);
    OcclusionSampleState occlusionState (state.rayState);

    const Vector         wo           = -state.rayState.wsRay.dir;
```

VolumeSampleState, 237

Using the **VolumeSampleState** that was passed to the function, each of the volumetric properties of the scene volume are sampled. When a volume is sampled, it returns both the sample value and the volume's phase function in the **VolumeSample** struct. The phase function is only relevant when the sampled property is scattering, but it is added whenever a volume is sampled, in case the **RaymarchSampler** needs to use it. When we get to Section 14.7.5, we will see how phase functions are handled for scenes with multiple **Volume** instances, but in the meantime, we just need to be aware that the phase function's state is valid only up until the next call to **Volume::sample()**. For this reason, we are careful to sample the scattering attribute last, preserving the integrity of the phase function.

Once the attributes have been sampled, reference variables are created to match the mathematical symbols used throughout the book: the scattering cross section σ_s, the absorption cross section σ_a, and luminance due to emission L_{em}.

Code 14.8. The **PhysicalSampler::sample** function

```
VolumeSample          abSample      = volume->sample(state, m_absorptionAttr);
VolumeSample          emSample      = volume->sample(state, m_emissionAttr);
VolumeSample          scSample      = volume->sample(state, m_scatteringAttr);

const Color &         sigma_s       = scSample.value;
const Color &         sigma_a       = abSample.value;
const Color &         L_em          = emSample.value;
```

Depending on the context in which the sampler is called, certain parts of the calculation may be skipped. For example, if the ray that spawned the sample is used only to determine transmittance, there is no reason to compute luminance. A second potential optimization is possible if σ_s is zero; in that case, no light will ever be reflected into the path of the current ray, and the luminance contribution of in-scattering is zero.

Code 14.9. The **PhysicalSampler::sample** function

```
// Only perform calculation if ray is primary and scattering coefficient is
// greater than zero.

Color                 L_sc          = Colors::zero();

if (Math::max(sigma_s) > 0.0f &&
    state.rayState.rayType == RayState::FullRaymarch) {
```

Next, the **LightSampleState** and **OcclusionSampleState** are updated with the current position so that the scene's **Light** instances and their **Occluder** counterparts may be sampled. The light and occluder types will be covered later in this chapter, so for now we will assume that they are sampled in a similar way as the sampler itself or the volumes.

Code 14.10. The PhysicalSampler::sample function

```
// Update light and occluder sample states
lightState.wsP      = state.wsP;
occlusionState.wsP  = state.wsP;
```

Once it's clear that the lights in the scene do need to be sampled, they are handled in order by traversing the **std::vector<Light::CPtr>** found in **Scene::lights**.

Scene, 203

Code 14.11. The PhysicalSampler::sample function

```
// For each light source
BOOST_FOREACH (Light::CPtr light, scene->lights) {

    // Sample the light
    LightSample lightSample = light->sample(lightState);
```

LightSample, 294

The result of sampling the light source is a **LightSample**, which contains both the incoming radiance and the position of the light source that was sampled. The light source's position is used by the occluder to determine the path of light that needs to have its transmittance computed.

Code 14.12. The PhysicalSampler::sample function

```
// Sample the occluder
occlusionState.wsLightP = lightSample.wsP;
Color transmittance     = light->occluder()->sample(occlusionState);
```

The next step in computing in-scattering is to find the scattering probability. We do this by evaluating the phase function for the angle between the incoming direction (from the light source) and the outgoing direction (along the camera ray).

Code 14.13. The PhysicalSampler::sample function

```
// Find the scattering probability
const Vector wi = (state.wsP - lightSample.wsP).normalized();
const float  p  = scSample.phaseFunction->probability(wi, wo);
```

Once the incoming light intensity, the occlusion and the scattering probability are known, we can proceed to update the **L_sc** variable according to Equation (13.1):

$$L_s = \sigma_s p(\vec{\omega}, \vec{\omega}_i') S_i(\boldsymbol{p}') T(\boldsymbol{p}', \boldsymbol{p}_i).$$

Code 14.14. The `PhysicalSampler::sample` function

```
// Update luminance
L_sc += sigma_s * p * lightSample.luminance * transmittance;
```

After looping over all the light sources, the final luminance is returned as $L = L_e + L_s$ and extinction as $\sigma_e = \sigma_s + \sigma_a$.

Code 14.15. The `PhysicalSampler::sample` function

```
return RaymarchSample(L_sc + L_em, sigma_s + sigma_a);
```

14.4   The Light Base Class

All light types in PVR derive from the **Light** base class. Each light type is expected to have an intensity associated with it, which the base class provides access to through the **setIntensity()** and **intensity()** calls.

Although all light sources in reality have some form of *falloff*, for a production renderer we often need to provide more control than just what is "correct." The user often wants control over both *if* and *how* this falloff behaves. To serve this purpose, the **Light** base class lets the user turn falloff on or off using the **setFalloffEnabled** method. Falloff is further discussed in Section 14.4.2.

Falloff, 295

Another important aspect of lighting is the concept of *occlusion*, which describes to what extent different parts of a scene are visible to one another. There are many ways in which occlusion can be computed and stored, and PVR provides several different solutions. In order for PVR to compute realistic lighting effects, each light source will need to answer queries regarding its visibility, and to do this, it uses a delegate class called **Occluder**. Each light source has a single **Occluder**, which is set and accessed using the **setOccluder()** and **occluder()** calls.

Occluder, 311

Code 14.16. The **Light** class's main methods

```
class Light : public Util::ParamBase
{
public:
...
```

```
  // Main methods
  void               setIntensity(const Color &intensity);
  const Color&       intensity() const;
  void               setFalloffEnabled(const bool enabled);
  bool               falloffEnabled() const;
  void               setOccluder(Occluder::CPtr occluder);
  Occluder::CPtr     occluder() const;
protected:
...
  // Data members
  Color          m_intensity;
  bool           m_falloffEnabled;
  bool           m_softRolloff;
  Occluder::CPtr m_occluder;
};
```

PVR's light-source interface is quite simple, and each light-source implementation needs to provide just a single virtual function, which is **sample()**. The **sample()** call takes as its single argument a **LightSample State** and returns the result of its calculations in the form of a **LightSam ple**.

Code 14.17. The **Light** class's virtual methods

```
class Light : public Util::ParamBase
{
public:
...
  // To be implemented by subclasses
  virtual LightSample sample(const LightSampleState &state) const = 0;
...
protected:
...};
```

The **LightSampleState** is primarily used to provide the light with a sample position (**LightSampleState::wsP**), but it also provides access to the current **RayState**, in case the light needs access to the current sample time or any other current or future render state variables.

Code 14.18. The **LightSampleState** class

```
struct LightSampleState
{
  LightSampleState(const RayState &rState)
    : rayState(rState)
  { }
  const RayState &rayState;
  Vector wsP;
};
```

Once the light has computed the radiance arriving at the given position, it returns that value in the **LightSample** struct. The struct holds not only intensity but also the light's position, which is later used to find the incoming light direction, needed for phase function and occlusion calculations.

Code 14.19. The **LightSample** class

```
struct LightSample
{
  LightSample()
    : luminance(Colors::zero()), wsP(Vectors::zero())
  { }
  LightSample(const Color &L, const Vector &wsPos)
    : luminance(L), wsP(wsPos)
  { }
  Color  luminance;
  Vector wsP;
};
```

14.4.1 Light Intensity

As we discussed in Section 9.5, when light integration is performed to determine how much of the light traveling through the scene is scattered towards the camera, the intensity of each light source is weighted by a phase function. The simplest of the phase functions, and the one that PVR uses by default, is the isotropic phase function, which models a material that scatters light equally in all directions. In order to preserve an energy equilibrium, the amount of light that is scattered must be equal to the incoming light. Thus, the integral over all outgoing solid angles ω must equal one:

Phase Functions, 172

$$\int_{\Omega=4\pi} p(\vec{\omega}, \vec{\omega}')d\omega = 1.$$

While using this formulation leads to physically correct results, it may be unintuitive for the user of a rendering system to have to set their light intensity to 4π in order to see a result that looks bright white. For this reason, PVR divides by the isotropic phase constant whenever the user requests that intensity be set to a given value. This ensures that calculations internally use a more physically based model, while still providing a more intuitive interface to the user.

Code 14.20. The **Light::setIntensity()** method

```
void Light::setIntensity(const Color &intensity)
{
  m_intensity = intensity / Phase::k_isotropic;
}
```

14.4.2 Falloff

The user will often need to control the way that light falloff behaves. The primary control is to turn falloff on and off completely using the **setFalloffEnabled()** function. Once falloff is enabled, it follows a physically based inverse square falloff law, where intensity falls off according to the equation

$$f(\mathbf{P}) = \frac{1}{|\mathbf{P}|^2}.$$

The inverse square law can be understood if we consider a light source L enclosed by two spheres, S_1 and S_2 (see Figure 14.3). The spheres themselves do not absorb light, but rather give us a point of reference for measuring the amount of light that passes through the scene. If S_1 has a radius $r_1 = 1$ and S_2 has the radius $r_2 = 2$, we find that the area of each sphere is

$$A_1 = \frac{4\pi 1^2}{3} = \frac{4\pi}{3},$$

$$A_2 = \frac{4\pi 2^2}{3} = \frac{16\pi}{3}.$$

If we assume that the scene is devoid of any light-absorbing media, the light from L will travel unimpeded, and the same amount of total light should pass through both S_1 and S_2, regardless of how far away each one is. The only difference is the area the light projects to, which scales by the factor r^2.

Thus, at a distance $d = 1$, the intensity of the light source is I. As distance increases, the intensity decreases. But conversely, for points where

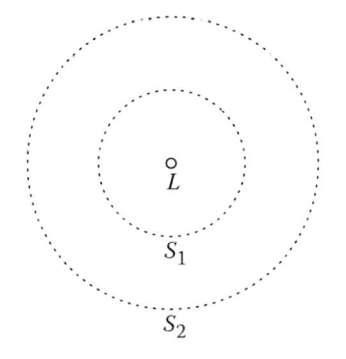

Figure 14.3. The amount of light arriving from L at S_1 is identical to that at S_2. Only the area of each sphere is different.

$d < 1$, intensity will be greater than I, increasing exponentially as the distance approaches zero. This increase, although physically correct, is often unwanted, and PVR instead uses an inverse square root falloff for very short distances.

Code 14.21. The `Light::falloff()` method

```
float Light::falloffFactor(const Vector &p1, const Vector &p2) const
{
  if (m_falloffEnabled) {
    float distanceSq = (p1 - p2).length2();
    if (m_softRolloff && distanceSq < 1.0) {
      return std::pow(1.0 / distanceSq, 0.25);
    } else {
      return 1.0 / distanceSq;
    }
  } else {
    return 1.0;
  }
}
```

14.5 Point Lights

The first light-source type we will look at is **PointLight**, which implements a light source that projects light uniformly in all directions. (See Figure 14.4.) This type of light source can be described using only a position for the projection origin; the rest of the necessary parameters are found in the **Light** base class.

Light, 292

Code 14.22. The **PointLight** class

```
class PointLight : public Light
{
public:
...
  // From Light
  virtual LightSample sample(const LightSampleState &state) const;
  // Main methods
  void            setPosition(const Vector &wsP);
  Vector          position() const;
private:
  // Private data members
  Vector m_wsP;
};
```

Figure 14.4. A **PointLight** surrounded by **ConstantVolume** instances.

The calculation of intensity for a point light is trivial. The light's intensity is found in the base class's **m_intensity** variable and is then scaled by **Light::falloffFactor()**. The result is returned along with the position of the light as a **LightSample** struct.

Code 14.23. The **PointLight::sample()** method

```
LightSample PointLight::sample(const LightSampleState &state) const
{
  return LightSample(m_intensity * falloffFactor(state.wsP, m_wsP), m_wsP);
}
```

Figure 14.5. A **SpotLight** projecting through a set of **ConstantVolume** instances.

14.6   Spot Lights

A small variation on the **PointLight** type is the **SpotLight**. Instead of projecting light in all directions, it has an orientation that determines in what direction light is emitted. (See Figure 14.5.) In PVR, this direction is specified using a **Camera**. The camera is used to determine the view direction of the light source, and the separate cone-angle controls determine the width of the light projection. Although a simple orientation vector could have done the same job, having a camera instance is convenient once we get to occlusion precomputation.

PointLight, 296

Camera, 213

Code 14.24. The **SpotLight** class

```
class SpotLight : public Light
{
public:
...
  // From Light
  virtual LightSample sample(const LightSampleState &state) const;
```

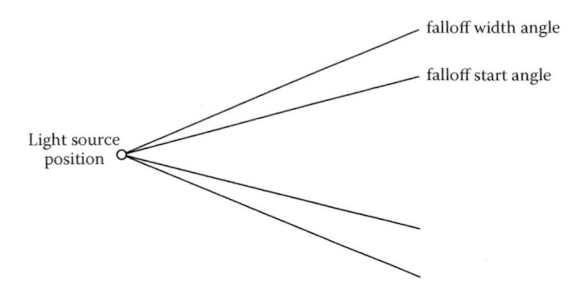

Figure 14.6. The falloff regions of a **SpotLight**.

```
// Main methods
void              setCamera(Camera::CPtr camera);
Camera::CPtr      camera() const;
void              setConeAngles(const float width, const float start);
private:
// Private data members
Vector      m_wsP;
Camera::CPtr m_camera;
float       m_cosWidth;
float       m_cosStart;
};
```

Internally, the **SpotLight** holds a variable **m_wsP** indicating the position of the light. This is only used as a convenience and optimization, rather than having to call on **Camera::position()** each time the light is sampled.

Camera, 213

The cone-angle falloff is computed by comparing the cosine of the sample point's camera-space position against the cosine of the falloff width and the falloff start (illustrated in Figure 14.6).

Code 14.25. The **SpotLight::sample()** method

```
LightSample SpotLight::sample(const LightSampleState &state) const
{
  Vector csP = m_camera->worldToCamera(state.wsP, state.rayState.time);
  float cosTheta = csP.normalized().z;
  float coneFalloff = 1.0;
  if (cosTheta < m_cosWidth) {
    coneFalloff = 0.0;
  } else if (cosTheta > m_cosStart) {
    coneFalloff = 1.0;
  } else {
    float delta = (cosTheta - m_cosWidth) / (m_cosStart - m_cosWidth);
    coneFalloff = delta * delta * delta * delta;
  }
  float distanceFalloff = falloffFactor(state.wsP, m_wsP);
  return LightSample(m_intensity * coneFalloff * distanceFalloff, m_wsP);
}
```

When we look at occluders in Section 14.8, we will see that different occluders use different projections. For example, the spotlight can use a normal perspective projection (**PerspectiveCamera**) for the view. On the other hand, a point light sees everything around it, requiring the use of a spherical projection (**SphericalCamera**).

Occlusion in PVR, 311

PerspectiveCamera, 220

SphericalCamera, 226

14.7   Phase Functions in PVR

In Section 9.5 we looked at how phase functions describe the directional distribution of light once a scattering event occurs in a volume. PVR implements several types of phase functions, and in this section, we will look both at some of the different types normally used in production rendering and also how the renderer can handle cases where multiple volumes exist in a scene, each with a different phase function.

Phase Functions, 172

14.7.1   The **PhaseFunction** Base Class

Each phase function in PVR inherits from the **PhaseFunction** base class. The only required virtual function implementation is **probability()**, which returns the scattering probability given an incoming and outgoing direction vector. The two vectors are presumed to be normalized, and the various phase function implementations take advantage of this fact, most notably that the cosine of the angle between the two vectors can be found using the expression

$$\cos(\theta) = \vec{\omega} \cdot \vec{\omega}'.$$

Code 14.26. The **PhaseFunction** base class

```
class PhaseFunction : public Util::ParamBase
{
public:
...
  // To be implemented by subclasses
  virtual float probability(const Vector &in, const Vector &out) const = 0;
};
```

Although phase functions may be wavelength dependent,[1] PVR makes the simplification that all wavelengths have the same scattering probability. Wavelength dependency is still supported through the scattering coefficient σ_s, just not for the phase function calculation.

---

[1]For example, Mie scattering behaves differently at different wavelengths.

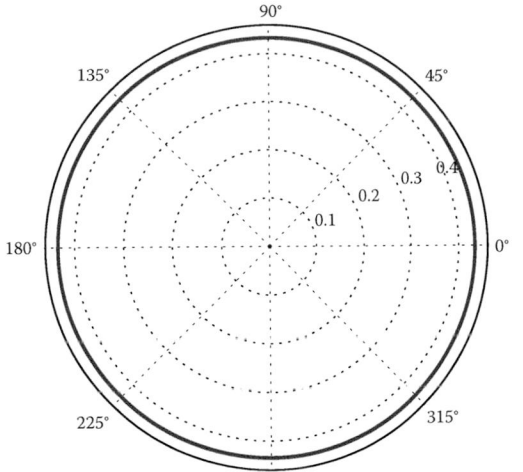
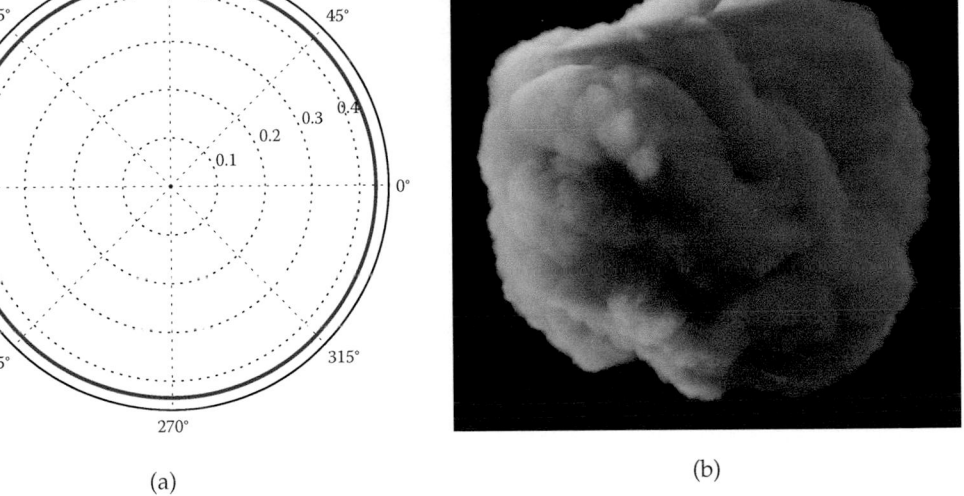

(a)
(b)

Figure 14.7. (a) Polar plot of isotropic phase function. (b) Rendered image using three colored light sources and the isotropic phase function.

14.7.2 The Isotropic Phase Function

Because the scattering probability of an isotropic phase function is well known, using a full class to represent it may seem a little superfluous. However, for the light integration code to be implemented cleanly, it is best to implement even the trivial isotropic case as a class in the same hierarchy as all the other phase functions. Thus, the **Isotropic** class acts mostly as a wrapper around the **k_isotropic** constant and always returns $1/4\pi$, regardless of the incoming direction vectors. (See Figure 14.7.)

Code 14.27. The **Isotropic::probability()** function

```
float Isotropic::probability(const Vector &in, const Vector &out) const
{
  return k_isotropic;
}
```

14.7.3 The Henyey-Greenstein Phase Function

One of the most widely used phase functions in computer graphics is the Henyey-Greenstein model. It was first described in the 1941 paper

"Diffuse Radiation in the Galaxy" [Henyey and Greenstein] and was originally devised as a model of scattering at galactic scales. Fortunately, it has proven useful in a wide range of contexts, and for computer graphics, it provides a straightforward way of describing anisotropic scattering using only a single *eccentricity* parameter g, which the **HenyeyGreenstein** class requires to be passed to the constructor. (See Figure 14.8.)

Code 14.28. The **HenyeyGreenstein** base class

```
class HenyeyGreenstein : public PhaseFunction
{
public:
...
  // Constructor, factory
  HenyeyGreenstein(float g);
  PVR_DEFINE_CREATE_FUNC_1_ARG(HenyeyGreenstein, float);
...
  // From PhaseFunction
  virtual float probability(const Vector &in, const Vector &out) const;
private:
  // Private data members
  const float m_g;
};
```

The Henyey-Greenstein function depends only upon the angle between $\vec{\omega}$ and $\vec{\omega}'$ and the asymmetry or eccentricity parameter g. It is defined as

$$p_{\mathrm{HG}}(\theta, g) = \frac{1}{4\pi} \frac{1 - g^2}{(1 + g^2 - 2g\cos\theta)^{3/2}}.$$

In the original paper, a third parameter γ is used to describe the spherical albedo of the phase function. Because PVR separates the overall scattering coefficient σ_s from the phase function, the γ parameter is assumed to be one and removed from the equation.

The implementation takes advantage of the fact that $\cos\theta = \vec{\omega} \cdot \vec{\omega}'$ but is otherwise a straight transcription of the mathematical formula.

Code 14.29. The **HenyeyGreenstein::probability()** function

```
float HenyeyGreenstein::probability(const Vector &in, const Vector &out) const
{
  const float cosTheta = in.dot(out);
  return k_isotropic * (1.0f - m_g * m_g) /
    std::pow(1.0f + m_g * m_g - 2.0f * m_g * cosTheta, 1.5f);
}
```

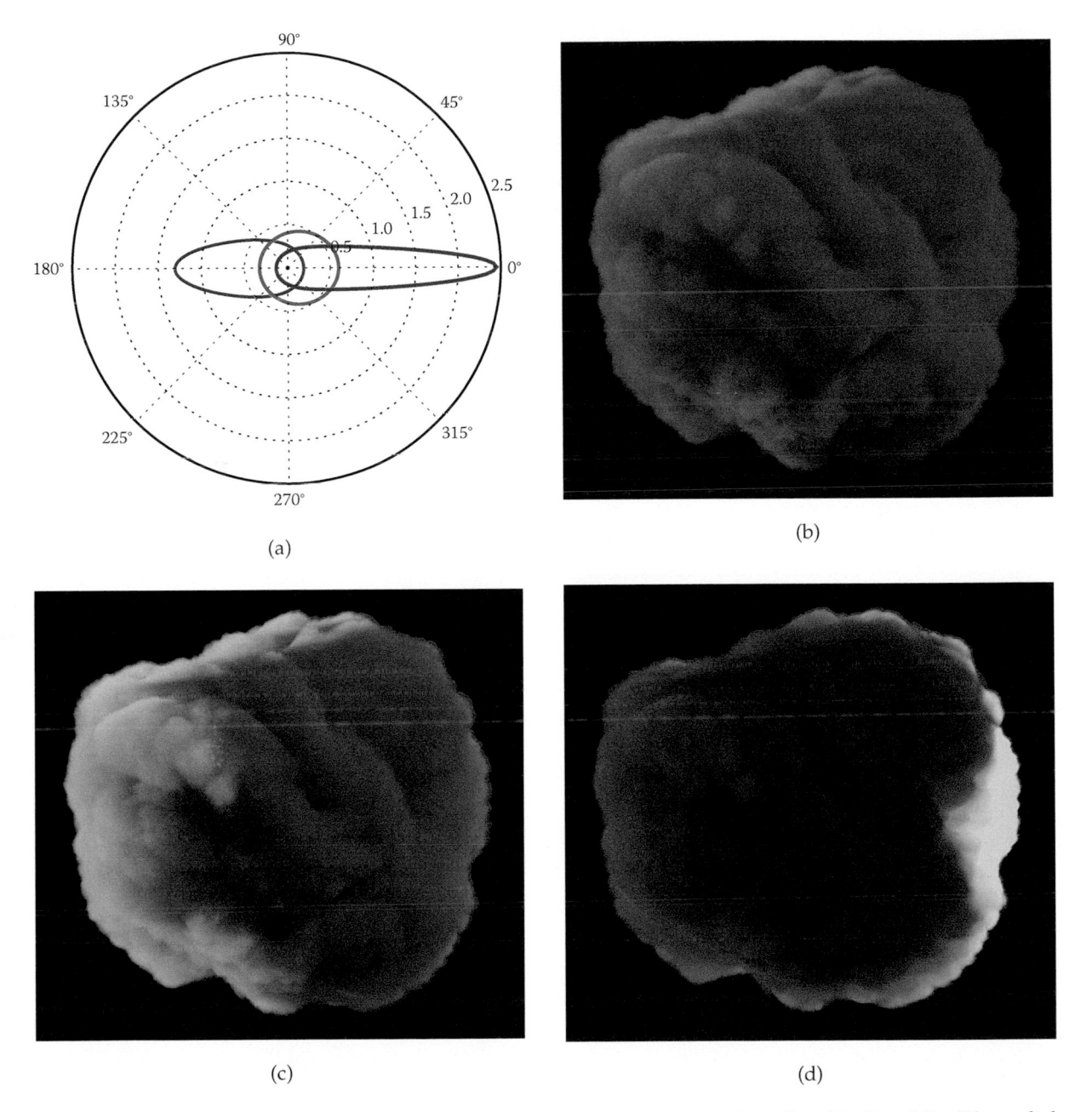

(a)

(b)

(c)

(d)

Figure 14.8. (a) Polar plot of Henyey-Greenstein with eccentricity R = −0.75, G = 0.3, B = 0.9. (The radial direction has been compressed.) (b) $g = -0.75$. (c) $g = 0.3$. (d) $g = 0.9$.

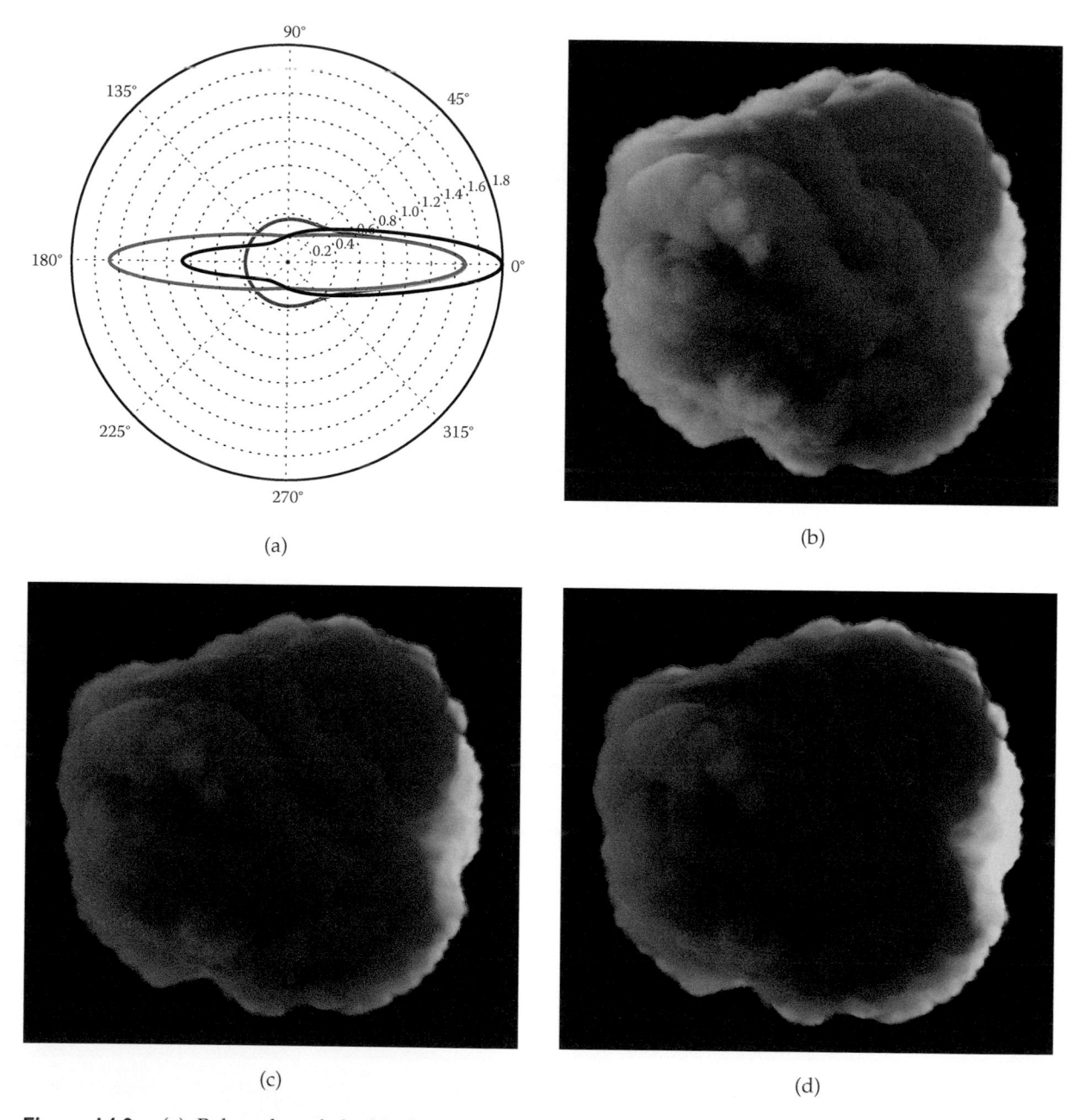

(a)

(b)

(c)

(d)

Figure 14.9. (a) Polar plot of double Henyey-Greenstein with parameters $R = p_{dHG}(0.85, 0.0, 0.5)$, $G = p_{dHG}(0.85, -0.85, 0.5)$, $B = p_{dHG}(0.85, -0.85, 0.9)$. (The radial direction has been compressed.) (b) $g_1 = 0.85, g_2 = 0.0, b = 0.5$. (c) $g_1 = 0.85, g_2 = -0.85, b = 0.5$. (d) $g_1 = 0.85, g_2 = -0.85, b = 0.9$.

14.7.4   The Double Henyey-Greenstein Phase Function

One of the drawbacks of the Henyey-Greenstein function is that the anisotropy acts in an all-or-nothing fashion. It can handle either isotropic behavior (if $|g| \approx 0$) or anisotropic behavior (if $|g| \gg 0$), but not both at the same time. If we consider the anisotropic behavior of a phase function to be somewhat similar to specular behavior in a surface BRDF, Henyey-Greenstein acts as a material with only a specular coefficient but no diffuse component; the specular can be made broad to the point where it approaches a diffuse surface, but there is no way to get both diffuse and specular behavior at the same time. For a BRDF, we would introduce a second *lobe* to our BRDF, and in the case of phase functions, we can simply use a combination of two or more phase functions.

One such combined phase function is the double Henyey-Greenstein function. It uses the same basic equation as the standard Henyey-Greenstein but computes the function twice, using two different eccentricity values, and then blends the two resulting values to find a single scattering probability:

$$p_{\mathrm{dHG}}(\theta, g_1, g_2, b) = b \cdot p_{\mathrm{HG}}(g_1) + (1 - b) \cdot p_{\mathrm{HG}}(g_2).$$

Using two Henyey-Greenstein functions means that complex phase functions can be approximated, even if they contain both forward and backward scattering properties. As an example, Mie scattering can be much better approximated using double Henyey-Greenstein than just using the single lobe version.

The **DoubleHenyeyGreenstein** constructor takes three parameters instead of **HenyeyGreenstein**'s single one: g_1 and g_2 control the eccentricity of the two phase functions, with 1.0 indicating full forward scattering and -1.0 full backward scattering. The blend parameter b has a range of $[0, 1]$, with higher values making the g_1 evaluation more prominent. (See Figure 14.9.)

HenyeyGreenstein, 301

Code 14.30. The **DoubleHenyeyGreenstein** base class

```
class DoubleHenyeyGreenstein : public PhaseFunction
{
public:
  ...
  // Constructor, factory
  DoubleHenyeyGreenstein(float g1, float g2, float blend);
  PVR_DEFINE_CREATE_FUNC_3_ARG(DoubleHenyeyGreenstein, float, float, float);
  ...
  // From PhaseFunction
  virtual float probability(const Vector &in, const Vector &out) const;
private:
```

```
// Private data members
const float m_g1;
const float m_g2;
const float m_blend;
};
```

The implementation of **DoubleHenyeyGreenstein::probability()** is similar to the single lobe version and first computes the result of each lobe before blending the values using **Math::fit01()**.

Code 14.31. The **DoubleHenyeyGreenstein::probability()** function

```
float DoubleHenyeyGreenstein::probability(const Vector &in,
                                          const Vector &out) const
{
  const float cosTheta = in.dot(out);
  float p1 = k_isotropic * (1.0f - m_g1 * m_g1) /
    std::pow(1.0f + m_g1 * m_g1 - 2.0f * m_g1 * cosTheta, 1.5f);
  float p2 = k_isotropic * (1.0f - m_g2 * m_g2) /
    std::pow(1.0f + m_g2 * m_g2 - 2.0f * m_g2 * cosTheta, 1.5f);
  return Math::fit01(m_blend, p2, p1);
}
```

14.7.5   Composite Phase Functions

So far, we have assumed that the volume can be described using just a single phase function. However, just as the raymarcher class needs to be able to integrate an arbitrary number of volumes, we must also let the user assign a separate phase function to each of the scene volumes. Integrating multiple phase functions wouldn't be too complicated if it weren't for the fact that the volumes may themselves be overlapping. The question is, what should the renderer do if one volume that uses **Isotropic** overlaps a second volume that uses **DoubleHenyeyGreenstein**? And even if we could resolve that case, what happens when any arbitrary number of volumes overlap?

Isotropic, 301
DoubleHenyeyGreenstein, 305

There isn't a simple answer to the question. In nature, volumes are not discrete, and if two different media mix, then the phase function is a result of the composition of the mixed volume. The molecular makeup and the different types of aerosols in the medium would all influence its scattering behavior. And the behavior of these mixed volumes is the whole *raison d'être* of the parameterized models, such as Henyey-Greenstein. (Figures 14.10 and 14.11 show scenes with multiple overlapping volumes using different phase functions.)

PVR's solution to the problem is to make a weighted average of all the scattering probabilities, based on the scattering coefficient of each

Figure 14.10. Set of **ConstantVolume** instances using the Henyey-Greenstein
phase function.

PhaseFunction, 300

volume. To fit the calculation in the **PhaseFunction** hierarchy, it is implemented as a subclass called **Composite** in the **pvr::Render::Phase** namespace.

Code 14.32. The **Composite** class

```
class Composite : public PhaseFunction
{
public:
...
  // From PhaseFunction
  virtual float probability(const Vector &in, const Vector &out) const;
  // Main methods
```

Figure 14.11. Set of **ConstantVolume** instances using the double Henyey-Greenstein phase function.

```
  void add(PhaseFunction::CPtr phaseFunction);
  void setWeight(const size_t idx, const float weight);
private:
  // Private data members
  std::vector<PhaseFunction::CPtr> m_functions;
  std::vector<float>               m_weights;
};
```

The handling of multiple phase functions takes place in the **Composite Volume**, which always uses **Phase::Composite** as its phase function. When a **Volume** instance is added to the composite volume, we not only add the volume to **m_volumes** but we also add its phase function to the composite phase function.

CompositeVolume, 262
Volume, 233

Code 14.33. Adding a child volume to **CompositeVolume**

```
void CompositeVolume::add(Volume::CPtr child)
{
  m_volumes.push_back(child);
  m_compositePhaseFunction->add(child->phaseFunction());
}
```

On the **Phase::Composite** side, the phase function pointer is recorded in **m_functions** and a dummy weight value of 0.0 is added to **m_weights**. Each phase function will be evaluated hundreds of thousands of times in a single render, so it is important that the evaluation of the composite function is quick. The assumption PVR makes is that the number of phase functions will remain constant during the course of the render, and only the vector arguments to **PhaseFunction::probability()** and the relative weights will change.

PhaseFunction, 300

Code 14.34. The **Composite::add()** function

```
void Composite::add(PhaseFunction::CPtr phaseFunction)
{
  m_functions.push_back(phaseFunction);
  m_weights.push_back(0.0f);
}
```

CompositeVolume, 262

Then, when the **CompositeVolume** is sampled, a check is performed to make sure that the ray type is **RayState::FullRaymarch**. If true, the **Composite** phase function is updated with the current sample value, which is used as the weighting factor for subsequent calls to **Composite::proba bility()**.

Code 14.35. Sampling the **CompositeVolume** updates the **Phase::Composite** instance

```
VolumeSample CompositeVolume::sample(const VolumeSampleState &state,
                                     const VolumeAttr &attribute) const
{
  if (attribute.index() == VolumeAttr::IndexNotSet) {
    setupAttribute(attribute);
  }
  if (attribute.index() == VolumeAttr::IndexInvalid) {
    return VolumeSample(Colors::zero(), m_phaseFunction);
  }

  Color value = Colors::zero();
  int attrIndex = attribute.index();

  for (size_t i = 0, size = m_volumes.size(); i < size; ++i) {
    const VolumeAttr &childAttr = m_childAttrs[attrIndex].attrs[i];
```

```
  const Color sampleValue = m_volumes[i]->sample(state, childAttr).value;
  value += sampleValue;
  if (state.rayState.rayType == RayState::FullRaymarch) {
    m_compositePhaseFunction->setWeight(i, Math::max(sampleValue));
  }
}
}

return VolumeSample(value, m_phaseFunction);
}
```

The `Composite::setWeight()` method just updates the weight of the volume with the given index.

Code 14.36. The `Composite::setWeight()` function

```
void Composite::setWeight(const size_t idx, const float weight)
{
  assert(idx < m_weights.size());
  m_weights[idx] = weight;
}
```

Once the weights have been updated for all volumes in the **Composite Volume**, the composite phase function is ready to be sampled just as any ordinary phase function. The final result is found according to the formula

CompositeVolume, 262

$$p_c(\vec{\omega}, \vec{\omega}') = \frac{\displaystyle\sum_{i=0}^{N} p_i(\vec{\omega}, \vec{\omega}') \cdot w_i}{\displaystyle\sum_{i=0}^{N} w_i}.$$

Code 14.37. The `Composite::probability()` function

```
float Composite::probability(const Vector &in, const Vector &out) const
{
  float p = 0.0;
  float weight = 0.0;
  for (size_t i = 0, size = m_functions.size(); i < size; i++) {
    p += m_functions[i]->probability(in, out) * m_weights[i];
    weight += m_weights[i];
  }
  return p / weight;
}
```

14.8   Occlusion in PVR

PhysicalSampler, 288

The final piece of the lighting model puzzle is *occlusion*. In the **Physical Sampler**, incoming light was computed by first sampling the intensity of the light source, and once the light-source position was known, the transmittance between the sample point and the light source was found. The two steps are kept separate because although light intensity attenuates over a distance,[2] the effects of volumetric occlusion are a different problem, best solved independently of each light's behavior.

PVR implements multiple different techniques for solving the occlusion problem, including both cache-based and non-cache-based ones. In the last parts of this chapter, we will look at the basics and a simple (but slow) non-cache-based implementation. In general production practice, some form of precomputation is used, and those solutions will be discussed in the next chapter.

14.8.1   The Occluder Base Class

The **Occluder** base class is similar to the other closure classes, having only a single virtual member function that takes a state parameter that encapsulates the relevant information needed for computation. Each **Occluder** is attached to a single light source and is only responsible for answering transmittance queries pertaining to that specific light source.

Code 14.38. The **Occluder** class

```
class Occluder : public Util::ParamBase
{
public:
  ...
  // To be implemented by subclasses
  virtual Color sample(const OcclusionSampleState &state) const = 0;
};
```

14.8.2   The **OcclusionSampleState** Struct

The **OcclusionSampleState** is similar to the other closure states, and its purpose is to provide the **Occluder** implementations with information about the current sample point's position, as well as the position of the light source that is casting light on the sample position.

The **makeSecondaryRayState()** member function serves a very important purpose. It creates a new ray, with its origin at the current sample

---

[2]Implemented in the falloff calculation.

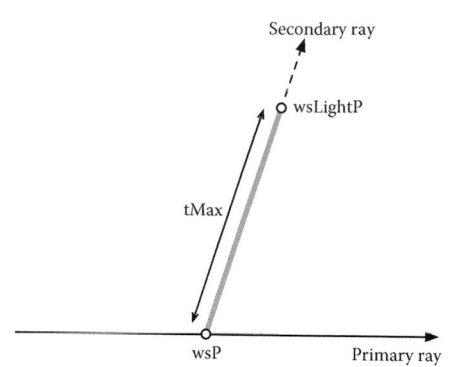

Figure 14.12. A secondary ray is spawned from the primary ray.

position and direction facing towards the light position. This new ray state can then be used to easily trace a new ray, directly answering the query about transmittance between the two points. (See Figure 14.12.)

When setting up the secondary state, we start out with a copy of the current state. The ray depth is increased, which lets the renderer track how deep the ray recursion is at any given moment. In general, the ray depth is zero or one, as PVR's only secondary ray type is the shadow ray.

The ray type is also changed to indicate that the ray only needs transmittance calculated, rather than performing a full raymarch including light integration. Skipping the lighting part of the raymarch helps speed up renders.

The last, but still important, step is to set **tMax** and **tMin**. The minimum distance along the ray will always be zero for a shadow ray, since we care about occlusion along the entire length of the ray between light source and sample point. Conversely, we must set **tMax** to ensure that only the portion of the ray between the two sample points is raymarched. If a ray was allowed to travel farther, a greater amount of occlusion would be found, giving the wrong result.

Code 14.39. The `OcclusionSampleState` struct

```
struct OcclusionSampleState
{
  OcclusionSampleState(const RayState &rState)
    : rayState(rState)
  { }
  RayState makeSecondaryRayState() const
  {
    RayState state(rayState);
    state.rayDepth++;
    state.rayType = RayState::TransmittanceOnly;
```

```
    state.wsRay.pos = wsP;
    state.wsRay.dir = (wsLightP - wsP).normalized();
    state.tMin = 0.0;
    state.tMax = (wsLightP - wsP).length();
    return state;
  }
  const RayState &rayState;
  Vector wsP;
  Vector wsLightP;
};
```

14.8.3 The `RaymarchOccluder` Class

With the `makeSecondaryRayState()` call in place, it is trivial to implement an **Occluder** that uses raymarching to compute occlusion for shadow rays.

The **RaymarchOccluder** is constructed with a pointer to a **Renderer**, which is used to actually trace the ray that **makeSecondaryRayState** sets up. Once the renderer returns the result of the traced ray, the result of the occlusion query can be found by looking at the **transmittance** member of

IntegrationResult.

Code 14.40. The **RaymarchOccluder** constructor

```
RaymarchOccluder::RaymarchOccluder(Renderer::CPtr renderer)
  : m_renderer(renderer)
{

}
```

Code 14.41. The **RaymarchOccluder::transmittance** function

```
Color RaymarchOccluder::sample(const OcclusionSampleState &state) const
{
  RayState raymarchState = state.makeSecondaryRayState();
  return m_renderer->trace(raymarchState).transmittance;
}
```

In PVR, the **RaymarchOccluder** is the only **Occluder** subclass that does not use any form of precomputation or caching. As such, it is very slow to use for actual rendering, and is most useful as a baseline comparison for other types of occluders.

Precomputed Occlusion

Answering the question "what hides what" is a fundamental computer graphics problem, and computing occlusion is a core task for any renderer, whether it handles surfaces or volumes. In fact, one of the most characteristic aspects of a given rendering algorithm is often the way in which it deals with occlusion.

In the previous chapter, we computed occlusion using a raymarching approach, and although it worked and was simple to implement, it was also quite slow. Fortunately, there are other approaches available, and in this chapter we will look at ways of speeding up occlusion queries using precomputation techniques.

15.1   Voxelized Occlusion

In their seminal 1984 paper "Ray Tracing Volume Densities" [Kajiya and Von Herzen 84], James Kajiya and Brian Von Herzen showed how a participating medium could be rendered using raymarching techniques. The most important contribution was in formulating the rendering equation for volumes; a less important, but still significant, contribution was that they saw the need to precompute the propagation of light through the volume, rather than evaluating it once every raymarch step. The approach they used (Section 3.2 in the original paper) was to build a three-dimensional array of light contribution values. For each light source S_i, they constructed a voxel buffer I_i, where

$$I_i(p) = S_i(p)T(p, P_{i,})$$
$$p = (x, y, z),$$
$$S_i = \text{source term for light source } i,$$
$$T(p, p') = \text{transmittance between points } p \text{ and } p'.$$

The array can be constructed in parallel and involves tracing a ray from each voxel center to the position of light source i. During final rendering, the light contribution at any given position can then be interpolated from the voxel representation, resulting in much faster renders.

The authors also observed that the values stored in the array were view independent and, assuming the volume itself was not animated, that they were valid for an entire animation. Precomputing lighting and occlusion was thus a great way to reduce render time without sacrificing correctness in the algorithm.

Voxelized occlusion is very efficient compared to a full raymarch solution, but it does introduce additional parameters to the system, most importantly the resolution to use for the voxel array. If too low a resolution is chosen, the lighting in the scene will lack detail. Conversely, if an excessively high resolution is chosen, the precomputation time may exceed the cost of raymarching the solution. No perfect solution exists when it comes to selecting the resolution, but a reasonable assumption would be that the size of a voxel should be chosen relative to the size of a pixel projected to the center of the volume.

15.2 Deep Shadows

One of the most important papers for production volume rendering is undoubtedly Tom Lokovic and Eric Veach's "Deep Shadow Maps" [Lokovic and Veach 00]. Before deep shadow maps, ordinary shadow maps had been in use since Lance Williams introduced them in his 1978 paper "Casting Curved Shadows on Curved Surfaces" [Williams 78]. A shadow map uses a *shadow camera*, positioned at the light source, to render an auxiliary view of the scene. Instead of shading the objects in the view of the camera, the distance to the closest one is found and stored in the shadow map as a distance. This calculation happens before the beauty render. For final rendering, occlusion queries can be answered by projecting the sample point into the view of the light and comparing the distance to the depth stored in the shadow map. If the sample point is farther away than the shadow map value, it is considered to be in shadow.

The breakthrough discovery with deep shadows was that fractional visibility[1] could be stored for multiple depths along the view of a shadow camera, making it possible to answer not just *if* a point was in shadow, but *how much* something was in shadow. Because as revolutionary as they were, ordinary shadow maps had several shortcomings. They could not support semitransparent or motion-blurring objects, and they could not easily be antialiased without using expensive filtering. Deep shadow maps solved all of these problems. Because they stored fractional visibility at all possible depths, they handled semitransparent objects, they could antialias partially covered pixels, and they could support motion-blurring objects.[2]

However, the most important feature of deep shadow maps (at least as far as we are concerned) was that they were suitable for storing occlusion in volumes. By raymarching each pixel from the shadow camera and storing the resulting transmittance function in the deep shadow map, there was finally a fast way to query continuously varying transmittance.

Deep shadows are, generally speaking, much more efficient than voxelized occlusion approaches. If we consider the voxelized occlusion case, we must perform a full raymarch for each voxel in the buffer. But looking at voxels A, B, and C, we can see that some information could be shared. If the transmittance at A is known, that could be used to compute the value of B and C, with only a few extra calculations. Unfortunately, the rays rarely line up with voxel centers, and in practice it is difficult to attempt these types of optimizations.

Deep shadow maps, on the other hand, take advantage of how light moves through the scene, since the generation process builds only the two-dimensional view from the shadow camera. Instead of tracing rays from the volume towards the light, they trace rays from the light into the volume. Thus, for each ray traced from the shadow camera, we build information corresponding to, on average, $N^{1/3}$ voxels, where N is the number of voxels in the voxelized occlusion buffer.

15.3   Strategies for Precomputation

There are two distinctly different approaches to building these cached representations of occlusion in a scene. In our descriptions of voxelized occlusion and deep shadow maps, we have assumed that the entire cache

---

[1] i.e., transmittance

[2] It should be noted that deep shadow maps store a single slice of time, and motion blur is "folded" into the spatial domain. It is not possible to undo the motion blur in a deep shadow map after it has been computed. It is also not possible to determine if a point is occluded at time t_1 but not at time t_2.

(i.e., the voxel buffer or deep image) is computed at once, before rendering of the final image is started. Although this is a perfectly valid approach, and potentially the only viable solution for algorithms such as REYES [Cook et al. 87], where geometry is discarded after portions of an image are completed, there are other options for a volume renderer where the entire scene is kept in memory. Instead of filling the entire cache at once, we can compute each cache value (a voxel or deep pixel) as it is needed. We will refer to the first approach as precomputation and the second as on-the-fly computation. On-the-fly computation of occlusion applies both to voxelized occlusion and deep shadow maps.

In PVR, the same occluder type is found both as a preprocess and as an on-the-fly variant. Generally, because the on-the-fly generation only gets triggered for visible parts of the scene, it is more efficient than precomputing all of the occlusion information in a preprocess. However, for purposes of illustration, both flavors are included in the code base.

15.4   The VoxelOccluder Class

In the next few sections, we will look at the implementation of several types of occluders. We will start with the voxelized occlusion approach, which is implemented in the VoxelOccluder class. The common pattern used between all of the Occluder subclasses is to perform all necessary setup work in the constructor, and then do as little work as possible in the sample() call.

Occluder, 311

The voxel occluder works by finding the bounds of the scene and configuring a voxel buffer to cover those bounds. Based on the shape of the bounds, a resolution is chosen for the voxel buffer such that the longest edge has the resolution passed by the user to the constructor.

The voxel occluder needs to perform a few different setup steps before it is ready to be used. First, it finds the bounds of the scene and builds a Field3D::MatrixFieldMapping that spans the bounds. Then, given the scene's bounding box size S and a longest-axis resolution r, the voxel buffer's resolution is computed as

$$R = \frac{S \cdot r}{\max(S)}.$$

Code 15.1. The VoxelOccluder constructor

```
VoxelOccluder::VoxelOccluder(Renderer::CPtr renderer,
                             const Vector &wsLightPos,
                             const size_t res)
{
  Log::print("Building VoxelOccluder");
```

```
BBox wsBounds       = renderer->scene()->volume->wsBounds();
Matrix localToWorld = Math::coordinateSystem(wsBounds);
MatrixFieldMapping::Ptr mapping(new MatrixFieldMapping);
mapping->setLocalToWorld(localToWorld);
m_buffer.setMapping(mapping);

V3i bufferRes = wsBounds.size() / Math::max(wsBounds.size()) * res;
m_buffer.setSize(bufferRes);

Log::print("  Resolution: " + str(bufferRes));
```

RayState, 210

The **RayState** used to trace secondary rays is set up in two steps. First, the properties that are constant for all voxels are updated.

Code 15.2. The **VoxelOccluder** constructor

```
RayState state;
state.rayType  = RayState::TransmittanceOnly;
state.rayDepth = 1;
```

A **Timer** and **ProgressReporter** is used to give the user feedback on how long the precomputation is expected to take and to offer a way of interrupting the calculation. In order to provide an accurate measure of progress, PVR keeps track of the number of voxels processed.

Code 15.3. The **VoxelOccluder** constructor

```
Timer timer;
ProgressReporter progress(2.5f, "  ");
```

Rasterization Primitives in PVR, 107

The next step in creating the precomputed occlusion buffer is to loop over each voxel and trace a ray to determine the transmittance between the light source and the voxel. The loop has the same structure as the rasterization primitives in Chapter 7 and starts with a check to **Interrupt:: throwOnAbort()**, followed by **progress.update()**, which prints progress to the log at given intervals.

Code 15.4. The **VoxelOccluder** constructor

```
size_t count = 0, numVoxels = bufferRes.x * bufferRes.y * bufferRes.z;
for (DenseBuffer::iterator i = m_buffer.begin(), end = m_buffer.end();
     i != end; ++i, ++count) {
  // Check if user terminated
  Sys::Interrupt::throwOnAbort();
  // Print progress
  progress.update(static_cast<float>(count) / numVoxels);
```

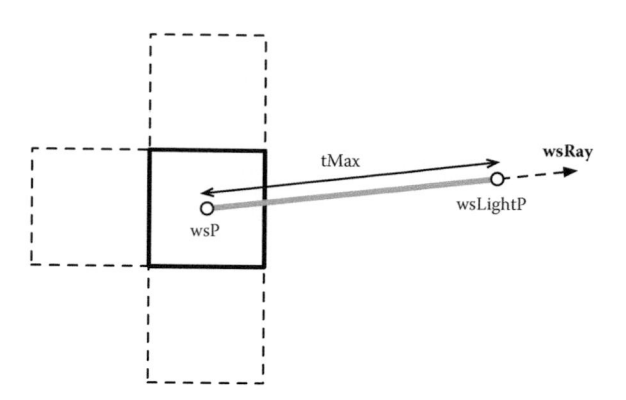

Figure 15.1. Setting up the **RayState** to be used for firing a secondary ray.

The last step is to set up the parts of the **RayState** that change from voxel to voxel, namely, the ray's origin, direction, and the maximum distance to raymarch. As with all transformations from discrete voxel space to world space, we have to call **discToCont()** to get a floating-point voxel-space coordinate before calling **voxelToWorld()**. Once the world-space position of the voxel is known, setting up the ray is simple. Figure 15.1 illustrates the relationships.

RayState, 210

Code 15.5. The **VoxelOccluder** constructor

```
// Do work
Vector wsP;
m_buffer.mapping()->voxelToWorld(discToCont(V3i(i.x, i.y, i.z)), wsP);
state.wsRay.pos      = wsP;
state.wsRay.dir      = (wsLightPos - wsP).normalized();
state.tMax           = (wsLightPos - wsP).length();
```

With the ray set up, the computation of transmittance between the light and the voxel is performed by calling **Renderer::trace()**. This triggers a new raymarch and, as such, is quite an expensive operation. Once the **Renderer** returns the integration result, the transmittance is stored at the current voxel location, ready to be used for rendering.

Renderer, 204

Code 15.6. The **VoxelOccluder** constructor

```
    IntegrationResult result = renderer->trace(state);
    *i = result.transmittance;
  }

  Log::print(" Time elapsed: " + str(timer.elapsed())));
}
```

Once the voxel buffer is filled, the virtual **sample** function is very similar to **VoxelVolume**'s **sample()** call. The world-space sample point found in the **OcclusionSampleState** is transformed into voxel space, checked against the bounds of the buffer, and then used to interpolate a transmittance value from the buffer.

Code 15.7. The `VoxelOccluder::sample()` member function

```
Color VoxelOccluder::sample(const OcclusionSampleState &state) const
{
  Vector vsP;
  m_buffer.mapping()->worldToVoxel(state.wsP, vsP);
  if (!Math::isInBounds(vsP, m_buffer.dataWindow())) {
    return Colors::one();
  }
  Color val = m_linearInterp.sample(m_buffer, vsP);
  return val;
}
```

At this point, it should be obvious that the **VoxelOccluder** performs the same basic work as the **RaymarchOccluder**. The call to **Renderer::trace()** is equally expensive in both cases, and the only real benefit to using voxelized occlusion is that the number of calls to **trace()** can be kept under control, based on the resolution of the voxel buffer.

15.5   The `OtfVoxelOccluder` Class

Before exploring other types of cached occlusion, we will look at a variation on the voxelized occlusion implementation. In Section 15.3 we discussed the two different approaches to precomputing occlusion: doing the work as a preprocess or on the fly. The **VoxelOccluder** implementation took the first route, performing all of the precomputation in the constructor and doing as little work as possible in the **sample()** call. One downside to this approach is that transmittance is evaluated for every voxel in the buffer, regardless of whether each contains any visible density or whether it is visible to camera.

Using the alternative method of computing transmittance values on the fly solves two of the problems. First, primary rays are only ever fired by the **Renderer** for pixels in the camera's view. This means that the only calls to the **RaymarchSampler**, and subsequently to the **Occluder**, will be for points that are in the camera's view. And second, the only times that the raymarch sampler will query the occluder is when the scattering coefficient is nonzero.

The **OtfVoxelOccluder**'s constructor is identical to the **VoxelOccluder**'s, except that no transmittance is computed, and the entire buffer is initialized to −1.0. The negative value is technically an invalid transmittance, and it is used only to mark a voxel as not yet having been computed.

Code 15.8. The `OtfVoxelOccluder` constructor

```
OtfVoxelOccluder::OtfVoxelOccluder(Renderer::CPtr renderer,
                                   const Vector &wsLightPos,
                                   const size_t res)
  : m_renderer(renderer), m_wsLightPos(wsLightPos)
{
  BBox wsBounds = renderer->scene()->volume->wsBounds();
  V3i bufferRes = wsBounds.size() / Math::max(wsBounds.size()) * res;
  m_buffer.setMapping(Math::makeMatrixMapping(wsBounds));
  m_buffer.setSize(bufferRes);
  m_buffer.clear(Color(-1.0));
}
```

The virtual `sample()` function is also similar to its `VoxelOccluder` counterpart. First, the world-space sample point is transformed to voxel space, then checked against the bounds of the buffer. However, before interpolating the transmittance value from the buffer, it checks to see if all of the relevant voxel values have been computed. If any of the required voxels have a negative value, it first needs to be computed using the `updateVoxel()` member function.

Code 15.9. The `OtfVoxelOccluder::sample` function

```
Color OtfVoxelOccluder::sample(const OcclusionSampleState &state) const
{
  Vector vsP;
  m_buffer.mapping()->worldToVoxel(state.wsP, vsP);

  if (!Math::isInBounds(vsP, m_buffer.dataWindow())) {
    return Colors::one();
  }

  int x0 = static_cast<int>(std::floor(vsP.x));
  int y0 = static_cast<int>(std::floor(vsP.y));
  int z0 = static_cast<int>(std::floor(vsP.z));

  for (int k = z0; k < z0 + 2; ++k) {
    for (int j = y0; j < y0 + 2; ++j) {
      for (int i = x0; i < x0 + 2; ++i) {
        int ii = Imath::clamp(i, m_buffer.dataWindow().min.x,
                              m_buffer.dataWindow().max.x);
        int jj = Imath::clamp(j, m_buffer.dataWindow().min.y,
                              m_buffer.dataWindow().max.y);
        int kk = Imath::clamp(k, m_buffer.dataWindow().min.z,
                              m_buffer.dataWindow().max.z);
        if (Math::max(m_buffer.fastValue(ii, jj, kk)) < 0.0) {
```

```
            updateVoxel(ii, jj, kk);
          }
        }
      }
    }

    return m_linearInterp.sample(m_buffer, vsP);
}
```

VoxelOccluder, 318

The implementation of **updateVoxel()** performs the same work as **VoxelOccluder**'s constructor. First, the world-space position of the voxel is found, and the information is then used to construct a ray from the current position towards the light source. The result of tracing the ray is finally recorded in the voxel buffer.

Code 15.10. The **OtfVoxelOccluder::updateVoxel** function

```
void
OtfVoxelOccluder::updateVoxel(const int i, const int j, const int k) const
{
    // Transform point from voxel to world space
    Vector wsP;
    m_buffer.mapping()->voxelToWorld(discToCont(V3i(i, j, k)), wsP);
    // Set up the ray state
    RayState state;
    state.rayType = RayState::TransmittanceOnly;
    state.rayDepth = 1;
    state.wsRay.pos = wsP;
    state.wsRay.dir = (m_wsLightPos - wsP).normalized();
    state.tMax = (m_wsLightPos - wsP).length();
    // Trace ray and record transmittance
    IntegrationResult result = m_renderer->trace(state);
    m_buffer.fastLValue(i, j, k) = result.transmittance;
}
```

15.6   The DeepImage Class

We have come across deep shadows and deep pixel functions in several contexts in this book. And while the **Curve** class is used to store individual deep pixel functions, PVR uses a special image class to store two-dimensional arrays of deep pixels that is called **DeepImage**. The implementation is in essence quite simple. Just as the **Image** stores an array

Image, 230

of pixel values, **DeepImage** stores an array of deep pixel functions.

When choosing the in-memory storage format for the image, a decision has to be made for how many samples to use for the transmittance function. It is possible to allow each pixel an arbitrary number of samples, but PVR's deep image class uses a fixed number of samples to store transmittance, identical for each pixel in the image.

The **DeepImage** class is very similar to the regular **Image** class. It is essentially just a two-dimensional array of **ColorCurve** objects, one for each pixel in the image. Just as with a normal image, the resolution is set using **setSize()**, but instead of setting the pixel values to a single color value, the **setPixel()** member function takes a **ColorCurve**. When called, **setPixel()** will convert the curve to a fixed number of samples so that all pixels in the image have the same number of sample points.

Curve, 16

Code 15.11. The **DeepImage** class

```
class DeepImage
{
public:
  ...
  // Main methods
  void        setSize(const size_t width, const size_t height);
  Imath::V2i  size() const;
  void        setNumSamples(const size_t numSamples);
  size_t      numSamples() const;
  void        setPixel(const size_t x, const size_t y, const Curve::CPtr func);
  void        setPixel(const size_t x, const size_t y, const Color &value);
  Curve::Ptr  pixelFunction(const size_t x, const size_t y) const;
  Color       lerp(const float rsX, const float rsY, const float z) const;
  void        printStats() const;
private:
  ...
  // Private data members
  PixelsVec   m_pixels;
  size_t      m_width;
  size_t      m_height;
  size_t      m_numSamples;
};
```

15.7   The **TransmittanceMapOccluder** Class

Next, we will look at how PVR implements the deep shadow concept. Although there are some differences from the original paper [Lokovic and Veach 00], the fundamental ideas are similar. PVR's implementation skips the compression of each pixel's transmittance function and, as it uses the **DeepImage** class, employs a fixed number of samples per pixel.

DeepImage, 323

When the **DeepImage** class is used to represent transmittance, we refer to it as a transmittance map, and the task of creating transmittance maps for the **TransmittanceMapOccluder** is delegated to the **Renderer** class.

Renderer, 204

The first step of the computation is to configure the **Renderer** instance that will be used to render the transmittance map. The argument to the constructor is a **const Renderer** (**Renderer::CPtr**), but **Renderer::execute()** is non-**const**,[3] so we first clone the **Renderer**, creating a mutable copy.

Code 15.12. The `TransmittanceMapOccluder` constructor

```
TransmittanceMapOccluder::TransmittanceMapOccluder(Renderer::CPtr
                                                       baseRenderer,
                                         Camera::CPtr camera,
                                         const size_t numSamples)
  : m_camera(camera)
{
  // Clone Renderer to create a mutable copy
  Renderer::Ptr renderer = baseRenderer->clone();
```

Next, the **Renderer** is configured to render from the shadow camera rather than the primary camera and to disable generation of the primary image, since all we are interested in is the transmittance map. The number of pixel samples is also updated, since the setting may differ from the primary render's.

Code 15.13. The `TransmittanceMapOccluder` constructor

```
  // Configure Renderer
  renderer->setCamera(camera);
  renderer->setPrimaryEnabled(false);
  renderer->setTransmittanceMapEnabled(true);
  renderer->setNumDeepSamples(numSamples);
```

With the **Renderer** configured, we call **execute()** and then store the pointer to the transmittance map the **Renderer** created.

Code 15.14. The `TransmittanceMapOccluder` constructor

```
  // Execute render and grab transmittance map
  renderer->execute();
  m_transmittanceMap = renderer->transmittanceMap();
  // Record the bounds of the transmittance map
  m_rasterBounds = static_cast<Imath::V2f>(m_transmittanceMap->size());
```

In order to support multiple types of projections, the **Transmittance MapOccluder** constructor takes a pointer to the **Camera** base class, rather

Camera, 213

---

[3]For example, it modifies the final image.

than any one specific camera subclass. The occluder makes no assumptions about how the camera functions internally, as long as it provides transforms between world, camera, and raster spaces. The only thing the occluder needs to be aware of is whether the space behind the camera is a valid point to be transformed.

Code 15.15. The `TransmittanceMapOccluder` constructor

```
  // Check if space behind camera is valid
  m_clipBehindCamera = !camera->canTransformNegativeCamZ();
}
```

During rendering, `sample()` will be called each time the `RaymarchSampler` needs to determine the visibility of a light source. The steps involved are very similar to ordinary shadow maps. First, the world-space sample point is transformed into camera space and into raster space.

RaymarchSampler, 285

Code 15.16. The `TransmittanceMapOccluder::sample()` function

```
Color TransmittanceMapOccluder::sample(const OcclusionSampleState &state)
    const
{
  // Transform to camera space for depth and raster space for pixel
  // coordinate
  Vector csP = m_camera->worldToCamera(state.wsP, state.rayState.time);
  Vector rsP = m_camera->worldToRaster(state.wsP, state.rayState.time);
```

The camera-space coordinate is used to determine whether points behind the camera can be deemed to be outside the view of the camera. Some camera types (such as spherical projections) have perfectly well-defined screen and raster spaces even behind the camera, whereas others do not (e.g., perspective projections). The occluder also checks if the x, y raster-space coordinates are outside the valid range. If they are, it is also possible (in fact, necessary) to skip lookups into the transmittance map and instead return full transmittance.

Code 15.17. The `TransmittanceMapOccluder::sample()` function

```
  // Bounds checks
  if (m_clipBehindCamera && csP.z < 0.0) {
    return Colors::one();
  }
  if (rsP.x < 0.0 || rsP.x > m_rasterBounds.x ||
      rsP.y < 0.0 || rsP.y > m_rasterBounds.y) {
    return Colors::one();
  }
```

Once the sample point is determined to lie in the domain of the transmittance map, we can proceed with interpolating the transmittance value. First, we need to determine the depth at which we will sample the transmittance map. Although it may seem reasonable to use the camera-space z-coordinate for depth, we must remember that the transmittance function in each pixel was built by the **Raymarcher**. The raymarcher classes are agnostic of what particular camera type is used to render, and as such, we cannot assume that a perspective transform was used to build the transmittance function; in fact, even if the ray traced by the raymarcher was spawned from a **PerspectiveCamera**, the transmittance function is still stored using world-space distance.

Code 15.18. The `TransmittanceMapOccluder::sample()` function

```
// Compute depth to sample at
float depth = (state.wsP - m_camera->
                                     position(state.rayState.time)).length();

// Finally interpolate
    return m_transmittanceMap->lerp(rsP.x, rsP.y, depth);
}
```

15.8   The `OtfTransmittanceMapOccluder` Class

The `TransmittanceMapOccluder` is much more efficient than both raymarch-based occlusion and voxelized occlusion, but it is possible to improve it further by generating the transmittance map on the fly during rendering, as we did with **OtfVoxelOccluder**.

Not much needs to change from the preprocess occluder, but the structure is different enough to warrant a different class. The constructor records the resolution of the camera and updates the **DeepImage** that stores the transmittance map. It also initializes the **m_computed** variable, which stores information about which pixels have been computed. A value of zero indicates that the ray for a given pixel has yet to be traced.

Code 15.19. The `OtfTransmittanceMapOccluder` constructor

```
OtfTransmittanceMapOccluder::OtfTransmittanceMapOccluder(Renderer::CPtr
                                                        renderer,
                                            Camera::CPtr camera,
                                            const size_t
                                                numSamples)

  : m_renderer(renderer), m_camera(camera)
```

```
{
  // Record resolution of camera
  m_resolution = m_camera->resolution();
  m_floatRasterBounds = static_cast<Imath::V2f>(m_resolution);
  m_intRasterBounds = m_resolution - Imath::V2i(1);
  // Update transmittance map size and sample count
  m_transmittanceMap.setSize(m_resolution.x, m_resolution.y);
  m_transmittanceMap.setNumSamples(numSamples);
  // Reset the list of computed pixels
  m_computed.resize(m_resolution.x * m_resolution.y, 0);
  // Check if space behind camera is valid
  m_clipBehindCamera = !camera->canTransformNegativeCamZ();
}
```

The work done by **OtfTransmittanceMapOccluder::sample()** is very similar to the preprocess variant. The sample point is transformed to camera and raster spaces, checked to make sure it is valid, and finally used to find the depth value to use for lookups.

Code 15.20. The **OtfTransmittanceMapOccluder::sample()** member function

```
Color OtfTransmittanceMapOccluder::sample(const OcclusionSampleState &state)
  const
{
  // Transform to camera space for depth and raster space for pixel
  // coordinate
  Vector csP = m_camera->worldToCamera(state.wsP, state.rayState.time);
  Vector rsP = m_camera->worldToRaster(state.wsP, state.rayState.time);

  // Bounds checks
  if (m_clipBehindCamera && csP.z < 0.0) {
    return Colors::one();
  }
  if (rsP.x < 0.0 || rsP.x >= m_floatRasterBounds.x ||
      rsP.y < 0.0 || rsP.y >= m_floatRasterBounds.y) {
    return Colors::one();
  }

  // Compute depth to sample at
  Vector wsCamPosition = m_camera->position(state.rayState.time);
  float depth = (state.wsP - wsCamPosition).length();
```

Before interpolating a value from the transmittance map, the occluder must first ensure that the relevant pixels have been computed.

Code 15.21. The **OtfTransmittanceMapOccluder::sample()** member function

```
  // Ensure all samples are available
  updateCoordinate(rsP);

  // Finally interpolate
  return m_transmittanceMap.lerp(rsP.x, rsP.y, depth);
}
```

Since the interpolation used in the occluder is linear, we know that only the four pixels adjacent to the sample point will be used in the calculation. The **updateCoordinate()** function checks whether each neighbor pixel's value in **m_computed** is valid and, if not, calls **updatePixel()**.

Code 15.22. The `OtfTransmittanceMapOccluder::updateCoordinate()` member function

```
void
OtfTransmittanceMapOccluder::updateCoordinate(const Vector &rsP) const
{
  size_t x = static_cast<size_t>(std::floor(rsP.x));
  size_t y = static_cast<size_t>(std::floor(rsP.y));
  for (uint j = y; j < y + 2; j++) {
    for (uint i = x; i < x + 2; i++) {
      uint iC = Imath::clamp(i, 0u, static_cast<uint>(m_intRasterBounds.x));
      uint jC = Imath::clamp(j, 0u, static_cast<uint>(m_intRasterBounds.y));
      if (!m_computed[offset(iC, jC)]) {
        updatePixel(iC, jC);
      }
    }
  }
}
```

The **updatePixel()** function performs the most important work of the occluder. It must replicate the process of the **Renderer** so that the transmittance map it generates is identical to what the ordinary **Transmittance MapOccluder** would have returned to it.

In order to handle motion blur appropriately, the occluder will be firing multiple rays per pixel, based on **Renderer::numPixelSamples()**. Each ray will return an **IntegrationResult**, which in turn contains a transmittance function. The transmittance-function pointer will be valid if the ray intersects a volume, but if it does not, the pointer will be null. Because of this, the exact size of the vector of transmittance functions cannot be known, so the **tf** variable is reserved rather than resized to the number of rays that will be traced. Reserving the appropriate amount of memory ahead of time reduces unnecessary reallocation of memory, which would otherwise slow down the computation.

Code 15.23. The `OtfTransmittanceMapOccluder::updatePixel()` member function

```
void
OtfTransmittanceMapOccluder::updatePixel(const size_t x, const size_t y)
    const
{
  // Storage for transmittance functions
  size_t numSamples = m_renderer->numPixelSamples();
  std::vector<Util::ColorCurve::CPtr> tf;
  tf.reserve(numSamples * numSamples);
```

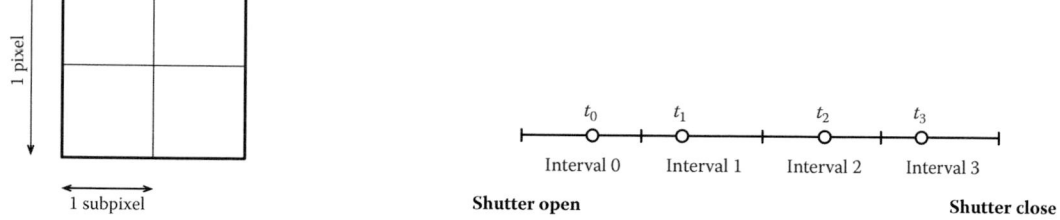

Figure 15.2. Given `numPixelSamples=2`, four subpixels are created.

Figure 15.3. Given `numPixelSamples=2`, four stratified time slices are used, with one randomized time value chosen in each stratum.

It is very important that the sequence of random numbers be coherent from one render to the next. As with the rest of PVR's sample distributions, it would be more optimal to use a distribution with good pixel-to-pixel distribution,[4] but for the sake of simplicity, a simple, stratified, independent random variable is used instead. It is initialized such that each pixel in the transmittance map gets a unique seed.

Code 15.24. The `OtfTransmittanceMapOccluder::updatePixel()` member function

```
// Ensure a unique sampling pattern for each pixel
Imath::Rand48 rng(x + y * m_resolution.x);
```

When the user specifies the number of pixel samples to use for rendering, the number represents how many x, y divisions each should pixel should use, resulting in N^2 samples. (See Figure 15.2.) Each division is assigned a different time value, which is used to produce motion blur effects. (See Figure 15.3.)

For each sample, the time value t_i is chosen based on the random variable ξ_i, such that

$$t_i = \frac{i + \xi_i}{N^2}, \qquad 0 \le i < N^2.$$

Code 15.25. The `OtfTransmittanceMapOccluder::updatePixel()` member function

```
// Fire N^2 rays, to match the number of rays used in main render
for (size_t i = 0; i < numSamples * numSamples; ++i) {
  // Set up the next ray with a random time sample
  RayState state;
  PTime ptime            ((i + rng.nextf()) / (numSamples * numSamples));
```

---

[4]Such as a low-discrepancy sampling pattern.

RayState, 210

The rest of the **RayState** is set up similar to the voxel-based occluders, which also needed to trace rays to determine transmittance. But whereas they only considered the final transmittance of the entire ray, the **OtfTransmittanceMapOccluder** uses the entire transmittance function built by the raymarcher. As mentioned above, the function is only created if an intersection was found between the ray and the scene, and as such, it will only be added to the list of transmittance functions if it is valid.

Code 15.26. The **OtfTransmittanceMapOccluder::updatePixel()** member function

```
state.wsRay          = setupRay(m_camera, Field3D::discToCont(x),
                                Field3D::discToCont(y), ptime);
state.time           = ptime;
state.rayType        = RayState::TransmittanceOnly;
state.rayDepth       = 1;
state.doOutputDeepT = true;
state.doOutputDeepL = false;
// Trace ray to find transmittance
IntegrationResult result = m_renderer->trace(state);
// Store transmittance function
if (result.transmittanceFunction) {
  tf.push_back(result.transmittanceFunction);
}
}
```

Once all the transmittance functions for the given pixel have been gathered, they are averaged into a single new transmittance function. This average will be a more accurate estimate the more samples are used. The average is then set as the transmittance function for the current pixel, and the **m_computed** variable is updated to indicate that the pixel has a valid value.

Code 15.27. The **OtfTransmittanceMapOccluder::updatePixel()** member function

```
// Update transmittance map
if (tf.size() > 0) {
  m_transmittanceMap.setPixel(x, y, Util::ColorCurve::average(tf));
} else {
  m_transmittanceMap.setPixel(x, y, Colors::one());
}

// Mark pixel as computed
m_computed[offset(x, y)] = 1;
}
```

Bibliography

[Abrahams 12] Dave Abrahams. "Boost.Python." *Boost C++ Libraries*. Available at http://www.boost.org/doc/libs/1_48_0/libs/python/doc/, 2012.

[Amanatides and Woo 87] John Amanatides and Andrew Woo. "A Fast Voxel Traversal Algorithm for Ray Tracing." In *Eurographics '87*, edited by Guy Maréchal, pp. 3–10. Amsterdam: North-Holland, 1987.

[Apodaca et al. 00] Anthony A. Apodaca, Larry Gritz, and Ronen Barzel. *Advanced RenderMan: Creating CGI for Motion Pictures*. The Morgan Kaufmann Series in Computer Graphics and Geometric Modeling, San Francisco: Morgan Kaufmann, 2000.

[Burum 07] Stephen H. Burum. *American Cinematographer Manual*, 1, Ninth edition. Hollywood: ASC Press, 2007.

[Catmull 74] Edwin E. Catmull. "A Subdivision Algorithm for Computer Display of Curved Surfaces." Ph.D. thesis, Department of Computer Science, University of Utah, Salt Lake City, UT, 1974.

[Cook et al. 84] Robert L. Cook, Thomas Porter, and Loren Carpenter. "Distributed Ray Tracing." *Proc. SIGGRAPH '84, Computer Graphics* 18:3 (1984), 137–145.

[Cook et al. 87] Robert L. Cook, Loren Carpenter, and Edwin Catmull. "The Reyes Image Rendering Architecture." *Proc. SIGGRAPH '87, Computer Graphics* 21:4 (1987), 95–102.

[Cook 86] Robert L. Cook. "Stochastic Sampling in Computer Graphics." *ACM Transactions on Graphics* 5:1 (1986), 51–72.

[Ebert et al. 02] David S. Ebert, F. Kenton Musgrave, Darwyn Peachey, Ken Perlin, and Steven Worley. *Texturing and Modeling: A Procedural Approach*, Third edition. San Francisco: Morgan Kaufmann Publishers Inc., 2002.

[Fedkiw et al. 01] Ronald Fedkiw, Jos Stam, and Henrik Wann Jensen. "Visual Simulation of Smoke." In *Proceedings of SIGGRAPH 2001, Computer Graphics Proceedings, Annual Conference Series*, edited by E. Fiume, pp. 15–22. Reading, MA: Addison-Wesley, 2001.

[Gritz 12] Larry Gritz. "OpenImageIO." Available at http://www.openimageio.org/, accessed February 17, 2012.

[Heckbert 90] Paul S. Heckbert. "What Are the Coordinates of a Pixel?" In *Graphics Gems*, edited by Andrew S. Glassner, pp. 246–248. Boston: Academic Press, 1990.

[Henyey and Greenstein] Louis George Henyey and Jesse Leonard Greenstein. "Diffuse Radiation in the Galaxy."

[ILM 12] ILM. "OpenEXR." Available at http://www.openexr.com/, 2012.

[Kajiya and Von Herzen 84] James T. Kajiya and Brian P. Von Herzen. "Ray Tracing Volume Densities." *SIGGRAPH '84* 18:3 (1984), 165–174.

[Kapler 02] Alan Kapler. "Evolution of a VFX Voxel Tool." In *ACM SIGGRAPH 2002 Conference Abstracts and Applications*, pp. 179–179. New York: ACM, 2002.

[Lokovic and Veach 00] Tom Lokovic and Eric Veach. "Deep shadow maps." In *Proceedings of SIGGRAPH 2000, Computer Graphics Proceedings, Annual Conference Series*, edited by Kurt Akeley, pp. 385–392. Reading, MA: Addison-Wesley, 2000.

[Mandelbrot and Van Ness 68] Benoit B. Mandelbrot and John W. Van Ness. "Fractional Brownian Motion, Fractional Noises and Applications." *SIAM Review* 10:4 (1968), 422–437.

[Mitchell and Netravali 88] Don P. Mitchell and Arun N. Netravali. "Reconstruction Filters in Computer-Graphics." *Proc. SIGGRAPH '88, Computer Graphics* 22:4 (1988), 221–228.

[Perlin and Hoffert 89] K. Perlin and E. M. Hoffert. "Hypertexture." *SIGGRAPH '89, Computer Graphics* 23:3 (1989), 253–262.

[Perlin 85] Ken Perlin. "An Image Synthesizer." *SIGGRAPH '85, Computer Graphics* 19:3 (1985), 287–296.

[Petty 04] Grant W. Petty. *A First Course in Atmospheric Radiation*. Madison, WI: Sundog Pub., 2004.

[Pharr and Humphreys 10] Matt Pharr and Greg Humphreys. *Physically Based Rendering: From Theory to Implementation*, Second edition. San Francisco: Morgan Kaufmann Publishers Inc., 2010.

[Stephenson 05] Ian Stephenson. *Production Rendering: Design and Implementation*. London: Springer, 2005.

[Watt 00] Alan H. Watt. *3D Computer Graphics*, Third edition. Essex, UK: Addison-Wesley, 2000.

[Williams 78] Lance Williams. "Casting Curved Shadows on Curved Surfaces." *Proc. SIGGRAPH '78, Computer Graphics* 12:3 (1978), 270–274.

[Wrenninge 12] Magnus Wrenninge. "Field3D." Available at http://github.com/imageworks/Field3D, accessed February 20, 2012.

Index

Class Index